MEMOIRS OF THE MUSEUM OF ANTHROPOLOGY
UNIVERSITY OF MICHIGAN
NUMBER 18

Studies in Latin American Ethnohistory & Archaeology

Joyce Marcus, General Editor

Volume 3

Aztec City-States

by

Mary G. Hodge

ANN ARBOR
1984

This series is partially supported by a grant-in-aid No. 4453 from the Wenner-Gren Foundation for Anthropological Research, whose Director of Research, Lita Osmundsen, offered both encouragement and help during the preparation of the grant proposal. Generous funds were also supplied by the Museum of Anthropology, University of Michigan, through the efforts of former Director Richard I. Ford.

© 1984 Regents of the University of Michigan
The Museum of Anthropology
All Rights Reserved

Printed in the
United States of America

ISBN
0-915703-02-5

Introduction to Volume 3

by
Joyce Marcus

Given the vast literature on the Aztec population, one might think that almost everything known about these people has been published already. However, we will see that this is not the case. First of all, many of the published studies deal only with the Aztec state in its role as an expansionist, tributary "empire." This "empire" was never a fully-integrated political entity. Rather, in its fullest development it was a confederation—a Triple Alliance—of three dominant polities, city-states, or señoríos, administered by Tenochtitlan, Texcoco, and Tlacopan, which jointly managed to subjugate 489 towns located in 38 "provinces" containing 15,000,000 people speaking several different languages. Most of these "provinces" lay beyond the Valley of Mexico; within them there were territorial groups that retained their autonomy, and groups that paid tribute to the Aztec Triple Alliance. This produced a complex mosaic of resistant, enemy peoples on the one hand, and cooperative, apparently loyal subjects on the other hand (Barlow 1949).

Rather than taking this expansionist, tributary "empire" as her primary theme, Mary Hodge takes as her principal concern the building blocks of the Aztec state—the city-states within the Valley of Mexico—focusing special attention on their diversity. As do so many major studies on the Aztec, this book is based squarely on the ethnohistorical documents, both published and unpublished, primarily because they afford us data that are rich and abundant, and they deal with topics for which we have no other source of information. However, Hodge also seeks to integrate these ethnohistorical data with available archaeological data (both survey and excavation) from the Valley of Mexico, thereby maximizing two complementary data sets.

One of the concerns of this book is to redress the imbalance created by other studies that are either capital-centric (Tenochtitlan-biased) or Mexica-biased, by presenting a multi-ethnic view that reveals the heterogeneous nature of all the polities that comprised the Valley of Mexico.

We know that somewhere between 40 and 60 city-states or señoríos constituted the center of the Aztec state and that they were occupied by the Chalca, the Acolhuaque, the Cuitlahuaca, the Culhuaque, the Xochimilca, the Mixquica, the Tepaneca, the Mexica, and the Otomí. Only the Otomí were non-Nahuatl speakers, employing an Otomanguean language. Each of the aforementioned ethnic groups had its own origin myths describing the difficulties encountered during its migration prior to arriving at its final destination in the Valley of Mexico. Additionally, each group recorded its own version of "history" and displayed a different type of internal political organization. Despite this ethnic, linguistic, and organizational diversity, various coalitions or alliances of two, three, or four members were formed, many of an ephemeral nature, with the Triple Alliance being merely one of the most well known, most powerful, and long lasting.

What is familiar to the Mesoamericanist is the saga of just one of these ethnic groups, the Mexica, who were the founders of Tenochtitlan ca. A.D. 1325 and later became the most prominent member of the Triple Alliance. Prior to this event, the Mexica were expelled from Chapultepec by their enemies the Tepaneca, the Culhuaque, and the Otomí. Upon settling in what came to be known as Tenochtitlan, the Mexica became part of a dependency of the Tepaneca capital, Azcapotzalco. The three earliest rulers of the Mexica were forced to pay tribute to Azcapotzalco. However, during the reign of the fourth Mexica ruler, Itzcoatl (A.D. 1427-1440), Tepaneca control was overthrown. From that time on, the Mexica began to form alliances, seeking military aid, labor, and tribute from various Tepaneca towns. Unable to usurp the land already occupied by other ethnic groups within the Valley of Mexico, they sought to establish working and tribute-paying alliances. This alliance-forming strategy meant that the lands continued to be occupied by a variety of ethnic groups, each semi-autonomous and each differing in internal organization. Within the Valley of Mexico these various groups can be listed in order of decreasing political power as follows: Mexica, Acolhuaque, Tepaneca, Chalca, Xochimilca, Cuitlahuaca, Mixquica, Culhuaque, and Otomí (Gibson 1964:21).

Just as the Mexica sought to elevate themselves above all other competitive ethnic groups, the ethnohistorians have usually followed suit, elevating the Mexica to an exalted position and allocating to them most of the space in the anthropological literature. At the same time, ethnohistorians often neglect to present a balanced, comprehensive view of the ethnic groups occupying the other 39-59 city-states (Bray 1972). That these ethnic divisions continued to be important at the time of the Spanish Conquest and into the Colonial period is clear from various sources. For example, we know that each ethnic group fought as a squadron in battle, or worked together as a labor force. For example, during the reign of Ahuitzotl (A.D. 1486-1502), work on an aqueduct was divided up into separate, specialized activities to be undertaken by the Acolhuaque, the Tepaneca, the Chalca, and the Xochimilca. Still later the Spaniards themselves deployed labor from four "provinces"—Mexico, Texcoco, Tlacopan, and Tlalmanalco—to repair significant flood damage in Mexico City during the Colonial period.

Hodge selects five of these city-states—Amecameca, Cuauhtitlan, Xochimilco, Coyoacan, and Teotihuacan—for detailed study of their internal organization. She is able to chronicle the changes that took place before, during, and after each of these city-states was incorporated into the Aztec "empire." She concentrates on the relationships among city-states (emphasizing these horizontal integrative mechanisms) and on the relationships between individual city-states and member(s) of the Triple Alliance (revealing vertical integrative mechanisms).

One of the conditions revealed by Hodge is that these city-states were often multi-ethnic polities, sometimes containing from 10,000 to 50,000 people (e.g. Bray 1972) with the only true metropolis being the atypical capital Tenochtitlan, with its 150,000 to 200,000 inhabitants (Calnek 1976:288).

Hodge presents a much needed view of the hierarchy, looking at the often neglected lower-order centers below the level of the capital. Prior to their incorporation into the Aztec state, these city-states were ruled by lineage leaders. Following incorporation, the state might retain these local lineage leaders if they were cooperative, or might replace them with pro-Mexica relatives. Another strategy pointed out by Hodge was the appointment of a temporary military ruler to be replaced later by a pro-Mexica (usually a relative of the former) ruler who was probably educated at Tenochtitlan. The Aztec capital was usually able to disrupt the succession to office within city-states when anti-Mexica leaders were about to rule.

Marriage alliances between the nobility of a lower-order center and a higher-order center were an effective means by which the Mexica could develop loyalty (Carrasco 1984), and constitute an example of a vertical integrative mechanism. Another example was the mandatory attendance of the city-state's ruler in the capital for part of every year. Additionally, the confirmation of city-state rulers took place at Tenochtitlan, and these rulers were required to attend special feasts or rites at the capital at specified times during the year.

As fundamental as the city-state was, so were the coalitions and confederations of city-states. This mosaic of polities with shifting loyalties and allegiances characterized not just the Valley of Mexico during the Late Postclassic period (A.D. 1300-1500), but much of Mesoamerica including the Mixteca (Spores 1967, 1983), the Valley of Oaxaca (Marcus and Flannery 1983), and the Yucatán peninsula (Roys 1957). Such señoríos or *cacicazgos* were encountered by the Spaniards in many other regions of Latin America as well.

INTRODUCTION TO VOLUME 3

Through a comparison of five city-states, Hodge is able to show that the imperial tribute hierarchy was highly centralized, and quite different from the administrative hierarchy. She also demonstrates that the more hierarchically organized an area was prior to incorporation into the Aztec "empire," the less the bureaucratic control imposed from above. For the most part, these city-states retained a surprising degree of political, cultural, and religious autonomy even after being incorporated into the Aztec "empire."

Bibliography

Barlow, Robert H.
    1949   The Extent of the Empire of the Culhua Mexica. *Ibero-Americana*, no. 28. Berkeley: University of California Press.

Bray, Warwick
    1972   The City State in Central Mexico at the Time of the Spanish Conquest. *Journal of Latin American Studies* 4(2):161-85.

Calnek, Edward E.
    1976   The Internal Structure of Tenochtitlan. In *The Valley of Mexico: Studies in Pre-Hispanic Ecology and Society*, Eric R. Wolf, ed., pp. 287-302. Albuquerque: University of New Mexico Press.

Carrasco, Pedro
    1984   Royal Marriages in Ancient Mexico. In *Explorations in Ethnohistory: Indians of Central Mexico in the Sixteenth Century*, Herbert R. Harvey and Hanns J. Prem, eds., pp. 41-81. Albuquerque: University of New Mexico Press.

Gibson, Charles
    1964   *The Aztecs Under Spanish Rule: A History of the Indians of the Valley of Mexico, 1519-1810*. Stanford: Stanford University Press.

Marcus, Joyce, and Kent V. Flannery
    1983   An Introduction to the Late Postclassic. In *The Cloud People: Divergent Evolution of the Zapotec and Mixtec Civilizations*, Kent V. Flannery and Joyce Marcus, eds., pp. 217-26. New York: Academic Press.

Roys, Ralph L.
    1957   The Political Geography of the Yucatan Maya. *Carnegie Institution of Washington, Publication 613*. Washington, D.C.: Carnegie Institution.

Spores, Ronald M.
    1967   *The Mixtec Kings and Their People*. Norman: University of Oklahoma Press.
    1983   The Origin and Evolution of the Mixtec System of Social Stratification. In *The Cloud People: Divergent Evolution of the Zapotec and Mixtec Civilizations*, Kent V. Flannery and Joyce Marcus, eds., pp. 227-38. New York: Academic Press.

Contents

Figures xi
Tables xiii
Acknowledgments xv

1. **Introduction** 1
   Evolution and Operation of States and Empires 2
      States and Empires Defined 2
      States as Complex Systems 2
      States as Regional Organizations 3
      Formation of Regional Political Systems 4
   Sources of Information on Aztec City-States 5
      Documents 5
      Archaeological Data on Aztec Culture 8
   Aspects of the Operation of Aztec City-States to be Examined 9
      Cultural Diversity Among Aztec City-States 9
      Internal Political Systems of Aztec City-States 9
      Interaction of City-States and the Capital 9
   Methodology 9
   Procedure 11

2. **City-States in the Valley of Mexico: An Overview** 13
   The Environmental Setting 13
   Occupational History of the Valley of Mexico 13
   Political Units in the Valley of Mexico 17
      City-States 17
      Confederations 18
   Aztec Capitals 18
      Tenochtitlan 18
      Texcoco 24
      Tlacopan 26
   The Empire 28
      The Triple Alliance 28
      Administration of Warfare 29
      Imperial Tribute Collection 30

3. **Amecameca** 33
   The Place and the People of Amecameca 33
      Settlement History of Amecameca 33
      The Urban Center of Amecameca 33
      Amecameca's People 34
      Rituals and Ideology in Amecameca 37
      Amecameca's Territory 40
   Amecameca's Political System 40

  Overview of Amecameca's Political Development 40
  Titles and Officials 41
  Support of Amecameca's Officials 43
  Rulers of Amecameca 44
  Succession to the Office of Teuctli in Amecameca 44
  Marriage Alliances of Amecameca's Rulers 46
  Amecameca as an Independent City-State 48
 Amecameca and the Aztec Empire 51
  Conquest by the Triple Alliance 51
  Effects of Conquest 51
 Summary and Conclusions 53
  History and Internal Organization of Amecameca 53
  Relations with Other Polities 54
  Conquest by the Empire 54

4. Cuauhtitlan 57
 The Place and the People of Cuauhtitlan 57
  Cuauhtitlan in 1519 57
  Evolution of the Urban Center of Cuauhtitlan 57
  Cuauhtitlan's People 60
  Rituals and Deities of Cuauhtitlan 60
 Cuauhtitlan's Political System 65
  Titles and Officials 65
  Support of Cuauhtitlan's Officials 65
  Territorial Organization of Cuauhtitlan 66
  Rulers of Cuauhtitlan 68
  Succession to Rulership in Cuauhtitlan 68
  Marriage Alliances of Cuauhtitlan's Rulers 70
  Political Alliances of the Independent City-State of Cuauhtitlan 70
 Cuauhtitlan and the Aztec Empire 73
  Conquest by Tenochtitlan 73
  Effects of Conquest 73
 Summary 76
  Cuauhtitlan's Political System 76
  Pre-Imperial Political Alliances 76
  Cuauhtitlan as a Dependency of Tenochtitlan 76

5. Xochimilco 81
 The Place and People of Xochimilco 81
  The Urban Center of Xochimilco 81
  The Xochimilca 82
  Xochimilca Deities and Rituals 84
  Extent of Xochimilca Territory 85
 Xochimilco's Political System 86
  Officials and Titles 86
  Economic Support of Xochimilco's Administrators 88
  Rulers of Xochimilco 89
  Succession to Rulership in Xochimilco 90
  Marriages between Xochimilco's and Tenochtitlan's Elites 90
  Xochimilco's Pre-Imperial Political Alliances 90
 Xochimilco and the Aztec Empire 93

    Conquest by the Triple Alliance 93
    Xochimilco as a Dependency of the Triple Alliance 93
  Summary and Conclusions 96

6. Coyoacan 99
  The Place and the People of Coyoacan 99
    The Urban Center of Coyoacan 99
    The People of Coyoacan 100
    Ideology and Religion in Coyoacan 100
    Coyoacan's Territory 102
  Political Organization of Coyoacan 103
    Officials and Titles 103
    Administration of Dependencies 104
    Economic Organization of the Tlatoani's Household 106
    Rulers of Coyoacan 108
    Ruler Succession in Pre-Hispanic Coyoacan 108
    Marriage Alliances of Coyoacan's Rulers 109
    Political Alliances of Coyoacan 109
  Coyoacan as a Dependency of the Aztec Empire 109
    Coyoacan's Obligations to the Triple Alliance 110
  Summary and Conclusions 113
    The Political Organization of Coyoacan 113
    Coyoacan's Alliances with Other City-States 113
    Coyoacan and Tenochtitlan 114

7. Teotihuacan: An Acolhua City-State 117
  The People and the Place of Teotihuacan 117
    The Urban Center of Teotihuacan 117
    The People of Teotihuacan 122
    Religion and Ritual at Aztec Teotihuacan 123
    Territorial Organization of Teotihuacan 123
  Teotihuacan's Political System 124
    Officials and Titles 124
    Rulers and Succession to Rulership 125
    Marriage Alliances of Teotihuacan's Rulers 125
    Income of Teotihuacan's Rulers 126
    Teotihuacan's Political Alliances 126
  Teotihuacan as a Dependency of Texcoco 129
  Teotihuacan as a Tributary Province of Tenochtitlan 130
  Summary and Conclusions 131
    Historical Summary 131
    Internal Organization 131
    Teotihuacan as a Dependency of the Triple Alliance Capitals 131

8. Conclusions: The Aztec Empire as Seen from Its Dependencies 133
  City-States 133
  Organization of Five Aztec City-States: A Comparison 133
    Territories 133
    Urban Centers 134
    City-State Officials 135
    Central-Place Functions of City-States 136

    Rulership 136
    Succession to Rulership 138
    Marriage Alliances of Ruling Lineages 138
    City-States Before the Empire 139
The Aztec Empire's Center 139
    Confederations of City-States in the Valley of Mexico 139
    Administration of Dependencies of the Empire 141
City-States and the Aztec Empire 142
    Goals of the Empire 142
    Effects of Conquest 142
    The Political Hierarchy 144
    The Tribute Hierarchy 145
    Tribute in Labor 147
    Marriage Alliances 147
    Centralization vs. Autonomy 148
Conclusions 150

Glossary of Some Nahuatl and Spanish Words 151

Bibliography 153

Resumen en Español 163

Figures

1-1. Location of city-states chosen for study	10
2-1. Location of the Valley of Mexico in Mesoamerica	14
2-2. The Valley of Mexico, showing the lake and major towns	15
2-3. Chronological sequences for the Valley of Mexico	16
2-4. Political confederations of the Valley of Mexico	18
2-5. Cities in the Valley of Mexico ruled by tlatoque, ca. A.D. 1519	19
2-6. Plan of Tenochtitlan	20
2-7. Genealogy of the rulers of Tenochtitlan	23
2-8. Lordships of the Acolhua state	25
2-9. Areas controlled by Triple Alliance members in 1519	28
2-10. Areas from which the Triple Alliance exacted tribute	31
3-1. Location of Amecameca in the Valley of Mexico	34
3-2. Map of Amecameca in 1599	35
3-3. Amecameca as portrayed on the Santa Cruz map, ca. 1550	36
3-4. Modern map of Amecameca showing its barrios	37
3-5. Late Aztec period settlements in the Amecameca area	38
3-6. Map of Amecameca and other Chalca settlements	43
3-7. Genealogy of rulers of Itztlacozauhcan and Tlayllotlacan	47
3-8. Marriages between nobles of Tenochtitlan and rulers of Amecameca	49
3-9. Location of tribute-collection points in Chalco province	52
3-10. Amecameca's internal administrative organization before and after conquest by the Aztec empire	55
3-11. Amecameca's position in the Valley of Mexico political organization	56
4-1. Location of Cuauhtitlan	58
4-2. Cuauhtitlan in 1550	59
4-3. Late Aztec settlement patterns, Cuauhtitlan area	61
4-4. Map of Cuauhtitlan area, ca. 1590	63
4-5. Cuauhtitlan's dependencies, 1390–1408	67
4-6. Dependencies of Cuauhtitlan, 1434–1495	69
4-7. Cuauhtitlan's dependencies, ca. 1519	71
4-8. Genealogy of the rulers of Cuauhtitlan	72
4-9. Changes in the administrative organization of Cuauhtitlan	75
4-10. Tribute-collection points in Cuauhtitlan province	77
4-11. The Codex San Andrés	78
4-12. Cuauhtitlan's position in the political hierarchy	79
5-1. Location of Xochimilco in the Valley of Mexico	82
5-2. Late Aztec settlements in the Xochimilco area	83
5-3. The city of Xochimilco in the mid-1500s	84
5-4. The Xochimilca confederation before 1430	86
5-5. Xochimilco's territory, ca. 1519	87
5-6. Organization of taxes and labor in Tepetenchi, ca. 1548	89
5-7. Diagram of fields granted to the cacique of Tepetenchi in 1582	91
5-8. Relationships of rulers of Tenochtitlan to tlatoque of Olac and Tepetenchi	95
5-9. Diagram of Xochimilco's political organization before and after 1430	97
6-1. Location of Coyoacan in the Valley of Mexico	100
6-2. Late Aztec settlements in the Coyoacan region	101
6-3. Coyoacan as pictured on the Santa Cruz map	103
6-4. Coyoacan's territory, with some of its dependencies	105
6-5. Coyoacan's administrative organization, mid-1500s	107
6-6. Genealogy of tlatoque of Coyoacan, Azcapotzalco, and Tenochtitlan	111
6-7. Acolhua and Tepaneca labor zones, with Coyoacan in the Tepaneca zone	114
6-8. Coyoacan's position in the political hierarchy at two different times	115
7-1. Location of Teotihuacan in the Valley of Mexico	118
7-2. Late Aztec period settlements in the Teotihuacan area	119
7-3. The town of San Juan Teotihuacan in 1580	121
7-4. Map of San Juan Teotihuacan's barrios in 1764	122
7-5. Sujetos of Teotihuacan, Acolman, and Tepexpan in 1580	124
7-6. Marriage alliances between rulers of Teotihuacan and Texcoco	127
7-7. Diagram of Teotihuacan in the Valley of Mexico political hierarchy	132

8-1. Comparison of estimated sizes of the territories of five city-states 134
8-2. Change in five local political hierarchies 143
8-3. Levels of decision-makers in the Triple Alliance 145
8-4. Actual versus idealized political hierarchy 146
8-5. Location of tributary provinces in the Valley of Mexico 147
8-6. Marriage alliances between the ruling lineages of Tenochtitlan and Texcoco and other Valley of Mexico city-states . 149

Tables

2-1.	Communities with a tlatoani in 1519	17
2-2.	Reorganization of the Acolhua (Texcocan) state ca. 1430	26
2-3.	Divisions of the Acolhua state which provided labor for the palace	27
3-1.	Amecameca's lineages and barrios	39
3-2.	Place of origin, ethnic affiliation, and deity of migrants to Amecameca	39
3-3.	Amecameca's sujetos, 1599	41
3-4.	Significant events in Amecameca's political history	42
3-5.	Rulers of the seven divisions of Amecameca	45
3-6.	Political organization of Chalco province before its conquest by Mexico, according to Chimalpahin	46
3-7.	Amecameca's political organization after its conquest by Tenochtitlan	46
4-1.	Rulers of Cuauhtitlan	62
4-2.	Events in the development of the polity of Cuauhtitlan	64
4-3.	Genealogical information on rulers of Cuauhtitlan	73
5-1.	Titles of Xochimilco's administrators	87
5-2.	Income of Don Martín, *cacique* of Tepentechi, 1548	92
5-3a.	Rulers of Tepetenchi Xochimilco	92
5-3b.	Rulers of Tecpan Xochimilco	92
5-3c.	Rulers of Olac Xochimilco	93
6-1.	Divisions of Coyoacan in 1553	102
6-2.	Dependents and/or administrators responsible to Don Juan, 1550	106
6-3.	Number of tribute payers and administrators in Coyoacan, 1553	107
6-4.	Income of Don Juan, tlatoani of Coyoacan	108
6-5.	List of Indians assigned to work the fields of Don Juan, *cacique* of Coyoacan, middle 1500s	109
6-6.	Rulers of Coyoacan	110
6-7.	List of work assigned to Coyoacan's sujetos on a single day in 1613	113
7-1.	Rulers of Teotihuacan	125
7-2.	Lands paying tribute to the tlatoani of Teotihuacan	128
7-3.	Property of Don Francisco Quetzalmamalitzin, from his will, 1563	128
7-4.	Tribute received by Teotihuacan's rulers	129
8-1.	Hierarchy of imperial tribute payment in the Valley of Mexico, according to Codex Mendoza	148

Acknowledgments

I wish to thank several individuals whose guidance aided me in the development and completion of this study. Dr. Joyce Marcus provided expertise in Mesoamerican archaeology, ethnohistorical research, and methodology; her constant enthusiasm and careful, critical attention to all stages of the research and manuscript preparation were invaluable. Dr. Jeffrey R. Parsons generously made available his data, his knowledge of Valley of Mexico archaeology, and his time for discussions of method and data. Dr. Henry T. Wright's knowledge of, perspectives on, and enthusiasm for research on the evolution of complex societies were especially helpful. Dr. William D. Schorger provided me with a broad overview of political anthropology and political processes in states and empires. Dr. John W. Eadie's perspective on the study of ancient empires was stimulating and helpful as well. I was aided in my first studies of Aztec history and in the initial development of my research by Dr. Charles Gibson, and I am grateful for his many practical suggestions. In addition, I wish to thank Dr. Kent V. Flannery for perspectives on Mesoamerican prehistory presented in lectures and discussions. I am grateful for the support of the staff of the University of Michigan Museum of Anthropology in my work there, particularly Richard I. Ford and James B. Griffin. An earlier version of this book was submitted in partial fulfillment of the requirements for the doctoral degree in the Horace H. Rackham School of Graduate Studies at the University of Michigan.

I would also like to thank Frederick Hicks, Elizabeth Brumfiel, and Edward Calnek for taking the time to read and comment on drafts of the manuscript for this book. Their comments on the work, as viewed from their areas of expertise, have been very useful. Drawings for the volume were prepared by Michael Hodge and Kay Clahassey.

My research was made possible by funds from the Wenner-Gren Foundation for Anthropological Research; the American Association of University Women; the Horace H. Rackham School of Graduate Studies, University of Michigan; the James B. Griffin Research Fund; and the Newberry Library, Chicago. Work in archives and collections in Mexico was facilitated by the staff of the Archivo General de la Nación, the Museo Nacional de Antropología e Historia, and the Instituto de Antropología, Universidad Nacional Autónoma de México.

Chapter 1

Introduction

Between A.D. 1430 and 1520, the Aztec[1] empire conquered and exacted tribute from much of Mesoamerica. Formed originally by the alliance of three city-states in the Valley of Mexico (Tenochtitlan, Texcoco, and Tlacopan), the empire expanded by absorbing other city-states. This empire was ultimately ruled by Tenochtitlan, the Mexica capital, before its conquest by Spaniards in A.D. 1521. This study examines political processes in the center of the empire by focusing on the evolution and organization of a selection of city-states in the Valley of Mexico.

According to traditional histories recorded in indigenous script and also committed to memory, the city-states of the Late pre-Hispanic period in the Valley of Mexico were founded by groups from Tula and from further north, who entered the valley following the demise of Tula (ca. A.D. 1150). Before the foundation of the Aztec empire, the valley was occupied by approximately 40-60 independent polities, or city-states. Each city-state was composed of an urban center and a territory containing villages and hamlets. A city-state was governed by one or more hereditary rulers. Each ruler and his palace dependents, as well as religious and military specialists, were supported by commoners. These city-states became part of the empire through alliance or conquest.

The city-states in the Valley of Mexico formed a number of political factions, and the histories of Aztec city-states record diverse traditions as well as political tensions between city-state lords and imperial rulers (for instance, *Anales de Cuauhtitlan* 1945; *Crónica Mexicáyotl* 1949; *Anales de Tlatelolco* 1948; *Códice Xólotl* 1951; Malacachtepec Momoxco 1953; *Tira de Tepechpan* 1978; Chimalpahin 1889, 1965, 1975; Alva Ixtlilxochitl 1975-77). On the other hand, histories written from the point of view of the capital (Alvarado Tezozomoc 1975; Durán 1967; Sahagún 1950-69)—which comprise the bulk of information on Aztec culture—present a normative description of Aztec political organization and have promoted a one-sided view of Aztec culture. The capital has been regarded as typical of Aztec city-states, and regional diversity has been largely ignored. This study attempts to develop a regional and comparative perspective on polities within the geographical center of the Aztec empire. Moreover, study of the interactions between the capital and other city-states, as recorded in the chronicles, can be used to analyze the political system of the Valley of Mexico in the Late pre-Hispanic period.

The following chapters investigate the structure and development of the political systems of five Aztec city-states. Although Aztec city-states have frequently been classified as similar because of their shared dependent status under the empire, they were not microcosms of the capital (an atypical city-state) nor were they uniformly rural dependencies existing at a much lower level of organiza-

---

[1]The term "Aztec" is employed here because the term readily identifies to the non-specialist the dominant polity of Late pre-Hispanic central Mexico. Herein, the term "Aztec" refers to all of the predominantly Nahuatl-speaking peoples and polities subsumed under the Triple Alliance (the political confederation of Tenochtitlan, Texcoco, and Tlacopan, which controlled central Mexico in 1519). In the following study, the entire political system headed by this confederation is called the Aztec empire, following the precedent in the literature (Gibson 1964b, 1971).

However, the term "Aztec" is too general a term to describe adequately all the varied polities that comprised the empire, and since the following study concentrates on diversity within the empire, subdivisions will be referred to according to more specific names. Such regional distinctions, which were made by the pre-Hispanic Nahuatl-speakers themselves, describe more specifically the variety of polities and historical traditions that existed within the Aztec empire. Viewing the "Aztec" empire as a number of component parts aids in developing a regional perspective and helps to delineate the texture of interwoven political connections that formed the system as a whole.

tion than the capital. Instead, they varied greatly in size and complexity. The chapters that follow examine how five Aztec city-states differed from one another, to what extent incorporation into the empire modified them, and to what extent they remained culturally or even politically autonomous after they became part of the empire.

Evolution and Operation of States and Empires

States and Empires Defined

Anthropological research into the evolution of political systems has given rise to definitions and theories which are useful for analysis of the Aztec political system. Anthropological theory proposes that human societies evolve from simple levels of organization to more complex ones, the most complex form being the state (Service 1971, 1975; Flannery 1972).

States are socio-political organizations, usually with populations numbering in the hundreds of thousands, that have a strong, centralized government, a professional ruling class, class stratification, and diversified economies that often are controlled by the elites. They maintain a monopoly of force and have law codes (Flannery 1972).

In its most developed form, the Aztec political system in the Valley of Mexico can be characterized as a state-level system. However, many of the activities of the Aztec political system resemble those associated with the type of political system identified as an empire.

An empire is a particular form of state. In general, ". . .ancient empires were territorially extensive, at least moderately durable, state systems that were substantially preoccupied with channelling resources from diverse subject polities and peoples to an ethnically defined ruling stratum whose authority ultimately derived from the repeated exercise of its military power" (Adams 1979:59).

Empires display several distinctive organizational qualities. Economically, empires attempt to monopolize the flow of goods within a large area, and often, to do this, they control trade routes. In scale, ancient empires were restricted by their ability to maintain communications between all parts; thus, ancient empires invested in communication facilities such as roads, messengers, and tribute record keeping. Ecologically, empires expand to control all of the zones within a large area. In relation to their social environment, empires expand to control all stratified and hierarchically organized societies (that is, all societies that can be controlled from the top) or they create such structures in conquered areas if they do not already exist there (Lattimore 1962). Ideologically, ancient empires attempted to achieve legitimacy by creating a pan-imperial ethos or philosophy, characterized by an abstract deity or a fundamental proposition which chartered their existence (Eisenstadt 1963; Caso 1966; H.T. Wright, personal communication, 1983).

States as Complex Systems

Early states and empires operated in societies which were less differentiated than modern society, and to study the development of these systems, it is necessary to define some specific processes relevant to the operation of political systems. For analytical purposes, this study focuses on political systems as organizations which control decision-making and information flow. Analyzing change in the systems through which political information flows allows the research to focus on political processes (which may occur outside of formal structures or roles, and which in early complex societies may have been fused with religious or economic activities) rather than on structure alone.

Thus, for analytical purposes, states may be viewed as information-processing systems, and the operation of state political systems may be analyzed through changes in their decision-making systems. For such purposes, a state is viewed "as a society with specialized decision-making organizations that are receiving messages from many different sources, recoding these messages, supplementing them with previously stored data, making the actual decision, storing both the message and the decision, and conveying decisions back to other organizations" (Wright 1978:56). Furthermore, for such purposes, a "state can be *conceptualized* as a sociocultural system in which there is a differentiated, internally specialized, decision-making subsystem that regulates varying exchanges among other subsystems and with other systems. Regulation involves information flow, even if it is expressed in the flow of material items" (ibid.).

This definition of states implies that (1) "information flow obeys the principle of channel capacity" (Wright 1978:56); that is, individuals can process information at only so fast a rate. If information flow increases, more administrators are needed, and more levels of hierarchy may be needed to coordinate activities. As information flow expands, the number of administrators expands horizontally and hierarchically (Johnson 1978:88). (2) Information flow is revealed in the form of materials and energy; and (3) Materials and human resources usually are limited relative to the demands of the system. "Therefore decision-makers will usually engage in whatever competition and/or collusion might be possible without destroying the system in order to maintain their segment of the hierarchy. Such political action will further define the internal structure of the decision-making system" (Wright 1978:56).

States as complex systems are differentiated, that is, the society's members are formally divided into positions, ranks, or subunits. Differentiation is vertical, i.e., decision-makers at different levels do different things and centers at different levels perform different functions. It is also horizontal, that is, decision-makers and centers at the same level may perform different functions or supply different goods. The development of vertical or horizontal differentiation in an administrative system creates different problems for administrators. Horizontal differentiation—the addition of many units at one level—increases the administrative workload at the top, but vertical differentiation—the addition of levels in the hierarchy—reduces direct control at the top. Structural differentiation, whether vertical or horizontal, involves more units, and these require increased managerial manpower to process increasing amounts of information. These managers have an increasingly specialized span of control (Blau and Schoenherr 1971:301-39).

As a state evolves, new hierarchical levels arise where none had previously existed; that is, as states become more complex and larger, more levels are added to the administrative hierarchy and more units are added to each level to process information (Johnson 1978). For some archaic states, archaeologists have identified regional administrative hierarchies, using economic or political texts (Wright and Johnson 1975; Marcus 1973, 1976). State systems are believed to have at least four levels in their administrative hierarchies.

Empires expand by absorbing other states. The administrative system of an empire may be horizontally differentiated, that is, different parts of the system perform different tasks (for instance, the center polities may carry out different tasks than border polities). Vertical differentiation occurs as units are assembled into a number of levels, with those at higher levels controlling those at lower levels. Imperial systems, which are built from a number of hierarchically organized units (states), can be assembled quickly, since each individual component is already organized into a system of control (Simon 1969).

The Aztec empire developed from a number of small city-states with their own internal hierarchies. Analyzing the processes involved in creating a centralized decision-making hierarchy was one goal of this study.

States as Regional Organizations

State political organizations operate in space as well as in time, and to understand the operation of archaic states better, anthropologists have turned from studying capitals in isolation to regional studies of capitals and their supporting areas. A regional approach concentrates on the relationships between centers and their support areas, allowing for the variation between the two, to produce more accurate generalizations, for, "With other approaches, generalization requires one to assume that what is true of the whole is also true of the parts. Regional analysis can build system variability into its models of explanation, so that generalization is neither far-fetched nor banal" (Smith 1976:5).

Regional theory suggests that functionally defined regions represent several levels of integration within a hierarchy of human settlements that theoretically culminates in a single all-inclusive system (ibid.). In complex societies, a hierarchical system of information or material exchanges exists. The lower-order and more commonly used functions will be located in numerous small centers, while higher-order functions will be located in fewer centers having correspondingly larger hinterlands (Haggett 1966; Berry, Conkling, and Ray 1976). Centers provide services that allow communication of information, division of labor, exchange of goods, and delegation of authority and control, sustaining the places and territories dependent upon them, and conversely, being sustained by these areas.

Basic units for regional studies are (1) local systems—those in which material and nonmaterial exchanges are organized around at least one higher-level node that regulates otherwise equivalent communities as places, and (2) regional systems—those nodal systems that include a number of levels of hierarchically organized communities. They have truly "urban" centers, complex linkages between communities and higher-level centers, and an organized pattern of nested local systems within them.

Regional settlement hierarchies have been recognized in several archaic state systems, based on site-size data and economic and political data (Johnson 1973; Marcus 1973, 1976, 1983b; Wright and Johnson 1975; Wright 1978). In some cases, economic or administrative hierarchies have been found to be paralleled by settlement patterns; that is, states have a capital with subsidiary administrative centers around it, and around them are smaller centers which are administered by them, all of which fall into predictable geographic patterns which promote efficiency in distributing services, goods, and information (Skinner 1977; Blanton et al. 1982). The range of variation in state settlement patterns is still being investigated and debated (Blanton 1976a; Willey 1979; Santley 1980; Sanders 1981).

Formation of Regional Political Systems

When polities merge either by voluntary alliance or conquest, hierarchically organized polities, or states, are absorbed quickly into larger systems such as empires (Simon 1969). That is, ". . .complex systems will evolve from simple systems much more rapidly if there are stable intermediate forms than if there are not. The resulting complex forms in the former case will be hierarchic" (Simon 1969:98-99). Similarly and hierarchically organized polities are easier to add to an empire than are ones organized very differently; and polities at a lower level of integration, which require intensive management, are harder to incorporate into an empire (Service 1955; Simon 1969). However, unless measures are taken by the center to crosscut the already-existing hierarchies in a region, segments are likely to secede, and a problem for empires is to maintain control of previously independent states.

Although an empire may be formed of previously separate units with hierarchical administrative structures replicated in each, following conquest by or affiliation with an empire, the decision-making systems of dependencies will change. Research on empires has disclosed that a number of specific effects may be expected.

As autonomous polities become part of an empire, the ways in which they are affected may vary in relation to their locations. Neighboring polities are more likely to be incorporated into a centralized administrative system, whereas those farther away may be conquered solely for tribute exaction. For instance, the Chinese empire's border dependencies had different obligations to the capital than did nearby polities which were part of an administratively homogeneous central area. The administrative systems of nearby polities conformed to a uniform pattern, as did their political economies. The frontier territories, on the other hand, supplied raw materials not available in the central area, paid taxes, and served as border guards (Lattimore 1962:469-91). Some of the Aztec empire's peripheral dependencies guarded borders in lieu of paying tribute (Davies 1973:114).

In empires, the capital competes with other centers for goods, and capitals generally contain more people, more sumptuary goods, more religious specialists, more artisans than dependencies, as well as the highest level decision-makers. Dependencies may lose income, specialists, and decision-makers; however, there are limits to centralization (Flannery 1972), and most imperial systems encourage centralization to the extent that it promotes efficient flow of information and goods to the capital (Eisenstadt 1963).

In empires, local economies are manipulated so that economic relations benefit the center (Adams 1979:59). The local assets (goods, land, and labor) of provincial rulers diminish, and they become dependent on the capital. The center of an empire gains at the expense of the dependent, conquered polities.

In order to control formerly autonomous regions, the capital attempts to effect greater interaction between the capital and its dependencies than between and among dependencies. The capital attempts to weaken former alliances and may create competition for favors among local rulers.

Rulers of conquered areas incorporated into an imperial structure may gain strength relative to their previous position by taking on imperial offices and hence gaining the empire's support. This way, they can become more powerful than local rivals (Lattimore 1962:475-76). On the other hand, if these provincial rulers become too dependent upon the empire's support, they may lose local support and hence lose their ability to rebel. For instance, rulers of Roman client states were often in insecure positions, for although they used Roman force to maintain their positions, fear of Roman force used against them kept them loyal (Luttwak 1976:31). "By channelling money and favors through chosen client chiefs, the Romans helped the latter gain power over their subjects, while the Romans gained power over them" (Luttwak 1976:36).

Conquest of formerly independent states by empires does not imply simply annexation of territory or removal of rulers; conquered rulers usually accept terms in order to retain some of their autonomy (Bosch Gimpera 1966:29). As a result, change in conquered areas can be gradual, and in the Roman empire, rulers of large, important states had more leeway for negotiation than did those of smaller, less important states (Luttwak 1976:31). Thus, centers incorporated into an empire do not lose all their previous functions; instead, they become part of a hierarchical political system in which the capital contains the highest-level administrators who make policy affecting the entire system, second-level centers have administrators whose span of control is less, and third- and fourth-level administrators make decisions and carry out policy involving even smaller areas and numbers of people.

In ancient empires, general policy decisions about pan-imperial matters were made at the capital, with provincial centers having diminishing spans of control with descending levels in the hierarchy. Archaeological evidence of early states and empires shows that provincial administrative centers may contain smaller versions of the capital's public administrative buildings, special indicators of their administrator's status (such as Maya stelae [Marcus 1976]), or special-purpose architecture such as administrative buildings (Wright and Johnson 1975). They may also contain garrisons, exchange areas, palaces, courts, temples, ball courts, and workshops, indicating specialized functions.

In summary, following conquest by or affiliation with an empire, the administrative centers of previously independent states (1) become secondary or tertiary administrative centers; (2) remain foci for the movement of goods and information in their own regions; (3) operate at a lower level economically than the capital they are supplying; (4) are smaller and may be less differentiated than the capital. Furthermore, the more hierarchically organized a polity before absorption into an empire, the less administrative organization will need to be imposed; the less hierarchically organized an area, the more administrators must be imposed. Empires have used indigenous elites as their decision-makers or replaced them with bureaucrats from the capital, depending on the situation. Because of constraints of scale, local centers seldom are done away with completely, for they serve a purpose as lower-order centers in the new hierarchy, though they may be assigned specialized tasks, as the decision-making system of the state or empire becomes increasingly differentiated into a number of hierarchies (e.g., tax collection versus political administration). Hierarchical integration such as this may reduce the ability of segments to fragment from the whole.

While the processes of centralization and hierarchy formation apply to all complex systems, it remains to be discovered whether these processes always unfold in the same sequence in state formation, or whether, and more likely, there may be a predictable variety of developmental sequences which culminate in state-level organizations. Likewise, there may be a predictable sequence of forms in the evolution of administrative systems of empires (Eisenstadt 1963; Johnson 1978).

The following study examines the evolution of the administrative system of the Aztec empire, a system which absorbed autonomous city-states at first by conquest and alliance, but later integrated them more fully by administrative measures. Emphasis will be placed on the effects of conquest on previously autonomous city-states and upon the capital's strategies for dealing with regional variation among the city-states in the Valley of Mexico the area in which the rulers of the Aztec empire sought most to form a stable support area.

Sources of Information on Aztec City-States

Documents

Aztec society can be reconstructed from native oral histories and and pictographic codices, chronicles by explorers and conquerors, histories and descriptions gathered by Spanish friars and Colonial administrators, dictionaries of the Aztec (Nahuatl) language, and early Colonial administrative or legal documents. The kinds of sources used in this study and the types of information they provide are described below.

Pictographic codices were painted in an indigenous Aztec style on native bark paper (*amatl*) or on European paper. Although most codices were destroyed, and only one or two now in existence may date from before the Spanish Conquest (Robertson 1959; Cline 1973-75), many others were painted shortly after the conquest at the request of the Spaniards. For instance, the *Codex Mendoza*, made in 1541-42 at the request of Viceroy Mendoza, lists polities conquered by Tenochtitlan, towns that paid tribute to it, and aspects of Aztec domestic and civil life. Historical annals such as the *Historia Tolteca-Chichimeca* (1976), the *Codex Xolotl* (1951), the *Codex Boturini* (1964) report events year by year according to the Nahua calendar. Though written with pictographs and Aztec phonetic signs, many include glosses in Nahuatl and/or Spanish which were added to aid European readers.

Though many historical codices were destroyed, the narratives they recorded were preserved. Many of the codices depicted elaborate texts which were memorized and recited, with the personal and place name glyphs on the codices serving as mnemonic devices (Thompson 1933:250; León-Portilla 1969:11; Dibble 1971:323). These oral histories, written down in Nahuatl and also translated into Spanish, are even richer in historical detail than the pictorial codices. The *Anales de Cuauhtitlan* (1945), *Anales de Tlatelolco* (1948), *Crónica Mexicáyotl* (1949), and the works of Chimalpahin are historical narratives of this type.

Another type of historical text was written by descendants of Aztec elites, who learned to write Nahuatl and Spanish in alphabetic script from Spanish friars, and who then recorded the histories of their families and cities. Among these are Alvarado Tezozomoc of Tenochtitlan, Alva Ixtlilxochitl and Pomar of Texcoco, and Chimalpahin of Chalco-Amecameca. Since these individuals represented different areas of the Valley of Mexico, a comparison of their narratives allows the modern scholar to reconstruct pre-Hispanic inter-city competition and regional differences.

Another class of document is the conquistadores' accounts. These individuals were the only Europeans to witness the Aztec empire before its demise. Cortés' letters to King Charles V of Spain and the narratives of Bernal Díaz and the Anonymous Conqueror provide analyses of the political conditions in 1519 as well as first-hand descriptions of the cities and the landscape.

Yet another type of document is the chronicle or ethnographic work which combines information from many native documents and informants. These chronicles were often written by Spanish friars, who, in their goal of converting the Indians to Christianity, tried to understand Aztec culture while changing it. Among these was Sahagún, who gathered an enormous collection of information and wrote many volumes, including a 12-volume work, the *Florentine Codex*, which describes Aztec history, mythology, social life, economic activity, and the conquest. Others, such as Durán, Motolinía, Mendieta, and Torquemada used Indian informants, codices, other chronicles, and oral histories to produce narrative histories synthesizing many sources, including some which are now lost.

Spanish Colonial administrators were asked to provide information to be used by officials in Spain. Documents written by these individuals contain information explicitly describing aspects of Aztec life during the early Colonial period that may sometimes parallel practices in the pre-Hispanic era. A questionnaire issued in 1577 provides answers to the same questions from all of New Spain. Some answers to the *Relaciones geográficas* questions, such as those of Pomar (*Relación de Texcoco* 1941) and Muñoz Camargo (1892) were extensive, and even many of the shorter answers provide very specific data on cities and their surrounding regions, including maps made by Indians at the request of the Spanish officials.

From the early Colonial period also come linguistic data embodied in dictionaries and Nahuatl texts. Dictionaries of Classic Nahuatl include those by Molina (1571 [1970]) and Siméon (1885). Sahagún's works include definitions that help in reconstructing Aztec classificatory schemes and world view. Modern Nahuatl dictionaries and modern ethnographic studies also provide data on Nahua belief systems and classification (Redfield 1930; Lewis 1951; Cook de Leonard and Lemoine V. 1954-55; Madsen 1960; Andrews 1975; Karttunen 1983).

Legal documents from the early Colonial period record (1) petitions from Indian pueblos to the Spanish Crown, (2) legal disputes between Indian nobles, Indian commoners, and Spaniards; and (3) inheritance claims concerning property, land, and titles. These documents provide detailed information about land ownership and land use, tribute payment, genealogies of noble families, and possessions of Indian elites both in the Colonial period and in the pre-Hispanic period (see Anderson, Berdan, and Lockhart 1976). In response to some of these legal disputes, *visitas* by government officials and by church officials were produced. These describe the appearance, population, and economic state of villages and towns in the sixteenth century and after (for instance, see Carrasco and Monjarás-Ruiz 1976, 1978; Lemoine Villicaña 1961).[1]

The documentary sources discussed above have both strengths and weaknesses for the study of local political organization in the Valley of Mexico. For instance, although pictographic codices provide chronological sequences of events according to Nahua calendrical dates, several calendars were in use simultaneously in Central Mexico in the Late pre-Hispanic period, and so exact dates must be carefully evaluated—both because there were different calendars, and also because Nahua time was cyclical and each date was repeated every 52 years (Kubler and Gibson 1951; Caso 1971; Davies 1981). Another limitation of the native sources is that most postdate the Spanish Conquest, and while they may be close copies of pre-Hispanic ones, they also may have been edited (Robertson 1959). A final problem is that of provenience. Some codices that are clearly products of specific areas or towns (*Códice Xolotl* [1951], *Tira de Tepechpan* [1978], *Mapa Quinatzin* [Robertson 1959:Pl.46]) were used in this study, but others of unknown origin were not useful for comparing specific areas. Similar problems exist for historical, prose narratives. However, anonymous histories are often marked by locale (as in the *Anales de Cuauhtitlan* [1938, 1945], *Anales Mexicanos—México-Azcapotzalco* [1903], etc.). A vast critical literature helps the modern scholar to unravel these sources and to evaluate specific data in them (see Cline 1973-75—*Handbook of Middle American Indians*, Vols. 12-15).[2]

The potential biases in the Nahuatl traditional histories must be evaluated, because history was a form of propaganda for the Aztecs. Itzcoatl, the fourth ruler of Tenochtitlan, burned all the books and rewrote Mexica history following his coronation, according to one chronicle (León-Portilla 1969:118). Likewise, despite the use of calendrical dates and writing, the earliest histories—of chiefs and migrations—are mixtures of myth and fact. The early king lists have ritual dates in some texts, i.e., each ruler has a set length of reign and hence the accession dates for rulers of several communities are all very similar (Davies 1981). In Aztec polities, historical myths were revised to suit immediate ideological needs.

As with any research, sources must be subjected to textual analysis to determine biases, and comparisons of texts can help to assess their veracity. The basis of disagreement can be as interesting as the resolution of differences among texts, and systematic distortions have their own meaning.

Another bias of the documents is that they describe primarily the activities of the elite class. Since the texts are almost always histories of elites and capitals, information about commoners and rural areas is never equally represented.

Another bias, noted by Kirchhoff in 1954 is that sources traditionally used to study Aztec culture were those stating general rules, and he noted that progress could be made only by using sources "which, instead of stating general rules, describe individual instances. . . . Another type of data of an individualizing nature . . . is contained in the documents. . .that were presented by the Indians to the Spanish courts, in land disputes that arose as a result of the Spanish Conquest. . . . they contain those quantitative data which are almost completely lacking in our generalizing sources" (Kirchhoff 1954-55:352-53).

More recently, it has been re-emphasized that much misunderstanding of pre-Hispanic social and political organization has occurred as a result of overgeneralizing from a few sources, and that many of the problems in comprehending pre-Hispanic

---

[1] In sixteenth-century documents, Spanish and Nahuatl orthography vary greatly. In this text, well known place and personal names have been standardized. Lesser-known names remain as found in the sources used. English versions of passages from Spanish, Nahuatl, and German sources were prepared by the author.

[2] Dates for pre-Hispanic events that are given in European calendar years in this text are approximate correlations with Nahuatl years, based on modern scholarship and on the dates given by sixteenth-century authors.

forms of social organization are a result of the fragmentary character of the information; its analysis has been greatly complicated due to the tendency of researchers to mix data of different periods and places (Olivera 1976:183). Specific examples should be used whenever possible to promote the identification of local and regional patterns; with such data both regional variation and general trends can be meaningfully studied.

A final bias to be noted is that sixteenth-century Colonial documents frequently emphasize the interests of the Spaniards. These interests are reflected in the organization of collections in archives—for instance, the Archivo General de la Nación, Mexico, includes sections labeled Tierras, Mercedes, Indios, Contaduría, Tasación, Civil, Congregaciones, and Inquisición, to name a few (see Civiera Taboda and Bribiesca 1977). That is, the Spanish Colonial administrators were interested in land, land use and ownership, production and labor, tribute, tax assessment, law enforcement, and religious conversion. Often, as a consequence, ethnohistorians using these documents have let the data direct their research and have followed the biases of the Spaniards. What the Spaniards omitted or suppressed can be just as important as what they recorded. Problem-oriented research can help order the data so that the omissions as well as the explicitly stated facts contribute to our knowledge of Aztec culture.

Archaeological Data on Aztec Culture

Archaeological research has provided several types of data on the Aztecs, and these data allow investigation of aspects of Aztec life that were not recorded in documents, as well as providing corroboration of aspects that were. Studies of ceramic sequences—stratigraphic data—and radiocarbon dating have established the sequence of occupation in the valley. Mapping and excavation of the sites of Teotihuacan and Tula have provided information about the civilizations that occupied the valley and its environs before the Aztecs. However, since most Aztec-period cities were either destroyed shortly after the conquest or are now covered by modern cities—particularly Tenochtitlan, which is covered by modern Mexico City—the outlook for large-scale excavation of Aztec sites is dim. Excavation of the Aztec Templo Mayor—the ceremonial center of Tenochtitlan—has been carried out recently (Matos 1978), and salvage excavations in conjunction with the building of the subway in Mexico City may provide additional information about Aztec life in the capital. Specific data from archaeological investigations are not reviewed here but will be discussed in the chapters to come.

The lack of excavation data has been partially offset by a survey by William T. Sanders, Jeffrey R. Parsons, and other archaeologists, of the parts of the Valley of Mexico not obscured by modern occupation. In this survey most of the valley was mapped, producing a record of settlement patterns for all ceramic cultural periods (Sanders, Parsons, and Santley 1979).

Regional analysis of the settlement patterns in the central portion of the Aztec empire has been made possible by the Valley of Mexico Survey Project. The survey drew attention away from conspicuous large sites with ceremonial centers or pyramids to the variety of smaller settlements in the valley. From the Valley of Mexico survey data, archaeologists have defined a hierarchy of site sizes (see Chapter 2).

The archaeological survey data have been interpreted as indicating that there was a centralized economic system, in which the population of the valley produced agricultural goods to sustain the specialists and elites living at the capital (Sanders, Parsons, and Santley 1979; Parsons et al. 1982). In contrast, documentary sources from cities other than the capital indicate that elites and craft specialists lived in them and that ritual activities took place at them (Carrasco 1980). More data are needed to clarify how political, economic, and ritual activities related to this settlement pattern, particularly at lower levels of the hierarchy. A major question pursued in this book is to what extent political, economic, or ritual activities were centralized in the Aztec system and to what extent they followed other patterns.

A related question is whether and/or how these activities correspond to regional settlement patterns (see Smith 1979; Evans 1980a). One researcher (Smith 1979) suggests that the settlement pattern of the Acolhua area in the Late Aztec period indicates the presence of centralized market functions. Another view (Evans 1980a) is that the settlement pattern is more a result of proximity to agricultural land than a result of marketing patterns. Yet another point of view, developed from work with settlement patterns and documents from another archaic state (China), suggests that settlement patterns may not show the effects of short-term political changes at all (Chang 1983). The following study of the operation of local systems in the Valley of Mexico in the Late pre-Hispanic and early Colonial periods is intended to resolve some of the questions that have been raised by studies of archaeological settlement patterns (see also Brumfiel 1980 and comments).

In sum, ethnohistoric sources on Aztec city-states reveal political and cultural diversity (Carrasco 1980), but archaeological survey data suggest great economic uniformity (Sanders, Parsons, and Santley 1979). As a result, much recent discussion about the Aztec state has focused upon the degree to which the capital acculturated its dependencies. This book addresses this problem by investigating the operation of individual dependencies of the Aztec state to determine which activities were locally and which were regionally controlled. The following chapters present the results of a diachronic study of the formation of local and regional administrative systems in the Valley of Mexico in the Late pre-Hispanic period, and the final chapter discusses some of the processes involved in the operation of the political system of the Aztec state in the Valley of Mexico.

Aspects of the Operation of Aztec City-States to be Examined

Cultural Diversity Among Aztec City-States

Tenochtitlan, the Aztec capital, and the urban centers of other Aztec city-states are now largely covered by modern occupation, making archaeological excavation of these sites difficult. The fact that the archaeological sites of Aztec city-states could not be completely surveyed by archaeologists leaves many questions about them unanswered. A major goal of this work was to assemble systematically information on a number of Aztec city-states.

The Aztec imperial capital received the most attention in early chronicles (such as Sahagún 1950-69; Durán 1967; Torquemada 1975; Alva Ixtlilxochitl 1975-77; *Crónica Mexicáyotl* 1949) and in secondary studies (Bandelier 1877, 1880; Vaillant 1941; Soustelle 1962). Although the capital has been taken as the ideal type for Aztec city-states, the non-capitals were the more typical form of organization in pre-Hispanic Central Mexico. The fact that the city-state as a political form survived pre-Hispanic empire-building and empire destruction as well as the Spanish Conquest, indicates that this was the case (see Lockhart 1982).

Internal Political Systems of Aztec City-States

This study attempted to discover what characteristics of Aztec city-states were constant and what differences existed among them, and to what extent differences in their organizations correlated with geographical location, political affiliation, "ethnic" background, or size. It examines the history of city-state political systems, investigating questions about structure such as whether multiple rulerships were a result of fission or accretion.

Chapters 3–7 examine the internal political organizations of five city-states, focusing on the patterns of rulership and succession to rulership, the officials and bureaucracies, territorial size and organization, political economy, and political relations of these city-states. These are related to each city-state's political history, the growth of its urban center, its settlement history, its people's ethnic affiliation, and the central-place functions of its center, such as religious rites, markets, craft production, political administration, etc. These basic data were sought for each city-state studied.

Interaction of City-States and the Capital

This study examines a number of city-states' political alliances before the Aztec empire conquered them. It investigates their later obligations to the empire and the variation in these obligations resulting from the city-states' locations and previous political affiliations. Data on selected city-states were evaluated in light of the general propositions about the formation of and operation of states and empires which have been outlined in this chapter.

Methodology

A case-study and comparative method was chosen because these methods, it was felt, would best elucidate *processes* in the development of the political system. By comparing and contrasting a number of city-states, the difficulty of community studies—which present one example as typical—

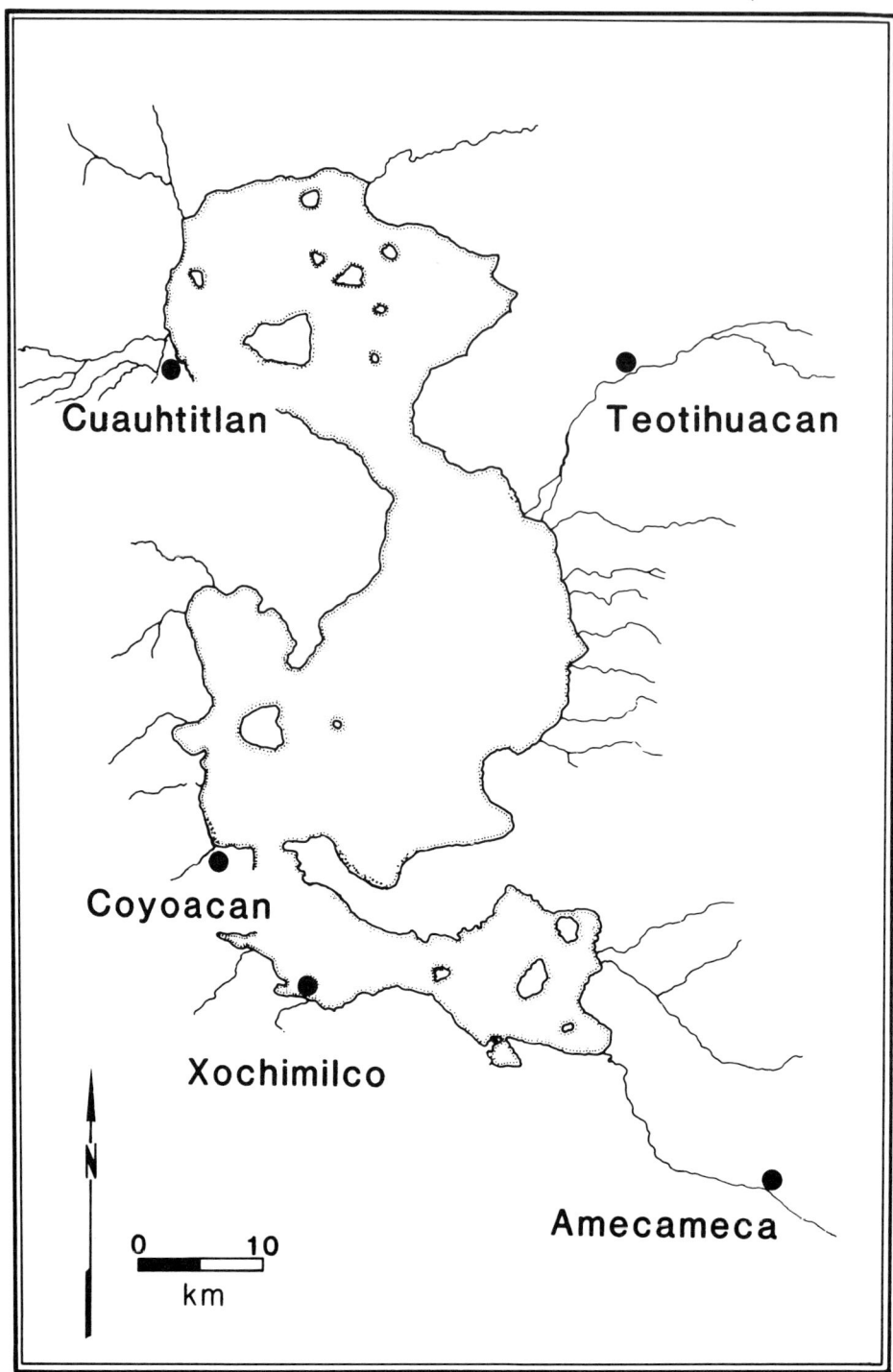

Fig. 1-1. Location of city-states chosen for detailed study.

would be avoided, and from several cases, more accurate generalizations could be made about city-states, their relations with neighboring polities, and with the capital.

The city-states chosen for study were selected from all the Valley of Mexico polities having hereditary rulers, or *tlatoque,* at the time of the Spanish Conquest (Gibson 1964b; Sanders and Price 1968; Bray 1972; Calnek 1978). Although there were 40–60 city-states in the valley, only a few, other than the capitals, produced chronicles of their history that provide great time depth, and few are described much by documentation produced before 1550.

Five of the most well-documented city-states were studied, to allow in-depth analysis of the political organizations of a few areas. The choice of polities for study was a compromise between a desire to choose city-states from various sections of the valley and the need to choose polities for which there were adequate data. Nevertheless, documents and archaeological data were never uniformly available even for the most well-documented city-states, due to the differential recording of data as well as differential preservation of Colonial documents during the approximately 400 years since their creation.

Since the aim was to study city-states with a variety of political affiliations and locations, but yet to study several city-states in detail, five of the best-documented city-states were selected for study. Those chosen were Amecameca, Cuauhtitlan, Xochimilco, Coyoacan and Teotihuacan. They represent several political confederations (Chalca, Tepaneca, Xochimilca, Tepaneca and Acolhua) and different geographic areas of the valley (see Fig. 1-1). Others (such as Culhuacan, Chalco-Atenco, Xaltocan) might have provided similar quantities of documentation; however, time and funding precluded detailed analysis of these systems. Comparing political processes in five city-states—while not incorporating every possible example—has permitted an analysis of political processes in Aztec city-states of different political affiliation, size, and complexity, and this is a first step in obtaining an empirically-based regional view of the organization of the center of the Aztec empire.

Procedure

The study proceeded as follows. (1) City-states in the central area of the Aztec political system were identified and described (see Chapter 2). (2) Five polities were selected for in-depth study. (3) Data on the selected city-states were collected from unpublished documents in archives, published collections of documents, and archaeological reports. (4) Data were analyzed to determine (a) the structure of each city-state's internal organization and changes in it over time, (b) the city-state's relationships with nearby polities, both its equals and its dependencies, in order to reconstruct its vertical hierarchy and examine horizontal integrative mechanisms within its regional system, and (c) relationships between selected city-states and the empire.

The following chapters present the results of a systematic study of local political systems in the Valley of Mexico and a reconstruction of the regional political hierarchy. This analysis of the hierarchy of local and regional systems within the Aztec empire's center provides a structure in which both the regional diversity evident in documentary sources from outside the capital and the pan-imperial activities emphasized in documents produced in the capital can be understood.

Chapter 2

City-States in the Valley of Mexico: An Overview

The Environmental Setting

The Aztec empire was centered in the Valley of Mexico (Figs. 2-1, 2-2), an area approximately 120 km north-south by 70 km east-west, located on the central mesa of Mexico between two mountain ranges, the Sierra Madre Occidental and the Sierra Madre Oriental. While much of Mexico's environment is mountainous, the valley provides approximately 8000 km^2 of relatively flat land (Sanders 1976:59).

Although surrounded by mountains as high as 5000 m, the valley itself is low enough in altitude (2240 m) to permit one agricultural season per year in which maize, beans, squash, amaranth, and other crops can be grown. In prehistoric times, the slopes were covered with forests, and the valley was partially filled with shallow lakes in which lived fish, waterfowl, crustaceans, insects, and other fauna consumed by the Aztec. In addition, the lakes contained economically important plants such as reeds and edible algae. Saline Lake Texcoco deposited salt that was extracted from soil by the lakeshore residents. The lake system, which consisted of lakes Xaltocan and Zumpango in the north, Lake Texcoco in the center, and lakes Chalco and Xochimilco in the south, provided food, water, and a means of speedy movement across the valley via canoes. The shallow water of the lakes permitted the development of chinampas, intensively cultivated raised fields. In southern lakes Chalco and Xochimilco, large numbers of chinampas constructed on the same grid apparently were created as a single state-planned project, in Late Aztec times (A.D. 1350-1520; Parsons 1976). This intensive agricultural system, which facilitated cultivation of maize and vegetables without dependence on rainfall, is one of the technological hallmarks of Aztec civilization (West and Armillas 1950; Coe 1964; Sanders, Parsons, and Santley 1979).

Occupational History of the Valley of Mexico

The Valley of Mexico has been occupied from Paleo-Indian times, and sites of all periods have been located by archaeological survey (Sanders, Parsons, and Santley 1979; see Fig. 2-3). Throughout the Early, Middle, and Late Formative periods (1500 B.C.–300 B.C.), residents of the valley occupied villages scattered around the lake. In the Terminal Formative period (300 B.C.–A.D. 150), the focus of occupation shifted to the sites now called Cuicuilco and Teotihuacan, polarizing population in the southwest and northeast sections of the valley.

After the demise of Cuicuilco following a volcanic eruption, Teotihuacan expanded in the Classic period (A.D. 150-750) into a center of ca. 125,000 inhabitants, with monumental architecture, foreign contacts as far south as Kaminaljuyú in Guatemala, a professional ruling class, and occupational specialists (Millon 1973, 1976). Meanwhile, the population living in the Valley of Mexico was sparse, with the bulk of the population living in the Teotihuacan Valley (Parsons 1976; Sanders, Parsons, and Santley 1979).

Following the general abandonment of Teotihuacan, the city of Tula, north of the Valley of Mexico in what is now the state of Hidalgo, probably dominated the area, although it may have been competing during this time (approximately A.D. 900–1150) with the city of Cholula to the southeast. This period is characterized as one of "Balkanization," during which the valley was a buffer zone between two large, competing centers outside the valley (Blanton 1975; Sanders, Parsons, and Santley 1979).

Oral history begins at this time, and the fall of Tula following a religious and political conflict is recounted in several versions (*Anales de Cuauhtitlan* 1938, 1945; Sahagún 1950-69; Durán

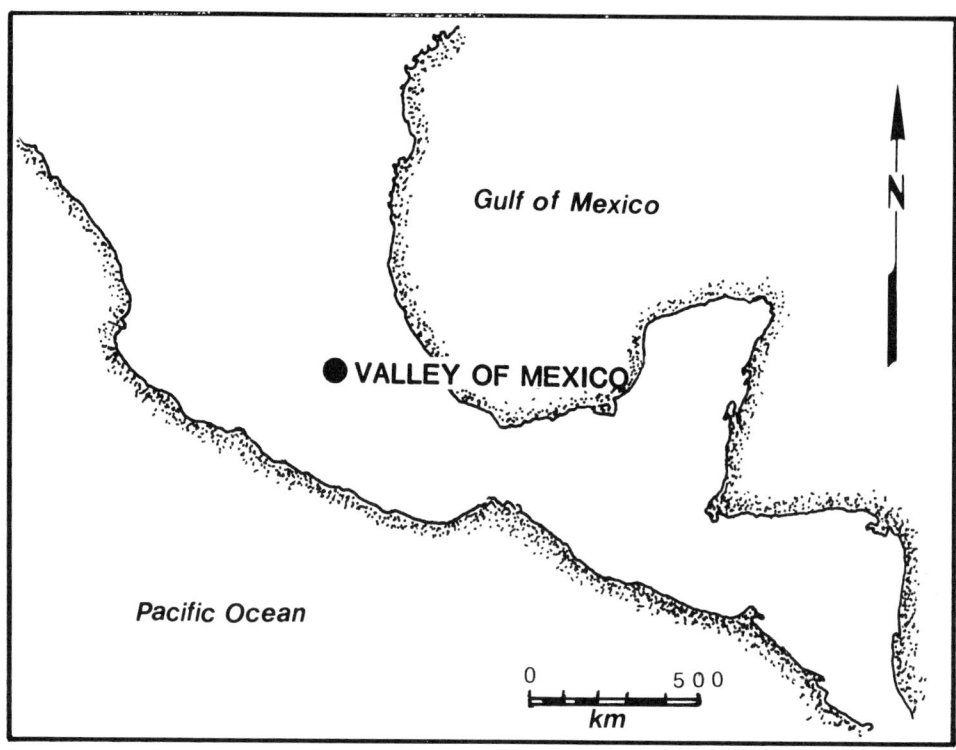

Fig. 2-1. Location of the Valley of Mexico in Mesoamerica. Since it has no outflow, it is technically a basin; however, in the text I refer to it as a valley, following the precedent in the literature.

1967; Chimalpahin 1958). After Tula's collapse, the historic narratives say that numerous groups, both from Tula and from farther north, entered the Valley of Mexico, establishing many small polities. These groups became important in the Postclassic socio-political environment and are the focus of this study. Although these polities were at first separated by buffer zones of unsettled land, their narratives record political interactions, coalitions, and confrontations which created the complicated political situation out of which the Aztec empire developed.

In the Early Aztec period (ca. 1150–1350), the largest and most influential sites were Azcapotzalco on the western side of the valley, and Huexotla and Coatlinchan on the eastern side. These centers became less influential in the Late Aztec period (ca. 1350–1520), when Tenochtitlan on the west and Texcoco on the east were the valley's most important political powers (Parsons 1974; Sanders, Parsons, and Santley 1979).

The Valley of Mexico survey project classified the total range of Late Horizon (Late Aztec) period sites. Based on site size and monumental architecture, the settlement categories included supraregional centers, primary regional centers, secondary regional centers, large nucleated villages, dispersed villages, small nucleated villages, hamlets, camps, isolated households, and isolated ceremonial centers. The supraregional centers, Tenochtitlan and Texcoco, had populations of 150–200,000 and 25–30,000 respectively. They were the centers of large polities, had monumental architecture, stratified societies, and were inhabited predominantly by elites and occupational specialists rather than by primary food producers. The primary regional centers were large, nucleated communities of 10–15,000 people, with distinct ceremonial architecture, indicating the presence of individuals who carried out roles in a socio-political hierarchy, and craft specialists. Secondary regional (local) centers contained well-defined public architecture and populations of 1,500–10,000. Large nucleated villages had populations of 500–1,000 people and little or no remains of civic-elite architecture. Small nucleated villages also had no public

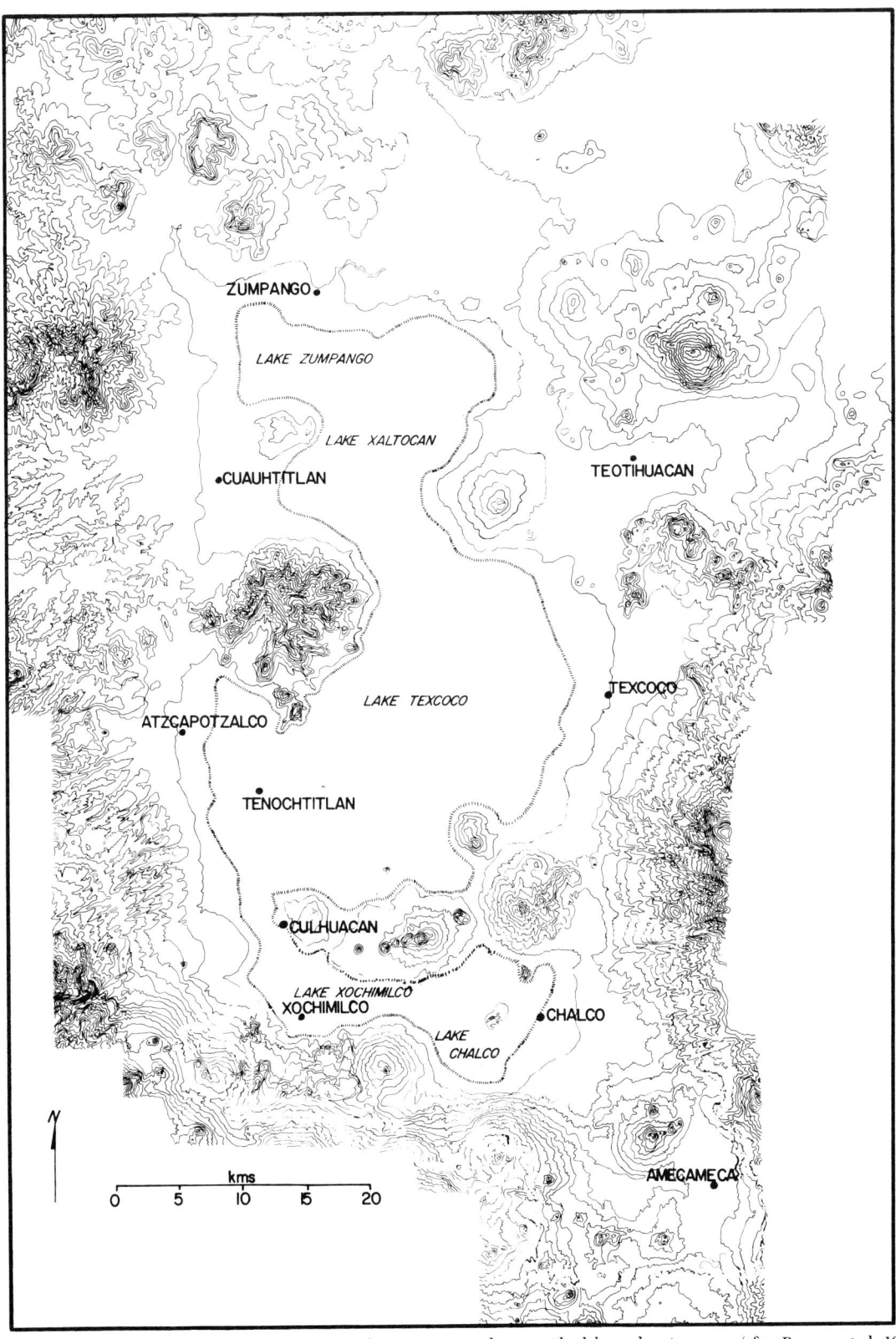

Fig. 2-2. The Valley of Mexico, showing the location of mountains in relation to the lake and major towns (after Parsons et al. 1982).

Absolute Chronology	Major Archaeological Periods and Phase Names				
	New System		Old System		
1500 1400	Late Horizon		Late Aztec	Tenochtitlan	1520 1350
1300 1200	Second Intermediate	Phase Three	Early Aztec	Culhuacan/Tenayuca	1150
1100 1000	Second Intermediate	Phase Two	Late Toltec	Mazapan	950
900 800	Second Intermediate	Phase One	Early Toltec	Coyotlatelco	750
700 600 500	Middle Horizon	Phase Two	Late Classic	Metepec	
	Middle Horizon			Xolalpan	500
400 300	Middle Horizon	Phase One	Early Classic	Tlamimilolpa	250
200		Phase Five		Miccaotli	150 A.D.
100 A.D. 0 B.C. 100		Phase Four	Terminal Formative	Tzacualli	B.C. 100
200		Phase Three		Patlachique	300
300 400 500 600	First Intermediate	Phase Two	Late Formative	Ticoman	
700 800	First Intermediate	Phase One-B	Middle Formative	Cuautepec La Pastora	650
900 1000 1100	First Intermediate	Phase One-A	Middle Formative	El Arbolillo Bomba	900 1050 1150
1200 1300 1400 1500	Early Horizon	Phase Two Phase One	Early Formative	Manantial Ayotla Coapexco	1300 1400 1500

Fig. 2-3. Chronological sequences for the Valley of Mexico (after Sanders, Parsons, and Santley 1979:93).

buildings and had only 100–500 people living in them (Sanders, Parsons, and Santley 1979:55-57, 160-71; Parsons et al. 1982:71).

Based on population, Sanders (1970:409) classified the Valley of Mexico's Late Horizon settlements as follows. Level 1 included only Tenochtitlan/Tlatelolco, with a population of 150–200,000; Level 2 was comprised of Texcoco, with 25–30,000; Level 3 included Xochimilco, Amecameca, Tlalmanalco, Tacuba/Tlacopan, and Ixtapalapa, each with ca. 15,000 residents. Level 4 consisted of 40 other towns with 4–5,000 inhabitants, and Level 5 included villages and hamlets of less than 1000 residents.

The total population of the valley in 1519 is estimated to have been 1–1.2 million (ibid). The survey detected a considerable population increase during the Late Aztec period, evident from the appearance of more and larger sites. The settlement pattern survey data suggest that although population expanded most markedly in Tenochtitlan, throughout the valley it was higher in the Late Horizon period than in any other previous period (Sanders, Parsons, and Santley 1979).

Political Units in the Valley of Mexico

City-States

In Nahuatl, the basic unit in political organization was altepetl, a word whose roots are atl, or "water" and tepetl, or "hill" (Andrews 1975:419). Molina (1970:4) defines altepetl as "pueblo, or rey," and Siméon (1885:21) defines the term as "poblado, ciudad, estado, rey, soberano"—settlement, city, state, king, sovereign. The term altepetl is associated with the idea of rulership as much as with territory, for under "rey" or king, Molina lists "vey tlatoani, altepetl" (Molina 1970:103). Thus, a city with attendant lands, governed by a tlatoani or ruler was the basic Nahua political unit, which the Spaniards called a señorío, or lordship, and which has been called a city-state in recent anthropological literature (Bray 1972; Calnek 1978).

Fundamentally, "in political terms, a Mexican city state can be defined as a sovereign territory with its own government and with one or more rulers chosen from a royal lineage" (Bray 1972:164). The territory contained a capital or central place, plus rural dependencies. The town was the center of government; it contained the major temples and was a center of redistribution and exchange via markets held at 1-, 5-, or 20-day intervals. The town was the cultural, political, artistic, religious, and economic focus of its surrounding region (ibid.).

Each city-state was governed by a hereditary ruler who lived in the urban center. Other elites, as well as occupational groups such as craft specialists, artisans, warriors, priests, and bureaucrats also lived in the urban center. Within the urban center of a city-state were residential wards, which were the smallest unit of political organization

TABLE 2-1
VALLEY OF MEXICO COMMUNITIES
WITH A TLATOANI IN 1519[1]

Confederation	Town	Name of Tlatoani	Confederation	Town	Name of Tlatoani
Mexica	Tenochtitlan	Moctezuma	Tepaneca	Citlaltepec	Aztatzontzin
	Tlatelolco	(Cuauhtlatoani)		Huehuetoca	"
	Ecatepec	Panitzin		Zumpango	"
	Azcapotzalco	Teuhtlehuacatzin		Coyoacan	Cuappopocatzin
Culhua	Culhuacan	Tezozomoc		Tacubaya	Yzquas(?)[3]
	Huitzilopochco	Huitzilatzin II		Huepoxtla	?
	Mexicaltzingo	Tochihuitzin		Tacuba/Tlacopan	Totoquihuatzin
	Ixtapalapa	Cuitlahuatzin		Tenayuca	Moteucçomatzin
Mixquica	Mixquic	Chalcayaotzin		Tepotzotlan	Quinatzin
Xochimilca	Xochimilco			Tequixquiac	?
	Tepetenchi	Tlatocatzin		Tultitlan	Citlalcohuatl
	Olac	Macuilmalinaltzin		Xilotcingo	?
	Tecpan	Tlilcoyohualtzin	Acolhua	Acolman	Coyoctzin
Cuitlahuaca	Cuitlahuac			Chiauhtla	?
	Tizic	Atlpopocatzin		Chiconauhtla	Tlatecatl
	Teopancalcan	Ixtotomahuatzin		Chimalhuacan Atenco	Acxoyatlatoatzin
	Atenchicalcan	Mayehuatzin		Coatlinchan	Xaquinteuctli
	Tecpan	Acxochitzin		Huexotla	Tzontemoctzin
Chalca	Amecameca			Ixtapaluca	
	Itztlacozauhcan	Cihuaillacatzin		Otumba	Cuechimaltzin
	Tlayllotlacan	Cacamatzin		Teotihuacan	Mamallitzin
	Tzacualtitlan			Tepetlaoztoc	Tlilpotonqui
	Tenango	Yotzintli		Tepexpan	Teyaoyaualouatzin
	Tecuanipan	Miccacalcatl Tlaltetecuintzin		Texcoco	Cacamatzin
	Panohuayan	Cuauhcecequitzin		Tequizistlan	?
	Tlalmanalco			Tezoyuca	?
	Opochhuacan	Necuametl		Tezontepec	?
	Itzcahuacan	Itzcahuatl			
	Acxotlan Cihuateopan	Huitznecahual			
	Tenango Tepopula	Tlacayaotl			
	Chimalhuacan	?			
Tepaneca	Azcapotzalco[2]	Tlaltecatlçin			
	Cuauhtitlan	Aztatzontzin			

[1] Based on *Anales de Cuauhtitlan* (1945) and Gibson (1964b).
[2] Azcapotzalco is listed twice because it had two tlatoque in 1519: one was Mexica and the other was Tepaneca and represented the indigenous ruling lineage.
[3] Carrasco and Monjarás-Ruiz 1976:66.
? = name unknown

(Bray 1972). Documents call a residential ward by a number of terms: barrio (Spanish), tlaxillacalli, and calpulli (Nahuatl: pl. tlaxillacaltin; calpultin), and there is still some ambiguity about the usage of the terms barrio, calpulli, and tlaxillacalli.

The hereditary ruler of a city-state was generally called tlatoani, or "speaker." In all city-states, society was stratified into two levels: pipiltin (elites) who were often descendants and relatives of the tlatoani, and commoners, or macehualtin (sing. macehualli). The nobles were supported by tribute which the commoners paid to them. These characteristics define what Aztec city-states had in common in 1519; in the case studies that follow, differences among them will be emphasized.

Confederations

The unit of political organization larger than the individual city-state in the Valley of Mexico in the late pre-Hispanic period was the league, or confederation, of city-states. Because a single polity would have less power in valley politics than a coalition, it was a long-established practice for polities to join together for mutual defense and to go to war together. Leagues were territorial blocs of city-states with shared interests. Since confederation members often shared a mythology about common origins, they have sometimes been described as "ethnic" groups or "tribes" (Gibson 1964b; Bray 1978). There were eight leagues in the Valley of Mexico in the Late Postclassic period: the Tenochca (Mexica), Tepaneca, Acolhuaque (Texcocan), Chalca, Xochimilca, Culhuaque, Cuitlahuaca, and Mixquica (see Fig. 2-4). The Aztec imperial system was formed originally from three of these confederations. The following section briefly describes the political organizations of the three cities and confederations that led the empire.

Aztec Capitals

Since most generalizations about Aztec polities are based on the capitals, I will briefly outline the political organizations of Tenochtitlon, Texcoco, and Tlacopan. Tenochtitlan and Texcoco are the best-known Aztec city-states, and the following overview of these paramount cities is intended to place non-capitals in perspective. Two important differences between the capitals and other city-

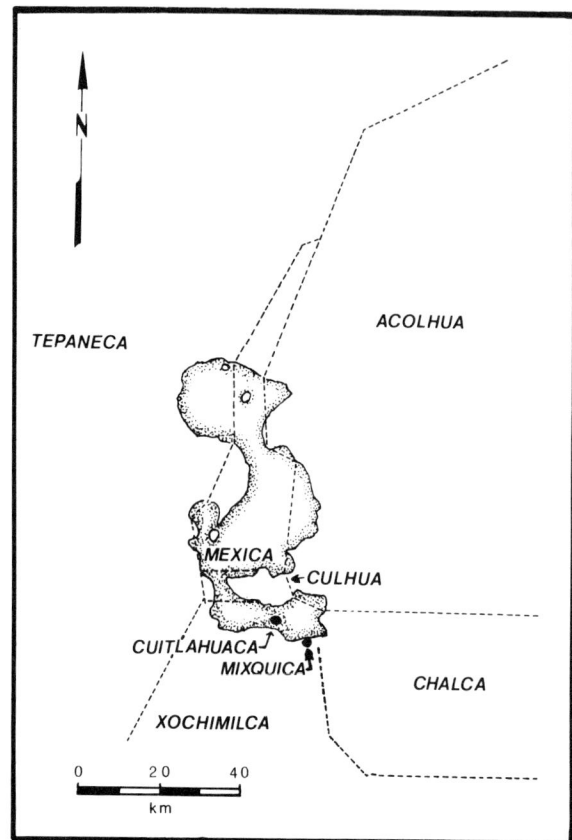

Fig. 2-4. Political confederations of the Valley of Mexico in Aztec times (after Gibson 1964b).

states were their regional span of control and the large numbers of people and quantities of resources at their command.

Tenochtitlan

Most generalizations about Aztec culture are drawn from Tenochtitlan. Tenochtitlan was located in the "highest part of New Spain and in the highest mountains. . . . Mexico is entirely surrounded by mountains and has a very beautiful crown of ranges around her, and the city itself is situated in the middle. This gives it great beauty and adornment and great security and strength" (Motolinía 1950:203).

Cortés described the capital as follows:

> This great city of Temixtitlan is built on the salt lake, and no matter by what road you travel there are two leagues from the main body of the city to the mainland. There are four artificial causeways leading to it, and each is as wide as two cavalry lances. The city itself is as big as Seville or Córdoba.

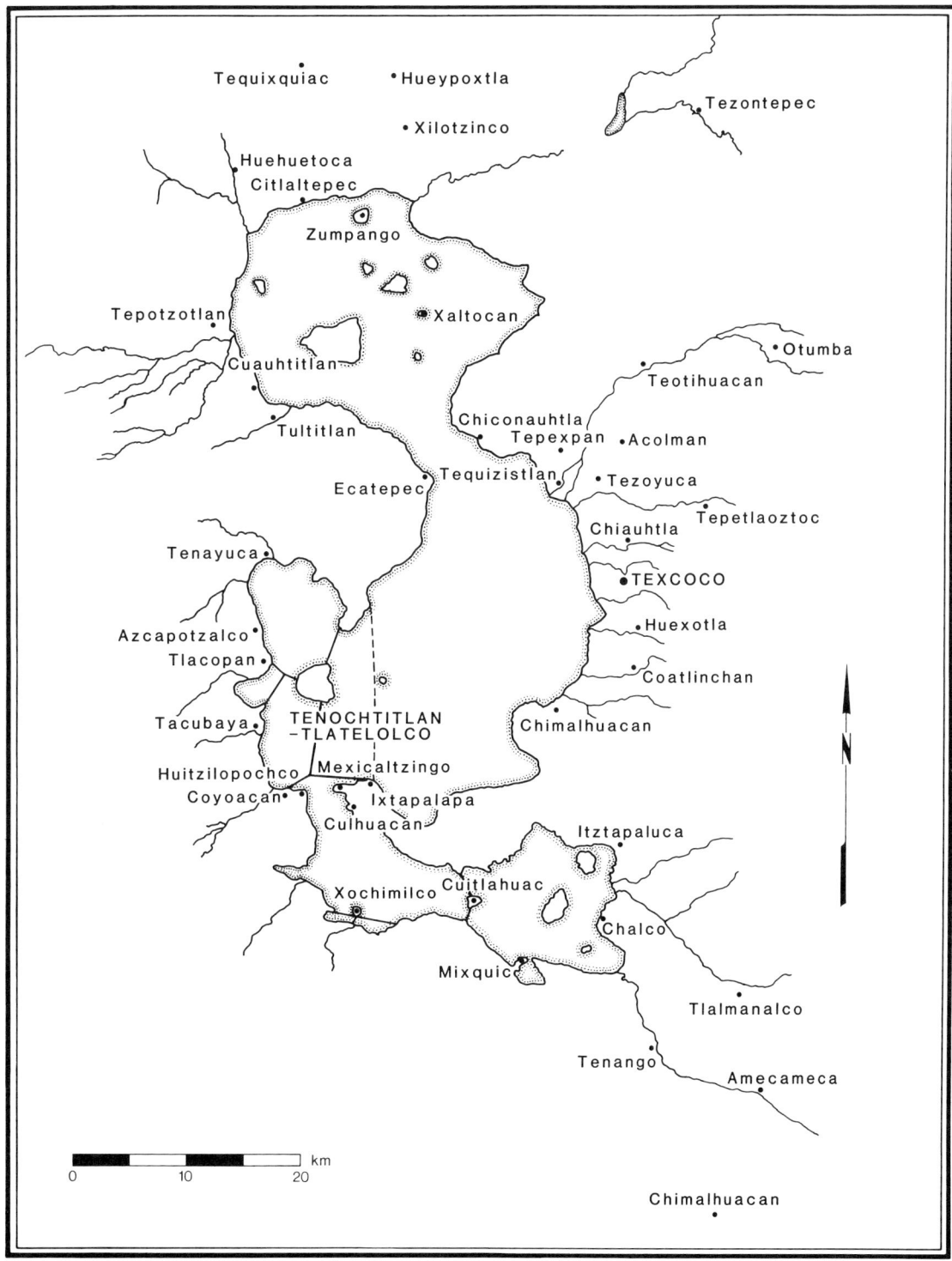

Fig. 2-5. Cities in the Valley of Mexico, ca. A.D. 1519, that were the residence of a tlatoani.

The main streets are very wide and very straight; some of these are on the land, but the rest and all the smaller ones are half on land, half canals where they paddle their canoes. . . . there are bridges made of long and wide beams joined together very firmly and so well made that on some of them ten horsemen may ride abreast. [Cortés 1971:102-03]

He adds that "The city has many squares where trading is done and markets are held continuously" (ibid.:103).

There are, in all districts of this great city, many temples or houses for their idols. They are all very beautiful buildings, and in the important ones there are priests of their sect who live there permanently. . . . [Cortés 1971:105]

Amongst these temples there is one, the principal one, whose great size and magnificence no human tongue could describe, for it is so large that within the precincts, which are surrounded by a very high wall, a town of some five hundred inhabitants could easily be built. All round inside this wall there are very elegant quarters with very large rooms and corridors where the priests live. There are as many as forty towers, all of which are so high that in the case of the largest there are fifty steps leading up to the main part of it; and the most important of these towers is higher than that of the cathedral of Seville. They are so well constructed in both their stone and woodwork that there can be none better in any place, for all the stonework inside the chapels where they keep their idols is in high relief, with figures and little houses, and the woodwork is likewise of relief and painted with monsters and other figures and designs. [Cortés 1971:105-06]

Tenochtitlan occupied an island and was connected by causeways to the mainland (Fig. 2-6). In addition to the wide roads, canals allowed canoe transport of people and goods in and out of the city.

The city had between 150,000 and 200,000 occupants in 1519, and it covered an area of 12 to 15 km² (Sanders, Parsons, and Santley 1979; Calnek 1976). The causeways ran into avenues which divided the city into four quarters; since the founding of the city, these quarters had been administrative divisions. Each of the divisions had a large temple or ceremonial center within it, and these quarters were subdivided into wards which some documents call a calpulli and others a tlaxillacalli (Calnek 1976:296).

Each ward contained a temple for the patron deity, a telpochcalli, or young men's house, and a plaza. All were on a smaller scale than the main temple and plaza, perhaps on the scale of the excavated pyramid which is visible today in Mexico City's Pino Suárez metro stop. These ward temples were typically low platforms, each with a houselike structure on top of it. "In addition to providing the locus for public and private rituals dedicated to

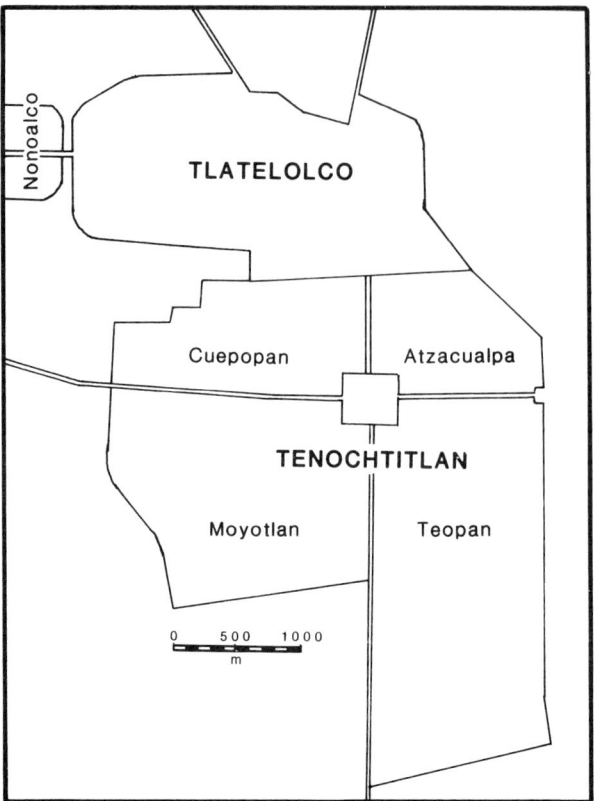

Fig. 2-6. Plan of Tenochtitlan, showing its causeways and four divisions (redrawn from Calnek 1976: Map 20).

local deities, the temple was also the meeting place for barrio elders and the focal point for large ceremonials organized by occupationally specialized groups" (Calnek 1976:297).

Residences in Tenochtitlan ranged from sumptuous palaces to less elaborate dwellings. Residential units were walled compounds enclosing a number of separate dwellings. They faced inward on an open patio. Most compounds were occupied by a "bilateral joint family" (ibid.:298). The houses of commoners were located in various wards, whereas the rulers lived at the center of the city in the palace-temple complex. Residential architecture was a sign of social status, for persons of elevated status had finer and larger houses than those of the lower classes (Trautmann 1968; Calnek 1976:300).

Tenochtitlan, as well as the Classic-period city of Teotihuacan, had a cruciform layout (Marcus 1983a). Each quarter may correspond to or be associated with one of the four world directions. The four quadrant layout may represent the Nahua world divided into four quarters, each associated with a world direction, and each with its own color symbolism, deity, and aspect (Nicholson 1971). Motolinía, in 1541, said, "It was a sight worth seeing, to look from the top of the principal temple and see how, from all the lesser towns and districts, the roads came in very straight and ended in the courtyard of the temples" (Motolinía 1950:86).

Social Organization of Tenochtitlan

> The people of this city are dressed with more elegance and are more courtly in their bearing than those of other cities and provinces, and because Mutezuma and all those chieftains, his vassals, are always coming to this city, the people have more manners and politeness in all matters. [Cortés 1971:108]

The populace of Tenochtitlan in 1519 formed two ascribed social strata, elites and commoners. Among the elite were (1) rulers, (2) chiefs, or teteuctin, who held administrative titles and offices, and (3) noblemen by birth, or pipiltin (literally meaning "noble children"). The nobles were free from tribute payment. (In some cases, freedom from tribute payment was earned by outstanding non-elite warriors. Those who achieved the status were called quauhpipiltin, "eagles' sons") (Carrasco 1971:354).

Commoners were called macehualtin. The commoner class included commoners who lived in land-holding wards, and others who were tenant farmers working on patrimonial lands of the elites. At the bottom of the social scale were the tlacotin, or slaves. People became slaves to pay debts, as punishment for crimes, or by being captured in war (Carrasco 1971:351-57; Torquemada 1975, II:563-67; Ramírez de Fuenleal 1870 [1532]:256).

Tenochtitlan's Administrators

The political system was headed by one ruler whose title in Nahuatl was tlatoani, or "he who speaks." Between ca. 1376 and 1521 nine tlatoque, all of whom were related, ruled Tenochtitlan (Fig. 2-7). The rules of succession stated that the office of the tlatoani went first to the eldest son of the principal wife of the ruler; if this individual was not acceptable, then the second or another qualified son would be chosen. After that, the choices were the grandson of the ruler, then his brothers in order of age, and last of all, other kinsmen of the ruler. If a ruler did not designate a successor, one was chosen by the council of lords—elite advisors to the tlatoani (Zorita 1963:91).

The tlatoani of Tenochtitlan, alternatively called hueytlatoani ("great tlatoani") or tlacateuctli ("lord of men") was chief priest, commander-in-chief of the army, highest judge, and controller of the main market at Tlatelolco as well as overseeing the activities of the pochteca, or long-distance traders in sumptuary goods. The ruler lived in a palace adjacent to the main temple, where he appeared for ceremonies. In these ceremonies the ruler sometimes appeared as ixiptla or spokesman-representative of the chief deity. The ruler's council lived near him, and the high level courts were held in the palace (Sahagún 1954, Book 8:41-45). Recent excavations in Mexico City have begun to corroborate the arrangement of the ceremonial center as described by eyewitnesses at the time of the Spanish Conquest and as depicted in codices (Matos 1978).

In Tenochtitlan, the most important official after the tlatoani was the cihuacoatl, or "snake woman," an official whose responsibilities encompassed those of chief judge, viceroy, captain general, and second king (Sahagún 1954, Book 8:55; Torquemada 1975, II:352). The cihuacoatl led the council in selecting a new ruler when needed (Durán 1964:220-21). Cortés described Tlacotzin, the cihuacoatl of Moctezuma II, as ". . .captain and governor of them all and directed matters concerning the war" (Cortés 1971:263). The cihuacoatl was Tenochtitlan's chief administrative officer. In matters dealing with religion, the ruler actively led important state rituals, but the cihuacoatl was charged with supervising the priesthood, the temples, and the performance of rites (Vaillant 1941:95). Although the qualifications for being appointed to the office of cihuacoatl were the same as that of ruler, the office of cihuacoatl was held consecutively by members of one branch of Tenochtitlan's ruling lineage (Durán 1967:369; Carrasco 1971; see Fig. 2-7).

The next level in the administrative hierarchy was the Council of the Four, or the war chiefs. Incumbents of these offices were potential rulers. "After the election of a king, four brothers or nearest relatives of the king are elected who take orders from the king. One of these may be elected king and no others" (Durán 1964:103). Itzcoatl's council was composed of four of his brothers (ibid.). Two of these four officials are almost always called tlacateccatl and tlacochcalcatl. The others are sometimes referred to as tlillancalqui and ezauacatl (Durán 1967:103), uitznauatlailotlac, pochtecatlailotlac, or ticociauacatl (Sahagún 1954, Book 8:61). In the chronicles, a number of diverse titles appear because many honorific titles were granted to individuals, and since eligibility for these offices apparently was based largely on lineage, qualified persons with any of a number of titles were appointed to the four offices.

The exact duties of these four advisors are not clearly defined. The tlacateccatl always is described as commander of the army, and this title probably appears frequently because there was a high mortality rate among them. The tlacochcalcatl and the ezauauacatl are reported to have served as judges in the palace, along with the cihuacoatl (Sahagún 1954, Book 8:55).

The members of the Council of the Four, then, were related to the tlatoani, were proven warriors, and had been awarded titles for this. The upper level of the political hierarchy of Tenochtitlan, consisting of the six highest offices, was monopolized by a single dynasty (Rounds 1979; Brumfiel 1983).

Other advisors—"old men, seasoned warriors, leaders of youth, lords, keepers of gods, and fire priests" (Sahagún 1954, Book 8:61)—comprised an additional group of officials who advised the ruler. These middle-level hierarchies dealt with military, religious, economic, judicial, and tributary matters. Members of these hierarchies were appointed from the elite class.

Military Officials. Since the Aztec state had no standing army—despite its emphasis on war—every adult male was called upon to fight. Those who took captives received the titles "quaquachite, otomí, tlacatecatl" (Sahagún 1958, Book 9:47). Orders of soldiers were distinguished by different insignia, and the nobility had their own warrior societies, distinct from the commoners (Durán 1971:187, 194-202). Particularly by taking captives, a warrior could earn titles, exemptions from taxes, sumptuary items and the status to wear them, or the post of governor of conquered towns. "From there they came to rule, to govern cities; and at that time they seated them with [the nobility] and they might eat with Moctezuma" (Sahagún 1954, Book 8:73). They received special clothing, shields, and jewelry, "and he gave them stewardships ['calpixcantli'] possibly in two places or in three he gave them [such offices] for truly they had taken [captives]" (ibid.:74).

Religious Officials. The cihuacoatl was the overseer of the priesthood, and the next two highest religious officials were the priests of the two most important Tenochca deities, Huitzilopochtli and Tlaloc. The assistant to them, called Mexicateohuatzin, was overseer of religion in the provinces and in Tenochtitlan. The hierarchy of priests in Tenochtitlan had many levels (see Acosta Saignes 1946). According to Durán, priests were given titles such as "tlacatecuhtli, mexicaltecuhtli, tlacochcalcatl-teuchtli, tepannecatl, mistoncatltecuhtli, amiztlato" (Durán 1971:138). However, some of these titles are also mentioned in Sahagún's list of highest judges (1954, Book 8:55; 1959, Book 9:47), and much remains to be learned about the religious or priestly duties of nobles, particularly the highest-level officeholders who participated in religious activities along with priests who had purely sacerdotal functions. The religious hierarchy directly affected the political hierarchy by (1) advising the rulers through oracles, and by interpreting the tonalpohualli, or sacred almanac, to select propitious days for coronations and other state events (Sahagún 1957, Books 4 and 5; Díaz 1956:183; Carrasco 1966), and (2) by educating the sons of rulers and nobles, who were educated by the fire priests from the age of ten or twelve (Sahagún 1954, Book 8:71-72).

Judicial Officials. The tlatoani, who was the supreme judge, appointed judicial officials. He held court every 10-12 days to judge important cases which came from the tlacxitlan, the court where cases involving nobles were tried, as well as difficult cases from lower courts. This court had 13 judges, among whom were the cihuacoatl, the tlacochcalcatl, and the ezauauacatl. If an individual was tried and condemned to die, he was executed by officials called achcacauhtli, quauhnochtli, and atempanecatl (Sahagún 1954, Book 8:55). Highest in the hierarchy was the court for cases involving nobles, followed by the regional courts. Then came courts for judging commoners. Each level in the judicial hierarchy had executioners and enforcement officials (ibid.:54).

Tribute Collectors. The tribute collectors, having many ranks and titles, were nobles and warriors appointed to these offices. They operated outside Tenochtitlan and are described below in the section on the empire.

Market Officials. The great market in Tlatelolco required administrators, and market directors oversaw exchanging and pricing of merchandise. They

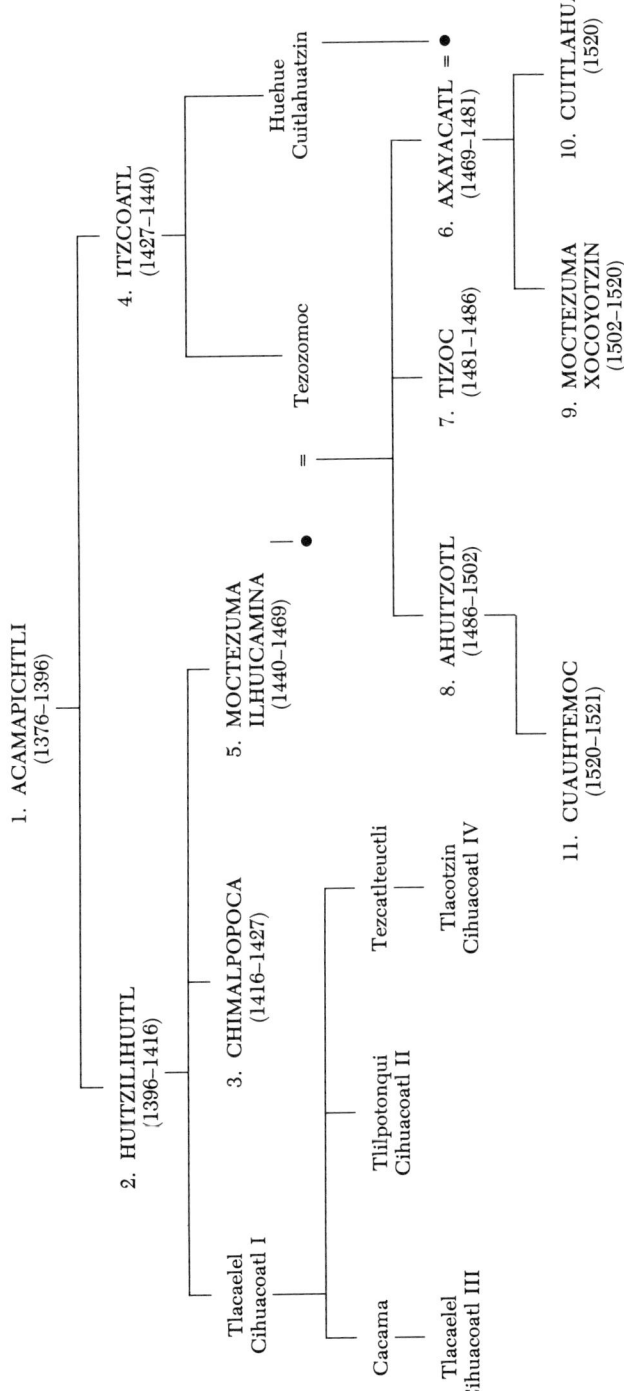

Fig. 2-7. Genealogy of the rulers of Tenochtitlan, including their relatives who held the office of cihuacoatl. Individuals who held the office of tlatoani are shown in capital letters; those holding the office of cihuacoatl are followed by roman numerals, indicating the order in which they served (after Carrasco 1971:350; Durán 1964:368).

also collected taxes from the sellers, and they enforced regulations concerning the market, including rules regarding theft and escapes of slaves (Sahagún 1954, Book 8:67-69).

According to Sahagún (1959, Book 9:24), the overseers of the Tenochtitlan marketplace (held in Tenochtitlan's sister-city, Tlatelolco) were the pochteca, or traders. The pochteca were long-distance traders who dealt primarily with sumptuary goods. During the expansion of the empire, they worked closely with the ruler of Tenochtitlan, carrying goods for him to places of exchange outside the boundaries of the empire, and exchanging them for feathers and other raw materials used in the crafting of sumptuary goods (ibid.:17). The head pochteca (puchtecatlatoque) had the titles Quappoyaualtzin (who led the disguised merchants, who also served as spies for the imperial ruler), nentlamatitzin, uetzcatocatzin, canatzin, and uei ocomatzin (Sahagún 1959, Book 9:24). Pochteca lived in their own residential wards and worshipped distinctive gods. There were pochteca barrios in 12 Valley of Mexico cities: Tenochtitlan, Texcoco, Huexotla, Tlatelolco, Coatlinchan, Chalco, Huitzilopochco, Mixcoac, Azcapotzalco, Cuauhtitlan, Xochimilco, and Otompan (Otumba) (ibid.:17, 24, 48-49; Durán 1967:185).

Lower-Level Officials—Ward Administrators. Within the state hierarchy, the ward or calpulli was the smallest unit of administration. For warfare and communal labor, workers were grouped first into units of 20 and then into larger units of 100. The ward was also the basic tribute-paying unit (Zorita 1963:110).

The principal administrator of a ward was responsible for justice and heard legal cases, assisted by a group of elders and other officials called teochcautin. The members of the ward met in the principal administrator's house to deliberate concerning the group's needs and the payment of tribute, and to plan their festivals. "This is very expensive for the elder, for to keep his guests happy and peaceful, he must support them with food and drink at these meetings, which are held frequently throughout the year" (Zorita 1963:110). Other ward officials oversaw the telpochcalli, or school for young men, and the barrio temple, for which lands were set aside and worked, in order to support festivals.

There was a difference between urban and rural wards. In Tenochtitlan, there were wards of specialized craftsmen such as the featherworkers' barrio which was established by Moctezuma I.

> And when finally the craft [of] feather design became important, it came to pass in the time of Moctezuma. For when he ruled, precisely when he was reigning, then quetzal feathers arrived, and all kinds of precious feathers. In just his time [this commerce flourished]. So he settled, he housed separately, those who were his feather workers, who pertained to him. He gave them a house of their own. The feather artisans of Tenochtitlan and Tlatelolco mingled with one another. [Sahagún 1958, Book 9:91]

Featherworkers produced costumes for rulers, warriors, and deities. "And some were known as featherworkers of the treasury store house; their domain was everything which was in Moctezuma's treasure store house" (ibid.).

In summary, Tenochtitlan in 1519 was the largest urban center in the Valley of Mexico, with hierarchies of administrators for both internal and external affairs. It contained monumental architecture, befitting an imperial capital, and it has served as the model for understanding the organization of central Mexican cites. Now let us briefly examine the organization of another Triple Alliance capital, Texcoco.

Texcoco

The City of Texcoco

Texcoco, located in the eastern Valley of Mexico, was capital of the kingdom of Acolhuacan. Texcoco evidently was not a tightly nucleated city, like Tenochtitlan. Although its Aztec-period nucleus covered ca. 4.5 km^2 and contained about 25,000 people (Parsons 1971:120), Texcoco's total metropolitan area covered some 80 km^2, an area estimated to have been inhabited by about 100,000 people (Hicks 1982:231). Though the city had a nucleus of palaces, it consisted mostly of dispersed clusters of houses, organized into barrios or calpultin.

The city's ceremonial center contained temples, palaces, storehouses, and a daily market. The city contained as many as 400 temples, and its main temple, like that of Tenochtitlan, was a twin temple, where Huitzilopochtli and Tlaloc were worshipped.

The city contained six major barrios or sections. Each section was governed by its own noble lineage and consisted of a palace, ceremonial center, and dependent commoners (Hicks 1982:236-37). Within these divisions were subdivisions of crafts-

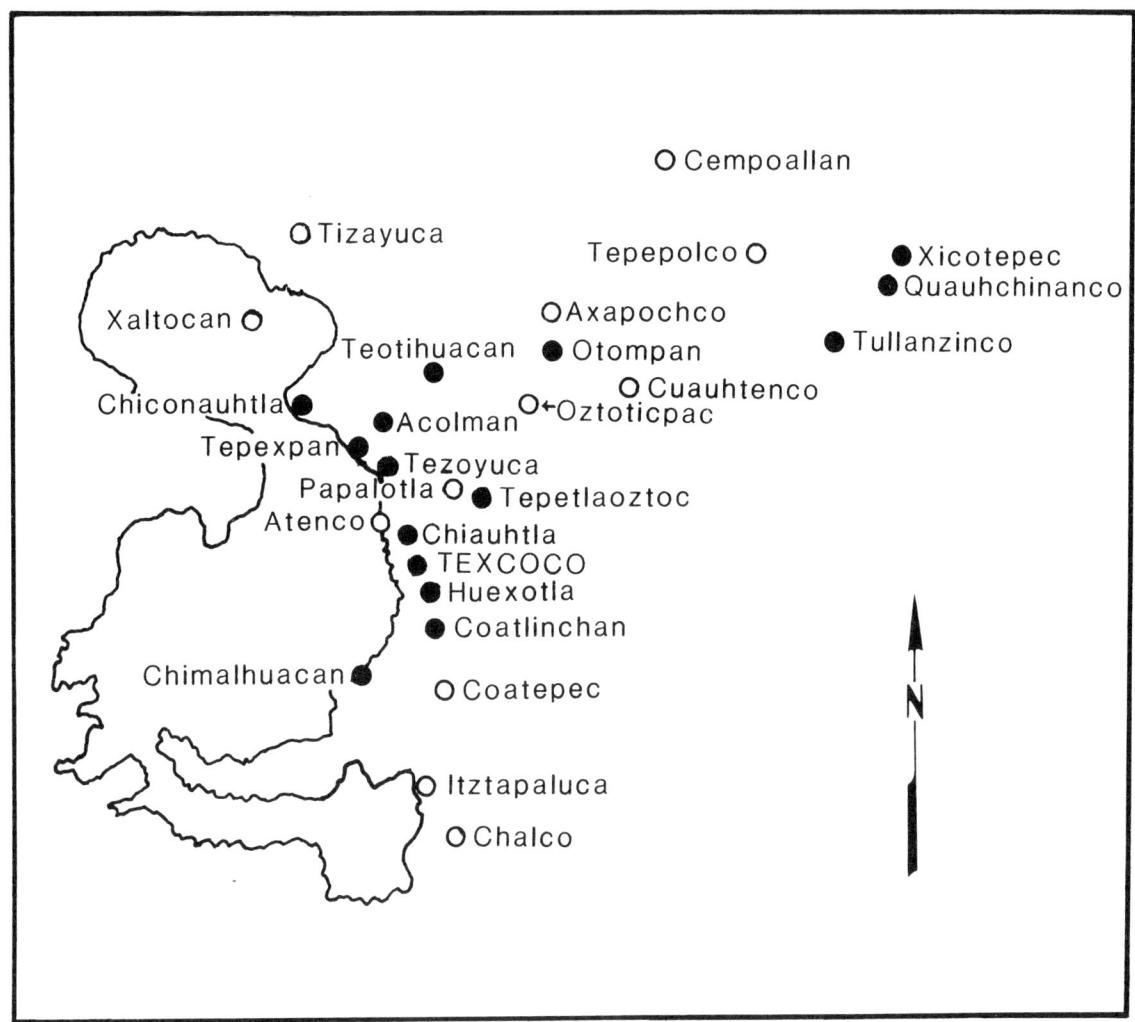

Fig. 2-8. Lordships of the Acolhua state. Those marked with solid dots are centers with a tlatoani, those with circles are centers that were governed by calpixque.

men and other specialists. This arrangement of discrete lineage-based units resembles the organization of the entire Acolhua (Texcocan) state, in which 14 provinces were administered by second-level lords subject to the Acolhua ruler.

Organization of the Acolhua State

Nezahualcoyotl became the ruler of Texcoco and the Acolhua state ca. 1430, having overthrown the Azcapotzalcan rulers, who had killed his father, Ixtlilxochitl, the previous Acolhua ruler. In 1430 or 1434, after Nezahualcoyotl and Itzcoatl of Tenochtitlan had defeated Azcapotzalco, Nezahualcoyotl reorganized the Texcocan state as follows.

Administration. Nezahualcoyotl appointed 14 hereditary rulers (tlatoque), some of whom had been deposed by the Azcapotzalcans, to rule 14 provinces, or second-level city-states. He also created 8 tributary provinces, each governed by administrators, or calpixque (see Table 2-1 and Fig. 2-8).

Twenty-nine towns served the Texcocan palace. These 29 were divided into two groups, each of which provided goods and labor for 6 months of each year (Table 2-2). The other dependencies provided tribute at different intervals, as assigned by the ruler. These two groups, along with the central section of Acolhuacan, made up three admin-

TABLE 2-2
REORGANIZATION OF THE ACOLHUA (TEXCOCAN) STATE, CA. 1430

Rulers appointed to govern 14 señoríos or provinces:	Huexotla Coatlinchan Tepetlaoztoc Acolman Tepexpan Tezoyuca Chiconauhtla Chiauhtla Chimalhuacan Otompan (Otumba) Teotihuacan Tullanzinco Quauhchinanco Xicotepec
Tribute-paying provinces, governed by administrators (calpixque):	Texcoco and its barrios Atenco Tepepolco Axapochco Quauhtlatzinco Ahuatepec Tetitlan Coatepec Ixtapalapa Tlapechhuacan Tecpilpan
Towns paying tribute to the ruler of Texcoco and his palace were:	Coatepec Iztapaluca Xaltocan Papalotla

(Alva Ixtlilxochitl 1975–77, II:89)

istrative divisions of the Acolhua state: the Sierra division, the Milpa division, and the Central division (Alva Ixtlilxochitl 1975-77, II:89-90).

Judicial Officials. The three administrative groups (the Milpa, the Sierra, and Central divisions) of the Texcocan state were judicial units as well (Corona-Sánchez 1976:91). Two judges for each division were appointed, one for the nobles and one for the commoners.

Military Officials. The 14 great lords served as advisors to the Texcocan ruler and also as war chiefs (Alva Ixtlilxochitl 1977, I:444-47; Torquemada 1975, II:355).

The Acolhua State's Provincial Rulers. The Acolhua administrative system employed city-states as administrative units for providing laborers and soldiers and for judicial matters, but the tlatoque were by no means isolated in their realms. Nezahualcoyotl reassigned lands so that the Texcocan city-state rulers were supported by produce from lands in each other's territories (as described in the chapter on Teotihuacan). Even the sizes of rulers' lands were dictated by Nezahualcoyotl: each portion measured 400 by 400 units (medidas) exactly (Alva Ixtlilxochitl 1975-77, II:91; Paso y Troncoso 1912).

Descriptions of the Acolhua state suggest a well-organized political system based on an extensive territory ruled by an interrelated group of elites (Offner 1979; Carrasco 1984). Although the capital city, Texcoco, was less nucleated than Tenochtitlan, it did not lack monumental architecture (Parsons 1971) and even outside the capital the state invested considerable labor in public works and palaces, such as those at Tetzcotzinco (Parsons 1971). Our picture of the Texcocan state is influenced by the content of the histories, which emphasize the Acolhua rulers' administrative talents and philosophical and aesthetic contributions to Nahua culture (Nezahualcoyotl believed in an invisible deity; Alva Ixtlilxochitl emphasizes the quality of Texcocan rhetoric [Alva Ixtlilxochitl 1975-77; see also Piña Chan 1976; Offner 1979]). Recent research has investigated the local economic basis of the Acolhua state (Brumfiel 1980; Hicks 1978, 1982). Overall, the Acolhua state appears to have been a tightly organized political system administered by a combination of elite rulers and appointed administrators (Hicks 1978). The orderly, centralized hierarchy of provincial rulers and administrators was purported to have been created in a single decree; it contrasts with the Mexica system, which the histories report was forged more gradually and less neatly by Tenochtitlan, out of a number of city-states in the western and southern sections of the Valley of Mexico.

Tlacopan

The third city-state member of the Aztec Triple Alliance was Tlacopan (called Tacuba in the Colonial period). This city-state headed the Tepaneca division, or the city-states formerly ruled by Azcapotzalco. The rulers of Tenochtitlan and Texcoco defeated the Azcapotzalcans ca. A.D. 1428.

> . . . Tlacaelel was victorious over the Tepanecs. . .
>
> And together (with Itzcoatzin) he did the same with those of Tacuba, although their lord, who was called Acolnahuacatl Tzacualcatl, later surrendered and he himself came to Mexico to recognize and to give obeisance in the name of his people to King Itzcoatzin and to Tlacaeleltzin. The King of Tacuba and his successors thereafter remained as counsellors to Mexico. . . . [Chimalpahin 1978:33]

TABLE 2-3
DIVISIONS OF THE ACOLHUA STATE
WHICH PROVIDED LABOR FOR THE PALACE

Acolhuacan Center Zone: Provided Labor for The Ruler's Palace 6 Months per Year	"Milpa" Zone: Provided Labor for Texcocan Ruler's Palace During the Other 6 Months	"Sierra" Zone: Dependencies Provided Labor and Goods at Irregular Intervals
Huexotla	Teotihuacan	Tullanzinco
Coatlinchan	Tepepolco	Xicotepec
Chimalhuacan	Cempoallan	Cuauhchinanco
Tepetlaoztoc	Aztaquemecan	Pahuatlan
Acolman	Ahuatepec	Tlachilotepec
Chiauhtla	Axapochco	Papaloticpac
Coatepec	Oztoticpac	
Ixtapaluca	Tizayuca	
Tepexpan	Tlalanalpan	
Palalotla	Coyoacan	
Chiconauhtla	Cuauhtlapan	
Tezoyuca	Cuauhtlacca	
	Cuauhtatzinco	
	Oztotlauhcan	
	Achichilacayocan	
	Tetliztoc	

(Alva Ixtlilxochitl 1975–77, II: 89–90)

After the rulers of Tenochtitlan and Texcoco had defeated the Azcapotzalcans, they appointed Totoquihuatzin I (who ruled between 1431 and 1470) as the Tepaneca ruler and relocated the Tepaneca seat of government in neighboring Tlacopan. Azcapotzalco was reduced in rank to a dependency of Tlacopan.

While the city of Tlacopan had previously been ruled by a son of Tezozomoc, Acolnahuacatzin, or Aculnahuacatl Tzacualcatl (*Anales de Tlatelolco* 1948:22; *Crónica Mexicáyotl* 1949:101), under the Triple Alliance, it had four more rulers: Totoquihuatzin I (1431-1470), Chimalpopocatzin (1470-1490), Totoquihuatzin (1490-1519), and Tetlepanquetzanitzin (1519-1521) (Zantwijk 1969:131). It is likely that these four rulers were related to Tenochca rulers. Certainly they ruled with the approval of Tenochtitlan (Chimalpahin 1978:33; Motolinía 1950:284).

There is no history with great time-depth describing the development of Tlacopan. This is not surprising since this city-state was promoted to administer the Azcapotzalcan domain, and the lack of dynastic information suggests a disjunction in rulership following Tlacopan's promotion to head of the Tepaneca realm (Alva Ixtlilxochitl 1975-77; Torquemada 1975, I:145, 175; Barlow 1947-48).

Despite the lack of information about the early periods in Tlacopan's development, Colonial documents have provided clues to how the Tepaneca territory was organized and administered under the Triple Alliance (*Memorial de los Pueblos*, in Paso y Troncoso 1940, XIV:118-22; *Códice Osuna* 1947; see also Gibson 1964a). The head town, Tlacopan, ruled a number of towns within its immediate territory (13 in the mid-sixteenth century; in pre-Hispanic times it had governed 16 additional towns that were held by a Spanish encomendero in the mid-1500s). Thirty-seven towns obeyed Tlacopan in warfare, paid tribute to Tlacopan, and supplied Tlacopan with stone, lime, wood, mats, shields, pottery, and other materials. A total of 32 estancias paid tribute to Tacuba's ruler, worked his lands and provided fuel for his palace for 80 days of each year. At the head of these towns and estancias were 8 administrative units (each called a tlatocayotl and governed by a tlatoani): Tlacopan, Coyoacan, Cuauhtitlan (including the lordships of Tultitlan, Tepotzotlan, and Tepexic), Tullan, and Apazco (Zantwijk 1969:131-33).

Thus, within Tlacopan's domain were towns directly in its jurisdiction, plus a number of provinces and their dependent towns, some of which were ruled by tlatoque. All of these dependencies paid tribute and labor to Tlacopan. Towns that paid tribute directly to Tlacopan's ruler were yet another category.

Superimposed on this organization was an imperial tribute structure, including towns paying tribute to all three capitals (*Memorial de los Pueblos,* in Paso y Troncoso 1940, XIV:119-22; Barlow 1949:33-50). Tlacopan's ruler was supposed to have received ⅕ of the imperial tribute (Torquemada 1975, I:145, 175), or perhaps even less (*Anales de Cuauhtitlan* 1945:65). According to the *Codex Mendoza* (as interpreted by Barlow 1949:33-50), the imperial tribute provinces in Tlacopan's territory were Quahuacan, Xocotitlan, Atotonilco, Quauhtitlan, Xilotepec, Axocopan, Huepuchtla.

The lord of Tlacopan was one of the main administrators of the empire, led the Tepaneca division warriors in imperial battles, and called up labor from the Tepaneca zone for imperial projects (Durán 1967:227-28, 373, 381, 389; see Fig. 6-7). Unlike Tenochtitlan and Texcoco, there is no mention of palaces being built in Tlacopan for the ruler; although the ruler at Tlacopan shared in feasts and imperial ceremonies, he may not have received as many of the benefits of imperial leadership as the rulers of Tenochtitlan and Texcoco. As we will see in the chapters on Coyoacan and Cuauhtitlan, large parts of the Tepaneca city-states were directly administered by Mexica nobles, and the *Anales de Cuauhtitlan* describes Tenochtitlan's continual meddling with city-state government, economics, and ritual in the Tepaneca area. Through its apparently rather firm control over Azcapotzalco and Tlacopan, Tenochtitlan was able to govern the old Tepaneca empire, which covered the area of the valley from southwest to north (see Fig. 2-9).

Led by Tenochtitlan, Tlacopan, and Texcoco the city-states of the Valley of Mexico together embarked on conquests of polities outside the valley, forming the Aztec empire. Triple Alliance policies for dealing with polities outside the Valley of Mexico are decribed in the following section.

The Empire

The Triple Alliance

The Triple Alliance, or confederation of Tenochtitlan, Texcoco, and Tacuba (Tlacopan) came into being after these and other subject polities rebelled against and defeated Azcapotzalco in 1428. The Triple Alliance was formed in 1430, and this new confederation replaced the Azcapotzalcan polity as dominant in the Valley of Mexico.

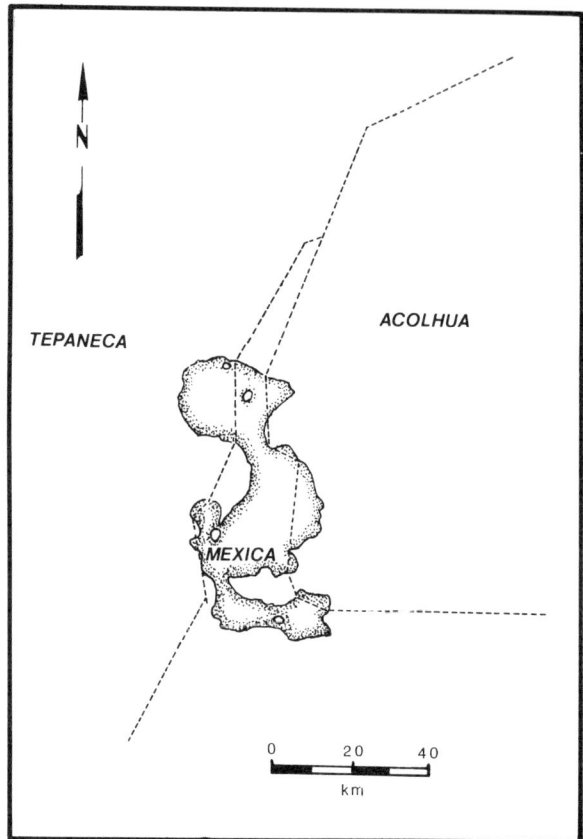

Fig. 2-9. Areas of the Valley of Mexico controlled by the Triple Alliance members in 1519 (after Gibson 1964b).

There are different versions of how this confederation came about. Tenochca (Mexica) sources recount that Nezahualcoyotl and other rulers allied themselves with Tenochtitlan voluntarily, rather than chancing a confrontation with the Mexica (Chimalpahin 1978:32-33; *Codex Ramírez* 1920:109). According to Chimalpahin, the ruler of Tlacopan,

who was called Acolnahuacatl Tzacualcatl, later surrendered and he himself came to Mexico to recognize and to give obeisance in the name of his people to King Itzcoatzin and to Tlacaeleltzin. The King of Tacuba and his successors thereafter remained as counsellors of Mexico until the arrival of Captain Don Hernando Cortés. He did the same with those of Coyoacan. By wars Tlacaeleltzin defeated Xochimilco and Cuitlahuac. After this the four lords who governed the Republic of Four Capitals [Culhuacan, Ixtapalapa, Mexicaltzingo, and Huitzilopochco] . . . [and] the king. . .of Mizquic. . . came to Mexico to render obedience to the said lords. And thus Nezahualcoyotl, the king of Texcoco did the same; he did not want war but came himself to Mexico to render obedience in the name of his city to his kinsman

Itzcoatzin and to his uncle Tlacaeleltzin, his mother's brother. The king of Texcoco and his successors thereafter then also remained as counsellors of Mexico until the arrival of Captain Don Hernando Cortés. [Chimalpahin 1978:32-33]

A Texcocan version disagrees with this reconstruction. The Texcocan historian Ixtlilxochitl relates that the empire of Azcapotzalco was initially divided between Texcoco and Tenochtitlan; however, Itzcoatl later reconsidered, demanded more territory, and had to be defeated by Nezahualcoyotl [Alva Ixtlilxochitl 1975-77, I:87-88, II:445-46]. Following this conflict, Texcoco received tribute from some areas within the Mexica half of the Valley of Mexico.

The foundation of the Triple Alliance is sketchy, but the formal agreement on which it was chartered was as follows:

> In Mexico City and its province there were three principal lords. They were the ruler of Mexico, the ruler of Texcoco, and the ruler of Tlacopan now called Tacuba. All the other inferior lords served and obeyed these three rulers. Since they were confederates, they divided all the land they conquered among themselves.
>
> The rulers of Texcoco and Tacuba obeyed the ruler of Mexico in matters of war. They were equals in all the rest, for none could meddle in the affairs of another. They held some towns in common, however, dividing among themselves the tribute paid by these towns. In some cases they divided the tribute into five parts: Two fell to the share of the ruler of Mexico, two to the ruler of Texcoco, and one to the ruler of Tacuba. [Zorita 1963:89]

Torquemada states that only tribute from joint conquests was divided and that each of the three participating cities was allowed to conquer and exact tribute independently. He adds that in addition, the world was divided into three territories. The land between the cardinal points east, south, and west was Tenochtitlan's. Tlacopan's territory stretched from the points west to north. The Texcocan area began slightly southwest of north and extended to east (Torquemada 1975, I:175), and while tribute was to be divided among the participants, only the ruler of each section was considered the political paramount of that area (see Fig. 2-9). Their titles were Culhua Tecuhtli (Tenochtitlan), Acolhua Tecuhtli (Texcoco), and Tepanecatl Tecuhtli (Tlacopan), or lord of the Culhua, lord of the Acolhua, and lord of the Tepaneca.

While the aforementioned agreement is the stated rule, in practice, by 1519, both Tenochtitlan and Texcoco received tribute from towns within each other's territory (Gibson 1971). Texcoco received tribute from chinampa lands in Coyoacan and Xochimilco and from lands in the territories of Tlacopan, Azcapotzalco, Tenayuca, Tepotzotlan, Cuauhtitlan, Tultitlan, Ecatepec, Huexachtitlan, Cuexomatitlan (Alva Ixtlilxochitl 1975-77, I:446, II:86-88). Most of these lands are in areas formerly ruled by Azcapotzalco and may have been assimilated following the war of 1428. Others in the productive chinampa area were taken over by Texcoco later. In turn, Tenochtitlan received tribute from 36 towns in the Acolhua area (Barlow 1949:66-72). A study of the variation in tribute payment showed that

> the outer territories of Tlacopan and Texcoco, even though those towns were capitals and partners in the Triple Alliance, are listed as tributary [to Tenochtitlan]. Apparently only the capitals and part of the land in their immediate vicinities were exempted from the imperial tribute system. The exemption of other nearby towns, such as Azcapotzalco may be explained by their having been absorbed closely into the fabric of the capitals by distribution of land to the nobility of the Triple Alliance. [Borah and Cook 1963:75-76]

Apparently the tributary areas changed over time; the preserved tribute lists freeze only a few moments in the history of the empire (Gibson 1971). It is also believed that polities longest under the domination of the Triple Alliance paid heavier tribute quotas per family than newly-conquered regions. Rebellions increased the tribute assessment in regions of older subjugation to amounts approaching their capacity to pay (Borah and Cook 1963:62).

Administration of Warfare

> I have not yet been able to discover the extent of the domain of Mutezuma, but in the two hundred leagues which his messengers traveled to the north and to the south of this city, his orders were obeyed, although there were some provinces in the middle of these lands which were at war with him. . . . The greater part of the chiefs of these lands and provinces, especially those from close by resided, as I have said, for most of the year in the capital city, and all or most of their eldest sons were in the service of Mutezuma. In all these domains he had fortresses garrisoned with his own people, and governers and officials to collect the tributes which each province must pay; and they kept an account of whatever each one was obliged to give in characters and drawings on the paper which they make, which is their writing. Each of these provinces paid appropriate tributes in accordance with the nature of the land; thus Mutezuma received every sort of produce from those provinces, and was so feared by all, both present and absent, that there could be no ruler in all the world more so. [Cortés 1971:109]

The main goals and activities of the Triple Alliance were obtaining captives and collecting tribute. The chronology of expansion is recorded in the Mexica conquest lists, which give the towns and territories conquered by each ruler (see Kelly and Palerm 1952). The initial military campaign of a ruler was carried out to obtain prisoners for sacrifice and tribute for distribution as gifts and rewards, both of which would affirm and reinforce the capital's position. Other campaigns were carried out, in which the Mexica sought to obtain more prisoners, more tribute, or secure trade routes. Figure 2-10 illustrates the area from which the Triple Alliance was exacting tribute in 1519.

Triple Alliance wars were directed by the ruler of Tenochtitlan. To declare war, Mexica ambassadors, called teucnene, approached the enemy ruler to ask whether he wanted peace (and to do whatever the Mexica asked) or war. To symbolize a declaration of war, these ambassadors carried shields and spears to the opposing ruler (Durán 1964:99, 1967:109, 156).

When war was declared, the ruler of Mexico notified the rulers of Texcoco, Tlacopan, and the rest of the valley to proclaim war in their domains. He sent capes and insignia to the rulers. The commoners were ordered to go to war, and the keepers of the storehouses were instructed to give them arms (Sahagún 1954, Book 8:51-52).

The army was composed first of priests, who chanted and beat drums, and then of the rulers and armies of Tenochtitlan, Texcoco, and Tlacopan, followed by armies of Chalca, Xochimilca, Tepaneca, Chinampaneca, Malinalca, Tlahuica, etc. (Sahagún 1954, Book 8:51-52; Durán 1967:156-57). Cadres of warriors marched in order, arranged by political affiliation, and one writer estimated that Moctezuma could muster 100,000 soldiers from his subject provinces (Durán 1967:164).

In war, the object was to take prisoners alive and uninjured for sacrifice, and to capture the opposing city. A demonstration of victory was to burn the main temple of the enemy city. The conquered city's idols were taken from the city back to Tenochtitlan and kept in a temple reserved for captured gods (Sahagún 1951, Book 2:168).

Imperial Tribute Collection

When the outcome of a war was a Triple Alliance victory, the terms of surrender were set.

And when the city which they had destroyed was attained, at once was set the tribute, the impost. [To the ruler who had conquered them] they gave that which was there made. And likewise, forthwith, a steward was placed in office, who would watch over and levy tribute. [Sahagún 1954, Book 8:53-54]

Tribute was delivered every 80 days, sometimes by an imperial official and in other cases by the conquered ruler. In addition to regularly scheduled tribute, conquered areas sometimes were ordered, as a peace settlement, to furnish labor and materials or to perform special tasks for Tenochtitlan. For instance, the conquered lords of Tepeaca (now in the state of Puebla) were ordered to furnish bearers to carry supplies, warriors, slaves for sacrifice, protection for Mexica merchants and travelers, a market area where exotic goods could be exchanged, and sustenance for the Mexica governor. In addition, they gave "gifts" to Moctezuma and his council, and the priests from Tepeaca went to Tenochtitlan to worship the Mexica deity, Huitzilopochtli (Durán 1967:159-60).

The empire imposed a "clearly defined system" of tribute collection on each conquered province (Berdan 1975:74). This chain went upwards from residential district or calpulli, to community, to regional center, to provincial capital, to Tenochtitlan. "Similar instances are found throughout the *Relaciones geográficas*, and this system probably existed with little variation throughout the empire" (ibid.). In Tenochtitlan, the principal tribute administrator was titled petlacalcatl. Provincial tribute collectors and their assistants were called calpixque (Gibson 1971:390; Berdan 1975:118; Carrasco 1976). The 38 provinces which paid tribute to Tenochtitlan are listed in the *Codex Mendoza* (1925; Barlow 1949; see also Fig. 2-10).

There is a lack of quantitative information about the distribution of tribute after it was delivered to Tenochtitlan. However, it is known that after wars, Mexica rulers gave sumptuary items to participating warriors and rulers. During the war with Tehuantepec, soldiers were stopped from sacking the city by Ahuitzotl and promised that they would get a part of the spoils (Durán 1967:388-89). Tribute was used for sustenance of state officials: the tlatoani and his court, judges, military officials, priests, provincial tlatoque, calpixque, artisans, singers, dancers, and laborers working on public projects. Tribute was also used to support state functions, such as festivals and rituals, constructing

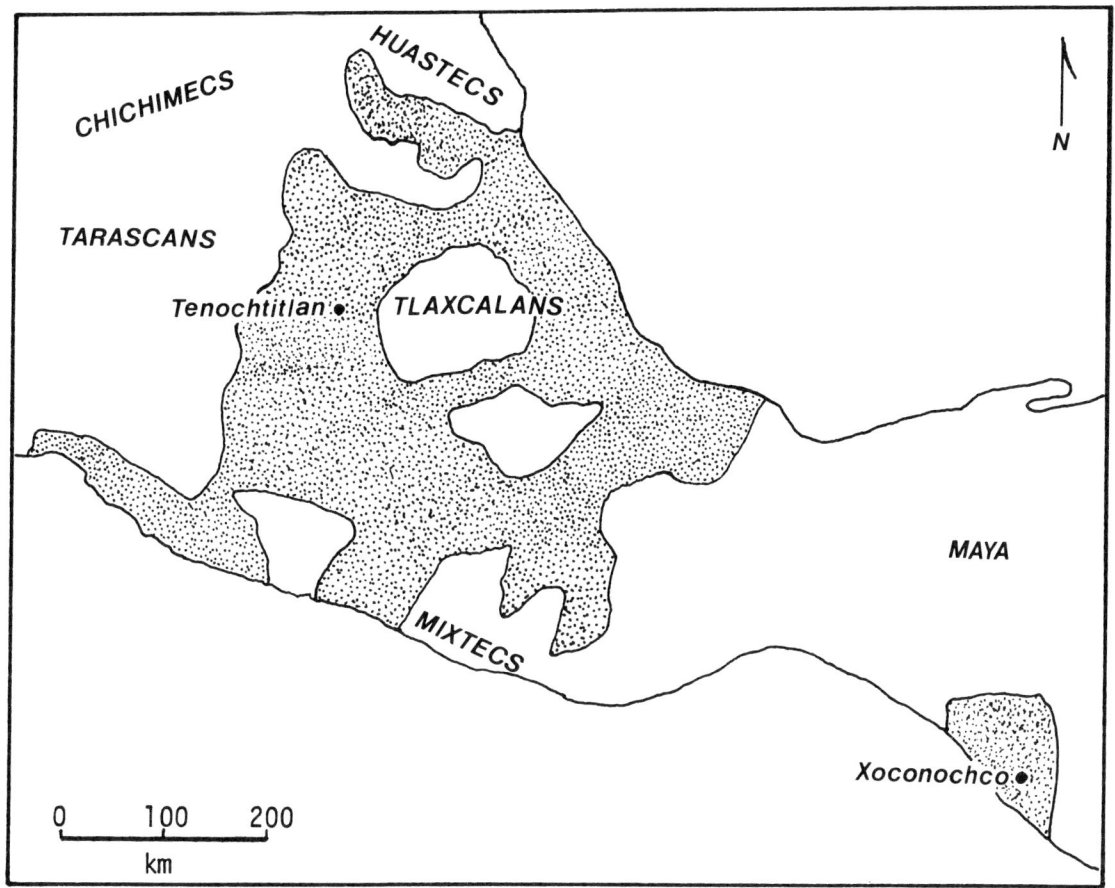

Fig. 2-10. The areas in Mesoamerica from which the Triple Alliance was exacting tribute in 1519 are indicated by shading (after Bray 1968).

public buildings, war expenses, social expenses such as food distributed during famine and to indigents, support of colonies, and political relations—for instance, gifts to foreign rulers (López Austin 1961:124-25).

I will now turn to a detailed processual analysis of five city-states—of their internal organizations, their development, their participation in regional confederations, and their interaction with the Aztec capital. Comparison of the development of individual city-states can suggest how the Aztec empire (best known from reports of its developed form, in 1519) evolved and how neighboring city-states and confederations were affected by, and in turn affected, its expansion. The city-states whose political systems were studied intensively and which are described in Chapters 3-7 are Amecameca, Cuauhtitlan, Xochimilco, Coyoacan, and Teotihuacan. The case studies are presented in the order of the last-conquered city-state to the first-conquered city-state; that is, we will look at the least acculturated or most recently assimilated polity first.

Chapter 3

Amecameca

The Place and the People of Amecameca

Amecameca is in the southeast corner of the Valley of Mexico (Fig. 3-1). In pre-Hispanic times, Amecameca was part of the Chalca confederation, a group of city-states which banded together for mutual aid and protection. After being conquered by the Mexica, the Chalca city-states were recast into a tributary and administrative province.

The town of Amecameca lies at the foot of the volcano Popocatepetl, at the lowest point in the Amecameca Valley, a 99 km^2 area, in which the Río Amecameca forms from the confluence of several small streams. At 2470-3000 m in elevation, the valley is bordered on the east by deep barrancas which are part of the steeply rising slopes of the Sierra Madre Oriental. The mountainsides above Amecameca are covered by oak-conifer forests, and the valley floor is covered by agricultural fields. In 1599, typical crops were maize, beans of several types, squash, fruit, and grains (Lemoine Villicaña 1961).

The southern quarter of the Amecameca Valley slopes southward, toward the warmer valleys in the modern state of Morelos, and the town of Amecameca was a stopover on the route between the Valley of Mexico and the Gulf Coast and other southern locations (ibid.; Parsons et al. 1982:5-14; Fig. 3-1).

The name Amecameca, or Amequemcan, which means "place costumed with ceremonial paper," is derived from the Nahuatl words amatl, meaning "paper," queme, meaning "ceremonial vestments," and -can, indicating place (Chimalpahin 1965:297). The name refers to religious rites which involved placing sheets of ceremonial paper on the hill which overlooks the town (Chimalpahin 1965:77; see Figs. 3-2, 3-3, 3-4).

Settlement History of Amecameca

Settlements in the Amecameca Valley date from the Early Formative period, and the valley populace then and later resided in small, dispersed settlements. This dispersed pattern continued until the Late Aztec period when over 90% of the population lived at the site of Amecameca (Sanders, Parsons, and Santley 1979; Parsons et al. 1982:294).

Throughout the Valley of Mexico, the Late Aztec period showed an increase in population, and the Amecameca Valley did as well. However, the Amecameca Valley contained only one large settlement—the town of Amecameca—which consisted of 5-10,000 inhabitants. Most of the outlying settlements were villages of 100 or fewer people (Parsons et al. 1982:277-78; Fig. 3-5).

The Urban Center of Amecameca

The Chalco-Xochimilco archaeological survey project identified remains of the Late Aztec-period community of Amecameca protruding out of the present-day community and reported that

> ...most of the Aztec community is covered by the modern town. The area visible to us probably represents a population of 350-700 people. Assuming that most of the modern town overlies Aztec occupation, we are apparently dealing with a local center of some 400 hectares and perhaps 5,000-10,000 people. We suggest the Early Aztec settlement is roughly 200 hectares and perhaps 2500-5000 people. The latter figures are little more than guesses. [Parsons et al. 1982:162]

Since the Aztec town of Amecameca is covered by modern occupation, we must turn to documentary sources for an idea of the town's pre-Hispanic appearance. In 1519, Cortés reported that Amecameca had well-built houses and was the residence of a ruler or lord.

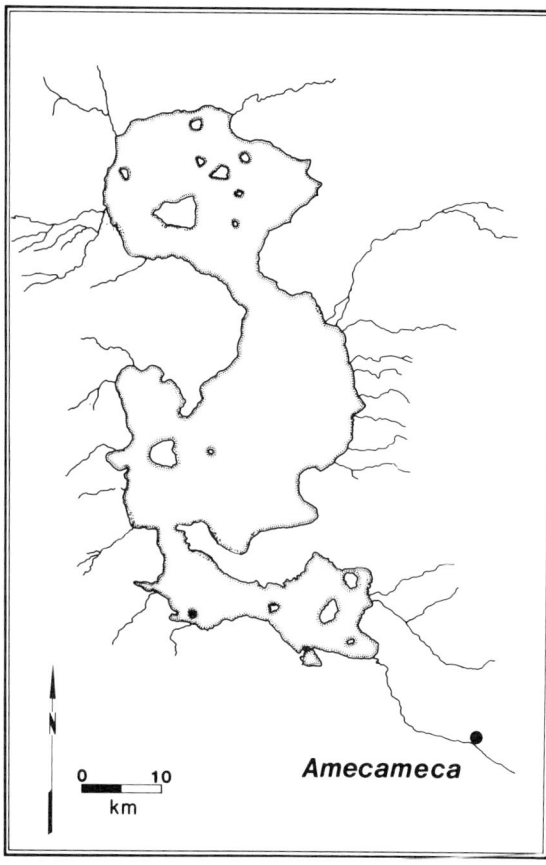

Fig. 3-1. Location of Amecameca in the Valley of Mexico.

> At daybreak I departed for a town which . . . is called Amequeruca. It is in the province of Chalco, which contains, in the principal town and in the villages which are two leagues away, more than twenty thousand inhabitants. In the aforementioned town we were quartered in some very good houses belonging to the lord of the place. And many persons who seemed to be of high rank came to speak with me, saying that Mutezuma, their lord, had sent them to wait for me there and to provide me with all that I might need. The chief of this province and town gave me as many as forty slave girls and three thousand *castellanos* [gold pieces], and, in the two days that we were there, he provided us very adequately with all the food we needed. [Cortés 1971:80]

Although Cortés did not record the exact population of the town, he estimated that there were 20,000 residents in it and in the surrounding villages. Later, a Colonial-period writer described Amecameca as a town traversed by streams, surrounded by fields, and ringed by mountains.

> I personally visited the site of Asumpción Amecameca and its six barrios . . . it is located and situated in a flat area beginning with the foothills of the volcano and Sierra Nevada. . . .

> There are in residence in the cabecera and its barrios 697 Mexican tribute payers. Its streets are well laid out. It has two natural arroyos for [transporting] good and plentiful water, one of which passes to the side and the other through the middle of the pueblo. They originate in the foothills of the volcano and Sierra Nevada, so that they plunge into it and run through its streets.

> The mountains are one-half league away and are the highest, and from them they take many, very good planks and beams that they buy for Mexico City and other places, and it is one of the principal products from there. Outside the town, they plant much corn, beans, lima beans, squash, and other native grains, in quantity. They raise Spanish and native fowl; they have many fruit trees—peaches, pears, apples, cherries—that they likewise have for sale. Eight-hundred and ninety-seven are taxed. [Lemoine Villicaña 1961:17-20]

The six barrios of Amecameca mentioned above were Ayapango, Caltenco, Panoaya (Panohuaya), Atenco, Tlailotlacan, (Tlayllotlacan), and the nucleus of the town, or Amecameca itself. Panoaya and Tlailotlacan were residences of two pre-Hispanic teteuctin, or lords, of Amecameca (see Table 3-1; Fig. 3-4).

Amecameca's People

Chimalpahin, Chalco's historian and a descendant of Amecameca's pre-Hispanic rulers, wrote a history of Amecameca in 1620 based on pictorial documents, prose histories, and local informants (Chimalpahin 1889, 1958, 1965). He reports that Amecameca was settled by people from north of the Valley of Mexico. The migration myths that he relates resemble those of other Nahua groups. However, he says that the first groups to enter the Valley of Mexico were the Xochimilca, Chalca, Tepaneca, Acolhuaque, Tlahuica, Tlaxcalteca, Teotenanca, Amaqueme, and Totolimpaneca (omitting the Tenochca, or Mexica) (Chimalpahin 1958:152). The lineages that founded Amecameca represented two major traditions of Postclassic central Mexico, the Chichimec and the Toltec (Alva Ixtlilxochitl 1975-77, I:306-07).

The first group of Chalca (the Axoteca) departed from Aztlan in A.D. 1072 and arrived at Chalco Atenco, on the shore of Lake Chalco, in 1241. By A.D. 1267, groups had fissioned off, and some had moved south to Tenango and Tlalmanalco. As they moved southward, the Chichimeca conquered, killed, or drove away the occupants of the area (Chimalpahin 1958:84-86, 1965:77). In regard to the occupants of the Amecameca area, Chimalpahin says:

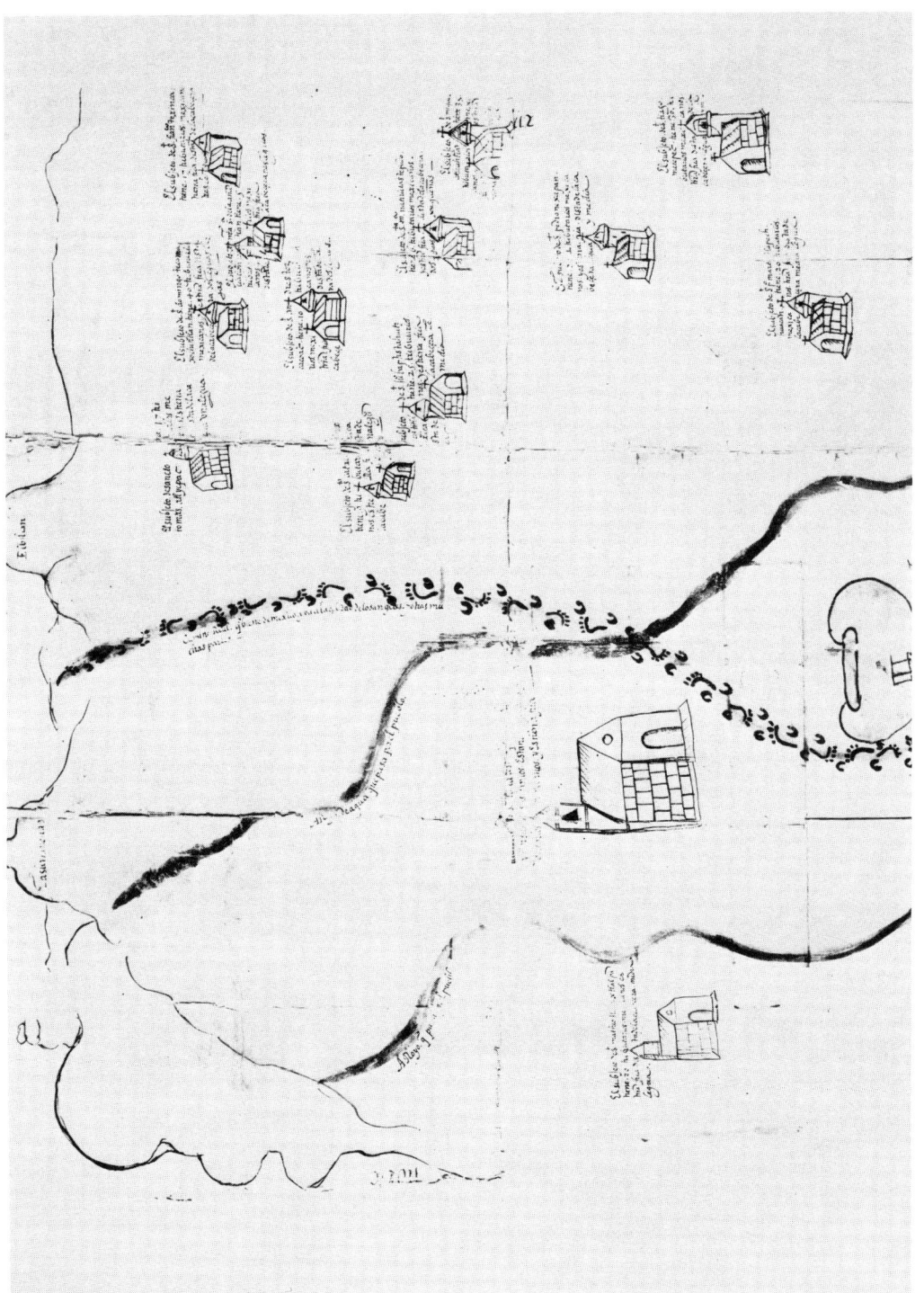

Fig. 3-2. Map of Amecameca in 1599 (AGN, Tierras, Vol. 2783, Exp. 1, Fol. 19). The villages subject to Amecameca are located to the south and east, as are villages located on the archaeological survey map of Late Horizon settlements in the area. From left to right, and top to bottom, the names for the places read: Santo Tomás Atlicpac, St. Domingo Tecomaxochititlan, St. Francisco Texinca, Ntra. Sa. de la Anunciación Coatlan, St. Andrés Tezcacoac, Sta. Catalina Texinca, St. Juan Baptista Huitzcuauhtitlan, Sta. Ma. Nativitas Tepanco, St. Miguel Atluahtla, Amecameca, St. Pedro Nexapan, St. Mateo Tlachixtlalpa, Santiago Metepec, St. Pedro Mártir Tlapechhuacan. [Photograph reproduced by permission of the Archivo General de la Nación, Mexico.]

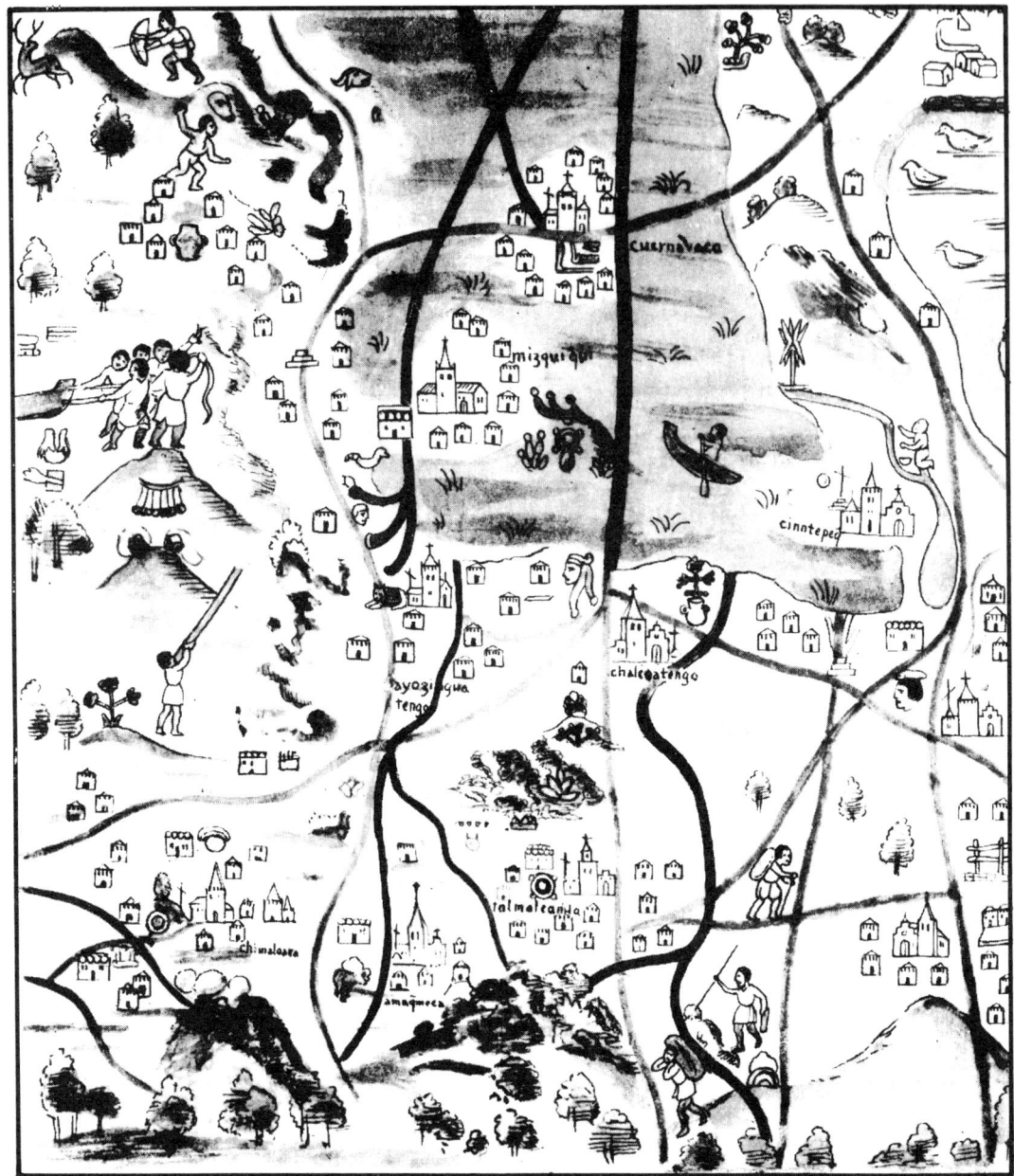

Fig. 3-3. Amecameca (lower center) as portrayed on the Santa Cruz map, ca. 1550 (Linné 1948).

They lived there, the common folk called Xochteca, Olmeca, Quiyauhteca, and Cocolca. These were four very depraved groups, given to the art of sorcery. They were magicians who could take on at will the appearance of animals and wild beasts. Moreover . . . they were nahual sorcerers and very carnivorous. The Tlaxcalteca passed by them in their travels. These were the people who lived where Amecameca is now.

But the Totolimpaneca and Amecame Chichimeca, when they arrived where Amecameca is today, put up a hostile front until they defeated and destroyed them, finally managing to drive them from their lands and towns. [Chimalpahin 1965:77]

Elsewhere in Chalco, conquered towns and people were divided among the rulers of Chalco and Tlalmanalco, so that each would receive equal amounts of tribute, suggesting that some natives stayed on the land and paid tribute to the conquer-

cuanipa settled the areas called Pochtlan and Huixtoco Amecameca (Chimalpahin 1965:73, 171). Finally, ca. 1304, a non-Chichimec group called the Poyauhteca settled Panohuayan Amecameca (ibid.:73, 150, 174, 205; see Table 3-1).

While most of the immigrants to Amecameca were Nahuatl-speaking Chichimeca, the final group to arrive spoke a dialect of Nahuatl called Nonoalca and were described as tecpantlaca, or "palace people." Associated with the Toltecs, they painted codices, and they practiced xochiyaotl, or ritual warfare. They are said to have brought a market with them when they arrived in Amecameca in 1306. Called Nonohualca or Poyauhteca, they formed the barrio of Panohuaya (Chimalpahin 1965:150, 174, 205; see Table 3-1).

Rituals and Ideology in Amecameca

Each group that, according to legend, settled in Amecameca brought a different deity with it (Kirchhoff 1956; Durand-Forest 1974; see Table 3-2). The Poyauhteca, who claimed to have come from Tula, worshipped the Toltec deity Tezcatlipoca, whereas the Tecuanipa and Totolimpaneca worshipped a deity associated with Chichimec culture—Citecatl/Mixcoatl, the deity of the hunt. The Tenanca deity was called Nauhyoteuctli, or "Lord of the Four Directions" (Chimalpahin 1965:53). Thus, several distinct Nahua traditions existed side-by-side in Amecameca. Each deity represented its group's culture and perhaps represented each group's elite lineage. Let us now turn to a discussion of the religious practices of the people of Amecameca.

Amecamecans practiced religious rites in urban temples and at shrines located on hilltops and in caves. When the Chichimeca first arrived in the Chalco area, they built an oratory to Nauhyoteuctli (Chimalpahin 1965:53, 203-04). These new arrivals to Amecameca adopted the former occupants' sacred places, such as the nearby mountain on which which the water deity Chalchiuhtlique had been worshipped.

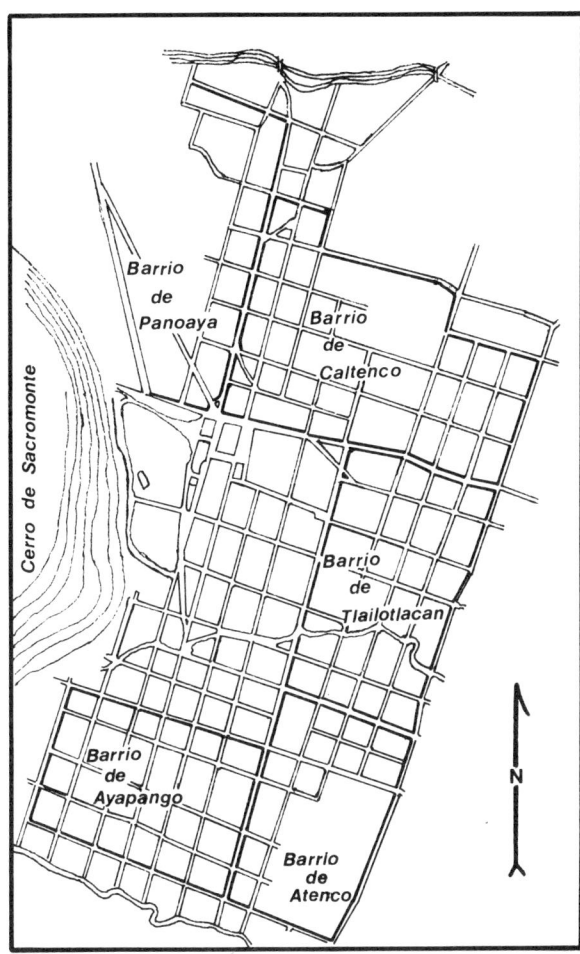

Fig. 3-4. Modern map of Amecameca showing its barrios (after Lemoine Villicaña 1961).

ing Chichimeca (Chimalpahin 1965:173). Though Chimalpahin describes only one dispute between the Totolimpaneca and the Tenanca over land; apparently the newcomers, having driven the natives from Amecameca, divided the land among themselves fairly amicably (Chimalpahin 1965:72).

The first group of Chichimeca to settle in Amecameca arrived in 1268, and they were called Totolimpaneca (Chimalpahin 1965:174-76). Later, another Totolimpaneca lineage came (ibid.:79-80). These two groups settled the barrios named Amecameca Itztlacozauhcan and Tlayllotlacan Amecamecan (Chimalpahin 1965:174). Next, another Chichimeca group, the Tenanca, settled the barrios of Tzacualtitlan Tenanco Amequemecan and Atlauhtlan Tzacualtitlan Amaquemecan (Chimalpahin 1965:73, 203). Later, in 1295, the Te-

> There in the same region, on the top of the mountain called Amaqueme today, existed an altar and temple that they called Chalchiuhmomozco ("altar of the goddess Chalchiuhtlique"), because there, water was worshipped and honored.
>
> And the mountain that thus was called Chalchiuhmomozco is no longer called that, since the Amaqueme took it and possessed the hill.... [Chimalpahin 1965:77]

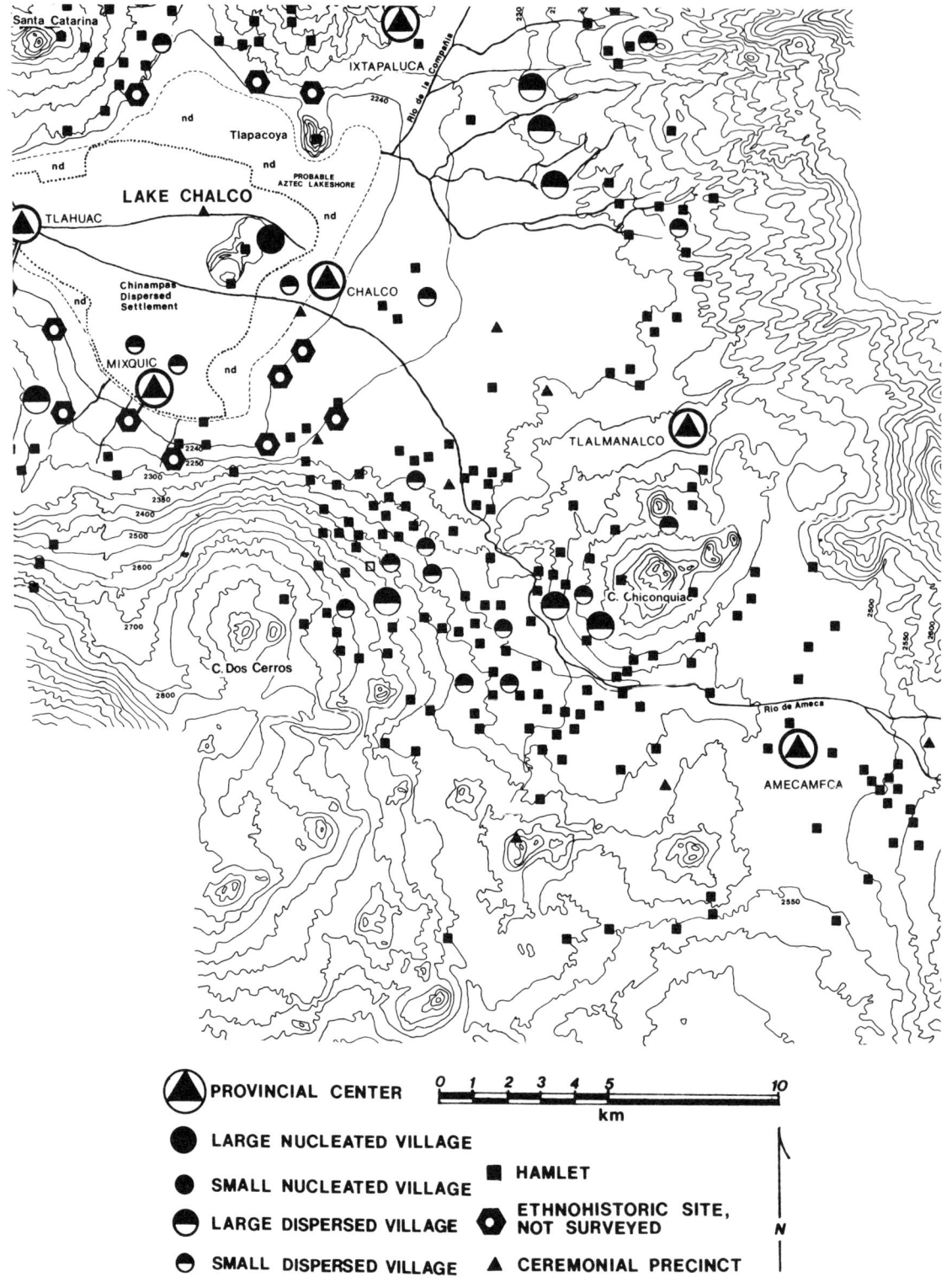

Fig. 3-5. Late Aztec period (A.D. 1350-1520) settlements in the Amecameca area. [Portion of Map 18, Late Horizon, reprinted from *The Basin of Mexico: Ecological Processes in the Evolution of a Civilization*, by William T. Sanders, Jeffrey R. Parsons, and Robert S. Santley. Copyright 1979, by Academic Press, Inc.]

TABLE 3-1
AMECAMECA'S LINEAGES AND BARRIOS

Name	Arrival[1]	Barrio Name	Ruler's Title
Totolimpaneca	1268	Itztlacozauhcan Tlayllotlacan	Chichimeca Teuctli Teohua Teuctli
Tenanca	1269	Tzacualtitlan Tenanco Atlauhtlan Tzacualtitlan	Tlayllotlac Teuctli Atlauhtecatl Teuctli
Tecuanipa	1295	Tecuanipan Huixtoco Tecuanipan Pochtlan	Chichimeca Teuctli Tzompahuaca Teuctli
Poyauhteca (Nonohualca)	1304	Panohuayan	Tlamaocatl Teuctli

[1] Dates of arrival are taken from Chimalpahin (1965:72–73); however, Davies (1981) believes that the Chalca calendar was different from the more widely known Tenochca calendar. According to Davies, if the Chalca year-count were corrected to match the Tenochca count, the arrival dates would be A.D. 1300, 1313, 1315, and 1324 (Davies 1981:268, 283). After 1428, according to Davies, Chimalpahin's correlations to the Julian calendar are the same as Tenochtitlan's, because the Chalca calendar was altered to correspond to that of the Mexica following Tenochtitlan's definitive conquest of the Chalco area.

TABLE 3-2
PLACE OF ORIGIN, ETHNIC AFFILIATION, AND DEITY OF MIGRANTS TO AMECAMECA

Name of Group	Place of Origin	Deity	Cultural Notes
Totolimpaneca	Aztlan/ Chicomoztoc	Mixcoatl, White Eagle, Red Jaguar	Called themselves "Teochichimeca"
Tenanca	Teotenango	Nauhyoteuctli	6 divisions: Tepaneca, Tlaillotlaque, Atlauhteca, Tlacatecpantlaca, Amilca, Teuhticpantlaca.
Tecuanipa	Aztlan	Citecatl (similar to Mixcoatl)	
Poyauhteca/ Nonohualca	Tlapallan- Nonohualco	Tezcatlipoca	"Palace people," or tecpantlaca. Spoke Nonoalca. Title of priest, or god-bearer was Tlotliteuctli. They painted codices, practiced ritual war or xochiyaotl, and brought a market with them

(Sources: Chimalpahin 1965; Kirchhoff 1956; Durand-Forest 1974)

On this mountain, they built a temple, and the priest of the Itztlacozauhque later sacrificed prisoners there (ibid.:203-4).

Cook de Leonard recorded modern folk rituals taking place on the mountain above Amecameca (called "Sacromonte" in Colonial and modern times), in which rocks and trees are draped with cloth. Any pre-Hispanic structures on the hill have been covered by the Colonial church located at the top of the hill, and the nearest pre-Hispanic ritual site which is visible today consists of a number of carvings on boulders (Site Number Ch-Az-47; Parsons et al. 1982:162-64). These carvings, which portray rabbits and calendrical glyphs, relate to the pulque deity, Tepozteco, for whom rituals were performed in the southern Valley of Mexico and in Morelos (Redfield 1930; Cook de Leonard and Lemoine Villicaña 1954-55; Madsen 1960).

While natural shrines were important for Amecamecan rituals, the Amecamecans also built urban temples (Chimalpahin 1965:53). Along with most of the remains of the pre-Hispanic town, these temples are obscured by modern occupation (Parsons, personal communication, 1982).

An archaeological survey report of the Chalco-Xochimilco area notes a tendency toward dispersed settlements in the Chalco region as a whole, compared to other parts of the Valley of Mexico (Parsons et al. 1982). Although this tendency may result from the late influx of Nahuatl speakers into the area and from the generally disrupted history of the area, which was a buffer zone between the Valley of Mexico and the Puebla area polities to the east (see Davies 1981), the absence of monumental architecture may also be related to the use of natural features—caves, springs, and mountains—rather than man-made pyramids, for rituals in this area.

Amecameca's Territory

In 1599, Amecameca had 13 sujetos (see Table 3-3), and its territory measured 2 leagues north to south and 4 or 5 leagues east to west (Lemoine Villicaña 1961:19), which adds up to an area of approximately 128 km² (1 league = 4.16 km).

The placement of Amecameca's dependent villages on a Colonial map made in 1599 (Fig. 3-2) shows a remarkable correspondence to the location of villages on the map of Late Aztec sites prepared from archaeological survey (Fig. 3-5). All of Amecameca's dependent villages had populations of less than 150 people in 1599 (Lemoine Villicaña 1961) and less than 100 people in the pre-Hispanic period (Sanders, Parsons, and Santley 1979). These villages fan out south and east of Amecameca; all were within 3 leagues (12.48 km) of the town of Amecameca. The villages lie along the edge of the mountainside rather than on the valley floor. These villages and hamlets produced agricultural crops in 1599 (Lemoine Villicaña 1961). The valley floor was probably cultivated by farmers who lived in the central settlement of Amecameca.

Amecameca's early Colonial territory is isomorphic with its extent in the Late pre-Hispanic period. After its initial settlement, it never expanded its territory by conquest. However, its span of control was increased in 1465, when the Mexica ruler Ahuitzotl demoted Atlauhtla from an independent lordship to a dependency of Amecameca (AGN, Tierras, Vol. 2674, Exp. 1; Chimalpahin 1965:102-03, 222).

Amecameca's Political System

Overview of Amecameca's Political Development

As mentioned previously, the town of Amecameca was founded ca. 1268, by groups of Chichimeca who migrated into the area and pushed out the previous occupants. Between ca. A.D. 1268-1304, several towns were settled by related groups, and these towns—Chalco Atenco, Tlalmanalco, Amecameca, Tenango, and Atlauhtla—became known as the Chalca polities, linked by common history and geographic proximity (see Fig. 3-6). The Chalca league expanded in 1301, when two Xochimilca lords joined the Chalca league. Their communities were called Chimalhuacan and Tepetlixpan (Chimalpahin 1965:173, 203; Parsons et al. 1982:81; see Fig. 3-6).

The Chalca polities joined together in 1367 to oppose the Tepaneca of Azcapotzalco and the Mexica. Conflicts, intermittent conquests, and rebellions against the Tepaneca and Mexica continued into the years of the Mexica rise to power. Finally, in 1465, the Mexica conquered the Chalca, replacing Chalca rulers with military governors, seizing agricultural lands for the support of Mexica nobles, and transforming the several polities into a unified tributary and administrative province, with the city-state of Tlalmanalco at the head. Twenty years later, some Chalca rulers were reinstated, with the teuctli offices in Amecameca being filled by sons of Mexica warriors and Amecamecan and Chalcan noblewomen. Amecameca and Chalco thus became part of the Aztec imperial system, participating with the other Valley of Mexico dependencies in wars outside the valley.

Table 3-4 is a chronological list of events in Amecameca's political history. The evolution of the Chalco-Amecameca political confederation, as well as Amecamecan dynastic succession, marriage alliances, tribute, and relations with the imperial capital, Tenochtitlan, will be discussed in detail in the pages that follow.

Titles and Officials

Amecameca's political organization consisted traditionally of seven hereditary rulers (teteuctin). By the time of the Spanish Conquest, the number had been reduced to five (Chimalpahin 1965:223;

TABLE 3-3
AMECAMECA'S SUJETOS, 1599

Name	Tribute Payers	Estimated Population[1]	Distance from Amecameca
St. Mateo Tlachixtlalpa	20	70	0.5 league
St. Tomás Atlicpac	17	60	1.0 league
St. Domingo Tecomaxochititlan	40	140	3.0 leagues
St. Franciso Texinca	17	60	3.0 leagues
Ntra. Sa. de la Anunciación Coatlan	5	18	3.0 leagues
St. Andrés Tezcacoac	10	35	2.0 leagues
Sta. Catalina Texinca	9	32	1.0 league
St. Juan Baptista Huitzcuauhtitlan	25	88	1.5 leagues
St. María Natívitas Tepanco	6	21	2.0 short leagues
St. Miguel Atlauhtla	35	123	2.0 leagues
St. Pedro Nexapan	22	77	1.5 leagues
Santiago Metepec	30	105	1.5 leagues
St. Pedro Mártir Tlapechhuacan	20	70	0.5 league

[1]Population estimate is number of tribute payers × 3.5.
(Source: Lemoine Villicaña 1961)

AGN, Indios, Vol. 1, Exps. 189, 245; Gibson 1960). Each office was hereditary, and its possessor was head of both a noble lineage and a political division. Each teuctli ruled a particular area and received tribute from his subjects; in one case Chimalpahin notes that a teuctli title was lost when the lord did not have enough commoners to support him (1965:188).

The term teuctli (also spelled teuhctli or tecuhtli) means "lord, chief, nobleman" (Andrews 1975:472). Teuctli was defined by Molinia as *cavellero o principal*, "knight or noble" (1970 [1571]:93), and Siméon defined the term as *noble, hidalgo, señor, alto personaje, primer magestad de una ciudad*—"noble, lord, elevated person, first authority of a city" (1885:454). The lords of Amecameca were called Chichimeca Teuctli, Teohua Teuctli, Tlayllotlac Teuctli, Tlamaocatl Teuctli, Atlauhtecatl Teuctli, and Tzompahuaca Teuctli. Chichimeca Teuctli simply means "lord of the Chichimeca"; Atlauhtecatl Teuctli means "lord of the barranqueros, or people of the slopes" (*Crónica Mexicáyotl* 1949:48). Teohua Teuctli means "ruler priest" (ibid.; Andrews 1975:470). Other Chalca towns had similarly numerous teuctli titles (see Kirchhoff 1956; Parsons et al. 1982:Ch. 5).

As we will see when discussing marriage alliances, the ruling families intermarried, titles changed from one lineage to another, and individuals seem to have changed titles rather easily (Gibson 1960:190-91). In two instances, women are reported holding teuctli offices.

The Amecamecan political leadership was in the hands of the elite lineages. At their arrival in Amecameca, the Itztlacozauhca were led by Atonaltzin, Chichimeca Teuctli, and his brother, who was called Yaotequihua, or "war leader" (Chimalpahin 1965:73). Their uncle and another brother, for whom no titles are given, assisted them in ruling. Rulership may also have included religious functions, for one Amecamecan lord was titled Teohua Teuctli, or "ruler priest" (*Crónica Mexicáyotl* 1949:47).

Only a few specialized offices existed, according to the historical sources. The Itztlacozauhca had a religious specialist, a "brujo" or sorcerer, recorded as having performed human sacrifices (Chimalpahin 1965:202). A Colonial-period document mentions the "guardapapeles de Amecameca," an individual who officiated at the boundary-setting of the community of Atlauhtla in 1579. This official, who kept land maps and deeds in the Colonial period, may be a carryover from boundary-setting officials of pre-Hispanic times (AGN, Tierras, Vol. 2674, Exp. 1). Other Colonial documents mention the five "*caciques*" (AGN, Indios, Vol. 1, Exp. 245) and the standard Colonial-period civil officials, including 34 tequitlatos, individuals who were perhaps barrio officials (AGN, Indios, Vol. 1, Exp. 189).

TABLE 3-4
SIGNIFICANT EVENTS IN AMECAMECA'S POLITICAL HISTORY

A.D.	
1073	Chichimec groups leave Aztlan, their legendary homeland. Among these are the Totolimpaneca, later called Amaquemes (68)[1]
1241	The Totolimpaneca arrive at Chalco (71)
1268	The Tenanca, another Chichimec group, and the Totolimpaneca meet at Amecameca. They share the land and set boundaries (72)
1295	The Tecuanipa arrive in Amecameca (171)
1304	Nonohualca and Poyauhteca arrive in Amecameca (173–74)
1324	The Axoteca Chalca and the Tlacochcalca begin the practice of xochiyaotl, or ceremonial war (177)
1376, 1381	Xochiyaotl takes place between the Mexica and Tepanec and the Chalca (182–83)
1385	The Chalca-Mexica war begins (*Anales de Cuauhtitlan* 1945:32)
1403	Because of a dispute between leaders, some people leave Tlalmanalco and move to the barrio of Tlayllotlacan in Amecameca; others go to different towns (184)
1407	The Mexica send tribute collectors, cuezconpixque, to the Chalco area. They were Chalca, but not from ruling lineages (184–87)
1407	The Mexica send soldiers to kill the rulers of Tenanco Tepopollan, Tlalmanalco Amaquemecan, Xochimilco Chimalhuacan, and Acxotlan Chalco (185), who flee to the mountains (186). The exiled leaders are replaced by cuezconpixque (187)
1410	All tlatoque in the Valley of Mexico protest the Mexica act of depriving the Chalca rulers of their offices, and they threaten war. The Mexica ruler restores the Chalca rulers to office (187–88)
1415	Xochiyaotl, or ritual war, becomes mortal war; captured warriors are sacrificed (189)
1425	The Chalca build walls to close off free transit by the Mexica (190)
1428	Chalca warriors capture Mexica warriors, including Moctezuma I, who escape with the help of a dissident Chalca lord (191)
1429	The Chalca stay neutral in the war of Azcapotzalco and Coyoacan versus Tenochtitlan and Texcoco (192)
1432–1434	The Mexica begin to conquer Chalco's neighbors—Xochimilco, Mixquic, Cuitlahuac (194)
1445	The Chalca refuse to carry stones to build a temple for Huitzilopochtli for the Mexica; war with Tenochtitlan begins in earnest (199)
1456	Mexica warriors capture the northern Chalca cities and Panohuayan (201)
1464	The Mexica reach Amecameca and burn the temples (203)
1465	The Chalca–Mexica war ends in Amecameca. Chalco's rulers are replaced by Mexica military governors. Land to pay tribute to Mexica nobles is apportioned. Many Chalca flee to Huexotzinco (102–03, 204–07)
1469	The Tlatelolca try to interest the Chalca in rebelling with them against the Mexica; the Chalca turn the Tlatelolca ambassadors over to the Mexica, who kill them (206–07)
1473	Axayacatl, ruler of Tenochtitlan, requires Chalca warriors to participate in Mexica wars (208)
1479	Chalca and Amecameca people go for the first time to ceremonies in Tenochtitlan (211–14)
1480	Laborers work land in Chalco, at Oztoticpan and Xoyocotepec, for Tenochtitlan's ruler, Axayacatl (214)
1482	The Chalca contribute trees and lumber to temple-construction at Tenochtitlan, at the order of Tizoc. Tizoc drives the Huexotzinca out of Chalco (216)
1486	The rulers of Tenochtitlan gradually begin replacing Chalca nobles as rulers of Chalca cities (218–23)
1499	Refugee nobles from Huexotzinco cause trouble in Amecameca (226)
1511	The Chalca participate in a Triple Alliance war against Huexotzinco (232)
1519	Cortés and his army pass through Amecameca on the way to Mexico (Cortés 1971:80)

[1]Numbers in parentheses refer to pages in Chimalpahin, 1965. References to other works are included following the item.

Following the Mexica conquests of Chalco, specialized administrators were appointed to perform tasks in Amecameca. The Mexica-appointed cuezconpixque, or "keepers of the granaries," collected maize tribute (Chimalpahin 1965:184-86). As elsewhere, imperial military governors were called quauhtlatoque ("eagle rulers") (Lehmann 1938:259; Chimalpahin 1965:198, 218-19).

In summary, there was not much emphasis on bureaucracy in Amecameca, and what there was, was small-scale. This small number of administrators demanded a correspondingly small amount of tribute for their living, as will be shown in the following paragraphs.

Support of Amecameca's Officials

Pre-Hispanic teteuctin and their dependents in Amecameca were supported by tribute in labor

AMECAMECA

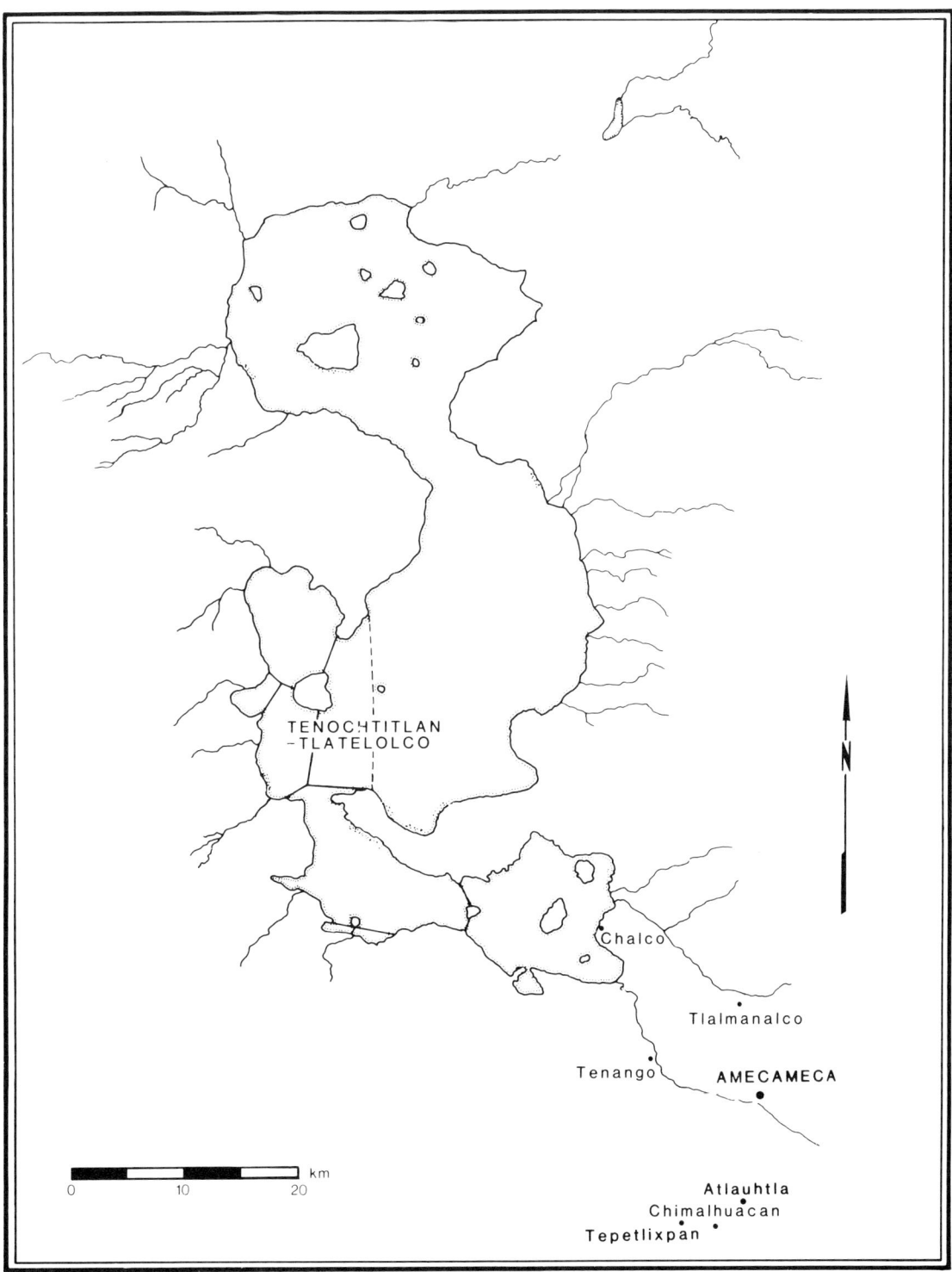

Fig. 3-6. Map of Amecameca and other Chalca settlements.

and goods from commoners and by produce from their own fields worked by commoners. In the Chalca town of Tlalmanalco, the rulers collected tribute from indigenous groups conquered by them (Chimalpahin 1965:173); whether or not conquered people were exploited in Amecameca is not explicitly stated anywhere.

An idea of the amount of tribute paid to one teuctli can be drawn from claims entered in a Colonial lawsuit, in 1600. A witness for Don Francisco Paez y Mendoza, the "casique y señor natural" of Panohuayan, said that from time immemorial,

> the Indians of the barrio of Panoaya [Panohuayan] . . . sent him each week 1 turkey, 300 cacao beans, 1 braza of wood, 1 Indian woman to grind corn, 20 Indian men to work in his fields, another Indian to work in his house, one-half fanega of corn, and they gave it to him each week, and every year a number of gold pesos from the community, though the witness doesn't know the quantity. [AGN, Tierras, Vol. 994:214v]

In 1579 and 1580, each of five *caciques* received ten fanegas of maize from community lands, and in addition, they owned fields in various part of the community of Amecameca. Likewise, in 1625, Doña Petronila de Furco owned land in Itztlacozauhcan, Tenango, Santa Rosario (Amecameca proper), Panohuayan, and in other locations (AGN, Tierras, Vol. 994:215-25; see also Barlow 1963:250-54), suggesting that Amecameca's teteuctin received income from similarly scattered and intermingled parcels of land.

There is absolutely no evidence for tribute taken from other polities by Amecameca, and there is no evidence of Amecamecan expansion into and conquest of other areas of polities, as practiced by Tenochtitlan and Texcoco. Amecameca's warriors participated in Triple Alliance wars, but none received land outside their territory as did rulers of some other city-states (Cuauhtitlan and Teotihuacan, for instance). Chalca rulers' rewards for participating in imperial activities were largely symbolic. Chalca nobles received Mexica warrior insignia and Mexica warrior titles after participating in Triple Alliance wars. For furnishing labor for public works in the capitals, the Chalca lords received gifts from Tenochtitlan's rulers (Anunciación 1940:259-66). Thus, it appears that Amecameca's rulers were supported by whatever was produced in their own territory or could be obtained through trade.

Rulers of Amecameca

Ruler lists for the seven teuctli offices are seen in Table 3-5. The dates during which the teteuctin ruled are those reconstructed by Chimalpahin's annals, and these dates are of course only Chimalpahin's approximations of dates which he gleaned from informants, traditional histories, and pictorial texts.

Succession to the Office of Teuctli in Amecameca

In Amecameca, father-to-son succession is the most common pattern (Chimalpahin 1965:174-75, 198, 218), but there is also evidence that if a son could not or would not accept the office, the title went to a younger son, or to a ruler's brother (Chimalpahin 1965:189). This pattern is a longstanding one, for in the period when Amecameca was being settled, three of the lineages were led by father, brother, and uncle combinations (ibid.:73, 174).

In two cases, women ruled. A daughter inherited the rulership of Tzacualtitlan in 1340, and a mother ruled for her son while he was too young to rule (ibid.:80, 188). One individual came to rule Tzacualtitlan Tenanco by achievement and by marriage: having earned the title "eagle warrior," for being a successful warrior, he married the daughter of the ruler of Tlayllotlacan, and thus became ruler (Chimalpahin 1965:198).

There is evidence that the noble lineages were interrelated. At two times (late 1300s and mid-1400s), Itztlacozauhcan and Tlayllotlacan were ruled by brothers (Fig. 3-7; *Crónica Mexicáyotl* 1949:46-48, 78-79; Chimalpahin 1965:187). In the Colonial period, individuals changed titles, and titles shifted from one lineage to another.

> The Tecuhtli ranks were preserved through the sixteenth century, and several individuals shifted from one Tecuhtli title to another. The comparable changes in office from one dynastic lineage to another . . . are suggestive of an interrelationship, an absence of isolation among the *cacique* families of Amecameca. [Gibson 1960:190-91]

Another line of evidence that suggests there was not much separation between the ruling noble in Amecameca is that in the Colonial period the *caciques* owned property in many areas of Amecameca, rather than in separate blocs (AGN, Tierras, Vol. 994, 995; Barlow 1963:250-54).

TABLE 3-5
RULERS OF THE SEVEN DIVISIONS OF AMECAMECA

ITZTLACOZAUHCAN AMECAMECA

1160–1174	Hecatl Teuctli
1174–1241	Huehue Chichimeca Teuctli
1241–1306	Atonal
1307	Acxitl
1308–1363	Huehue Teuctli II
1363–1392	Ipantlaquellotzin
1392–1407	Huehue Quetzalmacatzin
1407–1410	Tlacocihua
1411–1465	Ayocua I
1465–1486	(Mexica Military Governor: Quetzalpaoyoma)
1486–1499	Toyaotl Nonohualcatl
1499–1504	(No Ruler)
1504–1511	Ayocua Telpochtli II
1511–1521	Cihuaillaca

TZACUALTITLAN AMECAMECA

1611–1187	Totoltecatl Tzompachtli
1187–1238	Cualtzin
1238–1338	Cuahuitzatzin
1339	Nochhuetzin
1340–1348	Xiuhtoztzin
1348–1417	Itztlotzin
1418–1465	Cuauhtlehuac
1465–1488	(No Ruler: Mexica Military Governor)
1488–1520	Huehue Yotzintli and Xuihtzin

TECUANIPAN AMECAMECA

1221–1242	Cuitlach Teuctli
1242–1255	Cuauhtzin
1255–1287	Chalchiuhtlatonac
1287–1319	Ocelotl Teuctli
1319	Yaopol Tziuhtlacauhqui
1319	Mahuatzin
1319–1465	(Military Governor)
1465	Quetzal Tototl
1465–1492	(No Ruler: Mexica Military Governor)
1492–1527	Miccacalcatl

TLAYLLOTLACAN AMECAMECA

1336–1338	? (Founder)
1338–1352	Temizteuctli
1352–1367	Huehue Cacama Totec
1368–1406	?
1406–1411	(No Ruler)
1411–1465	Cohuazacatzin
1465–1469	(No Ruler)
1469–1486	(Mexica Military Governor: Cuauhtlaltzin)
1486–1519	Cacama Totec II

PANOHUAYAN AMECAMECA

1304–	Totec Nochuetzin
–1465	Teuhctlacozauhqui
1465–1488	(No Ruler)
1488–1519	Cuauhcececuitzin

TABLE 3-5, CONTINUED

ATLAUHTLA

1238–1273	Huehue Itzcuauhtzin
1273–1279	Cuauhuitzatzin
1279–1290	Illancueitl
1290–1341	Itzcuauhtzin
1341–1353	Tlotli Teuctli
1354–1359	Huecon Teuctli
1359–1361	(No Ruler)
1361–1392	Ozomatzin
1393–1441	Mactzin
1441–1443	(No Ruler)
1443–1465	Popocatl
1465–1486	(No Ruler)
1486–1488	Toyaotl Nonohualcatl, ruler of Itztlacozauhcan Amecameca
1488–	(No Ruler; governed by administrator, Tetlaltzin, and combined with the señorio of Amecameca)

TENANCO TEPOPOLLAN

1209–1238	Cualtzin
1238–1266	?
1267–1273	Cuahuitzatzin
1274–1459	?
1459–1465	Cuecuetlatla-Cuanochhuetl
1466–1486	?
1486–1519	(Military Governor: Cuauhhehcahuaz)

(Source: Chimalpahin 1965)

Conquest of the area by Tenochtitlan disrupted the regular inheritance of teuctli titles in Amecameca. All the rulers fled in 1465 when Amecameca was conquered. No local teteuctin ruled between 1465 and 1486; instead military governors (cuauhtlatoque, or "eagle rulers") from Tenochtitlan were appointed to govern. They married local noblewomen, and in 1486–88, when Amecameca's teteuctin were reappointed, some of the individuals so appointed were as closely related to Mexica nobles as to the former rulers (Fig. 3-8; Chimalpahin 1965:218-19; *Crónica Mexicáyotl* 1949:141) Moreover, the Mexica moved rulers' bases of operation, for in some cases, sons of rulers of one barrio were appointed to rule other barrios (for instance, Cacamatzin, son of the ruler of Tzacualtitlan became ruler of Tlayllotlacan). By 1486, five teteuctin were reinstated (see Tables 3-6, 3-7). These offices continued until 1519, and after (Gibson 1960).

In summary, the teteuctin of Amecameca were related to each other. Ideally, succession followed from father to son. However, following the area's

TABLE 3-6
POLITICAL ORGANIZATION OF CHALCO PROVINCE
BEFORE ITS CONQUEST BY MEXICO, ACCORDING TO CHIMALPAHIN

Town	Subdivisions	Title of Ruler
Amecameca	Itztlacozauhcan	Chichimeca Teuctli
	Tlaillotlac-Teohuaçan	Teohua Teuctli
	Tzacualtitlan-Tenanco	Tlaillotlac Teuctli
	Atlauhtlan-Tenanco	Atlauhtecatl Teuctli
	Pochtlan-Tecuanipan	Tzompahuaca Teuctli
	Huixtoco-Tecuanipan	Chichineca Teuctli
	Panohuayan	Tlamaocatl Teuctli
Atenco (Tlalmanalco)	Cihuatecpan-Acxotlan	Tecuachcauhtli
	Opochhuacan-Tlacochcalco	Teohua Teuctli
	Itzcahuacan-Tlacochcalco	Tlatquic Teuctli
Tenanco-Texocpolco-Tepopollan	—	Tlaillotlac Teuctli
Xochimilco-Chimalhuacan	Xochimilco-Chimalhuacan	Teohua Teuctli
	Tepetlixpan-Chimalhuacan-Xochimilco	Tecpanecatl Teuctli

(from Kirchhoff 1956)

TABLE 3-7
AMECAMECA'S POLITICAL ORGANIZATION
AFTER ITS CONQUEST BY TENOCHTITLAN

Division	Mexica Political Appointments
Itztlacozauhcan	Teuctli reappointed in 1486
Tlayllotlacan	Teuctli reappointed in 1486
Tzcualtitlan Tenanco	Teuctli appointed in 1488
Atlauhtlan Tenanco	No teuctli reappointed; governed by Tzacualtitlan Tenanco
Tecuanipan Pochtlan	Teuctli appointed in 1488
Tecuanipan Huixtoco	No teuctli reappointed; governed by Tecuanipan Pochtlan
Panohuayan	Teuctli appointed in 1488

(Chimalpahin 1965:206–07, 218–19)

conquest by and integration into the Mexica state, persons related to nobles in Tenochtitlan were favored for appointment to teuctli offices over those more closely related to former rulers. After 1465, the Mexica rulers controlled the teuctli offices, and the teteuctin were then part of the Aztec empire's administrative bureaucracy.

Marriage Alliances of Amecameca's Rulers

The chronicles mention only a few marriages between Amecameca's nobles and those of other nearby towns. Very early, Quiyauhtzin, son of the ruler of Huexotla, is reported to have married the daughter of Cacamatzin I, Teohua Teuctli of Tlayllotlacan (Chimalpahin 1958:46). In the mid-1400s, a woman from Amecameca married the ruler of Huexotzinco, and their son later ruled Huexotzinco (Chimalpahin 1965:217). Much later, a daughter of Cacamatzin II, ruler of Tlayllotlacan, married the ruler of Yacapixtla, a town to the south (ibid.:230). The alliances with Huexotzinco were sometimes convenient (such as when the Chalca fled there during battles with Tenochtitlan); at other times they were a problem (as when related nobles escaping from Huexotzinco moved to Amecameca, where they attempted to usurp the rulership there) (Chimalpahin 1965:102, 226). Altogether, the available documents suggest that there were marriage alliances between elites of Amecameca and other nearby polities, such as Huexotzinco.

The available histories, however, place much more emphasis on marriages between Amecameca's nobles and those from Tenochtitlan. These marriages no doubt occurred as part of Tenochtitlan's effort to form an administrative nucleus in the Valley of Mexico composed of hereditary provincial rulers who had the support of local leaders but who also would be responsive to Mexica policy and demands.

Marriage alliances with Tenochtitlan began after Amecameca was conquered in 1465. A daughter of the ruler of Iztlacozauhcan went to Tenochtitlan as a wife of Tlacaelel, cihuacoatl of Tenochtitlan

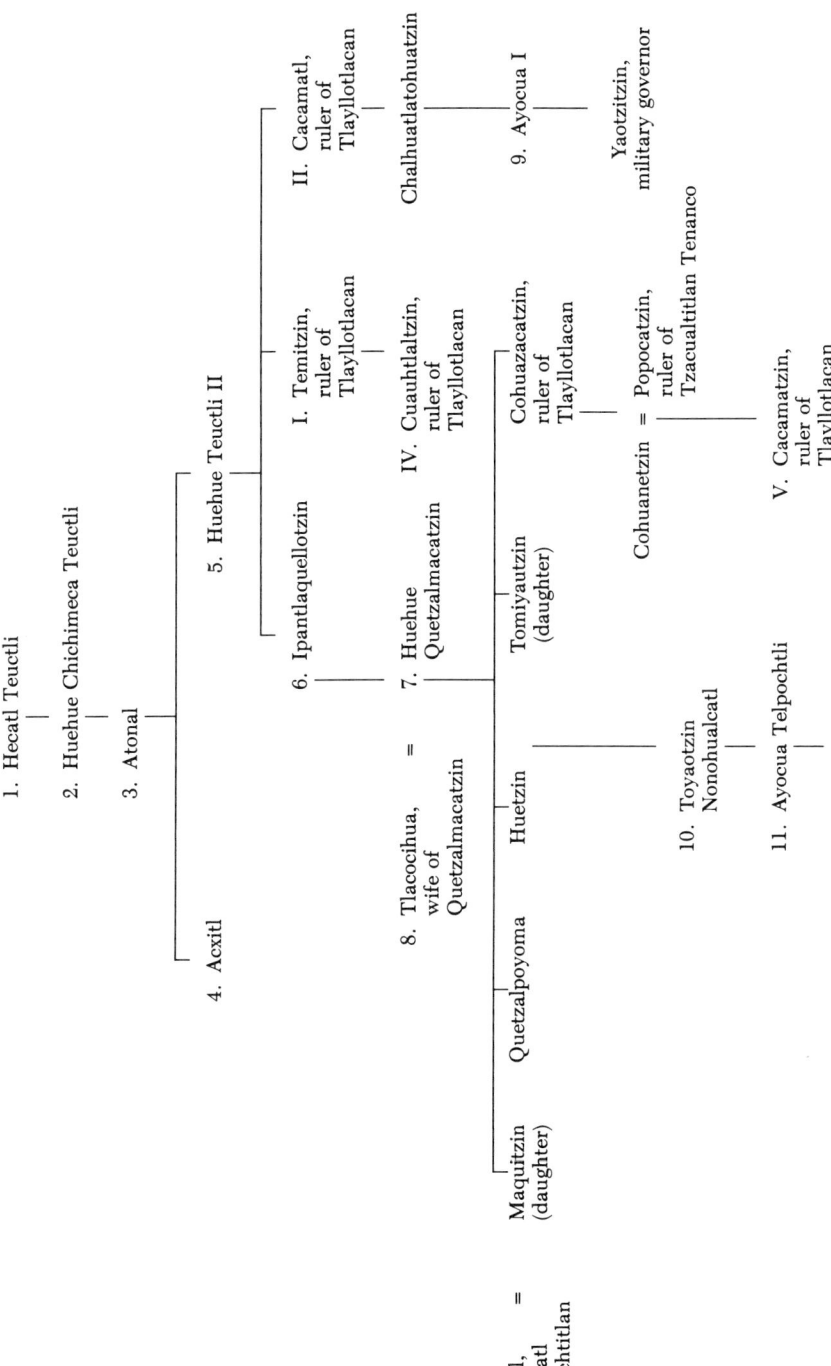

Fig. 3-7. Genealogy of rulers of Itztlacozauhcan and Tlayllotlacan Amecameca (based on Chimalpahin 1965).

(Chimalpahin 1965:187). One of their sons later became cuauhtlatoani of Amecameca and married a woman whose mother was Chalca and whose father was a Mexica military governor in Chalco. Their son later became a tlatoani in Tecuanipan Amecameca (ibid.:216-17; see Fig. 3-7).

The occurrence of marriage alliances between Tenochtitlan's rulers and elites from Amecameca parallels their occurrence in other Chalca city-states. A ruler of Chalco Itzcahuacan married a daughter of Acamapichtli (Chimalpahin 1965:199), and a ruler of Tlalmanalco married a daughter of Moctezuma II (*Crónica Mexicáyotl* 1949:140). However, it appears that rulers of Tlalmanalco and Chalco Atenco married Mexica rulers' daughters, while Amecameca's elite women married Mexica administrators who were from the cihuacoatl branch of Tenochtitlan's ruling family.

Amecameca as an Independent City-State

Amecameca and the Chalca Polities

Amecameca's relationship to the other Chalca polities is the topic of this section. What evidence from the histories supports the claim that they were a cohesive political force? How was this coalition organized? What functions did the individual polities perform in the organization? Did these roles change over time, and if so, how?

The term "Chalco" means "place of the green stones—turquoise or jade," and the term "Chalca" designates a person from that area. The name is derived from the one the previous residents gave the area—chalchuihmomozco—"altar of green stones," and the immigrants adopted this name (although at least one group migrated to the Valley of Mexico with that name—see *Codex Boturini* 1964, *Anales de Cuauhtitlan* 1945:13-19; Davies 1981; see also Table 3-6).

The original Chalca polities included Chalco Atenco, Tlalmanalco, Amecameca, Tenango, and Atlauhtla. Later, in 1301, two Xochimilca towns—Chimalhuacan and Tepetlixpan—joined with the Chalca (Chimalpahin 1965:173, 203; Parsons et al. 1982:81). Different Chalca polities were politically important at different times. In A.D. 1299, Chalco's leaders were from Tlalmanalco, Itztlacozauhcan Amecameca, and Atlauhtla (*Crónica Mexicáyotl* 1949:47-48). In 1367, Cacamatzin, ruler of Tlayllotlacan Amecameca (*Anales de Cuauhtitlan* 1945:36), led all the pueblos "that were grouped with the Chalca" against the Mexica, Tepaneca, and Ixtapalapaneca (Chimalpahin 1965:181). In 1407, Chalco was a "cabecera de cuatro partes," a head town of four parts: Tenanco Tepopollan, Tlalmanalco-Amecamecan, Xochimilco Chimalhuacan, Acxotlan Chalco (Chimalpahin 1965:185). At the time of the Mexica-Tepaneca war (1430), the two leaders of Chalco were from Chalco Atenco and Itzcahuacan (Durán 1967:89-90). In 1437, the Chalca leaders who met Nezahualcoyotl, ruler of Texcoco, included one each from Opochhuacan, Itzcahuacan, Acxotlan Chalco, Tlayllotlacan, Atlauhtla, Itztlacozauhcan Amecameca, Tenanco Tepopollan, two from Tzacualtitlan Tenanco, and four from Amecameca. Finally, Amecameca was the leader just before the Mexica conquest of the area, ca. 1465 (Durán 1967: 147-51).

These data suggest that Chalco had a segmentary organization with an impermanent hierarchy before the conquest by the Triple Alliance in 1465, with leaders chosen on an *ad hoc* basis. Amecameca's ruler led the Chalca in their final battle with the Mexica, perhaps because of Amecameca's southernmost location (since the Mexica conquerors began in the north and moved south toward Amecameca).

The non-centralized organization of the Chalca polities is also indicated by the amount of administrative apparatus which was imposed following their conquest. The Mexica imposed military governors, or cuauhtlatoque, in Tlalmanalco and Amecameca. Tlalmanalco became the tributary capital (Barlow 1949:74). When rulers from Chalco's tecpans were reinstated, the number was reduced, and they were ranked hierarchically in some cases. For instance, Atlauhtla's ruler was deposed and the town became subject to a military governor, and later the reinstated ruler of Amecameca governed this town (Chimalpahin 1965:233). The Mexica thus imposed a political hierarchy and a centralized administrative system on an area which previously was without formal, hierarchical organization but instead contained a number of similar, separate but equal units.

Amecameca's Alliances with Non-Chalca Polities

This discussion deals with Amecameca's relationships to non-Chalca polities (other than Tenochtitlan) in order to assess to what extent Amecameca independently formed political ties

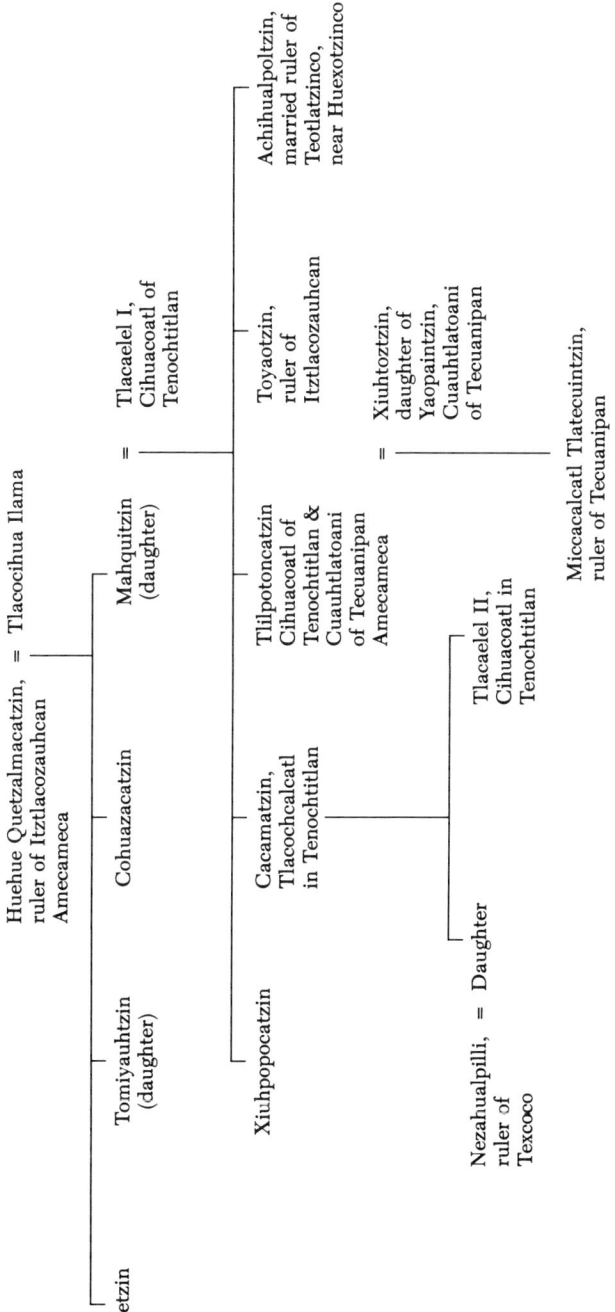

Fig. 3-8. Marriages between nobles of Tenochtitlan and rulers of Amecameca (Chimalpahin 1965).

with other polities. Amecameca's political role differed before and after its conquest by Tenochtitlan, as it moved from autonomy to dependency.

After the founding of Amecameca, groups from Amecameca moved to new areas, founding daughter settlements. Nine families were said to have left Amecameca and founded the settlement of Malacachtepec Momoxco, near Oztotepec and Milpa Alta (Malacachtepec Momoxco 1953:7). In 1403, as a result of a dispute between leaders, some of the Tlayllotlaca moved away, though others stayed (Chimalpahin 1965:184).

According to the chronicles, Amecameca had contact with communities to its south, and during the wars with Azcapotzalco and Tenochtitlan, Amecameca's people frequently fled to these towns. In 1407, the rulers fled south to Atlauhtla, Yecapixtla, Amilpa, and Acohualzingo to escape the Mexica (Chimalpahin 1965:185-86). Some Chalca remained in these areas (such as Amohmollocco Huitzillac) and even conspired to rule there (for example, an exiled ruler of Tlayllotlacan Amecameca killed and replaced the ruler of Mamalhuazocan in 1419 [ibid.:190]).

Huexotzinco, to the east, was a sometime ally and refuge for the Chalca. When the Mexica finally defeated the Chalca in Amecameca in 1465, Moctezuma had to block off a mountain pass to prevent large numbers of Chalca commoners and nobles from fleeing to Huexotzinco (Durán 1967:150; Chimalpahin 1965:102-03). Huexotzinco's and Amecameca's rulers were related by marriage, and although Huexotzinco's warriors participated in the conquest of Azcapotzalco (*Anales de Cuauhtitlan* 1945:46; Alva Ixtlilxochitl 1975-77, II:78), its relations with the Valley of Mexico deteriorated as it resisted the Triple Alliance's expansion.

Following Amecameca's conquest by the empire, its relationship to Huexotzinco became more adversarial. In 1499, Toltecatl, prince of Huexotzinco came to Amecameca to escape a war. He brought his relatives and other dependents. They came because his mother was from Amecameca (she was the daughter of the ruler of Itztlacozauhcan Amecameca). As soon as he had settled in his mother's relatives' house, however, Toltecatl began fighting with his relatives. He went to Tenochtitlan to see Ahuitzotl, the imperial ruler, plotting to set up his own kingdom in Amecameca. On hearing of this plot against them, the rulers of Amecameca captured and executed Toltecatl (Chimalpahin 1965:226). In 1511, Chalco participated in a Triple Alliance war against Huexotzinco, and in 1512, some Huexotzinca went to Tenochtitlan to escape the ongoing battles between Tenochtitlan, Cholula, and Tlaxcala (ibid.:232).

In 1407 all the rulers of Central Mexican city-states protested the Mexica replacement of the Chalca rulers with cuezconpixque (maize collectors), who, though nobles, were not in a position to inherit rulerships. The rulers of Cholula, Totomihuacan, Tlaxcala, Tliluilquitepec, Huexotzinco, Cuauhquechollan, Totollapan, Cuauhnahuac, Itzocan, Texcoco, Xochimilco, Culhuacan, Tullocan, Azcapotzalco, Tenayocan, Cuauhtitlan, Teocalhuiyacan, Matlatzinco, Mazahuacan, and Xiquipilco all threatened to start a war if the Mexica did not restore the Chalca nobles to their proper places. Although this incident may be inflated in importance by Chimalpahin, this drastic action by the Mexica may have threatened the position of all ruling lineages in the valley, and the outcry caused Huitzilihuitl and Itzcoatl to restore the Chalca nobles to their rightful offices (Chimalpahin 1965:187; Calnek 1972).

However, in 1429, when asked by both sides for help in the Tenochtitlan-Texcoco versus Azcapotzalco war, the Chalca polities remained neutral (Chimalpahin 1965:192; Durán 1964:62-63) although some Chalca participated in the assassination of Ixtlilxochitl, ruler of Texcoco, carried out by the Azcapotzalcans (Chimalpahin 1965:189).

Amecameca's relations with Texcoco are not documented in detail. The Texcocan historical sources claim that Chalco was a dependency of Texcoco and that the Chalca paid labor tribute to Texcoco (Alva Ixtlilxochitl 1975-77, I:384, 562; Hicks 1982). In keeping with this is a record of mutual dislike between the Chalca and the Texcocans. "Coatepec Chalco, an Acolhua town, bore a 'very special enmity' towards Chalco" (Barlow 1949:68), and its *Relación geográfica* records many wars between them (Paso y Troncoso 1905, VI:51). In correspondence to the documentary records, there is an archaeologically visible buffer zone—an area with few settlements—between the two polities that Parsons has termed the "Texcoco-Chalco Frontier" (Parsons 1971:229-30).

Thus, Amecameca was apparently in close contact with the lakeshore communities early in the 1300s but became more closely allied with the communities to its south and east as it began to be drawn into conflict with Azcapotzalco and Tenochtitlan. Surprisingly, the Amecamecan sources give very little information about Texcoco, its important neighbor to the north, and in the 1400s the chronicles emphasize instead interaction with Tenochtitlan, suggesting more direct lines of communication between the Mexica capital and Amecameca.

Amecameca and the Aztec Empire

Conquest by the Triple Alliance

Spanish and native chronicles document the development and resolution of a prolonged conflict between Azcapotzalco and later Tenochtitlan, and the Chalca polities. Recently, several scholars have analyzed these accounts critically (Davies 1973a, 1973b, 1981; Parsons et al. 1982:Ch. 5). In this section, I wish to emphasize Amecameca's role in these events and the effects of conquest on Amecameca. Accounts of the specific actions of Amecameca are few; most of the historical sources mention actions of the Chalca polities as a group more often than they mention Amecameca by itself. This is because the Chalca resisted the Aztec empire as a unit and because they were administered as a province of the empire after being conquered by it.

The Mexica conquest lists report that Huitzilihuitl (who ruled Tenochtitlan between 1396 and 1417, under Azcapotzalco) conquered Tlalmanalco, and Chimalpopoca (ruler of Tenochtitlan, 1417-27) put down a Chalca uprising (*Anales de Cuauhtitlan* 1945:66; *Anales de Tlatelolco* 1948:16, 53; *Codex Mendoza* 1925:3-4). Itzcoatl and Moctezuma I (1427-40 and 1440-69) definitively reconquered the area in 1465 (*Anales de Cuauhtitlan* 1945:53, 66; *Anales de Tlatelolco* 1948:59; *Codex Mendoza* 1925:7v).

The Chalca-Mexica conflict is reported to have been a 72-year struggle beginning in 1385 (10 Calli) (*Anales de Cuauhtitlan* 1945:32). And, in 1407, Chalco's rulers were replaced by tribute collectors but were reinstated in 1410 (Chimalpahin 1965:187-88). The Mexica-Chalca conflict consisted of long-term hostilities and several rebellions. In 1425, the Chalca built walls around their pueblos to prevent free passage by the Mexica (Chimalpahin 1965:190), and in 1428, they captured some Mexica nobles, including Moctezuma I (who escaped with the aid of a dissident Chalca ruler from Chalco Atenco) (ibid.:191). By 1440, the now-independent and expanding Mexica state started to reconquer parts of Azcapotzalco's empire, and it defeated city-states in the Valley of Mexico such as Cuitlahuac and Mixquic, and then attacked Chalco. By 1465, Amecameca was the last holdout of the Chalca (*Anales de Cuauhtitlan* 1938:29, 1945:53). As the Mexica armies burned the temple and entered the city, the Amecamecan women, children, and warriors tried to flee but were stopped by Mexica troops (Chimalpahin 1965:102-03; Durán 1967:150). After 1465, the Chalca rulers were replaced by Mexica military governors for approximately 20 years, finally being replaced by Chalca nobles more closely related to those of Tenochtitlan (as discussed above). Moctezuma II (who ruled Tenochtitlan from 1502-20) had to put down a revolt in Chalco Atenco (*Codex Mendoza* 1925:17v).

As for Texcoco, another Triple Alliance capital, Ixtlilxochitl reports that Nezahualcoyotl conquered Chalco in 1427 and again conquered at least the northern cities in 1463 or 1464 (Alva Ixtlilxochitl 1975-77, I:384; 1977, II:124-28). This chronology roughly parallels the Mexica conquests, suggesting that Texcoco shared in the victories. In 1437, Nezahualcoyotl visited all the Chalca rulers, including those of the "four courts of Amecameca" to secure arrows and drums for war (likely a ritual act) (Chimalpahin 1965:195).

Effects of Conquest

Rulership and Marriage Alliances. The main effect of conquest on the political system of Amecameca was the replacement of its rulers with military governors and the subsequent restructuring of its teuctli offices. For approximately 20 years, there were no hereditary rulers in Amecameca (Chimalpahin 1965:218-19), but in 1486-88, teteuctin from five of the seven ruling lineages were reinstated, creating the five-part organization of Amecameca which was still in effect when Cortés arrived in 1519 (see Table 3-7).

Political Organization. The Mexica policy produced the following general changes in organization. Lines of succession of rulers were broken. The Mexica simplified the organization and placed rulers in office who were responsive to Mexica demands and who had fewer hereditary ties to their local polities than former rulers. Some towns that had previously had a teuctli, such as Atlauhtla, were ruled as sections of other polities.

Territorial Organization. Another effect of conquest was the loss of land in Amecameca to Mexica nobles. In 1465,

> ... all of Chalco was divided *cemmitl* by *cemmitl* [a measurement equal to ca. 1.68 m (Gibson 1964:263-64)] throughout the four parts of the kingdom.

> Year 1-Flint, 1480. This year the land of Amecameca was traced in large furrows by the workers of Lord Axayacatzin. This was done in the place called Xocayoltepec and also in the place called Oztoticpan. From then on these lands began to be reckoned under the emblem of the chiefs of Mexico-Tenochtitlan. [Chimalpahin 1965:214]

Thus, fields in Oztoticpan and Xocayoltepec were appropriated for the support of Mexica nobles, diminishing Amecamecan control over its own labor and produce (see also *Relación de la Genealogía y Linaje de los Señores* 1941:255, 277-78).

Political Alliances. An effect of conquest, calculated or not, was to cause competition between Chalca towns. For example, Amecameca had always had a regional market, but in 1465, following its conquest by the Mexica, Tlalmanalco was ordered to provide Moctezuma, and presumably his soldiers, with food. The Tlalmanalca requested that the regional market be moved from Amecameca to Tlalmanalco; however, apparently this was not done, because the market at Amecameca was a tradition which belonged to the Poyauhteca, residents of Panohuayan (Chimalpahin 1965:205).

Tribute. Yet another result of conquest was to organize Chalco as a tributary province (see Fig. 3-9). Tribute-collection centers—other than the head town—were not placed in the Chalca political centers but instead were placed in small towns. The tribute-collection centers in Chalco were: "Chalco" (the head town, probably Tlalmanalco, according to Barlow [1949:74]), Quauxumulco, Tepuztlan, Malinaltepec, Temilco, and Xocoyaltepec. Xocoyaltepec is also listed as one of the towns directly responsible to Tenochtitlan's rulers (Chimalpahin 1965:214). Amecameca was presumably included in the Chalca tributary province (Fig. 3-9).

Chalco province gave one of the richest food tributes in the entire empire (Barlow 1949:73; Durán 1967:241), no doubt produced by its lakeshore chinampas (Parsons et al. 1982). The *Codex Men-*

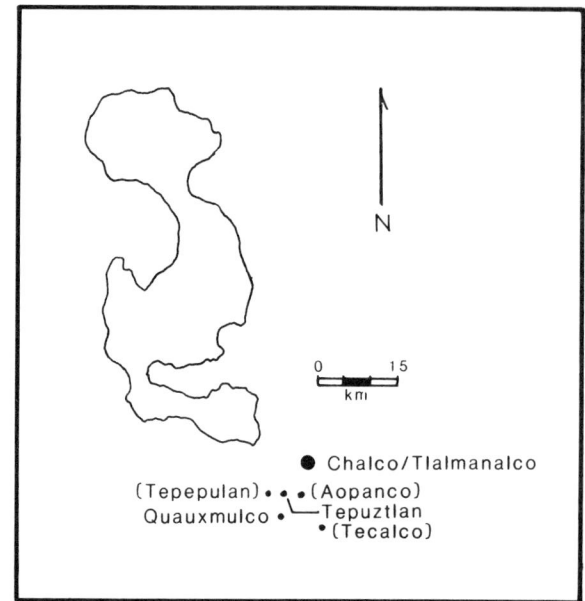

Fig. 3-9. Location of imperial tribute-collection points in Chalco province. Chalco (Tlalmanalco), Tepuztlan, and Quauxumulco, along with Xocoyoltepec (an unlocated part of Amecameca), Temilco, and Malinaltepec (both unlocated) appear on Folio 43 of the *Codex Mendoza*. Tepepulan, Aopanco, and Tecalco appear on Folios 20 and 21 of the *Codex Mendoza*, as part of another tributary province, Petlacalco (after Parsons, et al. 1982:89).

doza (1925:41) lists Chalco's tribute as 800 large mantas, 2 warriors' costumes with shields, 6 wooden bins of maize, 2 bins of beans, 2 bins of chia (sage or *Salvia*), and 2 bins of amaranth. One of the individuals questioned in the *Información sobre Tributos* of 1554 corroborates this, saying that

> the pueblo of Chalco with seven other pueblos that paid tribute with it gave to Moctezuma, each year, two warriors' costumes and four shields. ... And, moreover, they gave him 4100 fanegas of maize and an equal amount of chia. ...
> And every 80 days they gave him 800 fine mantas. ...
> And moreover, a large quantity of turkeys and mats and chili peppers and tomatoes and other vegetables [were given], and when they didn't give them all of the mentioned items, they punished them in the manner that they had. [Scholes and Adams 1957:81].

In addition to *scheduled* tribute payments, the Chalca polities had to contribute to Triple Alliance activities, and one pretext for the war with Chalco was that the Mexica wanted stone for monuments. Moctezuma demanded it, and the Chalca refused, saying they were not subjects but allies (Durán 1967:133-37; Reyes 1979:68).

Chimalpahin also does not emphasize, as does Ixtlilxochitl, the fact that after the Triple Alliance's conquest of the Chalca city-states in 1465, the Chalca had to provide materials and labor for all three capitals, including Texcoco. Ixtlilxochitl says that in 1465

> The Chalca began to build halls and rooms in the houses and palaces of the king, in those of the lords and gentlemen of his kingdom and in those of the other two kings and heads of the empire, as punishment for their stubbornness and rebellion, carrying from their province wood, rocks, and the other material for these buildings, with great and excessive labor. . . . [Alva Ixtlilxochitl 1975-77, II:128].

He adds that many laborers had died in the wars, so even the women and children worked; however, Nezahualcoyotl fed and housed the laborers (ibid.).

Tribute in labor was demanded by Tizoc in 1482, for the purpose of enlarging the temple of Huitzilopochtli in Tenochtitlan. The Chalca had to provide lumber as well.

> Then also, for the first time, he gave us, the Chalca, the labor tribute for which we had to take to lord Tizoc stout trees, gathering them from the slopes of Popocatepetl, from the place called Xochiquiyauhco, that is, in effect, the largest trees to be cut from this place, by order of those beloved nobles in whose care were all the Chalca towns. [Chimalpahin 1965:216]

The Chalca had to provide wood and volcanic sand for mortar to build the Coyoacan-Tenochtitlan aqueduct (Durán 1967:373). Later, Moctezuma II wanted a round stone, or temallacatl, for sacrifices, and a suitable large stone was found in Chalco province, in a place called Aculco, near Tepepula and the Amecameca River. Workers from the provinces of Xochimilco, Cuitlahuac, Ixtapalapa, Culhuacan, Mexicaltzingo, and Huitzilopochco delivered it to Tenochtitlan (Durán 1967:485-87).

Thus, Chalco supplied Tenochtitlan with goods and labor, and it supplied Texcoco with tribute in labor if not in goods (Chalco is included in the Texcocan repartimiento [labor] list [Gibson 1956, 1971:387]). However, the historian of Amecameca, Chimalpahin, emphasized its military and political relations with Tenochtitlan.

Imperial Wars. In 1473, Amecameca began to participate in Triple Alliance wars. "From here, Amecameca Chalco, he [the ruler] left for Mexico, at the front of the Amecamecan warriors, the prince named Quetzalpayomatzin, with orders to make war, in agreement with all of the Tlalmanalca Chalca" (Chimalpahin 1965:208).

Imperial Rituals. The nobles of Amecameca and Chalco also participated in ceremonies and rituals at Tenochtitlan (ibid.:211-14, 219). They also hosted Mexico and Texcocan rulers on their pilgrimages to nearby mountain shrines (Durán 1967:366, 1971:156-60; Sahagún 1951, Book 2:42-45).

According to a source from Chimalhuacan in 1554, the capital's demands increased over time. At first, the Chalca paid tribute in maize, and they cultivated land to provide produce directly to Moctezuma, Axayacatl, Tizoc, and Ahuitzotl. In return, Chalca nobles were rewarded with gold and cloth. Moctezuma II, however, increased the tribute greatly, and he required that the Chalca nobles go two to three times per year to festivals in Tenochtitlan. Two to three times per year the Chalca had to provide stone, sand, and wood for construction and carry it to Tenochtitlan by canoe, all in addition to the maize paid as regular tribute (Anunciación 1940:259-66). When Cortés arrived in Amecameca in 1519, the teuctli who met him complained greatly about the excessive demands of Moctezuma (Cortés 1971; Alva Ixtlilxochitl 1975-77, II:217).

Summary and Conclusions

History and Internal Organization of Amecameca

According to its own histories, Amecameca was founded in the 1200s by Chichimec peoples, along with other centers in the area. Like other locations in the Valley of Mexico, the incoming people conquered and/or displaced the residents of the area. From the beginning of settlement of the area, the Chalca peoples considered themselves related and shared a similar heritage. The Chalca polities all claimed to have been equal, though the rulers of Chalco Acxotlan were sometimes given special deference and were referred to as leaders because their settlement had been founded earliest. At various times single leaders or several leaders combined to head armies or make diplomatic journeys.

Though allied with the Chalca towns, Amecameca was governed independently of the rest of the Chalca city-states. Amecameca itself consisted of seven separate and equal tecpans—organizations consisting of a ruling nobleman (teuctli or lord) and his dependents (see Carrasco 1976 for a comparative discussion of such organizations), his extended family, perhaps other nobles, and dependent commoners, presumably organized in a residential ward. Although there is no explicit description of how the lower-level organization worked, in early Colonial times, in addition to the *caciques*, some principales (nobles), were on the municipal payrolls, and these individuals may have been barrio heads. Taking orders from them were tequitlatoque, functionaries of lesser rank.

Amecameca's seven tecpans—Itztlacozauhcan, Tlayllotlacan, Panohuayan, Tzacualtitlan, Atlauhtlan, Tecuanipan Huixtoco, and Tecuanipan Pochtlan—probably initially were associated with specific geographic locations, for several of these place-names are preserved in modern Amecameca. Panohuayan and Tlayllotlacan are modern barrios in Amecameca; Atlauhtla is south of Amecameca.

Amecameca's internal organization consisted of a town center with four wards around it, which were residences of rulers and their courts. Its territory, containing dependent villages, ranged east toward the mountains. These villages presumably paid tribute in goods and services to the lords.

Amecameca contained the market for the region, and it was situated on the well-traveled road to more tropical areas—the valleys of Morelos and the Gulf Coast. Apparently it did not participate in all the early ritual wars (xochiyaotl) of Chalco Atenco and Tlalmanalco. It did not pay tribute to any superior center until its conquest by Azcapotzalco and Tenochtitlan.

Thus, until 1407, Amecameca was an independent, territorially distinct polity with its own rulers appointed by its own elites. Its decision-making system consisted of separate but equal teteuctin, some of whom assumed special functions such as war leader when conditions demanded it. Its political organization was composed of several equal centers and their dependent villages (see Fig. 3-10).

Relations with Other Polities

Amecameca was more closely involved with its neighbor to the east, Huexotzinco, than with other non-Chalca polities, before its conquest by Tenochtitlan. Its teteuctin had diplomatic and marriage alliances with the lords of Huexotzinco, and Amecameca's rulers fled there at times to escape war or assassination plots. People from Amecameca settled in areas to the southwest; from early Colonial records, we can infer that there was some in-

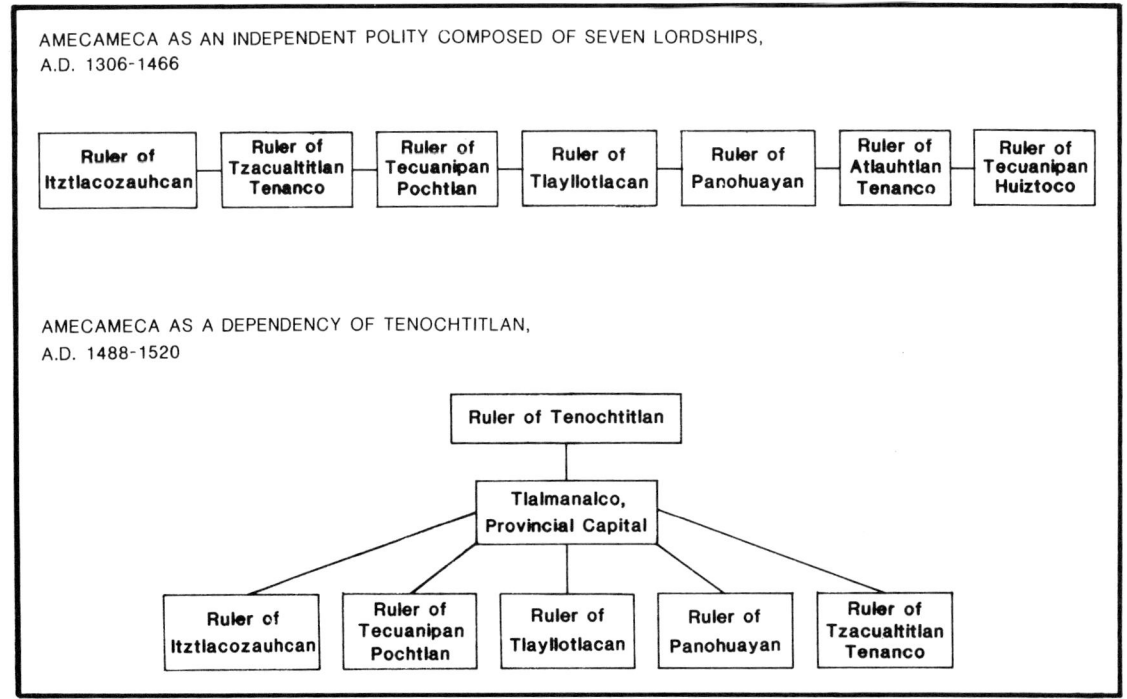

Fig. 3-10. Amecameca's internal administrative organization before and after conquest by the Aztec empire.

teraction with towns to the south, and histories report that towns in this area were also refuges for Chalca driven from their homes because of war.

As part of the Chalca league, Amecameca participated in the efforts to resist the Mexica armies, both when they were allied with the Azcapotzalcan state and subsequently when they represented the capital of the Triple Alliance. In the final period of the conflict with Tenochtitlan, Amecameca was the head of the Chalca organization because the polities further north had already been conquered. Amecameca fell in 1465, when the Mexica armies burned its temples.

Conquest by the Empire

Starting in 1407, the Azcapotzalcan polity tried to collect tribute in Chalco, and in 1410, it replaced Chalca rulers (who fled) with administrators who were local elites but not members of ruling lineages. However, the Chalca rulers were reinstated in 1411.

Following this were 54 years of intermittent conflict. The Chalca declined to participate in the war to topple the Azcapotzalcans and so were marked with the rest of the southern Valley of Mexico for early conquest by the Triple Alliance. The final

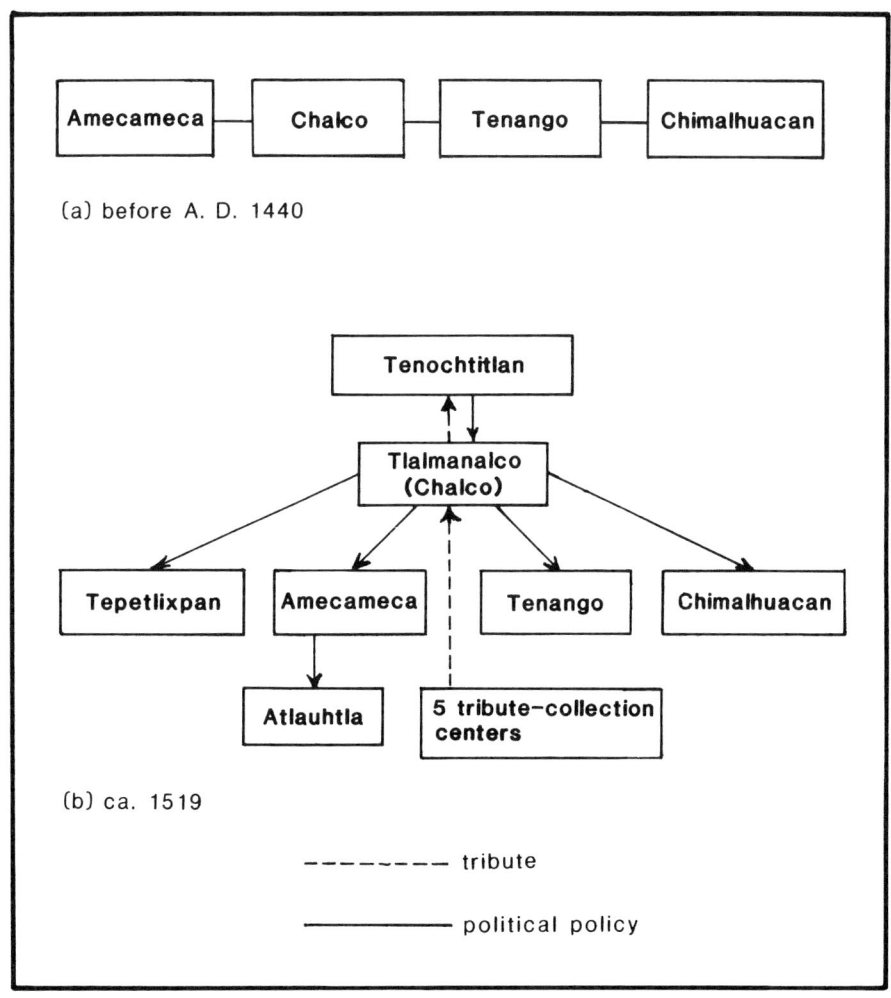

3-11. Amecameca's political organization; (a) before 1440, part of a confederation of separate and equal centers; (b) after A.D. 1519, part of a hierarchical system, with one center promoted to an administrative center.

conflict began in 1445, when Chalco refused to contribute stones for enlarging the main temple in Tenochtitlan.

Following the conquest of the Chalca, ca. 1465, Mexica nobles took lands in Chalco as tribute-producing estates. Some towns became directly subject to Tenochtitlan's ruler. Other towns became centers of tribute collection, organized under a single major center. The tribute-collection centers were not the same as the political or administrative centers.

For about 20 years, Mexica military governors replaced the local rulers. These Mexica nobles married Chalca noblewomen, and eventually, when Chalca rulers were reinstated, those more closely related to Tenochtitlan's rulers were appointed. For purposes unknown, but perhaps to simplify the indigenous organization, certain towns' rulers were never reinstated, and these towns became dependencies of other towns. The number of teuctli offices was reduced, perhaps to simplify administration, and also to create competition for tenure of offices, which now depended upon Tenochtitlan's rulers. Thus, the Chalca city-states, under the Triple Alliance, became an administered province and a tributary province, with a hierarchy created where there had been a more or less segmentary organization before (see Fig. 3-11).

As participants in the imperial system, the Chalca took part in imperial wars, contributed to ceremonies at Tenochtitlan, and supplied materials and laborers for public works in Tenochtitlan and Texcoco (particularly lumber and stone). Chalca nobles hosted Mexica rulers on their pilgrimages to sacred mountaintop shrines in Chalco, and Chalca nobles were rewarded with mantas, jewels, and Mexica war trophies for furnishing men and materials for construction and war. Under Moctezuma II, tribute of all kinds increased greatly, perhaps as a punitive measure, and Amecameca's nobles complained of this to Cortés in 1519.

In conclusion, before its conquest by Tenochtitlan, Amecameca was part of a segmentary, acephalous regional organization, but following its conquest, Tenochtitlan's rulers placed administrators in Amecameca and the other Chalca city-states. They simplified Amecameca's organization, and they placed it in a regional administrative hierarchy. The next case study concerns Cuauhtitlan, the center of a hierarchically organized polity.

Chapter 4

Cuauhtitlan

The Place and the People of Cuauhtitlan

The city of Cuauhtitlan is in the northwest corner of the Valley of Mexico. Before the lakes were drained in the 1600s, the city was on the edge of salty lakes Xaltocan and Zumpango (see Fig. 4-1). The city was surrounded by an alluvial plain, south of which lay the Sierra de Guadalupe. To the north were the Tepotzotlan mountains and the hill of Tultepec, and to the west was the piedmont of the Sierra de las Cruces. The Cuauhtitlan River, near the city, was diverted in the 1400s to prevent flooding (*Anales de Cuauhtitlan* 1945:49). Today the region is characterized as "high and dry" at 2240 to 2900 m (Gerhard 1972:127); however, it may have had more vegetation in pre-Hispanic times, since the name Cuauhtitlan means "place in the forest" (Peñafiel 1885:95-96).

The environment of Cuauhtitlan permitted cultivation of maize and other indigenous crops (Fig. 4-2). The tribute records report that a special requirement included in Cuauhtitlan's tribute to Tenochtitlan was mats woven of reeds. Reeds were a specialty of the area (Barlow 1949:42); no doubt they were gathered in the nearby shallow lakes and along the shore.

Cuauhtitlan in 1519

In 1519, Cortés reported seeing "a very large and beautiful city called Goatitlan [Cuauhtitlan]; this we found deserted and so slept there the night" (1971:187), and Bernal Díaz described Cuauhtitlan as a city with canals (1956:357-58). We have no detailed descriptions of the pre-Hispanic city's appearance; however, Motolinía described it as the residence of the fourth most important lord of the valley, following Tenochtitlan, Texcoco, and Tlacopan: "To the north, four leagues from Tenochtitlan, is the town of Cuauhtitlan, residence of the fourth lord of the land, who was the lord of many other towns" (Motolinía 1950:210). At the time of the Spanish Conquest, Cuauhtitlan was a city of 10-15,000 residents (Torquemada 1975, I:286-88; Sanders 1970:409; Sanders, Parsons, and Santley 1979:209-13).

Evolution of the Urban Center of Cuauhtitlan

The first villages in the Cuauhtitlan area date to the Early Formative period (1500-1150 B.C.), and like other parts of the Valley of Mexico, the Cuauhtitlan area was resettled following the demise of Teotihuacan (ca. A.D. 750) and Tula (ca. A.D. 1168). Between 1100 B.C. and A.D. 1200, settlements in the Cuauhtitlan area were concentrated on piedmont areas, but between A.D. 1350 and 1520, the population increased, covering the alluvial plain as well as the piedmont (Fig. 4-3; Sanders, Parsons, and Santley 1979:209-13).

According to legend, the Cuauhtitlan area was settled ca. A.D. 804 by Chichimeca who migrated from Chicomoztoc in the north. One group founded three towns: Cuauhtitlan, Macuexhuacan, and Huehuetoca (*Anales de Cuauhtitlan* 1945:4). The town's annals "picture Cuauhtitlan as a city-state founded, like nearby Tula, Hidalgo, after the ruin of Teotihuacan. The first inhabitants were new converts from nomadism, who moved their town around a bit, settled, and watched the blooming and destruction of Tula (twelfth century?) and the eventual formation of new centers—Azcapotzalco and Acolhuacan-Texcoco in the 1200's and 1300's" (Barlow 1947:520).

The *Anales de Cuauhtitlan*, an anonymous chronicle written in Nahuatl, tells of the development of the town. The *Anales* lists the early ruler's names, dates of reign, and the location of their residences (Table 4-1). Each ruler had a different place of residence until 1349. After that date, the

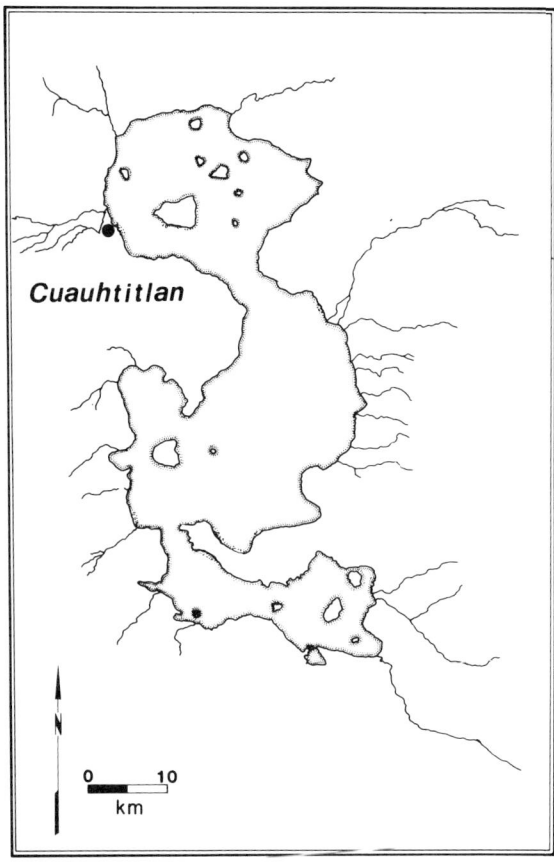

Fig. 4-1. Location of Cuauhtitlan.

rulers lived in a palace in the urban center of Cuauhtitlan, and from A.D. 1349 to 1390, Cuauhtitlan's rulers governed from this center.

The chronicler refers to early Cuauhtitlan as an altepetl inhabited by Chichimeca, who built a temple of reeds. All the reed-roofed temples were decorated with "mixcoas," or "cloud-serpents," representing the Chichimec deity, Mixcoatl. The people of Cuauhtitlan also built temples for their deity Itzpapalotl, whom they worshiped in the month of Quecholli (*Anales de Cuauhtitlan* 1945:30).

In time, Cuauhtitlan became a multi-ethnic community. In 1347, the town of Culhuacan was defeated by the Tepaneca of Azcapotzalco, and refugees fled the city to settle in Cuauhtitlan. The *Anales* attributes civilizing influences to them. (The acculturation of Chichimec or barbaric peoples by cultured Toltecs is a theme which recurs in much of Postclassic Mesoamerican historical mythology; see Bray 1978 and Davies 1981.)

The co-residence of the two groups in Cuauhtitlan is described in the *Anales* as follows:

> Year 12 Flint-13 House: In this year Huactzin, who was king of Cuauhtitlan, died; afterwards his lieutenant was seated. Shortly afterwards, the Culhua wished to have a king, electing the son of Huactzin, because they knew he was the grandson of the ruler of Culhuacan called Coxcoxteuctli. They built him a reed house in his barrio, where the house of the "devil" Mixcoatl was; it was at first only in his barrio, for the king Iztactototl was the priest of Mixcoatl. Moreover, these Culhua guarded and honored king Iztactototl and gave him many gifts. Also, they came to invent everything: new clothing, pottery, mats, jars, shields, and other such things. They gave form to the town of Cuauhtitlan and they settled on the land, because the Chichimeca were no longer moving from place to place. They introduced idolatry and added many gods, and as they already were well-liked by the Chichimeca, they began to work the land. Little by little they began to divide the lands and to organize their barrios. [*Anales de Cuauhtitlan* 1945:31]

At this point the locations of rulers' palaces became more standardized, for after Huactzin (1287-1348), the next three rulers' palaces were located near the temple of Mixcoatl (*Anales de Cuauhtitlan* 1945:32).

Xaltemoctzin, who ruled from 1390 to 1408, divided the city into four parts, around a central square. The temple in the square was enlarged, and each section of the city was assigned to maintain a quarter of the temple. (This incident is reminiscent of the division of labor ordered by Moctezuma I for building Huitzilopochtli's temple in Tenochtitlan [Durán 1967:227], and there is really no way to ascertain from the documents alone whether this incident really happened; however, the details do provide information about the Cuauhtitlan worldview.) The four sections of Cuauhtitlan were Tequixquinahuac, Chalmecapan, Nepantla, and Atempan, each of which was assigned to build a part of the temple, along with two dependent towns. According to the *Anales*:

> When Xaltemoctzin began his temple, at the same time he began to organize the city of Cuauhtitlan into four sections; it took on this pattern because to each corner of the square of his temple, he assigned one of the four parts of the city of Cuauhtitlan. He placed Tequixquinahuac at one corner, aided by the workers of Tepoxalco and Tzompanco. Chalmecapan, he placed at another corner with Cuauhtlaapan and Citlaltepec. Nepantla he placed in another corner, aided by Tepotzotlan and Huehuetoca. Atempan he placed in another corner, aided by Coyotepec and Otlazpan. The temple of Xaltemoctzin the elder was undertaken and finished in five years. [*Anales de Cuauhtitlan* 1945:34]

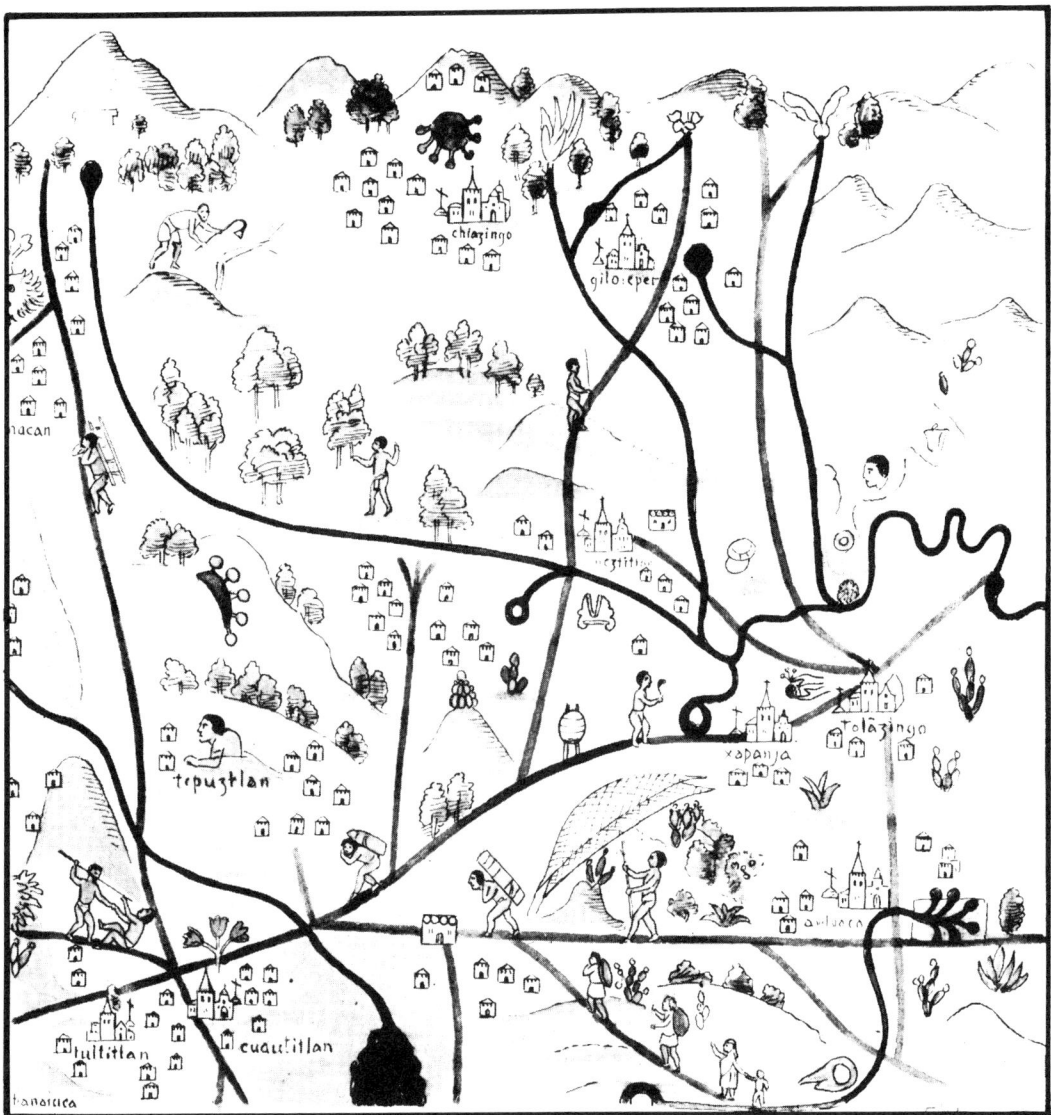

Fig. 4-2. Cuauhtitlan in 1550 (lower left), with Tultitlan (Linné 1948). The Santa Cruz map (ca. 1550) shows fishing and wood-gathering being done in the vicinity of Cuauhtitlan. It also shows maguey, nopal, and trees growing.

Following Xaltemoctzin's reign, Cuauhtitlan was conquered by Azcapotzalco. The temple was burned—a mark of defeat in Mesoamerican warfare—and as an added insult, the Tepaneca planted maguey in Cuauhtitlan's central plaza. The slave market was taken from Cuauhtitlan and moved to Azcapotzalco, where it stayed until the Spanish Conquest.

In the 1430s and under the Aztec empire's domination (1435-1519) the physical environment of the city of Cuauhtitlan was modified further. Outside the city, the Cuauhtitlan River was diverted in the year 1430, away from the center of Cuauhtitlan because it flooded frequently; the *Anales'* author says it was redirected over unoccupied houses in Tultitlan (*Anales de Cuauhtitlan* 1938:238, 1945:49). Irrigation canals also were built in pre-Hispanic times; some are shown on early Colonial maps (see Fig. 4-4). Finally, after A.D. 1500, when Cuauhtitlan was governed by Tenochtitlan, a structure for tribute collection was built, and a circular stone (temallacatl) was set up, presumably in the main plaza, for making human sacrifices (*Anales de Cuauhtitlan* 1945:59).

In summary, the city-state of Cuauhtitlan evolved from dispersed communities to an urban center with a main square, a temple, a palace, a marketplace, and, at times, four administrative divisions. Following its conquest by Tenochtitlan, a sacrificial stone and a tribute-collection post were built in Cuauhtitlan.

Cuauhtitlan's People

The people of Cuauhtitlan identified themselves as Chichimeca. (The term "Chichimeca" means "dog people," meaning wandering barbarians who hunted with bows and arrows and wore skins; however, the term did not have a derogatory connotation, for it implied fierceness, a characteristic valued by the Postclassic people of the Valley of Mexico [See Bray 1978; Davies 1981]). The people of Cuauhtitlan spoke the Nahuatl language (and in the early 1500s, some spoke Otomí); their legends report that, like other Chichimec groups, they migrated from the north, into the Valley of Mexico, where they settled.

Cuauhtitlan was located near Azcapotzalco, the Tepaneca political center. However, despite Cuauhtitlan's proximity to Azcapotzalco, according to the *Anales*' anonymous author, the people of Cuauhtitlan were never on good terms with Azcapotzalco or nearby Tultitlan. Instead, he stresses his people's acceptance of "Toltec" culture via immigrants from Culhuacan, and he almost always disguises his city's kinship with Azcapotzalco and other Tepanec towns. He instead stresses his people's alliance with the Mexica. Though it is a rich source, the *Anales* is not without bias (see Table 4-2).

The people of Cuauhtitlan also had enemies to the east, at Xaltocan, which was a settlement of Otomí speakers. They quarreled with the Nahuatl-speaking Chichimeca of Cuauhtitlan over hunting territory, and this disagreement became a war which lasted from as early as 1241 until 1395 (*Anales de Cuauhtitlan* 1945:22, 33-34; Barlow 1947:523; Carrasco 1950).

Although the rulers of Cuauhtitlan were conquered by those of Tenochtitlan by 1434 or 1435, according to the *Anales* they still took pride in their identity as a separate place and people. At one point, the ruler of Cuauhtitlan warned Moctezuma II of a plot against him and was offered as a reward the insignia and costume of a Mexica warrior. The ruler of Cuauhtitlan refused them but instead accepted gifts suitable for a Chichimec (*Anales de Cuauhtitlan* 1945:60).

Rituals and Deities of Cuauhtitlan

Mixcoatl, or "cloud serpent," was Cuauhtitlan's deity in early times. Its rulers were closely associated with this deity, for the *Anales* mentions specifically Ehuatlycuetzin (a woman who ruled between A.D. 1369 and 1373) and Tlacateotzin (who ruled between A.D. 1380 and 1390) being enthroned at the temple of Mixcoatl (*Anales de Cuauhtitlan* 1945:32).

Cuauhtitlan performed especially elaborate rites during the festival celebrating the eighteenth Nahua month, Izcalli. In 1431, all the towns and cities came to this festival (*Anales de Cuauhtitlan* 1945:48-49). Motolinía describes the rite as follows:

> But much more frightful than the general practice is what they did here in Cuautitlan, where I am writing this, where it seems that the devil showed himself more cruel than in other places. On the day before one festival in Cuautitlan they set up six great trees, like the masts of ships, with steps leading up to them, and on that cruel night—followed by a yet more cruel day—, they beheaded two female slaves at the top of the steps before the altar of the idols. Up there they flayed their bodies and faces and cut out their thigh bones. In the morning two of the leading Indians put on the skins, even the skin of the face, like a mask, and took the thigh bones, one in each hand, and slowly came down the steps, roaring like savage beasts. Down below in the courtyard a great crowd of people, all apparently terrified, cried: "Our gods are coming, our gods are coming!" When the two men reached the foot of the steps the people began to beat their drums, and to the backs of the men dressed in the skins they attached a quantity of paper, not folded, but sewed in the form of wings, a matter of some four hundred sheets. To each of them they gave a quail, already sacrificed and beheaded, and tied it to his lip, which was pierced. And thus the two danced, and many people sacrificed before them and offered them great numbers of quail, for it was also for the latter a day of death. And as the quail were sacrificed they were thrown before the two dancers, and there were so many that they covered the ground where they trod, for more than eight thousand quail were sacrificed that day. Everyone made great efforts to get them for this festival, to which people came from Mexico and from many other towns. At noon they took all the quail and divided them among the ministers of the temples and the principal lords. The two men dressed in the women's skins did nothing but dance all day. [Motolinía 1950:66-67]

Motolinía describes other sacrifices of the day, which included tying prisoners to the six poles,

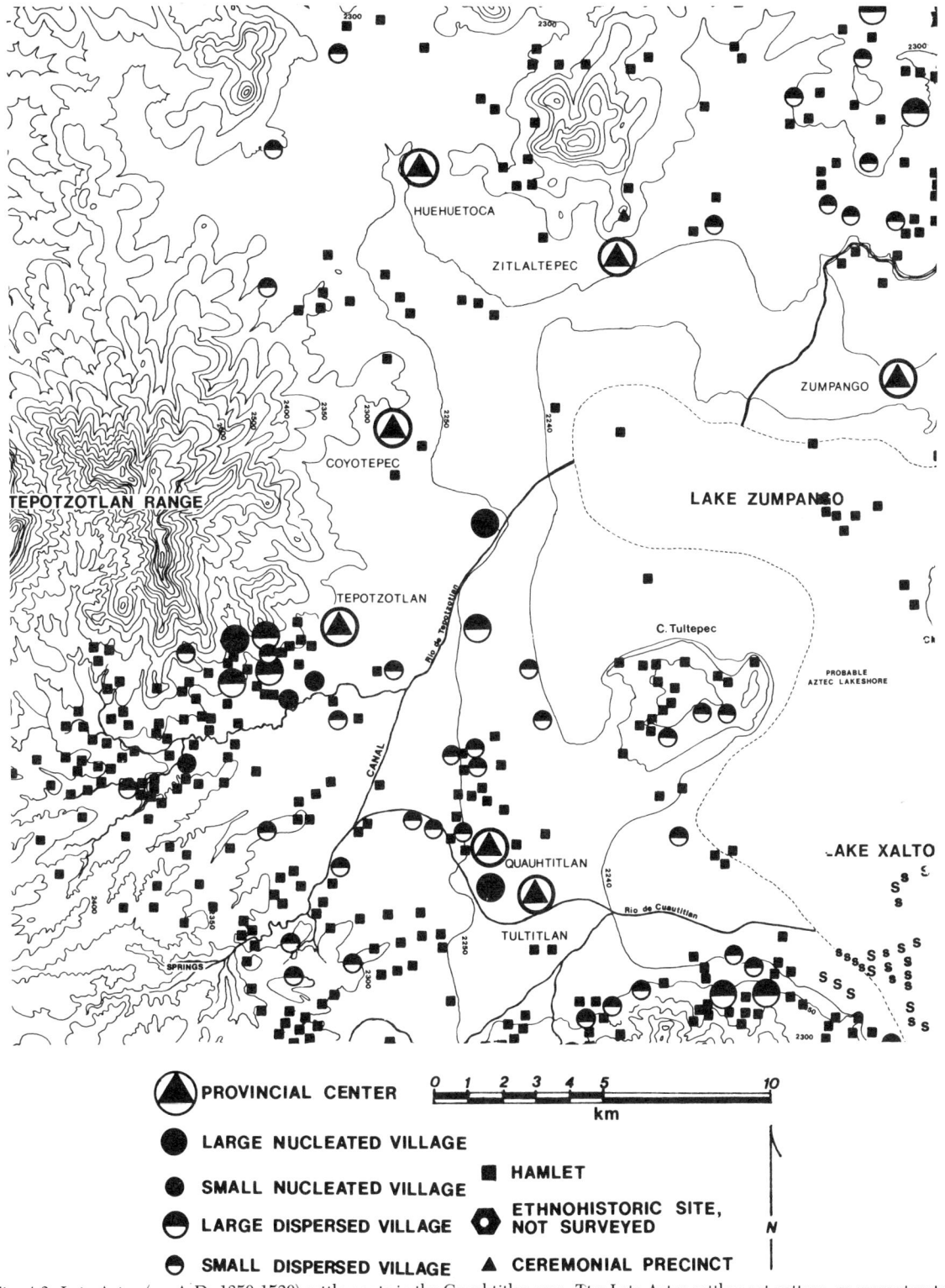

Fig. 4-3. Late Aztec (ca. A.D. 1350-1520) settlements in the Cuauhtitlan area. The Late Aztec settlement pattern, as reconstructed from the archaeological survey, shows Cuauhtitlan in the middle of the lakeshore plain, surrounded by 1 large nucleated village, 6 small nucleated villages, and 14 hamlets. Very near to the south, is another city, Tultitlan, which was also ranked as a Provincial Center, or a settlement with up to 10,000 inhabitants. Many hamlets dot the higher piedmont and high spots along the lakeshore. Most of these settlements were new in the Late Aztec period, and the area seems to have filled in greatly during that time. [Portion of Map 18, Late Horizon, reprinted from *The Basin of Mexico: Ecological Processes in the Evolution of a Civilization*, by William T. Sanders, Jeffrey R. Parsons, and Robert S. Santley, Copyright 1979, by Academic Press, Inc.]

TABLE 4-1
RULERS OF CUAUHTITLAN

Dates Ruled	Years of Reign	Name	Location of Residence	Reference[1]
First Lineage (ruled before arrival in Cuauhtitlan area)				
687–751	36	Chicontonatiuh	Macuexhuacan	5
752–803	65	Xiuhneltzin	Temilco and Quaxoxouhcan	
Second Lineage (ruled after arrival in Cuauhtitlan)				
804–865	72	Huactli	Nequameyocan	6
866–875	12	Xiuhtlacuilolxochcitzin (wife of Huactli)	Nequameyocan	7
876–930	65	Ayauhcoyotzin	Tecpanquauhtla	7
931–945	15	Nequamexochitzin	Miccacalco of Tepotzotlan	12
946–982	36	Mecellotzin	Tianquizalco of Cuauhtlaapan	12
983–1023	62	Tzihuacpapalotzin	Cuauhtlaapan	13
1024–1035	11	Iztacxillotzin	Izquitlanotla	13
1035–1091	55	Eztaquentzin	Techichco	15
1092–1107	15	Ezcoatzin	Techichco	15
1108–1175	57	Teyztlacoatzin	Xoloc	16
1175–1239	54	Quinatzin	Teptelapan, Tequixquinahuac, Huiztompa	17
1247–1286	39	Tezcalteuctli	Tequixquinahuac, Huiztompa	19
1287–1348	61	Huactzin	Techichco	23
1349–1368	19	Iztactototzin	Near Temple of Mixcoatl, Cuauhtitlan	31
1369–1373	4	Ehuatlycuetzin (wife of Iztactototzin)	Same as above	32
1374–1379	5	Temetzacocuitzin	Same as above	32
1380–1390	10	Tlacateotzin	Same as above	32
1390–1408	18	Xaltemoctzin	Çacacalco	33
1409–1418	(9)	No tlatoani; Military governor		36
1418–1430	12	Teçoçomoc	Huexocalco	36
1430–1433	3	Tecocohuatzin	Huexocalco	44
1434–1495	61	Ayactlacatzin	Huexocalco	49
1495–1503	(8)	Mexica governor, Tlacateccatl Tehuitzin	Cuauhtitlan	58
1503–1519	16	Aztatzontzin	Cuauhtitlan	59

[1]Page references are from *Anales de Cuauhtitlan* (1945).

sacrificing them by shooting them with arrows, and then cutting out their hearts. Their heads were taken to the chief priests and their bodies eaten by the nobles (ibid.).

When the Culhua immigrants moved to Cuauhtitlan, ca. 1347, they brought with them "idolatry" and many new deities (*Anales de Cuauhtitlan* 1945:30-31). Later, the Culhua complained to the ruler of Tenochtitlan, Itzcoatl (who ruled from 1427-40), that the Chichimeca of Cuauhtitlan wouldn't practice their rituals.

> Afterwards, when all of the people worshipped idols, when Itzcoatl reigned in Tenochtitlan, and there were still many Chichimeca, the Culhua went to Mexico to complain of those who didn't want to participate when everyone else fasted. For this reason, these Chichimeca came to be prisoners and were imprisoned in Mexico: Xiuhcac, native of Toltepec now called Xiuhcacco; then the grandchildren of Pitzallotl, who were in Tlalcoxpan and Hueytoctitlan; then Cocotl, native of Cocotitlan, and Pipilo, who also was from there, near Tzictla, and others. These went to die in Mexico, and then they dispossessed them of their lands, [lands] that are now called Acxotecatlalli and Mexicatlalli, in the same way as others of their companions. In this way, Maxtlaton, native of Xallan was killed, whose land is also called Acxotlantlalli and Mexicatlalli today. Thus it is that all of Çoltepec and Cuauhtepec and another place were Mexica land [mexicatlalli]. In this time there were Chichimeca; after this murder, without warning, they left and went to settle in Motocahuican and in Tlachco. [*Anales de Cuauhtitlan* 1945:31]

This passage suggests that the Mexica used a religious offense as an excuse for appropriating land.

Apparently, in time, the customs of the Aztec capital were followed in Cuauhtitlan, for later, in Triple Alliance wars, Cuauhtitlan's warriors are reported to have taken captives in battle to be offered as sacrifices at events such as the dedication of Nezahualcoyotl's temple (*Anales de Cuauhtitlan* 1938:261, 1945:54). For the new fire ceremony at the start of a new century in 1507, or 2 Acatl, a circular stone (temallacatl) was placed in

CUAUHTITLAN

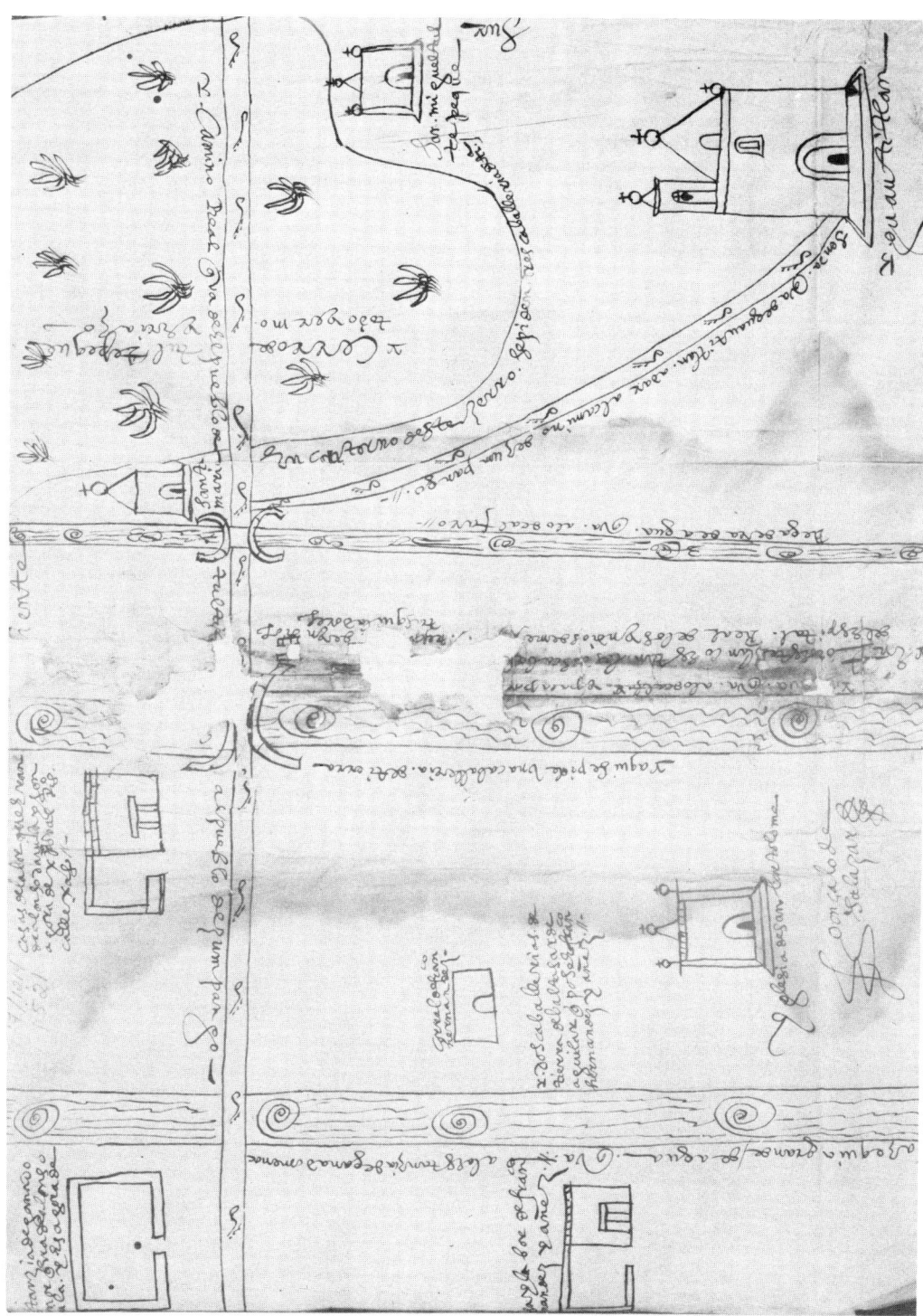

Fig. 4.4. Map from 1590-91 showing canals, roads, and buildings around Cuauhtitlan (from AGN, Tierras, Vol. 1521, Exp. 1, Fol. 69. Los naturales del pueblo de San Miguel Tultepec, contra Juan de Castillo. . .sobre Tierras). [Photograph reproduced by permission of the Archivo General de la Nación, Mexico]

TABLE 4-2
EVENTS IN THE DEVELOPMENT
OF THE POLITY OF CUAUHTITLAN[1]

A.D.	
635[2]	Chichimec people leave Aztlan and journey toward the Valley of Mexico (4–7)[3]
804	The Chichimeca stop in Tula and then travel on to found Cuauhtitlan (21)
1241	War begins between Cuauhtitlan and Xaltocan, a neighboring Otomí polity, and continues until 1395 (102)
1325	The Tenochca, or Mexica, found Tenochtitlan (117)
1347	Culhua people flee to Cuauhtitlan when their city, Culhuacan, is destroyed by Tepaneca from Azcapotzalco. They form a barrio in Cuauhtitlan (125–28)
1395	Cuauhtitlan defeats its enemy, Xaltocan, and Cuauhtitlan expands its territory to include much of Xaltocan's land (110–12). Xaltemoctzin, ruler of Cuauhtitlan, builds a temple in the city; he also fights the Chalca with the Azcapotzalcans and Mexica (134–35)
1408	Tepaneca from Azcapotzalco kill Xaltemoctzin and appoint a military governor to rule Cuauhtitlan for 9 years (138)
1408	Tezozomoc, ruler of Azcapotzalco, attempts to seat a tlatoani of his choosing in Cuauhtitlan. Because of local resistance to this, he appoints one of his sons to rule in Tultitlan, a nearby, rival polity (138)
1418	A Tepaneca ruler from Tlatelolco is seated in Cuauhtitlan (139)
1419	The Acolhua city-states are defeated by Azcapotzalco (140)
1427	Tezozomoc of Azcapotzalco dies; one of his sons, Maxtla, takes his place as Tepaneca ruler (144)
1428–1430	The Azcapotzalcans attack and conquer Cuauhtitlan. They burn the temple, plant maguey in the main plaza, and take the slave market to their city. Cuauhtitlan pays tribute to them. Cuauhtitlan's ruler kills himself in despair; in exile, Cuauhtitlan's nobles choose a new ruler (155–58)
1429–1430	Cuauhtitlan, Tenochtitlan, Tlatelolco, Texcoco, Tlacopan, Chalco, and Huexotzinco plot to defeat the Azcapotalcans. They defeat them by attacking, one by one, the cities governed by Tezozomoc's sons (160–65)
1431	Nezahualcoyotl becomes ruler of Texcoco, crowned by Itzcoatl of Tenochtitlan (172). Cuauhtitlan celebrates after the war (173)
1432	Itzcoatl of Tenochtitlan announces that he is ruler of the entire world, including Cuauhtitlan (176)
1433	Defeated Tepaneca are sent to live in Tultitlan. The ruler of Cuauhtitlan orders them to build a dam to divert the river there (178)
1435	Tenochtitlan, led by Itzcoatl, conquers Cuauhtitlan. Lands in Cuauhtitlan's territory are given to Mexica nobles (183). Cuauhtitlan's administrative system is reorganized by the new ruler, Ayactlacatzin (169)
1441	Warriors from Cuauhtitlan participate in Mexica wars outside the Valley of Mexico, as well as in conflicts with nearby Chalco and Tizic-Cuitlahuac (186–92)
1458	Mexico begins collecting tribute from everywhere (189)
1466–1473	The Triple Alliance capitals are improved—the Mexica build the Chapultepec aqueduct, and Nezahualcoyotl builds a temple in Texcoco (188, 192–94). Cuauhtitlan fights with the Triple Alliance again the nearby Tzompanca, Xillotzinca, and Citlaltepeca. Captives are taken for sacrifice at Nezahualcoyotl's temple. Cuauhtitlan's, Tultitlan's, and Cuitlachtepec's participants receive quauhtlalli or lands as spoils of war in Tezoyuca, a province ruled thereafter by Texcoco (194–96)
1472	Nezahualcoyotl, ruler of Texcoco, dies and his son Nezahualpilli replaces him (196)
1473	Cuauhtitlan aids Tenochtitlan during the Tenochtitlan-Tlatelolco civil war (197)
1494	Ayactlacatzin, ruler of Cuauhtitlan, dies and is replaced by a military governor, Tlacateccatl Tehuitzin, who governs until 1503 (206)
1503	Ahuitzotl, ruler of Tenochtitlan, dies and is replaced by Moctezuma II. In the same year, Moctezuma appoints Aztatzontzin as tlatoani of Cuauhtitlan. Aztatzontzin seats one of his brothers as tlatoani of Tepotzotlan (208)
1505	Aztatzontzin places tribute collectors in two of Cuauhtitlan's dependencies, Tlaxoxiuhco and Huexocalco (210). Famine occurs, and the people of Cuauhtitlan receive grain brought in from the Totonac area (210)
1507	For the ceremonies celebrating a new Aztec century, a sacrificial stone is set up in Cuauhtitlan, and war captives are sacrificed (212)
1508	Land in Tehuiloyoacan, part of Cuauhtitlan's territory, is divided among Mexica nobles (214)
1512	Moctezuma sends one of his daughters to Cuauhtitlan to marry its ruler, Aztatzontzin (216)
1519	The Spaniards arrive; Aztatzontzin is the ruler of Cuauhtitlan in 1519 (222)

[1]Source: *Anales de Cuauhtitlan* (1945).
[2]Dates in Christian calendar are approximate correlations published by P. F. Velázquez in *Anales de Cuauhtitlan* (1945).
[3]Numbers refer to paragraph numbers in *Anales de Cuauhtitlan* (1945).

Cuauhtitlan, and prisoners were sacrificed on it (though the author of the *Anales*, writing in the Colonial period, carefully points out that the people of Cuauhtitlan had only two captives, probably in order to deemphasize their role in human sacrifice) (*Anales de Cuauhtitlan* 1945:59).

Thus, Cuauhtitlan's people, and in particular the nobles, were required after they were conquered by Tenochtitlan, to perform Mexica rituals or be punished by loss of their land and/or death. Mexica rituals and deities were imposed upon traditional Chichimec rituals and deities. This is a pattern not always reported in Mexica dependencies, where it is often assumed that rule was indirect and that religion was not affected by incorporation into the empire. However, since the participation of nobles from other towns in Cuauhtitlan's yearly ritual is also recorded, a two-way assimilation of religious practices by the capital and the dependencies is indicated by these data.

Cuauhtitlan's Political System

Titles and Officials

Cuauhtitlan was governed by one tlatoani. In one case the ruler had the title atecpanecatl, or "lord of the water palace" (*Anales de Cuauhtitlan* 1945:35; Davies 1981:240); however, all other rulers are simply called tlatoani.

Other officials included leaders of the four divisions of Cuauhtitlan. They were (1) the chief priest of Tequixquinahuac, called teuctlamacazqui; (2) an individual from Nepantla, perhaps with the title tziuhcoacatl; (3) a named individual with no title from Chalmecapan; and (4) the tlacochcalcatl from Atempan Huauhtlan (*Anales de Cuauhtitlan* 1938:224, 1945:45). These officials went as ambassadors to Huexotzinco (a polity in what is the modern state of Puebla) (ibid.), and officials from these divisions, including the tziuhcoacatl from Nepantla and the tezcaccomecatl from Atempan, apportioned land taken from Matlatzinco in 1468 (*Anales de Cuauhtitlan* 1938:264).

The titles tlacochcalcatl, tziuhcoacatl, and tezcaccomecatl may indicate a status rather than an office, and the number of examples of these titles and of title-holders' activities is too few to be certain that the titles designated specific responsibilities. However, certain titles appear a sufficient number of times in an administrative context to suggest high positions or ranks if not specific duties. For instance, the titles tlacochcalcatl and tlacateuctli appear very often and with many different individuals. Two of the appointed officials governing outposts under Xaltemoctzin (ca. 1395) were called tlacateuctli, meaning "noble ruler" or "magistrate" in some contexts (Simeón 1885:538; Lehmann 1938:180), and Tollanzingo was ruled by an individual with the title tlacateuctzin in 1505 (*Anales de Cuauhtitlan* 1938:281). A title which seems to be equivalent to "war chief" is tiçocyauhacatl (*Anales de Cuauhtitlan* 1938:282; 1945:59). Yet another title was that of tlacochteuctli, mentioned in regard to a noble in Tehuiloyoacan (*Anales de Cuauhtitlan* 1938:286-87, 1945:60).

Officials with more explicit duties were tribute collectors and administrators of the arsenals, both called calpixque (*Anales de Cuauhtitlan* 1938:182, 280). Officials who guarded the borders, or perhaps garrisons, were called quaxochpixque (*Anales de Cuauhtitlan* 1938:148-49, 180, 1945:34).

Support of Cuauhtitlan's Officials

Cuauhtitlan's tlatoani and pipiltin received income from commoners, who provided tribute in goods and labor. Something of the scale of tribute collection within Cuauhtitlan's territory can be inferred from early Colonial documents. For instance, a court case of 1552 (AGN, Tierras, Vol. 2719, Exp. 8) involved a dispute between the inhabitants of Cuauhtlaapan, Tepujaco, and Xoloc, and their governor and nobles ("principales"). The inhabitants of these pueblos argued that they were being taxed excessively. The tribute in goods included fowl, cacao beans, cotton cloth (mantas), maguey fiber cloth, lime, wood, reed mats, as well as items that clearly were added in the Colonial period and were not traditional tribute items—tributos ordinarios (money), eggs, pigs, and cows. Labor requirements included women for grinding corn and workmen to maintain the nobles' houses.

In addition, a document from the middle 1500s reports a dispute between one of the Indian officials and potters who claimed they had not been paid for their work. This document (Barlow 1951) suggests that Cuauhtitlan housed craft specialists (potters in particular) who may have paid tribute to Indian nobles in the form of their crafts in the pre-Hispanic period.

Clearly the ruler of Cuauhtitlan received a fairly rich income as a result of governing many dependent towns, and under the Aztec empire, the rulers' income was supplemented by produce from lands taken from Azcapotzalco when that city-state was defeated in 1428. In 1435, Ayactlacatzin made grants of land to nobles of his court, assisted by officials from Tenochtitlan and Tlatelolco, and he took Citlaltepec's temple land for his own support (*Anales de Cuauhtitlan* 1945:48). Moreover, he redistributed items which he collected four times each year (ibid.:35). Although the ruler of Cuauhtitlan received income from estates granted after Triple Alliance wars, Cuauhtitlan and its dependencies also had to pay imperial tribute, thus losing income. (Imperial tribute will be discussed in the section on effects of conquest, later in this chapter.)

Territorial Organization of Cuauhtitlan

One indication of the success or failure of a polity at retaining local autonomy is the expansion or reduction of its territory. Below is a summary, based largely on the *Anales de Cuauhtitlan*, of how Cuauhtitlan's territory was organized while it was independent and how this organization changed when Cuauhtitlan was conquered by Tenochtitlan.

The Cuauhtitlan area was not governed from a single, central town or palace between the city-state's founding at approximately A.D. 804, and A.D. 1350, if the rulers' dwelling places are used an an index. Table 4-1 is a list of the rulers of Cuauhtitlan and their places of residence. The places that can be located because some of their names have been preserved—Xoloc, Tepotzotlan, and Tequixquinahuac—are near Cuauhtitlan. After 1349, the palace location appears to be consistently the urban center of Cuauhtitlan.

Xaltemoctzin, who ruled from approximately 1390 to 1408, expanded Cuauhtitlan's territory through conquests. He placed outposts around this territory and appointed administrators to rule the towns of Citlaltepec, Huehuetoca, Tzompanco (Zumpango), and Otlazpan (Fig. 4-5).

> In this year king Xaltemoctzin sent his emissaries to place border guards (quaxochpixque) in Tzompanco, Citlaltepec, Huehuetoca, and Otlazpan. To Tzompanco went Cayocacatzin, the principal lord, to govern; Itzcuintzin went to govern Citlaltepec; prince Cuauchichitzin, who went for the first time to govern, was seated in Otlazpan. [*Anales de Cuauhtitlan* 1945:34]

As noted earlier, these dependent towns aided in furnishing labor for building the temple. After this, Cuauhtitlan was defeated by Azcapotzalco, becoming subject to it and paying tribute. The annals do not mention the territorial organization of Cuauhtitlan until the defeat of Azcapotzalco, after which the territory was reorganized.

In the 1430s the ruler of Cuauhtitlan, Ayactlacatzin, assisted by Mexica and Tlatelolca, reorganized the territorial and administrative arrangement set up by Xaltemoctzin, which apparently had lapsed while the area was subject to Azcapotzalco.

> At this time, Cuauhtitlan was already divided into four parts, to which had been given dependencies. The order that had been and that Xaltemoctzin the elder had come to establish, was destroyed; of Tequixquinahuacan were formed Tepoxalco and Tzompanco, of Chalmecapan were made Cuauhtlaapan and Citlaltepec, of Nepantla were made Tepotzotlan and Huehuetoca, and of Atempan were formed Coyotepec and Otlazpan. After the war was over, the ruler of Cuauhtitlan (who was Ayactlacatzin, because of the death of Tecocohuatzin) took vengeance on those [Azcapotzalcans] who had occupied the city of Cuauhtitlan. He divided the land; he distributed it, and he made grants of it. Thus, the señorío [tlatocayotl] of the city of Cuauhtitlan came to be organized in the land; it was because of the war that the grants were made. On dividing the land of Tzompanco and Citlaltepec, the ruler Ayactlacatzin took the temple lands of Citlaltepec for himself, and the deputies who came to mark the boundaries were Tenochca from Tlatelolco. Following this, boundary markers were placed in Otlazpan; afterward, they were put in Tepoxalco and Tehuiloyoacan; finally tribute land was chosen in all parts where it has been related that the boundaries were marked. However, in Huehuetoca, none were apportioned out, because the people of Cuauhtitlan liked the Huehuetocans very much, for when they took refuge there in time of war, they were good allies. . . . This is a summary of the Song of the Tepaneca [Acapotzalcan] defeat. [*Anales de Cuauhtitlan* 1945:47-48]

Thus, Ayactlacatzin and the Tenochca changed the territorial organization of Cuauhtitlan, which had consisted of four divisions of the urban center of Cuauhtitlan and two dependent towns subject to each division. The four administrative offices, held by nobles of Cuauhtitlan, were abolished, and eight administrative divisions were created, each centered in a particular town (see Fig. 4-6). The division of land was overseen by Tenochca from Tlatelolco, to whom Cuauhtitlan was probably either an ally or a dependency. (The *Anales* gives 1435 as the date when Tenochtitlan conquered Cuauhtitlan [see Barlow 1947:525]; the *Anales*' author barely mentioned the event.) The passage quoted above demonstrates that by 1435 Cuauhtitlan's nobles were taking land for personal or official income, a practice frequently documented for the Mexica.

In 1508, land in Tehuiloyoacan was divided among Mexica nobles from Tenochtitlan, Mexicaltzingo, and Tlatelolco. Residents in at least one place were moved.

> Also in this year [1508] the Mexica leaders from Tenochtitlan took land. The Tlatelolca took land in Tehuiloyoacan in order to create cohuatlalli [tribute-paying land]. The land was divided up by the tlatoani of Tenochtitlan, Moctezuma, and the tlatoani of Cuauhtitlan, Aztatzontzin. In the following manner, the foreign land was given into the hands of the rulers of Acxotlan [a barrio of Tlatelolco in which pochteca lived]. It was *not* the deed of the pipiltin or the tlatoque of Cuauhtitlan.

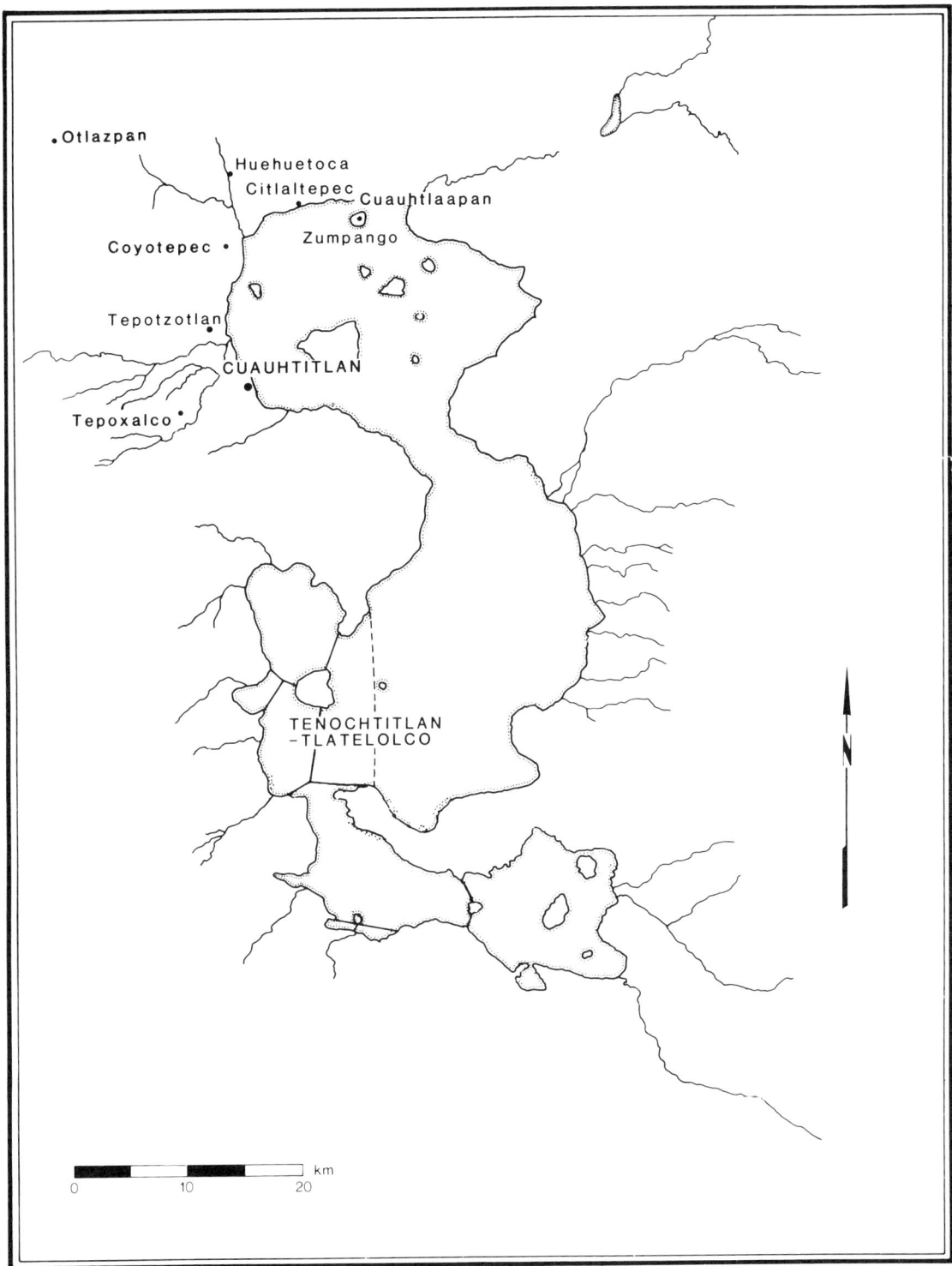

Fig. 4-5. Map of Cuauhtitlan's dependencies ruled by Xaltemoctzin, between 1390 and 1408. There were four administrative divisions composing the polity of Cuauhtitlan. The administrative division of Tequixquinahuacan consisted of the towns of Tepoxalco and Tzompango (Zumpango); the administrative division of Chalmecapan was composed of Cuauhtlaapan and Citlaltepec; the administrative division of Nepantlan included Tepotzotlan and Huehuetoca; the administrative division of Atempan included Coyotepec and Otlazpan (source of place-names, *Anales de Cuauhtitlan* 1938, 1945).

The land was taken by Tzihuacpopocatzin of Tlatelolco, whose portion was the Sierra of Tehuiloyoacan, now called Tlatelolca land [tlatilolcatlalli]. The second portion was given to Techotlallatzin of Itztapalapa; it was irrigated land called Atzaqualpan ["capture of water, or dam"]. The third grant was to Tochihuitzin of Mexicaltzingo and was irrigated land also by the dam. As a result, the Cohuatzinca who lived on the land were very angry. And then the land of Macuitzinco, which belonged to the palace of Teçoncaltitlan and on which lived the children of the tlacochteuctli of Tehuiloyoacan, by the dammed up water in Quauhacaltitlan, was taken.

In this manner, the nobles named above received land. [*Anales de Cuauhtitlan* 1938:286-87]

Finally, Aztatzontzin, who ruled Cuauhtitlan in 1519, also ruled the territories of Tzompanco (Zumpango), Citlaltepec, Huehuetoca, Otlazpan, and parts of Tultitlan, Tepexic, and Tepotzotlan. "In this year, 1 Acatl, the lords of the towns, at the time when the Spaniards arrived, were . . . Aztatzontzin of Cuauhtitlan and of the four kingdoms of Tzompanco, Citlaltepec, Huehuetoca, and Otlazpan, and of the woodlands of Tultitlan, Tepexic, and Tepotzotlan, and of the flat land near the woodlands" (*Anales de Cuauhtitlan* 1945:63). Hence, at the time of the conquest, Cuauhtitlan was the center of a province governing at least one lesser tlatoani (at Tultitlan) and four towns and their dependent territories that at one time had been independent city-states (see Fig. 4-7).

In summary, the boundaries of the territory of Cuauhtitlan changed over time. Before the Triple Alliance, Cuauhtitlan's rulers conquered and ruled four previously independent city-states. Administration of the territory was reorganized after it was conquered by Tenochtitlan. Cuauhtitlan lost control over some of its own land when Mexica nobles appropriated fields within the province but Cuauhtitlan's ruler and other nobles gained land when they received, or were granted, the income from tribute-paying lands outside Cuauhtitlan's territory, in reward for their participation in Triple Alliance wars. In all time periods from which there is documentary evidence, the province of Cuauhtitlan always dominated territory to its north and somewhat to its east; it never expanded south toward Azcapotzalco and Tenochtitlan.

Rulers of Cuauhtitlan

A list of the numerous rulers of Cuauhtitlan, according to the *Anales de Cuauhtitlan*, appears in Table 4-3. Any genealogical information given in the *Anales* is also presented; however, this information is fragmentary, and so although a complete list of rulers is available, their relationships to each other are not always clearly stated.

Succession to Rulership in Cuauhtitlan

The office of tlatoani is usually defined as an inherited office, since most descriptions of rulership in the Valley of Mexico state that offices were supposed to pass from father to son (cf. Zorita 1963:90; however, in Tenochtitlan and other city-states, there were variations [Alva Ixtlilxochitl 1975-77, I; Carrasco 1984]). In the *Anales de Cuauhtitlan*, there are no explicit descriptions of succession procedure, although heredity appears to have been important whenever Cuauhtitlan chose a ruler without outside interference. As Table 4-3 demonstrates, only twice were sons explicitly mentioned as inheriting the office of tlatoani. Three times women succeeded their husbands in the office. In other instances, nobles were chosen who had a forebear who had been a ruler (for instance, Aztatzontzin), because of noble Chichimec ancestors (Teçoçmoctzin) or Culhua ancestors (Iztactototzin).

The line of succession by rulers chosen internally is often broken by political events. Tezozomoc of Azcapotzalco had Xaltemoctzin assassinated (*Anales de Cuauhtitlan* 1945:35-36, 43-44). Then, when Azcapotzalco defeated Cuauhtitlan, a military governor was installed, and after him, a ruler was brought in from Tlatelolco (1418-30) (see *Anales de Cuauhtitlan* 1945:36; Barlow [1947] says this ruler was a pro-Mexica Tepaneca) and, in 1495, a military governor, the tlacateccatl Tehuitzin, was appointed by the ruler of Tenochtitlan (*Anales de Cuauhtitlan* 1945:58). Moctezuma II appointed the final ruler, Aztatzontzin, whose ancestor Quinatzin had ruled Cuauhtitlan and whose father ruled Tepotzotlan.

Aztatzontzin was established as lord; the ruler of Tenochtitlan called Moctezuma appointed him; he ordered that he be placed in the town of Cuauhtitlan, so that he would be king. His father, Quinatzin [ruler of nearby Tepotzotlan], had negotiated this with Moctezuma. In Cuauhtitlan, by this time, Achicatzin and Tlilpotoncatzin, sons of Ayactlacatzin, were deposed, and Cuauhtitlan was governed militarily: the tlacateccatl ['war captain'] Tehuitzin, a native of Tepetlapan, ruled the town. For eight years, it was thus ruled, until Aztatzontzin was enthroned. [*Anales de Cuauhtitlan* 1945:20]

The final ruler before the Spanish Conquest—Aztatzontzin—as noted in the paragraph above,

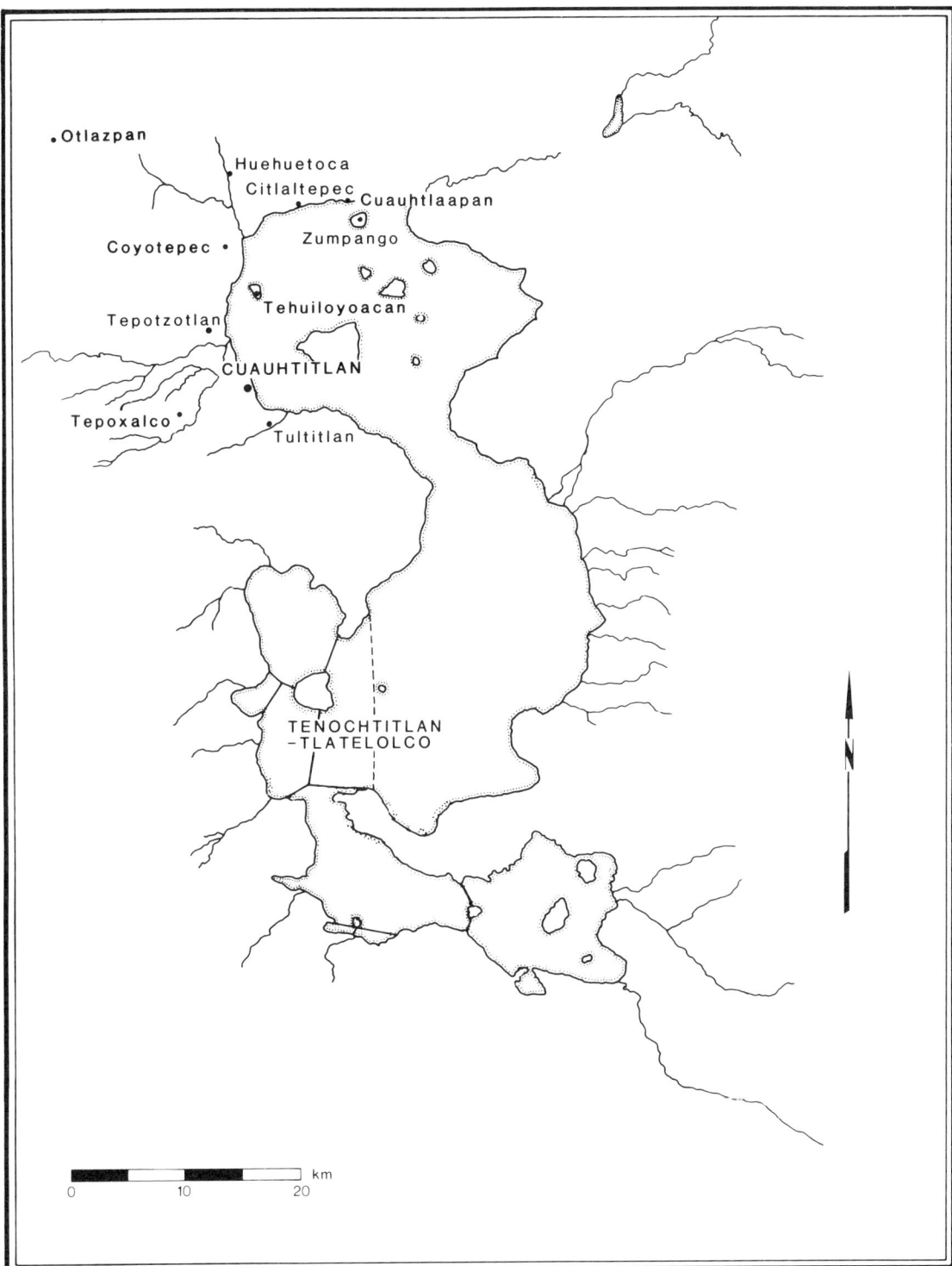

Fig. 4-6. Map of the dependencies of Cuauhtitlan during the reign of Ayactlacatzin (1434-95). Administrative divisions of the polity consisted of eight separate towns (source: *Anales de Cuauhtitlan* 1938, 1945).

was appointed by Moctezuma, instead of the sons of the former ruler. Significantly, Aztatzontzin married one of Moctezuma's daughters and apparently was fairly compliant with Mexica policy, since he set up a tribute-collection post despite protests by local lords (*Anales de Cuauhtitlan* 1938:280-21; see Fig. 4-8).

In summary, succession to rulership in Cuauhtitlan did not follow the father-to-son pattern so often suggested as the norm for Nahua polities (Zorita 1963), a pattern that was followed fairly regularly in Tenochtitlan and Texcoco. This divergence from the norm occurred not as a result of preference, but because of political and military interference—particularly assassination of rulers and meddling in succession by the rulers of Tenochtitlan and Azcapotzalco—which prevented the orderly inheritance of the office of tlatoani in Cuauhtitlan. Under the Aztec empire, the ruler was appointed by the ruler of Tenochtitlan, with heredity as a secondary factor, and with allegiance to Tenochtitlan being the more important factor. Thus, the initially hereditary office of tlatoani in Cuauhtitlan became an office that was less dependent on inheritance than on political appointment. The office became separated from the local nobles and local traditions and in practice was an imperial administrative office.

Marriage Alliances of Cuauhtitlan's Rulers

The rulers of Cuauhtitlan married women from elite lineages in towns in the southern Valley of Mexico, particularly Culhuacan, Chapultepec, and Xochimilco. Quinatzin, who ruled ca. A.D. 1175-1239, married Chimalaxochitzin, a daughter of the ruler of Chapultepec (*Anales de Cuauhtitlan* 1945:18). Later, Huactzin (who ruled from A.D. 1287-1348) married Itztolpanxochitl, a daughter of Coxcoxteuctli, ruler of Culhuacan, ca. 1325 (ibid.:27). When some Culhua people fled Culhuacan and went to Cuauhtitlan, ca. 1347, Huactzin's son—who was half Culhua—was a favored choice to be the next ruler because his ancestry satisfied both the faction from Culhuacan and the residents of Cuauhtitlan. The *Anales* (1945:31) also records that Cuauhtitlan's nobles gave daughters as wives to the newcomers, further cementing the bonds between the two groups.

The rulers of Cuauhtitlan received wives from noble lineages in other towns, and they gave their daughters in marriage to the rulers of nearby Tepaneca towns. For instance, Tecocohuatzin's daughter married a ruler of Tultitlan, ca. 1430 (*Anales de Cuauhtitlan* 1945:35-36). The documents record the rulers of Cuauhtitlan allying themselves with equal, more politically important, or more prestigious noble families by marrying women from these families, and in turn, giving their daughters in marriage to rulers in their province or nearby, to cement alliances with them, in keeping with a pattern of wife-giving to a subordinate lord.

The final pre-Hispanic ruler, Aztatzontzin, was the son of the ruler of nearby Tepotzotlan and the descendant of Quinaztin II, an early ruler of Cuauhtitlan. Foremost among his several wives was a daughter of Moctezuma II, whose name was Illancueitl (*Crónica Mexicáyotl* 1949:153) or Moceltzin (*Anales de Cuauhtitlan* 1945:61). He also married a noblewoman from Huitzilopochco, or Xochimilco, called "Doña María" after the Spanish Conquest, and a daughter of Tecoctzin, tlacochcalcatl of Cuauhyacac, is listed as the mother of his first child. Though the principal wives of the tlatoque may have been from high status lineages outside Cuauhtitlan, it appears that the rulers also married women from dependent towns, for Aztatzontzin's wives included women whose rank is not given, from Tequixquinahuac, Tollantzinco, Apazco, Azcapotzalco, and Tlatecayohuacan. Yet other women, whom he did not marry, produced children (*Anales de Cuauhtitlan* 1945:20-21).

Though the *Anales* lists only the most significant earlier marriages of Cuauhtitlan's tlatoque, these indicate several patterns of marriage. First, there were pre-Triple Alliance associations with towns in the southern Valley of Mexico, such as Culhuacan and Chapultepec. Second, there were marriages later with Tenochca nobility. Third, there were no marriage alliances recorded at all between Cuauhtitlan's rulers and those of Texcoco or Chalco, limiting marriage alliances to the Mexica and Tepaneca realms of the valley. Finally, the tlatoque of Cuauhtitlan also married women from dependent towns and nearby Tepaneca cities and gave their daughters as wives to rulers in these towns.

Political Alliances of the Independent City-State of Cuauhtitlan

While historical sources from other city-states in the Valley of Mexico tend to regard Cuauhtitlan as

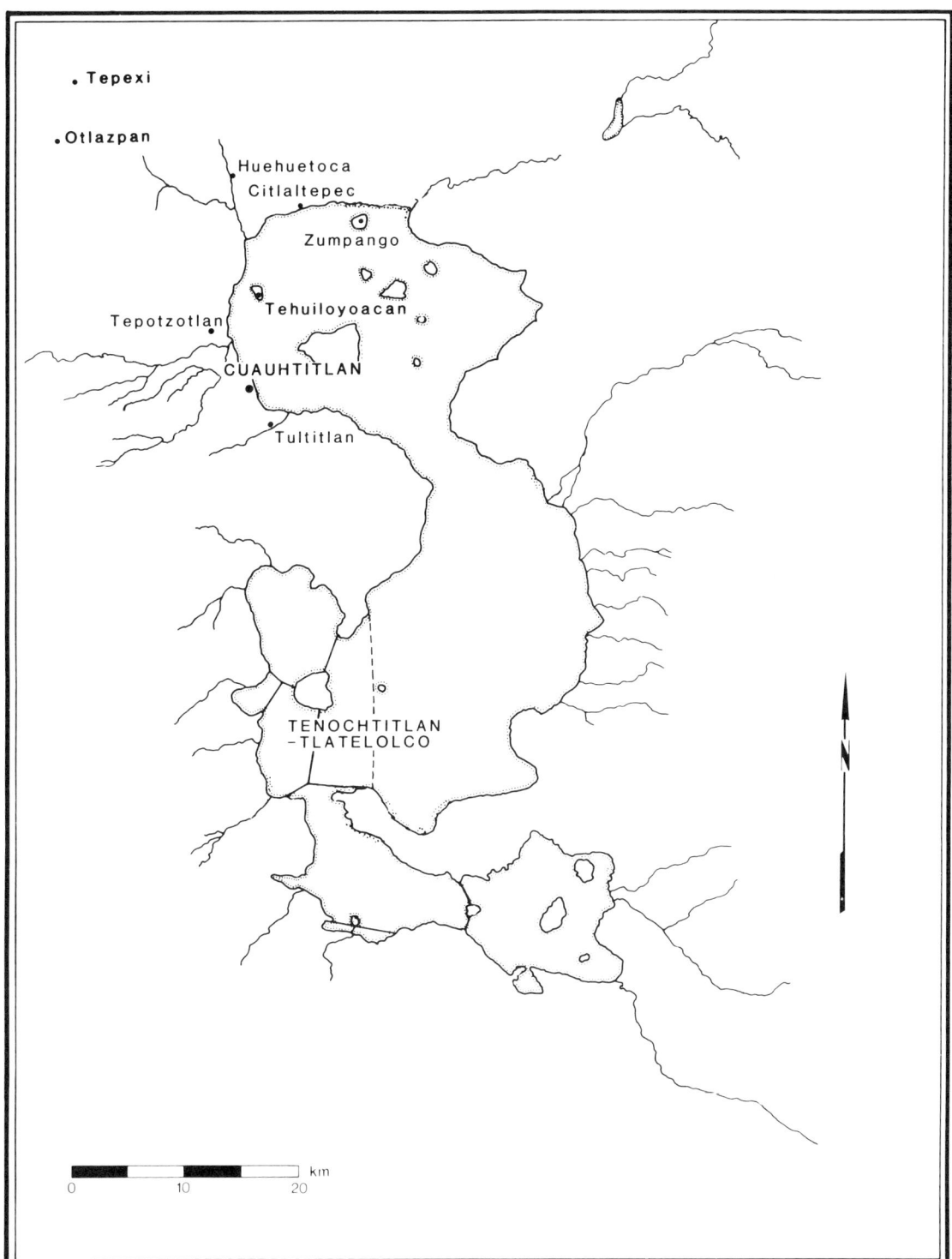

Fig. 4-7. Map of some of Cuauhtitlan's dependencies, ca. 1519. The *Anales de Cuauhtitlan* (1945:63) mentions differing statuses and obligations of these dependencies. Tzompango, Citlaltepec, Huehuetoca, and Otlazpan were "four kingdoms" whose rulership had been taken over by the tlatoani of Cuauhtitlan. Cuauhtitlan's ruler had lands in Tultitlan, Tepexic, and Tepotzotlan, and Mexica nobles had lands in Tehuiloyoacan.

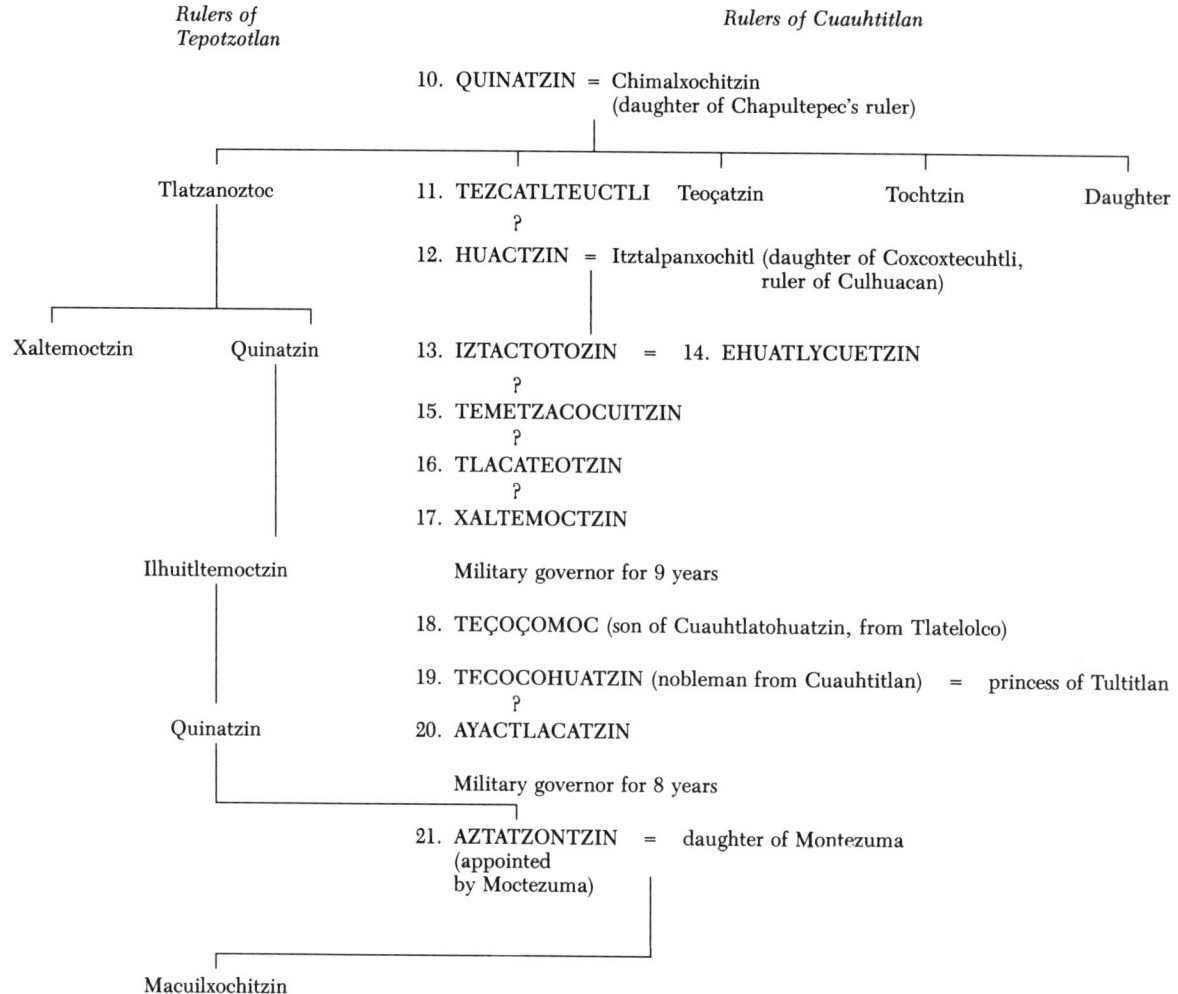

Fig. 4-8. Genealogy of the last twelve pre-Hispanic rulers of Cuauhtitlan (from *Anales de Cuauhtitlan* 1938, 1945).

either a Tepaneca city in league with Azcapotzalco or Tlacopan, or as a dependency of Tenochtitlan (Chimalpahin 1965; *Memorial de los Pueblos*, in Paso y Troncoso 1940, XIV:118-22), the author of the *Anales* stresses its independence and, in fact, almost succeeds in disguising its conquest by Tenochtitlan.

Apparently, before its conquest by Tenochtitlan, Cuauhtitlan operated independently. Cuauhtitlan's people fought over boundaries with Xaltocan's people, and the Mexica sided with Cuauhtitlan against Xaltocan at a time when they were subjects of Azcapotzalco (*Anales de Cuauhtitlan* 1945:18, 22-26; Davies 1973a; Carrasco 1950). As an independent polity, Cuauhtitlan waged wars and received ambassadors from other city-states (such as those from Cuauhnauac [Cuernavaca]), and it sent ambassadors to Huexotzinco to ask for help in its rebellion against Azcapotzalco (*Anales de Cuauhtitlan* 1938:234, 1945:45). After Azcapotzalco was defeated, Cuauhtitlan still skirmished with hostile Tepaneca factions, particularly those of Tultitlan (*Anales de Cuauhtitlan* 1945:48-49). Following Cuauhtitlan's defeat by Tenochtitlan (ca. A.D. 1435), independent functions of Cuauhtitlan —such as waging war and making diplomatic trips—were curtailed.

Cuauhtitlan was conquered by the Mexica rulers Huitzilihuitl (1396-1417), when the Mexica were allies of Azcapotzalco, and by Itzcoatl (1427–40)

TABLE 4-3
GENEALOGICAL INFORMATION ON RULERS OF CUAUHTITLAN

Date	Name	Relation to Previous Ruler(s)
687–751	Chicontonatiuh	Lineage founder
752–803	Xiuhneltzin	End of first lineage
804–865	Huactli	Starts new lineage
866–875	Xiuhtlacuilolxochitzin	Wife of Huactli
876–930	Ayauhcoyotzin	No information
931–945	Nequamexochitxin	No information
946–982	Mecellotzin	No information
983–1023	Tzihuacpapalotzin	No information
1024–1035	Iztacxillotzin	Wife of Tzihuacpapalotzin
1035–1091	Eztlaquencatzin	No information
1092–1107	Ezcoatzin	No information
1108–1175	Teyztlacoatzin	No information
1175–1239	Quinatzin	Married Chimalxochitzin, daughter of ruler of Chapultepec
1247–1286	Tezcalteuctli	Son of Quinatzin
1287–1348	Huactzin	He married the daughter of the ruler of Culhuacan
1349–1368	Iztactototzin	Son of Huactzin
1369–1373	Ehuatlycuetzin	Wife of Iztactototzin
1374–1379	Temetzacocuitzin	No information
1380–1390	Tlacateotzin	No information
1390–1408	Xaltemoctzin	No information
1409–1418	—	Break of 9 years with no tlatoani while a military governor ruled
1418–1430	Teçoçomoc	Son of Cuauhtlatohuatzin, from Tlatelolco
1430–1433	Tecocohuatzin	A noble from Cuauhtitlan whose daughter married Epcohuatl, ruler of Tultitlan and son of Tezozomoc
1434–1495	Ayactlacatzin	No information
1495–1503	—	No tlatoani; a military governor from Tenochtitlan ruled Cuauhtitlan
1503–1519	Aztatzontzin	Son of the ruler of Tepotzotlan; he was a descendant of Quinatzin, ruler of Cuauhtitlan, 1175–1239

(Source: *Anales de Cuauhtitlan* 1938, 1945)

(*Anales de Cuauhtitlan* 1945:66; *Codex Mendoza* 1925:3v, 5v). In 1428, Cuauhtitlan was definitively beaten by Azcapotzalco, as described by the author of the *Anales*:

> In this time the tlatoani was Teçoçomoc, who came from Tlatelolco. He was the tlatoani when the Tepaneca took the city of Cuauhtitlan, when they came planting the plaza with maguey and burning the temple. On taking the city of Cuauhtitlan, they made many prisoners, who were carried to Azcapotzalco. They killed many of the people of Cuauhtitlan, and those that weren't killed were taken prisoner. Thus the city of Cuauhtitlan was taken; for 80 days the people of Cuauhtitlan paid tribute in Tepanohuayan [another name for Azcapotzalco]. They went only two times to give tribute: the first, when the city was captured and the second when the 80 days were over. They paid tribute of cloth; each paid his debt with a small piece of paper, each one the size from one hand to one's elbow, and they paid with paper for offerings. . . . [*Anales de Cuauhtitlan* 1945:43–44]

Azcapotzalco apparently did not organize a tribute-collecting bureaucracy, but rather demanded payment for peace.

Cuauhtitlan and the Aztec Empire

Conquest by Tenochtitlan

Conquest by Tenochtitlan occurred in 1435, after a short period of independence following the defeat of Azcapotzalco. The definitive defeat of Cuauhtitlan was led by the Mexica ruler Itzcoatl. Under the Mexica, changes were instituted in Cuauhtitlan's organization, as described below.

Effects of Conquest

Rulership. As mentioned previously, the Mexica first appointed a military governor to rule Cuauhtitlan. Later, Cuauhtitlan's rulers were appointed by the Mexica ruler, and hereditary succession became less important than obedience to imperial orders.

Officials. Following Cuauhtitlan's incorporation into the empire, the individual at the highest level of decision-making (the tlatoani) was appointed by the ruler of Tenochtitlan. The second level—lords of the four quarters and administrators of the four divisions of Cuauhtitlan—was eradicated. Instead of the four advisors, eight towns (and presumably their administrators) became the second level of administration (Fig. 4-9). This new structure eliminated administrators who were probably receiving income that the empire preferred be sent to Tenochtitlan. The change also reduced what would have been a four-level hierarchy (Tenochtitlan, Cuauhtitlan's ruler, the lords of the four divisions, town administrators), down to a three-level hierarchy of administration (Tenochtitlan, Cuauhtitlan's ruler, eight dependent towns); a hierarchy of fewer levels would increase control by the top-most level over the lower-level centers (Blau and Schoenherr 1971). Moreover, at least one of the third-level towns— Citlaltepec—was governed by an individual appointed by Tenochtitlan's ruler, which would have made control by the capital even more direct (*Relación de Tequisquiac, Citlaltepec y Xilotzingo* 1957:297).

Tribute. As a dependency of Tenochtitlan, Cuauhtitlan paid tribute to it. Tenochtitlan sent to Cuauhtitlan specialized officials for tribute collection (*calpixque*) who operated at specific tribute-collection posts. Although some sources report that Cuauhtitlan paid tribute to Tlacopan, the city which governed the Tepaneca area under the Triple Alliance (Paso y Troncoso 1940, XIV:118-22; Gibson 1964a, 1964b; Zantwijk 1969), Cuauhtitlan's tribute to Tenochtitlan is better documented and more quantified. Apparently Tenochtitlan's demands increased over time, for in 1503, in response to Mexica orders:

> Aztatzontzin, tlatoani of Cuauhtitlan audited the tribute lands [calpixcatlalli] in Cuauhtitlan. He appointed officials to collect tribute in Tlaxoxiuhco and Huexocalco and built houses for tribute collection [calpollalli]. When he told Tzincopintzin, the tlacateuctzin of Tollanzinco, Tzincopintzin rebuked him (for doing this). . . . [*Anales de Cuauhtitlan* 1938:280-81]

The *Codex Mendoza* (1925:26) shows Cuauhtitlan as head of a tribute-collection province which was not isomorphic with the political province as of 1519. Cuauhtitlan is listed as the head town, followed by six subordinate towns where tribute was collected. These towns were Tehuiloyoacan, Alheuxoyoca, Xalapan, Tepoxalco, Cuezcomahuacan/Tequixquiac, and Xilotzinco (Fig. 4-10). These place-names are not those of the largest towns in the province; instead smaller towns served as calpixqui centers. Barlow (1949) added two other towns which he believed were included in Cuauhtitlan's tributary province—Huehuetoca and Tepotzotlan—because they are listed as subjects of Tlacopan (Paso y Troncoso 1940, XIV:118-22), although the tributary provinces of Tlacopan were not necesarily the same as political provinces (see Zantwijk 1969 and Calnek 1978).

The quantities of tribute paid by Cuauhtitlan to Tenochtitlan were as follows. Every 6 months, they paid 400 loads of richly embroidered cloth, 800 loads of small, fine blankets with colors woven in, 4000 mats woven of reeds, and 4000 seats woven of grass and reeds. Yearly they paid 2 richly feathered warrior costumes, and 2 shields decorated with costly feathers of different kinds and colors that made a design, 50 warrior costumes and another 60 shields decorated with costly feathers, plus 4 crates full of corn, beans, chia (*Salvia*), and amaranth seed. The rush mats were a distinctive tribute item, produced in large quantities in the province, from rushes that grew along the shore of lakes Zumpango and Xaltocan (Barlow 1949:40-42).

The *Información Sobre Tributos* adds that Cuauhtitlan and 14 pueblos were required to give 5 feathered warrior costumes and 43 shields as yearly tribute. Every 80 days they paid 1200 blue and white mantas (cotton blankets). They sent as many as requested of hens, mats, wood, torch pine, chili peppers, jugs, bowls, ollas, and as many commoners for labor as were requested by Tenochtitlan's ruler (Scholes and Adams 1957:36-37).

Although tribute paid by the entire province is listed in the *Codex Mendoza*; this list still does not enumerate perishable goods such as tortillas or turkeys that were collected, nor does it list the assignment of laborers for tasks at Cuauhtitlan or Tenochtitlan. Tribute of this type is suggested by another Colonial-period document, the *Codex San Andrés*. The *Codex San Andrés* illusrates services and goods sent via Cuauhtitlan to Tenochtitlan (Galarza 1963). The codex dates to approximately the mid-1500s, judging from the style (there is no European or Nahuatl date on the map). On the codex are written the words "cuauhtitlan calpixcatiaia," "san andres," and a glyph for Tenochtitlan (Fig.

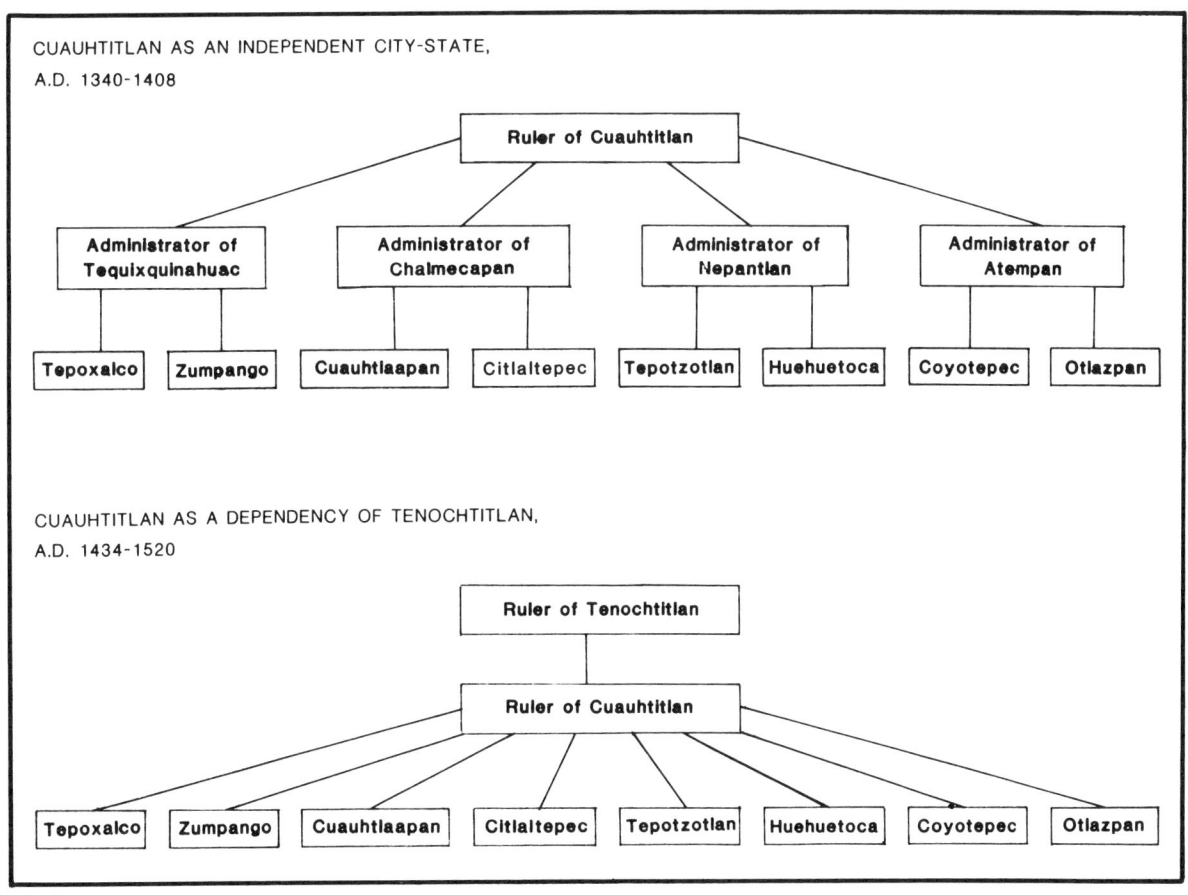

Fig. 4-9. Administrative organization of Cuauhtitlan before and after its incorporation into the Aztec empire.

4-11). The village of San Andrés, located just northeast of Cuauhtitlan (see Galarza 1963), at an unknown interval provided: 400 laborers (20 groups of 20, plus a leader), 4 women to grind maize, 12 mantas (or 12 loads of mantas), 80 turkeys, 200 tortillas (or perhaps 1600 tortillas and a bag of 8000 units of another item, perhaps cacao beans). These goods were collected at San Andrés and sent via Cuauhtitlan to Tenochtitlan.

In addition to labor for public works, Cuauhtitlan provided warriors for Triple Alliance wars. It supplied soldiers in cadres of 20 men, and its soldiers were organized according to which quarter of the city they came from (*Anales de Cuauhtitlan* 1938:267). As mentioned previously, Tenochtitlan's orders were carried out either by military governors or by tlatoque appointed by and rewarded by Tenochtitlan's rulers. Although the *Anales* does not mention it, it is likely that soldiers and laborers from Cuauhtitlan were organized through Tlacopan for some imperial activities, since Cuauhtitlan is listed as one of the cities that were in Tlacopan's labor zone (see Gibson 1964a, 1964b).

Territory. Under the Triple Alliance, the extent of Cuauhtitlan's territory did not change radically; however, its administrative arrangements were altered. Moreover, Mexica nobles took over land within the province, land which then contributed to their support and not to the support of Cuauhtitlan's ruler and nobles. Cuauhtitlan's ruler and nobles received lands outside the province for their support, as rewards for participation in Triple Alliance victories.

Marriage Alliances of Rulers. Following its incorporation into the empire, Cuauhtitlan's rulers

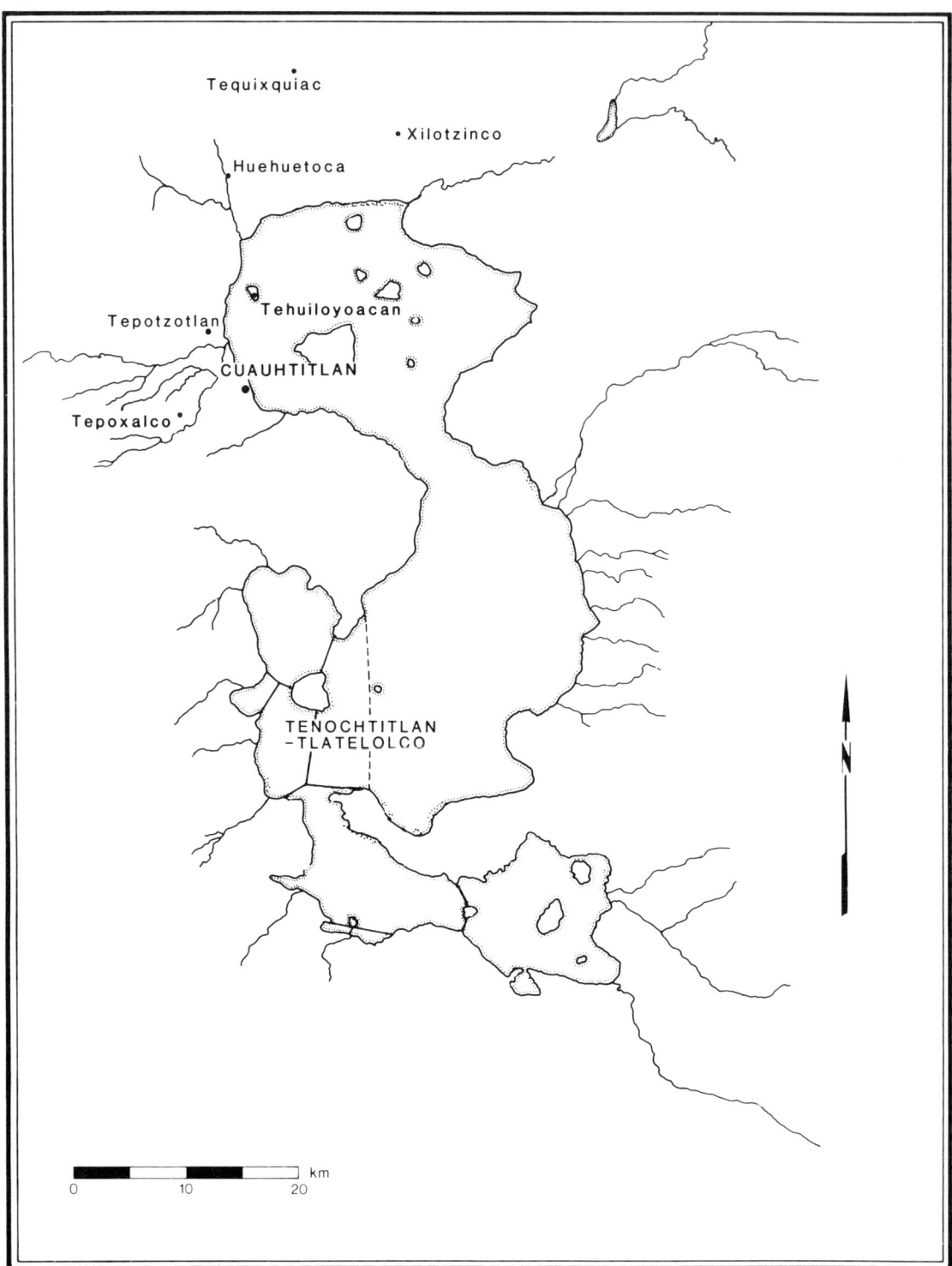

Fig. 4-10. Tribute-collection points in Cuauhtitlan province, as listed in the *Codex Mendoza* (1925:26). Tequixquiac/ Cuezcomahuacan, Xilotzinco, Tehuiloyoacan, and Tepoxalco have been located; Alhuexoyoca and Xalapan have not been located (Barlow 1949:41). Barlow added Huehuetoca and Tepotzotlan to the province because these towns were dependencies of Tlacopan.

married Tenochca elite women. For instance, the last ruler married the daughter of the ruler of Tenochtitlan, Moctezuma. Marriage alliances with communities in the area continued, with the ruler of Cuauhtitlan giving his daughters to subordinate rulers.

Political Alliances. Under the empire, Cuauhtitlan no longer made independent alliances or sent ambassadors to other city-states outside the valley.

Imperial Ceremonies. Cuauhtitlan's religious practices changed after its conquest. Some of Cuauhtitlan's nobles were killed or lost their land as a result of not practicing Mexica rites; religion was used as an excuse for taking land. The Mexica installed a sacrificial stone in Cuauhtitlan. However, Cuauhtitlan continued to perform an annual rite of its own, to which came nobles from throughout the valley.

Summary

Cuauhtitlan's Political System

The Cuauhtitlan area was settled by Chichimeca immigrants ca. A.D. 800. Archaeological survey shows only villages in the area until the 1300s. Cuauhtitlan was ruled by one tlatoani, and the political center, in accord with the archaeological data, was said to have been the village of the tlatoani. Only in the 1300s was an urban temple-palace center built. The city was divided into barrios to accommodate its residents and immigrant Culhua people, and the town and its territory con-

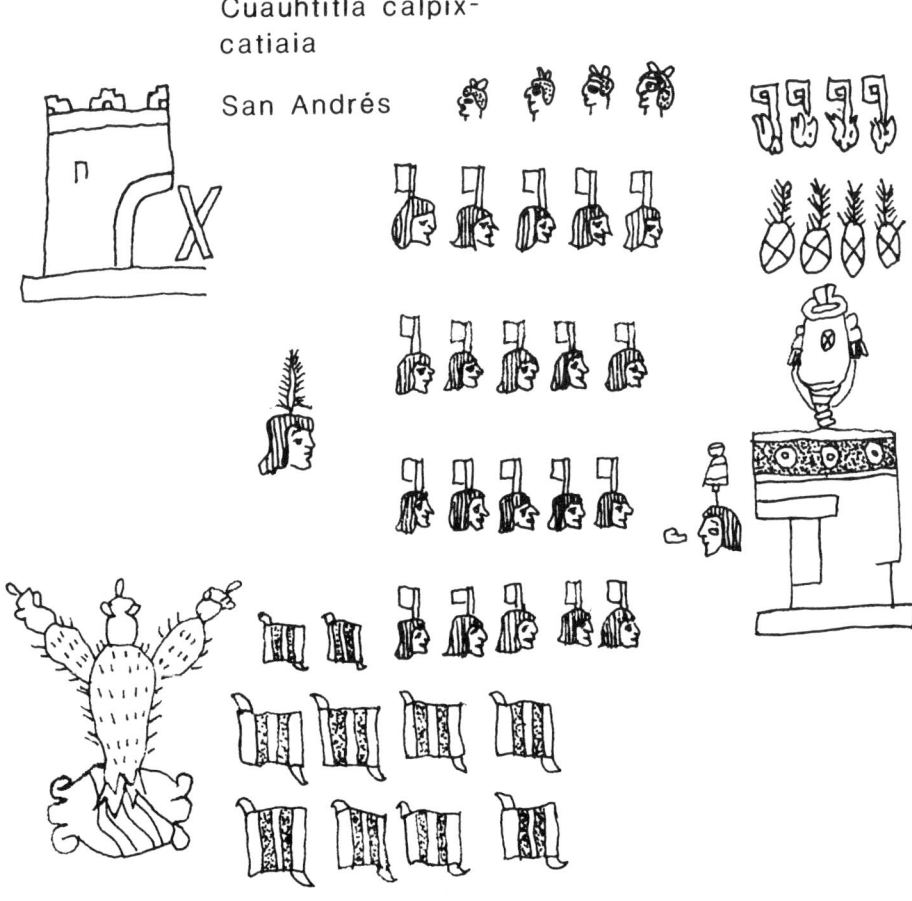

Fig. 4-11. Reconstruction of the Codex San Andrés (after Galarza 1963).

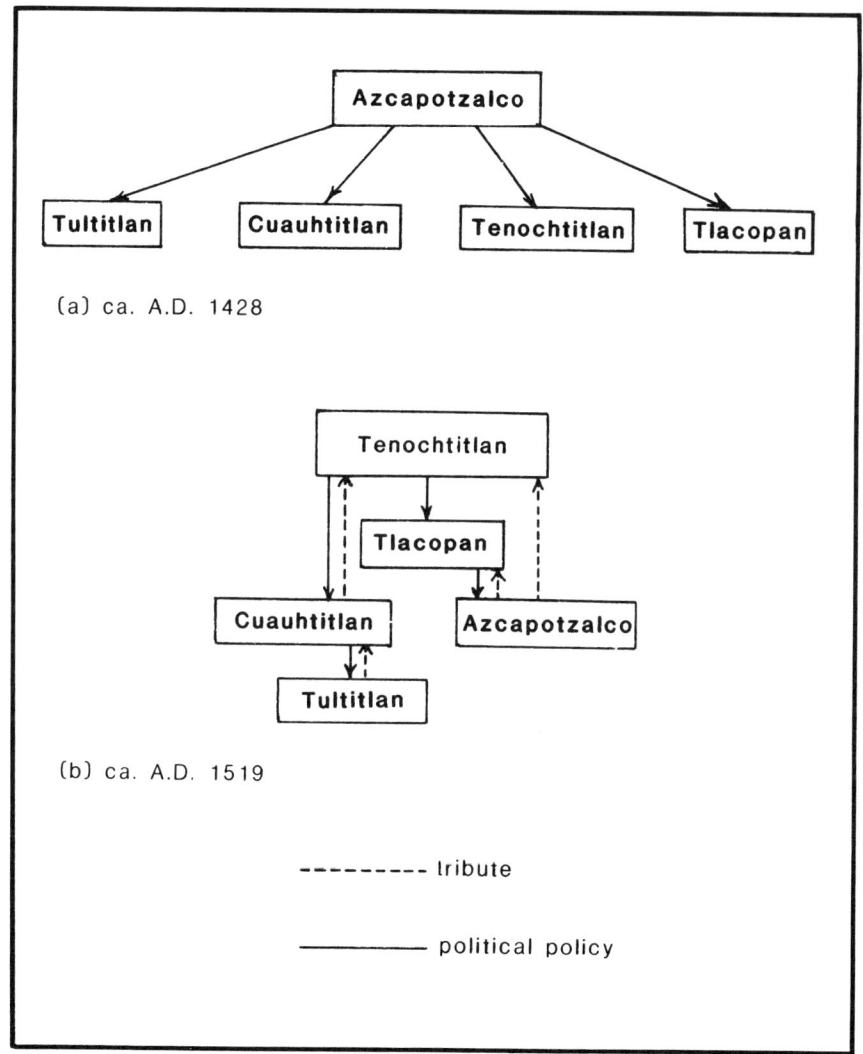

Fig. 4-12. Cuauhtitlan's position in the Valley of Mexico's political hierarchy at approximately 1428 and 1519.

sisted of four administrative sections. These divisions provided laborers for public works and men to serve as warriors. The leaders served as ambassadors and as advisors to the tlatoani. The political organization appears to have involved administrators—military governors in dependent towns, boundary setters, warriors to guard outposts—who were elites of the city. Cuauhtitlan was one of the 12 towns with resident pochteca, or long-distance traders in sumptuary goods, and Cuauhtitlan performed a distinctive ceremony each year, to which individuals came from other towns in the valley.

Pre-Imperial Political Alliances

An an independent city-state, Cuauhtitlan made political alliances with Culhuacan and Tepotzotlan. It was allied with Tenochtitlan and waged war against Xaltocan. Cuauhtitlan independently received ambassadors from Cuernavaca and sent ambassadors to Huexotzinco to ask for aid in overthrowing the Azcapozalcan city-state along with Tenochtitlan, Texcoco, and other polities. There was apparently much friction between nearby Tultitlan and Cuauhtitlan, a result of Azcapotzalco having placed a Tepaneca tlatoani in

Tultitlan and a military governor in Cuauhtitlan. These "horizontal" relationships were less evident after conquest by Tenochtitlan and imposition of a ruler sympathetic to Tenochtitlan.

Cuauhtitlan as a Dependency of Tenochtitlan

Between 1435 and 1519, Cuauhtitlan was governed by Tenochtitlan. Cuauhtitlan was ruled by a military ruler for a time and, later, a tlatoani appointed by Tenochtitlan's ruler was seated. Cuauhtitlan's internal administrative organization was streamlined after its incorporation into the Aztec empire, in such a way that some local elites' political and economic control were reduced. In the final years before the Spanish Conquest, Cuauhtitlan's ruler married a daughter of the ruler of Tenochtitlan.

After its conquest by Tenochtitlan, Cuauhtitlan's laborers were sent to assist in many Triple Alliance projects. Following 1434, no work on public buildings in Cuauhtitlan (except for sacrificial stones and tribute-collection depots) is recorded; before this time, work on local public works—canals, the ruler's palace, and temples—occurred.

The annals suggest there was an increase over time in tribute paid by the province to Tenochtitlan. Its territorial boundaries seem not to have changed greatly after its conquest by Tenochtitlan, but its boundaries shifted somewhat, and the tribute payment hierarchy was reorganized at various intervals. While estates were granted to Cuauhtitlan's ruler and nobles outside its territory, Mexica nobles had estates within its territory.

Cuauhtitlan furnished soldiers for imperial wars. In return, its ruler received booty and land from imperial conquests outside the Valley of Mexico. Cuauhtitlan's rulers attended state rituals and ceremonies. With several other important towns, including Tenochtitlan-Tlatelolco, Cuauhtitlan's pochteca carried on trade in sumptuary goods. In famine years, the people received imported maize from imperial storehouses. Cuauhtitlan was head of a tribute-collection province and ruled several towns, at least one of which had its own tlatoani. Though listed as a Tepaneca dependency on Tlacopan's list of its subject towns, Cuauhtitlan was actually administered more directly by Tenochtitlan. Its place in the political hierarchy of the Valley of Mexico is diagrammed in Figure 4-12.

Chapter 5

Xochimilco

The Place and the People of Xochimilco

The settlement of Xochimilco was located near the shore of freshwater lakes Chalco and Xochimilco at the southern end of the Valley of Mexico (see Fig. 5-1). The lakeshore was lined with swampy areas which the Xochimilca converted into chinampas, or raised fields with canals around them, an invention which greatly increased the agricultural productivity of the lakeshore area. Some chinampas remain to the present day and still produce vegetables and flowers.

To the west of Xochimilco lies an expanse of volcanic rock (El Pedregal), and most of its lakeshore is a narrow delta of deep soil rising quickly to the sierra in the south. Xochimilca territory extended from the settlement of Xochimilco to the south and east, over the Sierra de Ajusco and into the warm valleys of northern Morelos. Altitudes in Xochimilco's territory ranged from 2240 m at the lakeshore to over 2500 m in the upper piedmont, and to 2750 to 2900 m in the sierra, creating a variety of environments. The most productive areas were at lower altitudes; the areas over 2500 m were more susceptible to frost and hence less productive for agriculture. The area, classified as wet and cool, received moderate rainfall (Sanders, Parsons, and Santley 1979:188-89; Parsons et al. 1982:14-33).

From this varied environment, the Xochimilca obtained volcanic stone from the Pedregal, lumber from the sierra, and tropical crops such as cotton, fig tree paper (amatl) for painted codices, and warm-climate fruits from the southern side of the sierra (Paso y Troncoso 1905, VI:237-50, 283-90).

The Urban Center of Xochimilco

Xochimilco was described by Cortés as "a pleasant city called Suchimilco, which is built on the freshwater lake" (Cortés 1971:198-99). In 1519, Xochimilco was surrounded by chinampas and intervening canals. Bridges permitted entry into the city (Torquemada 1975, I:537, II:159).

Like other towns on the lake, Xochimilco had a port from which goods were loaded on canoes and sent elsewhere in the valley (Lewis 1951:170-71). The city contained a sizable market (Torquemada 1975, II:55). Within the city lived craftsmen—carpenters, masons, woodcutters, metalworkers, fishermen, and featherworkers (*Carta de los Caciques* 1970:296). Xochimilco was one of the 12 cities in the Valley of Mexico which had a group of resident pochteca in the Late pre-Hispanic period (Sahagún 1959, Book 9:49; Durán 1967:185).

Spanish chroniclers ranked Xochimilco as one of the five settlements which could be classified as ciudades, "cities" (along with Tenochtitlan, Texcoco, Coyoacan, and Tacuba), as opposed to smaller villas or pueblos (Gibson 1964b:32-33). Torquemada specified that Xochimilco ranked only after Tenochtitlan and Texcoco and that it was a city of more than 20,000 people (Torquemada 1975, I:450; Sanders 1970:409).

Archaeological survey around the periphery of the settlement provided data suggesting that in the Early Aztec period Xochimilco was a "Local Center" of 150 ha, populated by 3750-7500 people, and that in the Late Aztec period it covered 214 ha and contained 5,450 to 10,700 people (Parsons et al. 1982:238; Fig. 5-2). Colonial sources, of course, present varied population estimates for the city, due to the depopulation that occurred after 1520. One document from 1563 states that it contained around 6-7000 tribute payers and 400 nobles, or about 24-32,000 people (*Carta de los Caciques* 1970:299-300). In 1570, Xochimilco contained 5800 tribute payers, and the surrounding rural area contained 2800 tribute payers, suggesting that there

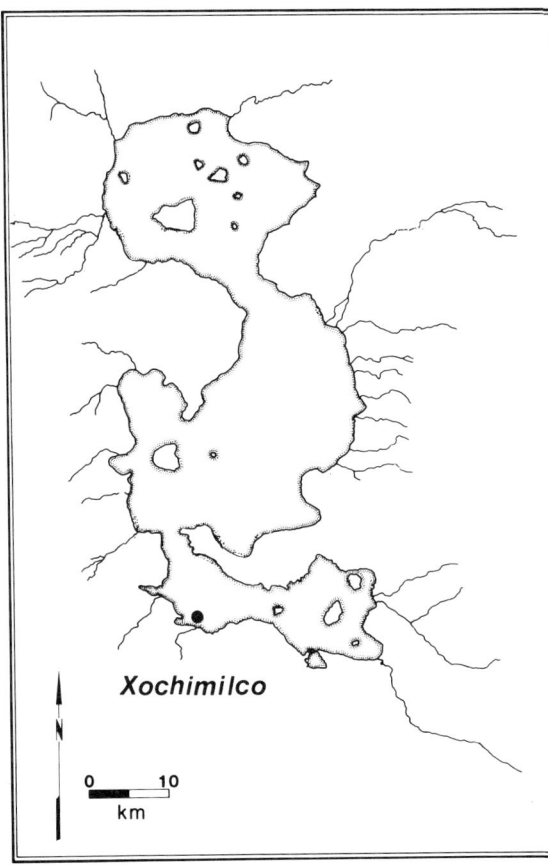

Fig. 5-1. Location of Xochimilco in the Valley of Mexico.

could be up to 23,000 in the city and 11,000 in the territory outside the city (López de Velasco 1971:105; see Fig. 5-3).

The Xochimilca

According to traditional histories, the Xochimilca migrated into the Valley of Mexico in the 1100s (*Codex Boturini* 1964:Pl. 2; Chimalpahin 1965:75). Durán says that

> The Xochimilca were the first to arrive [in the Valley of Mexico] and they made a circuit of the great lake. They saw that the place they occupy today was good earth, so they settled there. [Durán 1964:10]

On arriving in the valley, the Xochimilca settled the place called Xochimilco and occupied land extending over the sierra to the south and east.

Archaeological data now temper Durán's statement that the Xochimilca were the first people to arrive in the valley, for the archaeological survey has revealed that lakeshore and piedmont village settlements existed in the Xochimilco area as early as the Terminal Formative period (300 B.C.-A.D. 150) (Parsons et al. 1982:118, Map 20). Archaeological survey indicates that the area was almost depopulated between 100 B.C. and A.D. 150, perhaps due to movement of population to Teotihuacan. Between A.D. 300 and 750, the area began to be repopulated, and the population continued to grow until 1519 (Sanders, Parsons, and Santley 1979:189-90; Parsons et al. 1982). In addition, excavations in the Xochimilca urban center (Noguera 1970) indicated that although there was Early Aztec occupation (A.D. 1150-1350), the bulk of occupation occurred in the Late Aztec period (A.D. 1350-1520). Survey data likewise show a rise in population in the surrounding area between approximately A.D. 1200 and 1520 (Parsons et al. 1982:156-57, Maps 27-28). Both excavation and survey data indicate that a population increase occurred following the date that traditional histories give for the founding of the city, but they also indicate that settlement existed in the area before the Postclassic period.

According to Texcocan sources, the Xochimilca received the land they settled upon from Tlotzin, the second great Chichimecatl Tecuhtli (Alva Ixtlilxochitl 1975-77, I:411-12). However, the Xochimilca were more often associated with the heritage of the Toltecs. They are characterized as skilled people who were great masters of architecture, carpentry, and other technical arts. The Xochimilca were known for their craftsmanship, particularly lapidary work (Sahagún 1959, Book:79-80). And, as noted before, the city of Xochimilco housed many kinds of craft specialists, a group of pochteca, and a thriving market.

Collectively, the occupants of the chinampa-area towns of Xochimilco, Cuitlahuac, and Mixquic were sometimes called chinampaneca, "the people of the chinampas" (Sahagún 1954, Book 8:52), or "la gente de los setos or cercos de cañas," (the people of the hedges or reed enclosures) (Durán 1967:393). As will be discussed in the section on Xochimilco's territory, the geographical range of the people who called themselves Xochimilca was greater in 1519 than the extent of political control by the city of Xochimilco, suggesting a loss of political control over time and a shrinkage of the Xochimilca political confederation to the immediate environs of the city (Gibson 1964b:13).

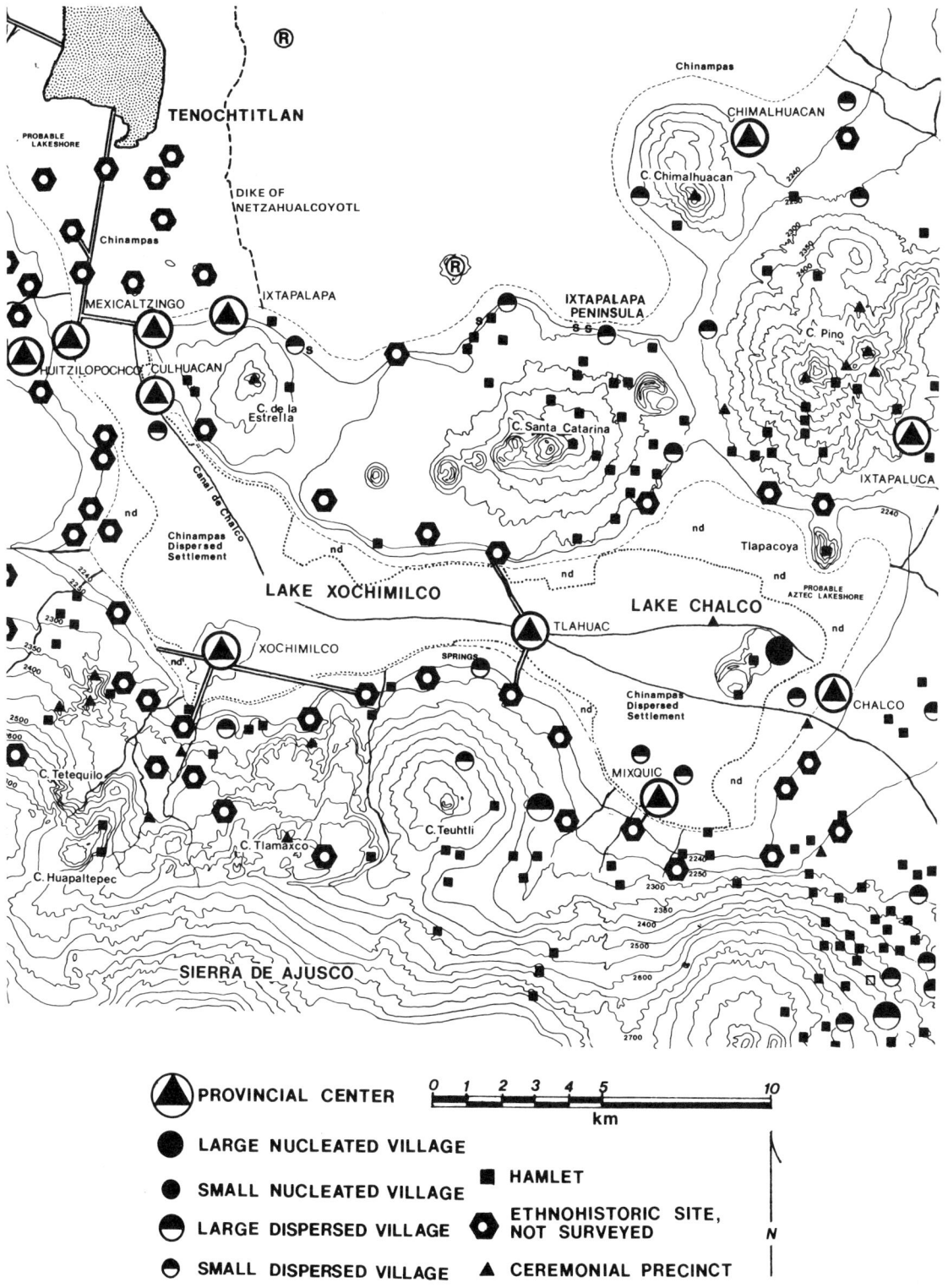

Fig. 5-2. Late Aztec settlements in the Xochimilco area. [Portion of Map 18, Late Horizon, reprinted from *The Basin of Mexico: Ecological Processes in the Evolution of a Civilization*, by William T. Sanders, Jeffrey R. Parsons and Robert S. Santley, Copyright 1979, by Academic Press, Inc.]

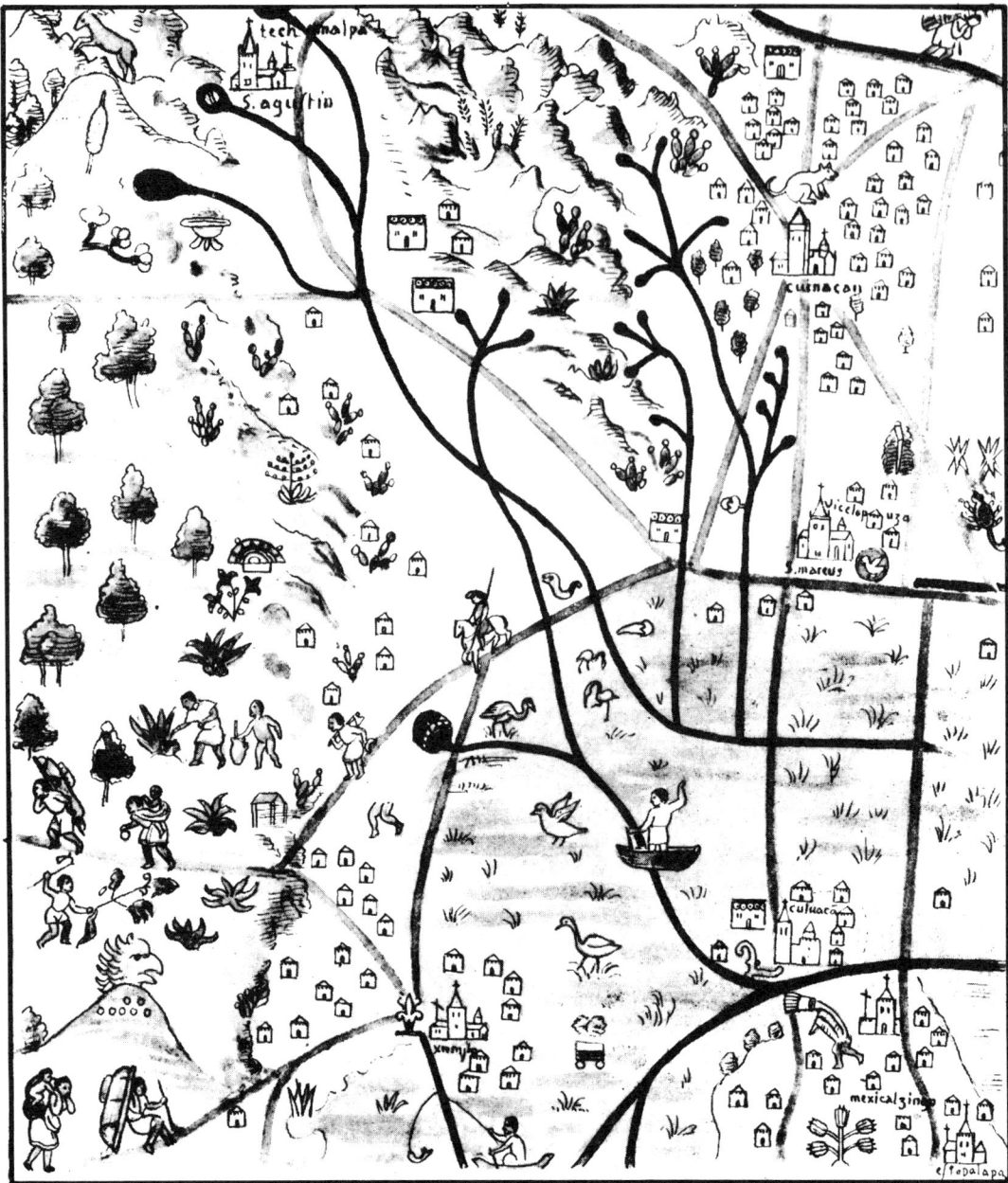

Fig. 5-3. The city of Xochimilco in the mid-1500s, lower center (from Linné 1948). The glyph "xochitl" or flower appears at the left of the church. Lake Xochimilco was fed by springs which originated about one-half league, or 1 mile from the town of Xochimilco; from these springs, streams carried water to the fresh-water lake. The lakeshore was a fertile area producing many flowers and vegetables. People went from place to place in the chinampa area by canoe. In the lake were many fish (Torquemada 1975, II:159).

Xochimilca Deities and Rituals

A number of deities and rituals characterized Xochimilca public life. The Xochimilca's foremost deity was named Cihuacoatl, or Quilaztli (Durán 1971:210; *Historia de los Mexicanos por sus Pinturas* 1941:219). Cihuacoatl, or "snake woman," was associated with fertility and the earth (Caso 1936; Nicholson 1971). She was the "deity of the people of Xochimilco, she was revered and greatly exalted in Mexico, Tetzcoco, and all the land" (Durán 1971:210). Nevertheless, in Xochimilco, her temple was more elaborate than in Mexico or Texcoco. This goddess was particularly worshipped on July 18th, according to Durán, during the festival known as Huey Tecuilhuitl. The goddess was made of stone, dressed like a woman but with ferocious teeth, and her figure was kept in a dark room at the top of the temple on an altar (ibid.:211).

According to Durán, the idol of Cihuacoatl and/or other idols associated with her (called tecuacuiltin, "images of stone," or idols in general) were kept in the outer chamber of her temple and taken out of the temple for ceremonies.

> The idols were taken out whenever it was necessary to perform a special feast for them or when their help was needed. They were carried out in a procession to the woods, to the mountains, or to the caves from which they had taken their names. There, in that cave or in that forest, they were presented with the usual offerings and sacrifices, and the mountain was invoked for some special need—lack of water, a plague or famine, or a future war. When the ceremony had ended, [the image] was returned to the hall, to the place where it always stood. [Durán 1971:211]

Some pilgrimages may have gone to the ceremonial site outside the town of Santa Cruz Acalpixcan, near Xochimilco, at which are found carved boulders inscribed with jaguars, effigy temples, a carved flower, and several other calendrical signs. Since no single motif predominates, the site many be a multi-purpose pilgrimage/ceremonial spot (see Beyer 1924; Noguera 1970; Cook de Leonard and Lemoine Villicāna 1953-54; Marcus 1982; Parsons et al. 1982). An archaeological survey of the site (Noguera 1970) disclosed that Aztec III pottery (A.D. 1430-55) was abundant, but that Aztec IV pottery (A.D. 1455-1519) was less plentiful. In style, the carvings resemble those of the Postclassic period in general, and perhaps they were carved in the Early Aztec period, with ritual activity and manpower being drawn to Tenochtitlan after Xochimilco's conquest by that city, ca. 1430.

Another ritual which took place in Xochimilco honored the four deities of the lapidaries "because the grandfathers [and] fathers of all the lapidaries came from there. There was the beginning; there they took their origin. It was their native land" (Sahagún 1959, Book 9:80). These deities—two male and two female—were called Chiconaui, Naualpilli, Macuilcalli, and Cinteotl. The celebration took place on the day 9 Dog, and four slaves dressed to resemble the four deities were sacrificed. "And at that time, when their feast day arrived, [their] old men, all the master lapidaries, provided song [and] held vigil during the night for those who were to die at dawn—all the likenesses [of these gods]. All rejoiced; they enjoyed the feasting" (ibid.). In Late pre-Hispanic times, ca. 1500, this festival began in Xochimilco and then moved to Tenochtitlan for completion.

Two additional deities particular to the Xochimilca were Amimitl and Atlahuac, deities of the chinampas and of the rivers (Noguera 1970:95). The Xochimilca worshipped other Nahua deities, as demonstrated by the excavation of figurines in Xochimilco which portray the deities Xolotl, Xochitl, and others (ibid.:108).

To summarize, Xochimilco had its own distinctive deities and festivals; it also originated an important festival for craftsmen. Its urban temple was the focus of an annual festival for its people, and ceremonial sites outside the city were the loci of rituals for its people.

Extent of Xochimilca Territory

According to tradition, the Xochimilca were one of the first Nahuatl-speaking groups that migrated into the Valley of Mexico from "Aztlan" in the 1100s (Durán 1964:10; *Codex Boturini* 1964:Pl. 2; Chimalpahin 1965:75). The Xochimilca territory originally extended into the sierra to the south and east of the urban center (Fig. 5-4).

> They took possession of the mountain ridge that today belongs to the Xochimilca nation and which stretched as far as a town called Tuchimilco or Ocopetlayuca, by another name. Other towns that form part of this nation and are called by the same name include Ocuituco, Tetelaneyapan, Tlamimilulpan, Xumiltepec, Tlacotepec, Zacualpa and Temoac, Tlayacapa, and Totolapa and Tepoztlan, Chimalhuacan, Ehecatzinco and Tepetlixpan, and with all the other towns subject to Chimalhuacan. All of these are part of the Xochimilca nation, including Cuitlahuac, Mixquic, and Culhuacan. [Durán 1964:10]

Dependencies of Xochimilco such as Tetela and Hueyapan reported in 1581 that in the past they had been subjects of Xochimilco and sent tribute and personal service to the city (Paso y Troncoso 1905, VI:283, 285). The pueblos of Tetela and Hueyapan sent tribute of honey, henequen (agave) mantas, fowl, and maize to Xochimilco (Paso y Troncoso 1905, VI:283).

The territory that Xochimilco controlled diminished over time. In 1301, two peripheral communities to the southeast—Chimalhuacan and

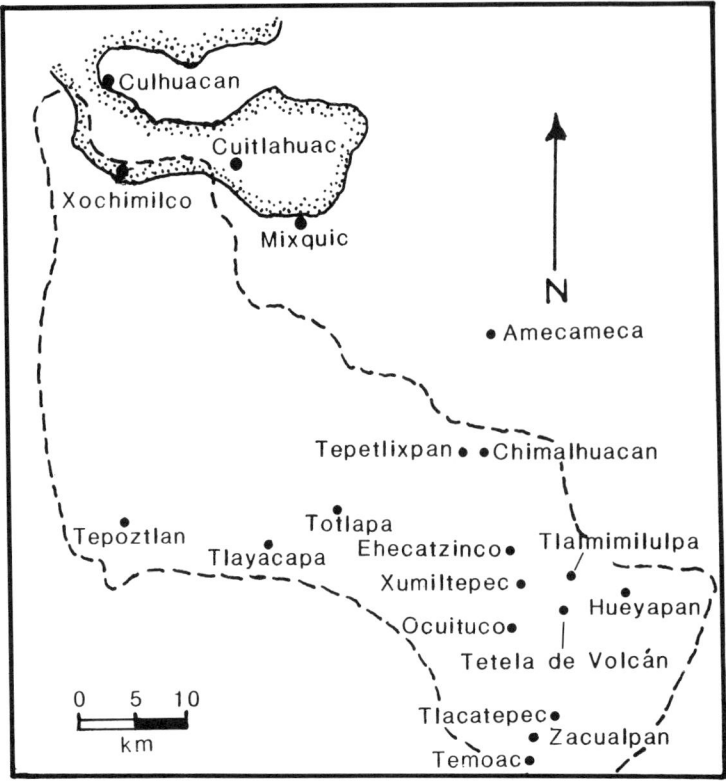

Fig. 5-4. Extent of the Xochimilca confederation before 1430 (after Parsons et al. 1982:77).

Tepetlixpan—seceded and joined the Chalca confederation (Chimalpahin 1965:173, 176, 178). If Mixquic, Cuitlahuac, and Culhuacan had ever been dependencies of Xochimilco, they were not in 1519 (and had not been for a long time, according to Chimalpahin [1958] and the *Relaciones geográficas* for Culhuacan and Cuitlahuac [Paso y Troncoso 1905, VI; Gibson 1964b]).

Furthermore, when the Triple Alliance conquered Xochimilco in 1430, the rulers of Tenochtitlan and Texcoco took tribute-paying plots for themselves and other nobles in the chinampa areas of Xochimilco and in other parts of its territory, reducing the income-producing territory of the Xochimilca rulers, and hence reducing their control over their territory. "Under Aztec authority the real area of influence of Xochimilco was reduced to the lakeshore between the Pedregal and the border of Cuitlahuac, and to the adjacent upland communities to the south" (Gibson 1964b:13; Fig. 5-5). By 1519, Xochimilco was no longer an allied group of city-states, but one city-state among many administered separately by the empire.

Xochimilco's Political System

Officials and Titles

Xochimilco had three tlatoque, each of whom governed a separate jurisdiction. These three divisions were named Olac, Tepetenchi, and Tecpan (*Carta de los Caciques* 1970:296; Carrasco 1977:230). Tepetenchi was the largest and most important divison, whereas Olac was the smallest and had the fewest nobles, though it was the center for tribute collection (Gibson 1964b). Each division, called a tecpan or cabecera in early Colonial documents, had subdivisions called tlaxillacaltin or barrios. In Tepetenchi, there were 12 barrios; in Tecpan there were 7, and in Olac, there were 7 (Carrasco 1977).

In addition to the general histories of the Valley of Mexico which mention Xochimilco in passing, Xochimilco's pre-Hispanic political organization can be partially reconstructed from Colonial documents which describe its administrators and the economic organization supporting them (*Carta de*

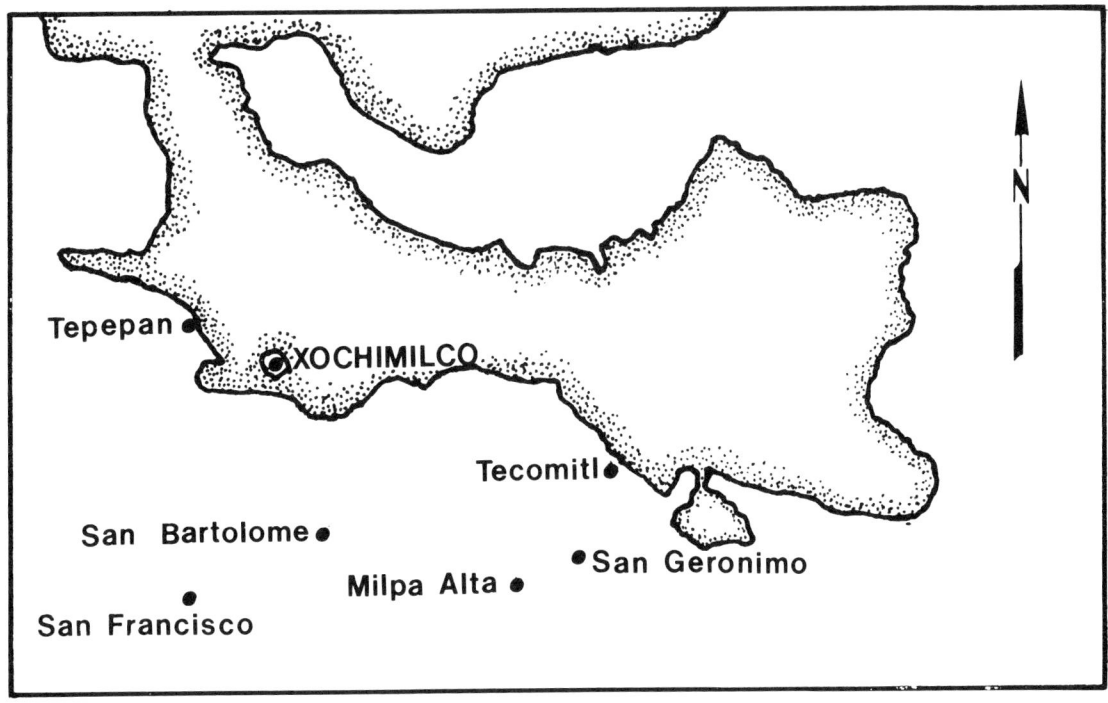

Fig. 5-5. Xochimilco's territory, ca. 1519, showing some of its dependencies.

los Caciques 1970; Kraus Collection, Library of Congress, MS 140 [1548] published by Carrasco 1977; AGN, Vínculos, Vol. 279). These documents suggest the kinds of officials that formed the organization of political decision-making in pre-Hispanic Xochimilco.

In 1563, in the three tecpans, or jurisdictions consisting of a tlatoani and his dependents, there were 3 *caciques* and 80 principales, or nobles, eligible for political offices. In each tecpan were four or five major officials who assisted their tlatoani. These officials had varied titles, including tlacochcalcatl, tlacateuctli, tecpanecatl, cuauhnochtli, tiçonquiquacatl, tzicouacatl, tiçonauacatl, and tepetenchicalqui (Carrasco 1977:230-31; see Table 5-1).

The titles of these major officals are familiar from descriptions of Tenochtitlan's officials. Tlacochcalcatl and tlacateccatl are always listed as members of the council of four advisors to Tenochtitlan's ruler, and the title of tizocyahuacatl refers to a military official. Quauhnochtli is an administrator or warrior (*Codex Mendoza* 1925:65, 67; Sahagún 1959, Book 9:47). In Tenochtitlan, these titles designated general-purpose advisors to the ruler rather than officials with specific duties, and in Xochimilco these officials apparently served as advisors to their tlatoque as well. These advisors performed diverse duties; as the document from 1548 says, "they helped them [the *caciques*] govern" (Carrasco 1977:235).

Appointment to administrative offices, according to the document of 1548, was through election by peers. If any official left office, the position was filled by election by the "principales y vezinos"—

TABLE 5-1
TITLES OF XOCHIMILCO'S ADMINISTRATORS

Tepetenchi	Tecpan	Olac
1. tlatoani	1. tlatoani	1. tlatoani
2. tepetenchicalqui or tepetenchicalcatl teuctli	2. tecpanecatl	2. cuauhnochtli
3. tlacateuctli	3. tlacatecuhtli	3. tiçonauacatl
4. tlacochcalcatl teuctli	4. tlacochcalcatl teuctli	4. tlacochcalcatl teuctli
5. tiçonquiyquacatl	5. tzicouacatl teuctli	—

(Source: Carrasco 1977)

nobles and residents—of their division or tecpan (Carrasco 1977:232). (However, since each officeholder described in the document also had patrimonial land, it seems probable that all these offices were filled by members of the elite class.) In the Colonial period, these four or five main offices survived independently of the Colonial municipal offices such as alcalde, regidor, and alguacil, which were tied to specific duties and salaries (*Carta de los Caciques* 1970:300).

Other officials, whose social status is less clear, were leaders of the craftsmen, mayordomos, and barrio functionaries. Twice a year, these officials received mantas and various products from the tlatoani of their tecpan, items that were collected from the tribute payers at 80-day intervals. Officials receiving this income were the master woodcutters, canoe makers, carpenters, tequitlatoque, mayordomos, singers, workers in the church, and other barrio officials (AGN, Vínculos, Vol. 279, Fols. 76-78; Carrasco 1977).

Economic Support of Xochimilco's Administrators

Elite officeholders received goods and labor from the commoners. Laborers performed daily household tasks and brought wood and food to elite households at specified intervals—daily, weekly, bi-weekly, and yearly. Twice a year, Xochimilco's tlatoque (referred to as *caciques* in Colonial-period documents) collected canoes made by craftsmen and mantas from the commoners; these items were redistributed twice a year among the principales, tequitlatos, mayordomos, leaders of craftsmen, singers and workers in the church, and other barrio officials. Although the document specifies that this procedure was requested in Colonial times by the commoners, it may represent a traditional practice. In addition, tribute in gold was paid out as salaries to all the officials of the town (AGN, Vínculos, Vol. 279, Fols. 76-78; Table 5-2; Fig. 5-6).

The three tlatoque had *tierras de señorío*, or lands of lordship that went with their offices. See Figure 5-7 for an illustration of fields granted to Don Martín Serón y Villasañes in 1582, by the community officials.

The tlatoque and other high officals also had patrimonial, or inherited lands which were worked by the commoners, and they were exempt from paying tribute because of their status. The 1563 document states that there were about 400 nobles in the city (plus 6000-7000 tribute payers):

> we say that in the said city, today are up to 400 natives, a little more or less, who are noble knights, nobles of known position and of free and known family; they and their ancestors from time immemorial, have been in the position not to pay tributes—neither service nor money—[they are] neither royalty nor appointed, and when Moctezuma tyrannized this kingdom, he preserved this nobility. [*Carta de los Caciques* 1970:299-300]

These nobles received tribute in labor from the commoners, who either worked their patrimonial lands, or if craftsmen, provided skilled labor for them.

> From time immemorial in this place and before the time when the Spaniards came, the *caciques* and heads of the said city of Xochimilco, by way of patrimony and lordship, were served by all the officials, carpenters, masons, woodsmen, smiths, fishermen, and feather workers, and those who made jewelry, and other officials, and [officials] of the market and other natives served them in tending their fields, and they gave them complete obedience, giving them tribute and gifts, and today they do not receive these things. They are dispossessed, and though it is a thing of inheritance and lordship, we beg Your Magesty to order restitution of these things. [*Carta de los Caciques* 1970:296]

Elites in Xochimilco possessed inherited lands which were tended by the commoners for them. The commoners worked one-quarter of the lands of office holders, and the other three-quarters were either left fallow or worked by sharecroppers (terrazgueros) who received one-quarter of the harvest as payment. In Xochimilco, patrimonial lands were a specific, standardized size—400 brazas (1 braza = ca. 1.6 m)—long and narrow proportions suitable to the measurement of chinampas, though the same measurements applied to the dry land fields (Carrasco 1977:233).

Thus, in the Colonial period, approximately thirty years after the Spanish Conquest, nobles in Xochimilco received produce and labor through a system similar to that of pre-Hispanic times. Moreover, the redistribution of goods to officials followed a traditional pattern of ceremonial giving at specific intervals (though mixed in Colonial times with monetary compensation in the form of monthly salaries).

From this discussion of the officials and their economic support, we turn to the patterns of rulership in the city-state of Xochimilco, as they can be reconstructed from traditional histories and Colonial-period documents.

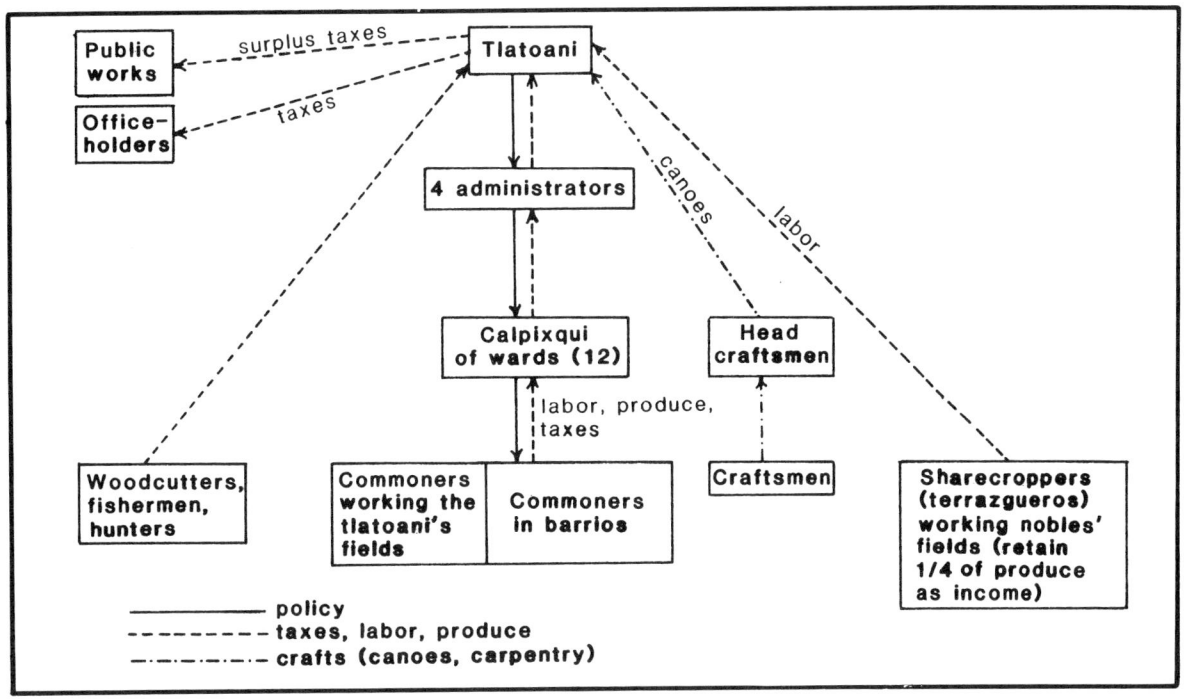

Fig. 5-6. Organization of taxes and labor in Xochimilco's tecpan or cabecera of Tepetenchi, ca. 1548 (derived from the document published by Carrasco [1977]).

Rulers of Xochimilco

In an early period, Xochimilco had two rulers—one from the urban center of Xochimilco (this individual was called Yacaxapo tecuhtli) and another from Milpa Alta (called Pachimalcatl tecuhtli) (Durán 1967:105-06). However, in 1519, Xochimilco had three tlatoque, one each governing Tepetenchi, Tecpan, and Olac (Gibson 1964b:41).

One problem in reconstructing the king lists of Xochimilco's tecpans is that general histories about the Valley of Mexico, which were written outside of the city of Xochimilco, often refer to a single Xochimilca ruler without naming from which division the individual came. However, scattered notes on Xochimilco's rulers found in native histories and in Colonial documents allow a partial reconstruction of the king lists of Xochimilco's three tecpans.

Xochimilco's leadership patterns were disrupted by political problems even before the formation of the Triple Alliance. Xochimilco was conquered by Azcapotzalco as early as the late 1300s (Anales de Cuauhtitlan 1945:66), and along with other conquered city-states, Xochimilco was ruled by one of Tezozomoc's sons. This Tepaneca ruler, named Tepanquizqui, ruled from 1426-27 (Anales de Cuauhtitlan 1938:193, 1945:37, 47) but was deposed by the Tenochtitlan-Texcocan alliance, which had destroyed the Azcapotzalcan state by 1430.

Native lords of Xochimilco regained the rulership of the Xochimilca in the short time that it was independent. When Xochimilco was conquered by the Triple Alliance in 1430, there may have been as many as five leaders (Alvarado Tezózomoc 1975:272; Pérez Zevallos 1981:108-09).

Tepetenchi appears to have had the longest-lasting dynasty in Xochimilco, and it may have been the most important, judging from its size and influence in the Colonial period. Alva Ixtlilxochitl, Texcoco's historian, lists the rulers of Xochimilco, and other documents, such as the Anales de Cuauhtitlan and Chimalpahin's histories, which identify the Xochimilca rulers' lineages, indicate that most of these names refer to rulers of Tepetenchi. Tepetenchi's king list covers as many as 16 rulers and at least 170 years, perhaps from approximately A.D. 1346 to 1519, (see Table 5-3a).

Tecpan's rulers are first mentioned in 1446, when one was deposed by Moctezuma I and Tlacaelel, as punishment for his participation in the

Tlatelolca rebellion (Chimalpahin 1965:98). This ruler, Quequecholtzin (d. 1446), was replaced by Xihuitletemoc, who ruled from 1460-77 (Table 5-3b lists the rulers of Tecpan and is based largely on Chimalpahin's brief notes on events in Xochimilco).

The dynasty of Olac appears late, and it is possible that it was created by Moctezuma II, who apparently placed his brother Macuilmalinaltzin in the office (Table 5-3c; see also Pérez Zavallos 1981:114-17).

> ...he began to tyrannize the lords of the towns and cities and to give lordships to his relatives and to take them from those to whom they came by law and thus ... another he placed in Xochimilco, who was named Omacatl... [Durán 1967:516]
>
> The sixth [son of Moctezuma], named Macuilmalinal, went to rule in Xochimilco; his son was named Don Francisco de Guzmán Omacatzin; and Macuilmalinaltzin died in a war in Atlixco. [*Crónica Mexicáyotl* 1945:137]

The genealogy of the rulers of Olac is found in a Colonial-period document which traces these rulers back to the ruling family of Tenochtitlan (Fig. 5-8; AGN, Vínculos, Vol. 279; Reyes 1977).

The creation of a new rulership and its superimposition on Xochimilco is one example of the Mexica creating a tlatoani office in a city which already had an indigenous ruler. A similar situation is documented in Azcapotzalco, where a Tenochca dynasty as well as a Tepaneca one existed at the time of the Spanish Conquest (Gibson 1964b). In these two cases the Mexica rulers created a new dynasty rather than taking over an established one, as they did in many other city-states. Unfortunately there is apparently no information about whether the Mexica rulers married the daughters of Xochimilca rulers, as occurred in other city-states (a result of which was that the offspring of the marriage were both heirs to the local rulership and relatives of the Mexica dynasty). It follows that Olac was the locus of imperial tribute collection for Xochimilco. Tribute collection may have been a task the ruler of Olac supervised.

Succession to Rulership in Xochimilco

Ixtlilxochitl reports that the office of tlatoani in Xochimilco was inherited from brother to brother, and if there were no brothers to inherit the office, rulership went to a close male relative of the ruler. He says that this practice explains why there are so many rulers listed for Xochimilco, with such short reigns (though the number of rulers in Ixtlilxochitl's list also is a result of combining the names of rulers of more than one tecpan into the list—see Table 5-3a-c). According to Alva Ixtlilxochitl:

> The reason that there have been so many lords in Xochimilco in so short a time is that sons did not succeed fathers, but brothers [succeeded] brothers, although they preserved the line so that a cousin inherited from a brother when all the uncles had perished. This is the true origin of the Xochimilca, taken from their ancient histories. [Alva Ixtlilxochitl 1975-77, I:411-12]

If the practice of brother-to-brother inheritance of office actually existed, it did not persist long into the Colonial period, for the document of 1548 states that if a *cacique* died, his oldest son would take over, and only if he couldn't would another near relative take the office (Carrasco 1977:244).

In the towns dependent upon Xochimilco, lordship was inherited, but the ruler had to be approved by the rulers of Xochimilco and, later, of Tenochtitlan.

> Their government was through the representatives and governors that the lords of the capitals, to which they were subjects, appointed them, natives of the same pueblo; those who governed, governed until their death, and they were not deprived of that office or charge except for a serious crime, and neither sons nor other relatives chosen by the said lords inherited the offices, and some say that one had to have that choice approved by the king and council of Mexico. [Paso y Troncoso 1905, VI:286]

Marriages between Xochimilco's and Tenochtitlan's Elites

As we have seen above, Olac's rulers were from the ruling dynasty of Tenochtitlan, and hence some of Xochimilco's nobles traced their genealogy back to the Mexica rulers Tizoc and Axayacatl (AGN, Vínculos, Vol. 279, Exp. 1; Reyes 1977; see Fig. 5-8). Unfortunately, the histories of the Valley of Mexico do not enlighten us about the Xochimilca rulers' marriage alliances with noble lineages from other city-states.

Xochimilco's Pre-Imperial Political Alliances

Said to have been founded in the 1100s, Xochimilco is reported to have been independent, subject to Culhuacan, and to have ruled Culhuacan in the 1300s (Durán 1967:22; Chimalpahin 1958:5; Alva Ixtlilxochitl 1975-77, I:411-12). This disagreement no doubt results from the early rivalry be-

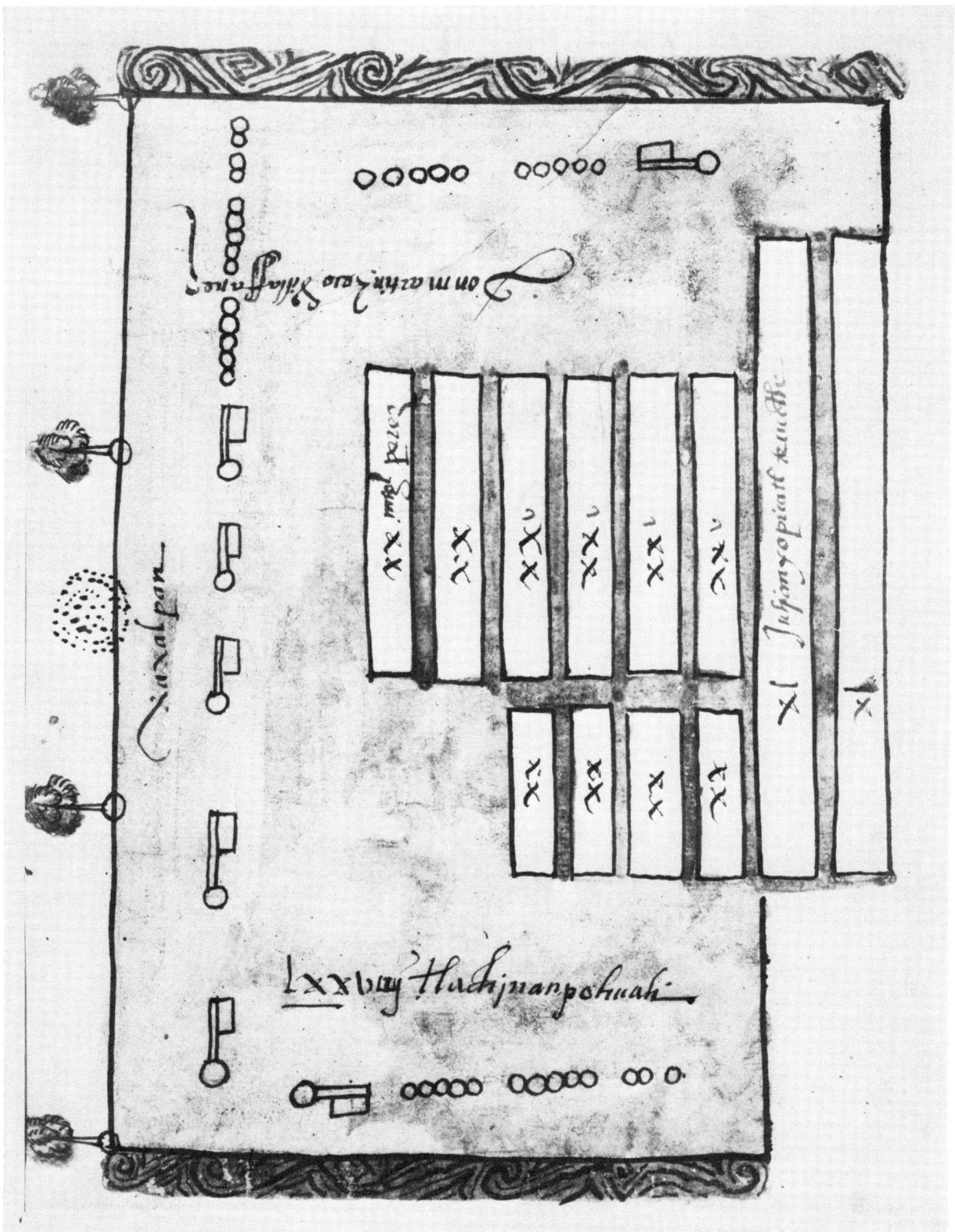

Fig. 5-7. Diagram of fields granted to Don Martín, *cacique* of Tepetenchi, Xochimilco, in 1582 (AGN, Vínculos, Vol. 279, Fol. 78). [Photograph reproduced by permission of the Archivo General de la Nación, Mexico.]

TABLE 5-2
INCOME OF DON MARTÍN, *CACIQUE* OF TEPETENCHI (TECPAN OF XOCHIMILCO), 1548

Land:
21 sections of land, 20 × 400 brazas were Don Martín's as a perquisite of his office. The 12 barrios worked 5 sections for him, half on dry land and half in the chinampas
20 sections of inherited land had the same dimensions. The community worked 5 sections for him, as above

Daily Income:
5 loads of wood
600 cacao beans
5 women to make bread for him
4 tlapixque (guardians) for his house

Weekly Income:
2 fowl
400 chili peppers
1 cake of salt
1 basket of pumpkin seeds
1 basket of tomatoes

Bi-Weekly Income:
2 loads of ocote (torch pine) from the woodcutters
10 loads of wood from the woodcutters
10 rabbits
2 handfuls of 20 each, of incense
1 "braza" of wood from the canoe makers

Twice Yearly:
240 canoes (120 each time)
⅓ were for Don Martín
⅓ were for the barrio principales
⅓ were for the barrios who worked Don Martín's chimampa land
1 manta per house, collected and then re-distributed to principales, tequitlatoque, mayordomos, carpenters, singers, workers in the church and other barrio officials

Every 80 Days:
50 pesos salary, collected in the form of cacao beans and/or coins from the tribute payers

(Carrasco 1977)

TABLE 5-3A
RULERS OF TEPETENCHI XOCHIMILCO[1]

Name	Length of Reign (Years)
1. Huetzolin	?
2. Actonale	23
3. Tlahuitecuhtli	7
4. Atlahuica	9
5. Tecuhtonale	11
6. Atlahuica II	10
7. Quauhquetzale Tecuhtli	12
8. Tlaxcozihuapili (woman)	12
9. Cazcotzin Tecuhtli	32
10. Xaopayntzin[2]	18
11. Oztlo	14
12. Ozelotl	4
13. [Quetzalpoyotzin][3]	[22]
14. Tlilhuatzin	5
15. [Xihuiltemoc][4]	[17]
16. [Ihuicatlaminatzin]	[14]
17. Xihuiltemoc II	16
18. [Tlacoyohuatzin][5]	[17]
19. Opochquiyauhtzin (Don Luis)[6]	
20. Don Martín Serón	

[1]According to Alva Ixtlilxochitl [1975–77, I:411–12], who lists rulers of all three tecpans of Xochimilco together.
[2]Tepanquizqui, ruler of Xochimilco under Azcapotzalco (1426–27), is not listed by Ixtlilxochitl, perhaps because he was Tepaneca and not Xochimilca (*Anales de Cuauhtitlan* 1938:193, 1945:37, 47).
[3]The rulers deposed by Moctezuma I and Tlacaelel in 1446 were Tepanquizqui of Tepetenchi (whom the *Anales de Cuauhtitlan* lists as a Tepaneca ruler; see above), and Quequecholtzin of Tecpan (Chimalpahin 1965:98).
[4]Ixtlilxochitl lists Xihuitletemoc as a ruler of Tepetenchi, but according to Chimalpahin, Xihuitletemoc was seated as ruler of Tecpan in 1460 and died in 1477. He was replaced by Ilhuicaminatzin (Chimalpahin 1965:203, 210).
[5]*Anales de Cuauhtitlan* (1945:63) lists Tlatolcatzin as the name of the Xochimilca ruler in 1519; Chimalpahin (1965:229) says the ruler of Tecpan at the time was named Tlicoyohualtzin, so probably this individual is a tlatoani of Tecpan. Based on sources other than Ixtlilxochitl, rulers 13, 15, 16, and 18, above, may be rulers of Tecpan. See Table 5-3b.
[6]The *caciques* in 1548 were Don Martín Cortés (Tepetenchi), Don Joaquin de Santa María (Tecpan), and Don Francisco Guzmán Omacatzin (Olac) (Carrasco 1977).

TABLE 5-3B
RULERS OF TECPAN XOCHIMILCO

Name	Years of Reign
Quequecholtzin	deposed 1446
Xihuitletemoc	1460–1477
Ilhuicaminatzin	1477– ?
Tlicoyohualtzin	1519
Don Joaquín de Santa María	1548

Source: Chimalpahin 1965:98, 203, 210, 229.

tween the two polities. In one war, ca. 1303, the Xochimilca fought the Culhua (who were aided by the Mexica). According to Mexica sources, the Xochimilca lost to the Culhua. This story is illustrated in the *Codex Boturini*, which shows the Mexica presenting bags of Xochimilca ears to the ruler of Culhuacan, to prove how many had been killed (1964:Pl. 21; see also Torquemada 1975, I:90; *Historia de los Mexicanos por sus Pinturas* 1941:226). Although the Xochimilca fled to the mountains, many were captured and sacrificed (*Anales de Tlatelolco* 1948:39-40).

The Xochimilca also experienced conflict with polities on their southern and eastern borders.

TABLE 5-3C
RULERS OF OLAC XOCHIMILCO

Name	Years of Reign
Macuilmalinaltzin	1503–1521
Don Francisco Guzmán Omacatzin	? –1548

Sources: AGN, Vínculos, Vol. 279, Exp. 1; Reyes 1977; *Crónica Mexicayotl* 1949:136–39.

Their southeastern border was a hostile one, and the Xochimilca from Totolapa and Tlayacapa fought with Huexotzinco, Tlaxcala, and Cholula (Gibson 1964b:13).

The Xochimilca resisted the expanding polity of Xaltocan in the northern part of the valley, which they fought in A.D. 1299, and also Azcapotzalco (Chimalpahin 1958:118). Xochimilco was reportedly conquered by Acamapichtli (ruler of Tenochtitlan from 1370 to 1396) as an agent or a mercenary of Azcapotzalco (*Codex Mendoza* 1925:2v; *Anales de Cuauhtitlan* 1945:66; *Anales de Tlatelolco* 1948:52; *Historia de los Mexicanos por sus Pinturas* 1941:299), and Xochimilco was finally defeated by Azcapotzalco, and its rulers were replaced in 1426-27 by one of Tezozomoc's sons (*Anales de Cuauhtitlan* 1938:193, 1945:37). Tezozomoc sent his sons to rule several newly-conquered dependencies, including Xochimilco, and these towns were the first ones attacked by the Tenochca and Acolhua when they began to attack the Azcapotzalcan empire (*Anales de Cuauhtitlan* 1938:232).

Xochimilco was allied with Chalco (Durán 1964:10), although two Xochimilca towns were said to have left the Xochimilca and joined the Chalca confederation in 1301 (Chimalpahin 1965:173-78). Xochimilco's rulers, along with those of other Valley of Mexico polities, protested the Mexica replacement of Chalco's rulers with tax collectors in 1410 (ibid.:187). In 1473, the Xochimilca aided the Tlatelolca in their rebellion against the Mexica of Tenochtitlan (Torquemada 1975, I:176).

Thus, prior to the Triple Alliance, the independent city-state of Xochimilco warred with its neighbor, Culhuacan, and was later conquered by Azcapotzalco. Though it was one of the first polities conquered by the Triple Alliance (as described below in the section on conquest and incorporation into the empire), its rulers attempted later, with the Tlatelolca, to rebel.

Xochimilco and the Aztec Empire

Conquest by the Triple Alliance

Xochimilco was one of the first cities conquered by the anti-Tepaneca armies, led by Itzcoatl, Nezahualcoyotl, and others. Xochimilco fell in 1430 to the Triple Alliance forces, and thus Mexica conquest lists claim it as a conquest of Itzcoatl (*Codex Mendoza* 1925:6; *Anales de Cuauhtitlan* 1945:47, 66; Torquemada 1975, I:148-49). The Tepaneca ruler of Xochimilco, along with Tepaneca from Tultitlan, Tenayuca, Azcapotzalco, Tlacopan, and Coyoacan, and some of the Xochimilca, fled to the mountains (*Anales de Cuauhtitlan* 1945:47; *Codex Ramírez* 1920:106; Torquemada 1975, I:148-49; Alva Ixtlilxochitl 1975-77, I:444).

The remaining Xochimilca surrendered to the Mexica:

> they discussed among themselves surrendering to Itzcoatl, which they did, entering his presence with rings of precious stones, chains or necklaces, of gold, and many other riches, with which they were presented [to him]. Itzcoatl received them with good will, and he accepted his present, and from this time they remained as his tribute payers. Returning from this war, the Mexica were very pleased.... [Torquemada 1975, I:148-49]

As a penalty, the Xochimilca were ordered by Itzcoatl and Tlacaelel to build a causeway 3 brazas wide (ca. 5 m) from Coyoacan to Tenochtitlan, along with the conquered Tepaneca city-states of Coyoacan and Azcapotzalco (Durán 1967:111-12). The Mexica and Acolhua rulers appropriated some fields in Xochimilco, giving as rewards two portions to nobles and two to warriors, and taking land as well for the support of the imperial rulers' palaces (Durán 1967:111-17; Alva Ixtlilxochitl 1975-77, I:445-46).

Xochimilco as a Dependency of the Triple Alliance

Effects of Conquest

Rulership. As discussed in the section on rulership, the limited data available on the empire's manipulation of rulership in Xochimilco shows that: (1) one ruler of Xochimilco was killed in 1477 for participating in the Tlatelolca rebellion (Chimalpahin 1965:210; Torquemada 1975, I:180-81); (2) in later years, Moctezuma II placed a relative in office as ruler of Olac. Thus, the data available show that over time, Tenochtitlan meddled considerably with rulership in Xochimilco.

Tribute. As a result of conquest, Xochimilco lost land within its territory to Mexica and Acolhua nobles. It paid tribute regularly through the central tribute collection province, Petlacalco.

Xochimilco itself does not appear in the *Codex Mendoza* as a tribute collection spot, but one division of Xochimilco, Olac, does (*Codex Mendoza* 1925:20). The place-name Xochimilco appears in the *Codex Mendoza*, in the list of the places conquered by Mexica rulers, as a stylized field with flowers on it (*Codex Mendoza* 1925), because Xochimilco means "in the field of flowers" (in Nahuatl, xochitl means "flower," and milli means "field," or "cultivated field," as in milpa). The glyph for Olac, which appears as part of the tribute province of Petlacalco in the *Codex Mendoza*, shows a rubber ball (Nahuatl: olotic) with water (Nahuatl: atl) over the glyph for Xochimilco. Olac thus is believed to be the section of Xochimilco where tribute was collected for Tenochtitlan (see *Codex Mendoza* 1925:20; Peñafiel 1885:155, 241).

The tribute of the entire Petlacalco province was clothing (65 warrior costumes, 2400 loads of mantas of "twisted cloth," 800 loads of colored mantas, 400 loincloths, and 400 items of women's clothing) and food (1 bin of chia, 2 bins of amaranth) (Barlow 1949:133). Tribute paid by Xochimilco alone is not quantified, but it is likely that Xochimilco provided produce grown in the chinampas (see below). In addition, the Xochimilca were assessed a unique tribute: they provided flowers for the fiestas at Tenochtitlan (Torquemada 1975, II:60).

The Xochimilca also supplied labor for imperial building projects. The Xochimilca provided up to 30,000 workers before the Spanish Conquest, and 6000-7000 in 1563 (*Carta de los Caciques* 1970:298). In 1563, they regularly supplied 300 men for labor and construction that the Spaniards requested (ibid.).

Xochimilco's dependencies paid tribute to Tenochtitlan, via Xochimilco (Paso y Troncoso 1905, VI:285). Ocuituco, Tetela, and Jumiltepec sent wood and flowers: "all of the province was under one lord and all together sent flowers to Moctezuma, except for the estancia of Ayaçingo that gave wood to Ocuituco. . ." (Gerhard 1970b:110). Following this precedent, in the early Colonial period, documents report that Xochimilca nobles were tax administrators in its dependencies (Ayer MS 1121, Fol. 88).

Territory. The archaeological survey data suggest that although between A.D. 1200 and 1400, most of the population in the southern Valley of Mexico lived in nucleated settlements on islands or on the lakeshore, that later there was state-planned development of chinampas in the area. Between A.D. 1400 and 1600, population spread out into the chinampa areas, as indicated by the many housemounds found in the now-drained areas that produced pottery dating to this period. The regular orientation of these chinampas, compared to more haphazard orientations of earlier chinampas, as well as the ceramic evidence, suggest that large numbers of chinampas were constructed at the same time, as planned projects. Ethnohistoric documents report that the large-scale, planned, and state-administered chinampa-building took place during the reigns of the Mexica tlatoque Itzcoatl (A.D. 1426-40) and Moctezuma Ilhuicamina (A.D. 1440-67) (Parsons 1976:236).

Furthermore, following the Triple Alliance conquest of Xochimilco in 1430, Mexica and Acolhua rulers took plots of land in Xochimilco for their support, and they distributed plots of land among officials and deserving warriors. These plots of land were in both the chinampa area and other parts of Xochimilco's territory, including the places called Coapan, Chilchoc, Teoztitlan, Xuchitepec, Motlaxauhcan, Xalpan, Moyotepec, Acapulco, Tulyahualco, Tlacatepec, "y todos las partes. . ." (Alvarado Tezózomoc 1975:276-77). The payment of produce from these places to the capitals reduced the income of Xochimilco's rulers, and it also represented a large amount of labor and goods taken from the population of Xochimilco.

As noted above, the nobles of Xochimilco lost control of sections of land, which were granted to Mexica and Acolhua nobles. The area of influence of the city-state of Xochimilco was also reduced, so that the political territory of Xochimilco, by 1519, consisted of only a small area extending from the lakeshore to the sierra (Gibson 1964b:13, Fig. 5-5).

Participation in Imperial Activities

As a dependency of the Triple Alliance, Xochimilco was involved in the empire's wars, long-distance trade, rituals, and construction of monuments in the capital. In addition to regularly scheduled tribute payments, the Xochimilca had to provide labor and goods for *ad hoc* imperial activities, some of which are detailed below.

Warfare. When the Triple Alliance leaders de-

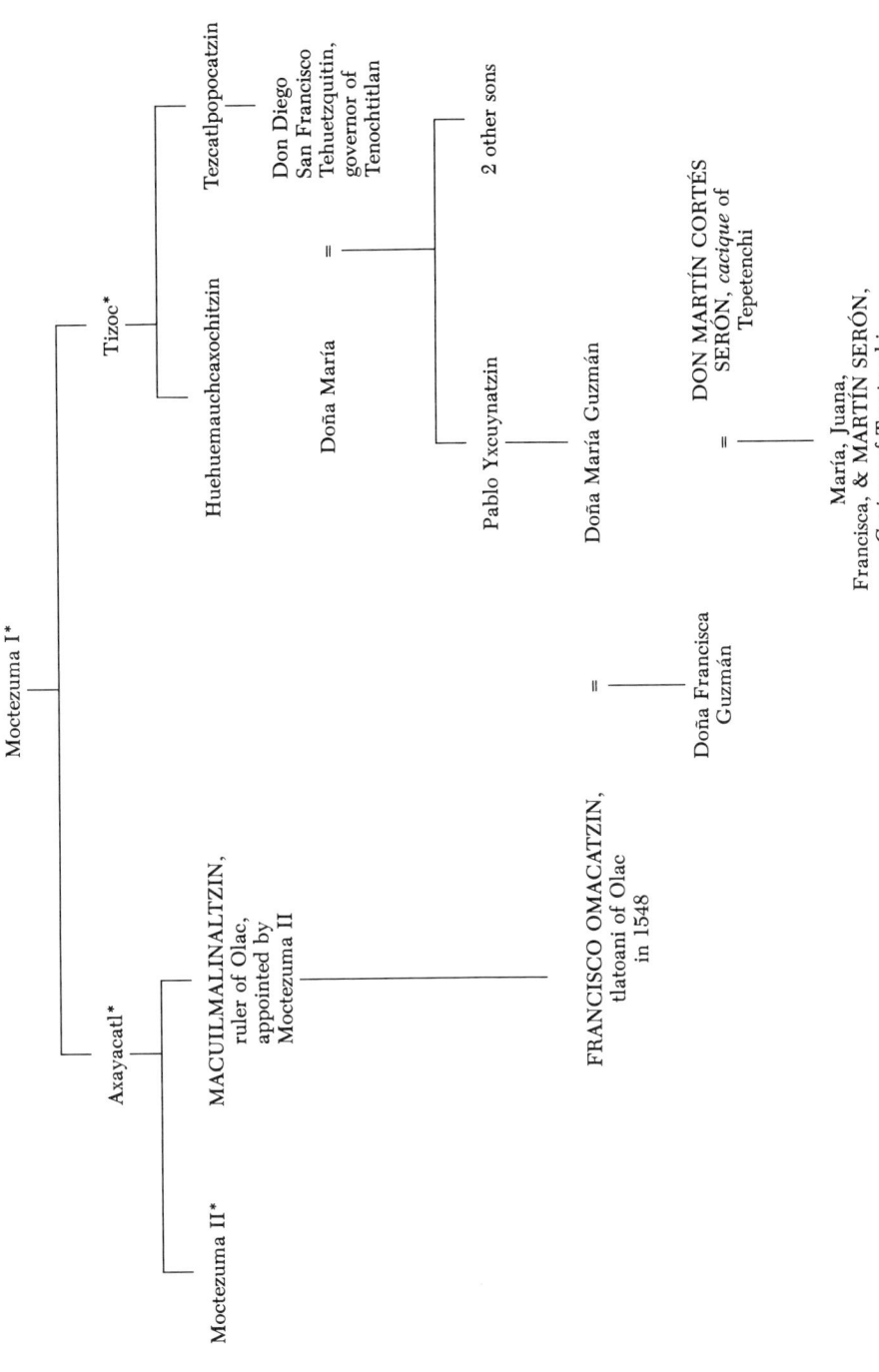

Fig. 5-8. Relationships of rulers of Tenochtitlan (marked with asterisks) to tlatoque of Olac and Tepetenchi, divisions of Xochimilco (AGN, Vínculos, Vol. 279, Exp. 1, published by Reyes, 1977. See also *Crónica Mexicáyotl* 1949:136-39).

cided on a military campaign, they called up supplies, implements, and manpower from the surrounding city-states. The ruler of Tenochtitlan sent messengers to Texcoco, Xochimilco, Culhuacan, Chalco, Cuitlahuac, Coyoacan, and Azcapotzalco to collect these things (Durán 1967:156-57, 164; Sahagún 1954, Book 8:51-52). According to Durán, who lists participants in the Triple Alliance wars, the Xochimilca participated in all the wars after their conquest (Durán 1967:133-34, 164, 179, 186, 237, 271, 285, 303, 319, 389, 407, etc.).

Labor for Special Projects. Along with the other nearby dependencies, Xochimilco provided craftsmen, materials, and manpower for construction of public works at the Triple Alliance capitals of Tenochtitlan, Texcoco, and Tlacopan (Alva Ixtlilxochitl 1975-77, II:133). For instance, to build the temple of Huitzilopochtli in Tenochtitlan, Moctezuma called on labor from Texcoco province, Xochimilco, Culhuacan, Cuitlahuac, Mixquic, Coyoacan, Azcapotzalco, and Tlacopan (Durán 1967:133, 227). Xochimilco and the chinampa cities built the right side of the temple (ibid.). The dependencies were called upon to build aqueducts and, after a flood in Tenochtitlan, they had to gather rushes and supply many canoes full of earth to dam the water (Durán 1967:373). In addition, when Nezahualcoyotl became ruler of Acolhuacan, he moved craftsmen from other cities, including Xochimilco, to Texcoco, to rebuild his capital (Alva Ixtlilxochitl 1975-77, I:444-45, II:84).

Colonists. When the Triple Alliance sent colonists to Oaxaca, Alauiztlan, Oztoman, and Teloloapan, Xochimilco sent people. Like other confederations, it sent 60 families to Oaxaca (Durán 1967:238, 352-53).

Political Ceremonies. Xochimilco participated in political ceremonies in Tenochtitlan. The lords of Xochimilco attended rulers' coronations, victory celebrations, and funerals (Durán 1967:301, 307-08, 392; Sahagún 1954, Book 8:64-65). They and other provincial rulers were installed at Tenochtitlan (Chimalpahin 1965:113, 223). The Xochimilca are reported to have sent mantas, jewels, gold, and slaves for sacrifice to the funeral of the Texcocan ruler, Nezahualpilli (Durán 1967:474).

Calendrical Rituals. Nobles from Triple Alliance dependencies attended calendrically-ordered ceremonies at Tenochtitlan. Xochimilco's ruler is mentioned specifically as having been invited, with all the neighboring and even enemy rulers, to view the sacrifice of prisoners at Tenochtitlan during the festival of the second month, Tlacaxiphualiztli (Durán 1967:172). During the ceremony of Huey Tecuilhuitl, the rulers of dependencies, including the Xochimilca rulers, provided feasts at Tenochtitlan (ibid.:439). The festival for the deity Cihuacoatl began at Xochimilco and continued in Tenochtitlan (ibid.:210-15). The rulers of Xochimilco and other dependencies also attended special imperial religious rituals, such as the dedication of the sun stone, and Xochimilca rulers and nobles participated in pilgrimages to Cerro Tlaloc. There they made offerings, after the rulers of Tenochtitlan, Texcoco, and Tlacopan had done so (Durán 1967:156-59, 192).

Xochimilco made a special contribution to rituals in Tenochtitlan. Both Xochimilco and its dependencies sent flowers, gathered in the mountains and grown in the chinampas, to rituals in the capitals (Torquemada 1975, II:60).

Long-Distance Trade. Xochimilco was one of 12 cities in the Valley of Mexico that had resident pochteca who carried out long-distance trading (Sahagún 1959, Book 9:49). These traders went to exchange points like Coixtlahuaca, where they could obtain gold, feathers, cacao, thread, and cloth (Durán 1967:357).

Summary and Conclusions

Xochimilco was the capital of a political territory founded by one of the first groups of Chichimeca to enter the Valley of Mexico. The Xochimilca people originally settled areas as far south as Morelos, and as far east as Chimalhuacan. The city of Xochimilco was located on freshwater lakes Chalco and Xochimilco and possessed chinampas which made its people capable of great agricultural productivity. Independent until its conquest by Azcapotzalco (ca. 1370), it was conquered again by the Triple Alliance about 1430, becoming an early dependency of the empire.

Internal Organization. Xochimilco had three tlatoani offices, with each ruler governing a designated area. Each tecpan's lands, worked by commoners, supported its nobles. Craftsmen and chinampa farmers were among the commoner subjects of these tecpans. One of 12 cities that had

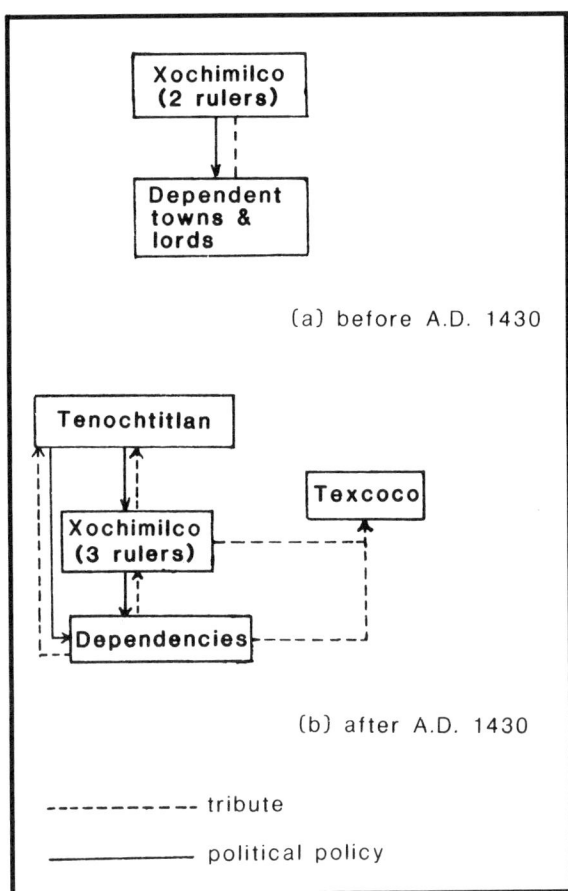

Fig. 5-9. Diagram of Xochimilco's political organization (a) before 1430 and (b) after 1430.

resident pochteca, or long-distance traders, Xochimilco had a large market, and from the town, canoes could transport goods to other towns on the lake. The city's inhabitants performed distinctive rituals connected with particular deities (although it also celebrated the other calendrical ceremonies of the Nahua year).

Relations with Other Polities. The Xochimilca were originally a confederation of towns covering the southern Valley of Mexico, and as such they composed a large political bloc in the Valley of Mexico's pre-imperial arena. Though apparently allied with the Chalca, their southern and eastern borders with the Tlahuica, Huexotzinca, and Cholulateca were hostile ones, and they also fought with city-states north of them—Xaltocan, Azcapotzalco, and Tenochtitlan—in the Valley of Mexico.

Conquered first by Azcapotzalco and later by Tenochtitlan, the Xochimilca confederation found its independence sharply eroded. By 1519, the city of Xochimilco was demoted from the leader of a confederation to a city with control of only its immediate hinterland.

Conquest and Administration by the Triple Alliance. After Xochimilco was conquered, sections of its territory were assigned to support the rulers of Tenochtitlan and Texcoco and other Triple Alliance nobles. The polity as a whole paid tribute at regular intervals to Tenochtitlan. A special penalty following conquest was that Xochimilco and the conquered Tepaneca cities had to build a causeway across the lake from Coyoacan to Tenochtitlan. At least one of the tlatoque of Xochimilco in 1519 was a relative of the ruler of Tenochtitlan, and his division was the tribute-collection center for the province. The other rulers were approved by the imperial ruler and appointed at the capital, Tenochtitlan.

As a dependency of the Triple Alliance, Xochimilco participated in all of the activities usually required of dependencies. It rebelled once, during the Tenochtitlan-Tlatelolco war, but at the time of the Spanish Conquest, it resisted the Spaniards. Although Xochimilco was long-dominated and well-integrated into the central part of the empire, Colonial-period documents suggest that the nobles of this city-state survived and even thrived, having maintained three rulerships, three tecpans, and a local organization in which they retained large amounts of property and influence over local exchange and production.

Chapter 6

Coyoacan

The Place and the People of Coyoacan

The pre-Hispanic city of Coyoacan was located in the southwest corner of the Valley of Mexico, about 1 km from the shore of Lake Texcoco, at ca. 2250-2300 m in elevation. Coyoacan and its neighboring villages were located near the springfed Río Churubusco, which flowed out of the hills and into Lake Texcoco. To the south was the Pedregal, a large lava flow, and further south and west rose the piedmont and sierra (Sanders, Parsons, and Santley 1979; see Fig. 6-1).

The nearby lake provided aquatic resources for the pre-Hispanic inhabitants of Coyoacan, and the alluvial plain provided flat land for growing maize and vegetables. The hills behind Coyoacan were sources of wood and charcoal, and volcanic stone from the Pedregal was used for monuments and buildings. Claybeds provided material for the city's Postclassic period specialization in pottery-making (Sanders, Parsons, and Santley 1979:292), and salt was extracted in Coyoacan and nearby villages (Cortés 1971:83; *Historia de los Mexicanos* 1941:223).

The Urban Center of Coyoacan

Coyoacan's size in the Late Aztec period is difficult to determine, since it is buried under the modern city of Coyoacan. Therefore, the town has not been surveyed by archaeologists, but archaeological excavations in the area have revealed remains dating from the Formative period and from the Early and Late Aztec periods (Díaz Lozano 1925). Coyoacan's territory was densely populated in the Late Horizon period (Fig. 6-2; Sanders, Parsons, and Santley 1979:161-63). Together, the town and its sujetos reported having 11,922 occupants in the early 1550s (Carrasco and Monjarás-Ruiz 1976:144-45).

The Spanish chroniclers describe Coyoacan as a city with well built houses and with "towers" (platforms) for the "chiefs'" houses (Cortés 1971:83). Cortés noted in 1519 that the city of Coyoacan had more than 6000 houses, or about 24,000 to 30,000 residents. The town was

> placed in dry land, [that is] very fertile, clean, and pleasant. . . . These three pueblos [Mexicaltzingo, Coyoacan, and Huitzilopochco] in pagan times had many temples, and very high towers, that were white-washed, that from afar shown like the sun, like silver, and they ornamented the towns greatly. [Torquemada 1975, I:450]

Motolinía ranked Coyoacan as the fifth most important political center in the valley, adding that its lord had "many vassals" (1950:210). The city contained temples, a ruler's palace, and a large market. Craftsmen and traders lived in the city. The city was divided into two major divisions which contained 14 and 18 wards, or tlaxillacaltin (Table 6-1). These two divisions, one in the east and one in the west, were called Tlalnahuac (meaning "next to the land," indicating the area near the urban center, or Coyoacan itself), and Annyr or Acouic (meaning "upwards," and including settlements in the hills west of Coyoacan). These two divisions functioned as administrative subdivisions on tax and land lists in the early Colonial period (Anderson, Berdan, and Lockhart 1976:148-49; AGN, Tierras, Vol. 1736, Exp. 2, Fol. 195; Carrasco and Monjarás-Ruiz 1978:188-89, 198-99).

Coyoacan became a center for the Spaniards right after the Conquest; in fact, Spaniards stayed there while they had houses built over the ruins of Tenochtitlan (Motolinía 1950:310; *Anales de Tlatelolco* 1948:76). As one of the seats of Cortés' government, the city's appearance changed very early in the Colonial period, leaving no surface evidence of the city's former spatial arrangement. Thus, the depiction of Coyoacan as a large urban

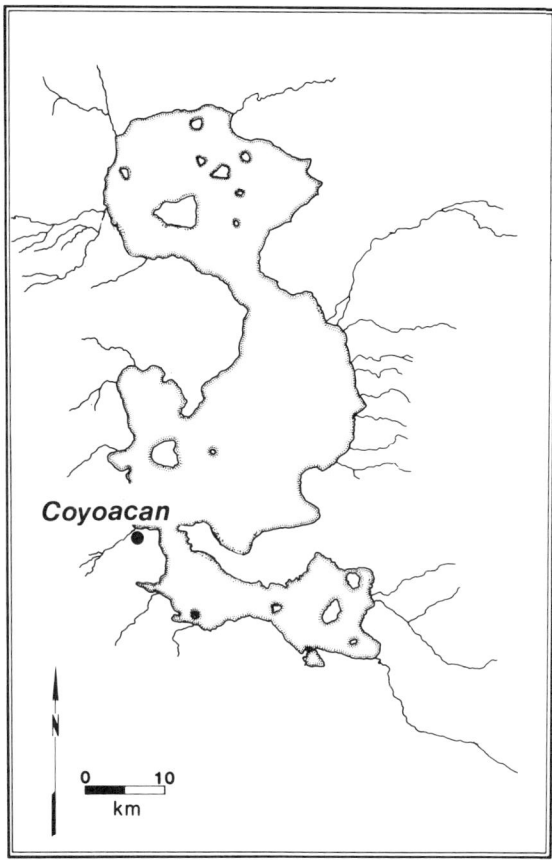

Fig. 6-1. Location of Coyoacan in the Valley of Mexico.

settlement at the meeting of several roads, as seen on the mid-sixteenth century Santa Cruz map (Linné 1948) must suffice as evidence of its urban design (see Fig. 6-3).

The People of Coyoacan

Coyoacan's early history is not reported in detail, and according to its own sources, it was founded by Tezozomoc, ruler of Azcapotzalco, A.D. 1366-1426 (AGN, Tierras, Vol. 1735, Exp. 2, Fols. 115-115v; Carrasco and Monjarás-Ruiz 1978:206). However, sources from other towns mention Coyoacan's existence in earlier times. For instance, the *Memorial Breve* by Chimalpahin says that Coyoacan was one of six cities ruled by Culhuacan at the time of the Toltecs (the six were Xochimilco, Cuitlahuac, Mixquic, Coyoacan, Malinalco, and Ocuilan) (Chimalpahin 1958:3-5). On their migration into the Valley of Mexico, the Mexica passed through Coyoacan (*Historia de los Mexicanos* 1941:223). Such comments suggest that Coyoacan was founded in the 1100s or 1200s, after Culhuacan or Xochimilco, and it was later taken over by the Tepaneca, who revised its history (see *Relación de la Genealogía* 1941:247; Davies 1981:28).

Coyoacan's people spoke Nahuatl and Otomí, and in the 1500s, they called themselves Tepaneca (Carrasco and Monjarás-Ruiz 1978:32-33, 206; AGN, Vínculos, Vol. 242, Exp. 1, Fol. 29). The Tepaneca were one of the Chichimec groups that, according to legend, migrated from Aztlan-Chicomoztoc to the Valley of Mexico with the Mexica, Chalca, Xochimilca, Acolhua, Tlahuica, and Matlatzinca (*Codex Boturini* 1964:Pl. ii), and they are the people of Azcapotzalco and Tlacopan, the city-states which ruled the northwest corner of the Valley of Mexico before the Aztec empire was formed.

Ideology and Religion in Coyoacan

Though Coyoacan's people participated in the yearly round of Nahua calendrical rites, they performed at least one distinctive ritual, which they celebrated in the tenth Nahua month. Called Xocotl Huetzi, it was "the principal feast of the Tepaneca, who were the nation and land of Tlacopan, Coyoacan, and Azcapotzalco" (Durán 1971:444). Motolinía describes the festival as follows:

> In another festival, in some places—Tlacopan, Coyoacan, and Azcapotzalco, for instance, they erected a great round pole ten fathoms long, made an idol out of seeds, wrapped it and tied it with strips of paper and put it on top of the pole. This pole and idol they erected on the day before the festival and danced around it all day. On the morning of the festival they took some slaves and some prisoners of war, and brought them tied hand and foot and threw them into a big fire prepared for this cruelty. They did not allow the victims to burn to death, not out of any sense of pity, but to make their torture greater, for after taking them out of the fire they sacrificed them and cut out their hearts. In the afternoon they pulled down the pole and all struggled to get some part of the idol to eat, for they believed that it would make them valiant in battle. [Motolinía 1950.65-66]

The translator (Foster 1950:65) notes that the intention was not to increase the victims' torture as Motolinía believed, but to maintain the vigor of the fire god by feeding the fire with living victims who must be taken out before they died. In many of the ceremonies described by Motolinía and others, the victims evidently impersonated the deity, and kill-

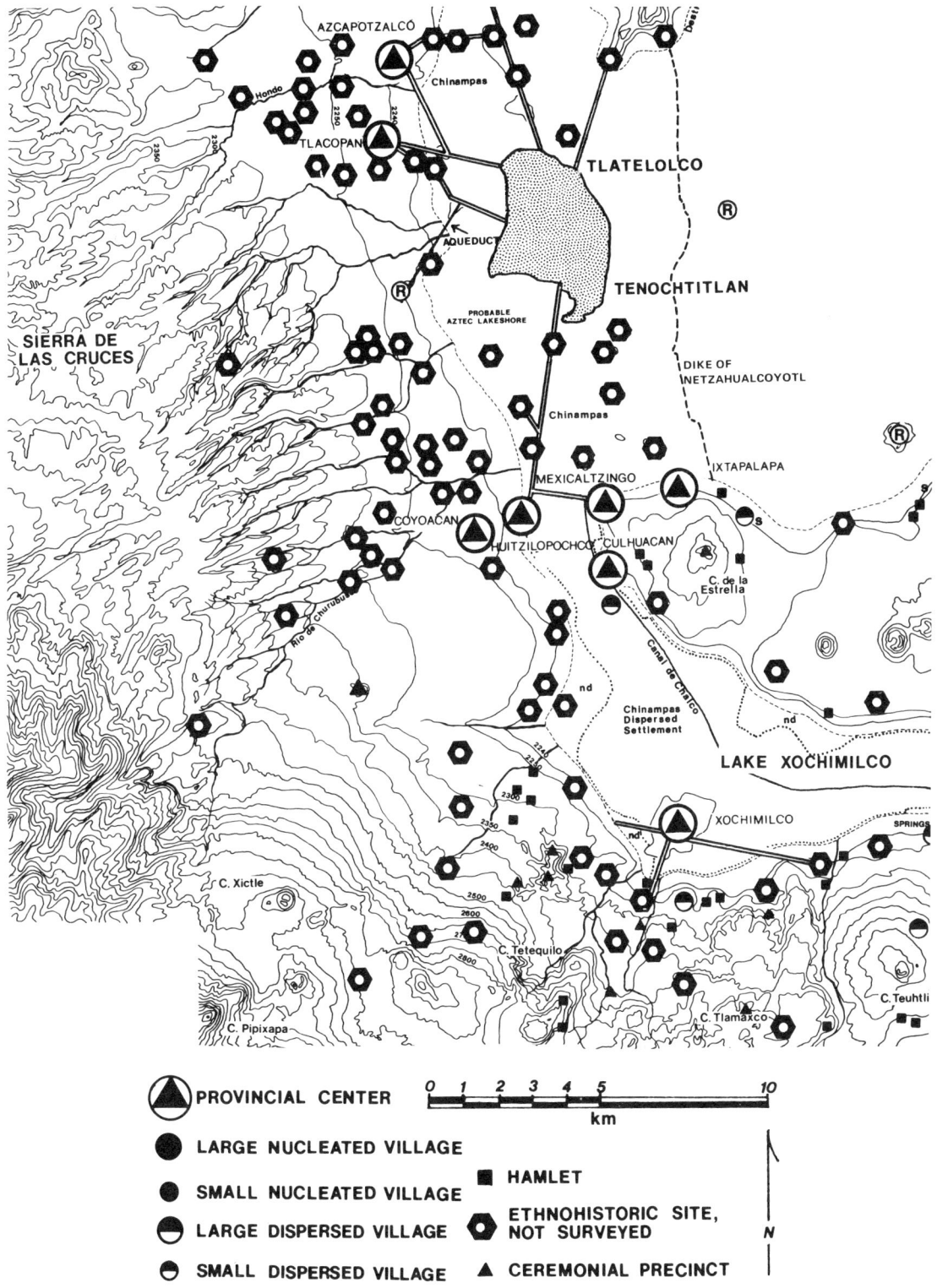

Fig. 6-2. Late Aztec settlements in the Coyoacan region, from archaeological and ethnohistoric data. [Portion of Map 18, Late Horizon, reprinted from *The Basin of Mexico: Ecological Processes in the Evolution of a Civilization*, by William T. Sanders, Jeffrey R. Parsons, and Robert S. Santley, Copyright 1979, by Academic Press, Inc.]

TABLE 6-1
DIVISIONS ("BARRIOS") OF COYOACAN IN 1553

Division 1: Acouic

Barrio Name	Number of Houses
San Gregorio Estetitlan	125
Atongo Omaque Santa Catalina	103
Tepetlapan	113
Chimalistaca	103
Tizapa	9
Tequentaca	105
Aquexutla	120
Tlacuva	69
Myscoaque Santo Domingo	107
Tilhuacan	67
Atiquipaque	107
Zimatlan	58
San Pedro Quaximalpan	15
Tecaltenango	30
San Bartolome	106
San Jerónimo	105
Atlitqui Santa María Magdalena	61
Atlistacatetitlan	63
Total	1466

Division 2: Tlalnahuac

Barrio Name	Number of Houses
Tlalxupa	103
Suchuque	103
Tlilaque	103
Tepetlapan	114
Azalco	100
Atlaquipague	98
Atloyaque	109
Unnamed Barrio	19
San Agustín Guitlan	100
Oquitetitlan	100
Quipalpan	88
Another Unnamed Barrio	26
San Andrés Totoltepeque	114
Santo Tomás Axusco	95
Total	1272

Total Number of Houses in Both Divisions	2738

(Source: Pérez Rocha 1978:8–9; Carrasco and Monjarás-Ruiz 1976:144–46)

ing them was supposed to keep the god always young and strong (ibid.). Eating a part of the idol which had been infused with strength by the sacrifice would bring a part of the deity's strength to the participant.

The ritual geography of Coyoacan is not well documented. However, near Coyoacan, in the area of San Bartolomé, a stone carved into a representation of "the devil" and covered by a cross was described in 1553 (Carrasco and Monjarás-Ruiz 1978:32). Apparently the major festivals took place in the town center.

Coyoacan's Territory

Coyoacan's territory included an urban center, a number of dependent towns near the lake, and smaller villages in the piedmont to the west and southwest. Its territory bordered on the provinces of Xochimilco, Mexicaltzingo, Culhuacan, Oquila, and Mexico-Tenochtitlan (Paso y Troncoso 1905-06, I:105-06; Trautmann 1968:79). Coyoacan's dependencies included Atlacuihuayan, also called Tacubaya (Carrasco and Monjarás-Ruiz 1976), Atlauhpolco, Capulhuac, Xalatlauhco, Coatepec (*Códice Osuna* 1947:250-51; located by Zantwijk 1969 and Barlow 1949 to the south and west of Coyoacan), and Mixcoac (Anderson, Berdan, and Lockhart 1976:139-49; Gerhard 1972:100-03). Figure 6-4 shows the location of some of the towns that were within Coyoacan's territory. Lists of smaller sujetos (all from the Colonial period) vary from one list to another, making Coyoacan's exact boundaries difficult to define (cf. AGN, Tierras, Vol. 1735, Exp. 2, Fol. 18; Gerhard 1972:100-01; Carrasco and Monjarás-Ruiz 1976; Pérez Rocha 1978).

Despite the lack of a definitive list of subject towns, Coyoacan's immediate territory can be characterized as containing several ranks of towns, villages, and hamlets. There were perhaps 12 important sujetos, because the early Colonial-period Indian government of Coyoacan included 12 regidores, one elected by each sujeto (Carrasco and Monjarás-Ruiz 1976:12, 1978:93-94; AGN, Tierras, Vol. 1735, Exp. 2, Fol. 18). Some of the dependent towns were large, like Tacubaya, which had a population of 543 tribute payers, or ca. 2100-2700 residents in 1553 (Carrasco and Monjarás-Ruiz 1976:16-19). Mixcoac was another important dependency, which in pre-Hispanic times housed a division of pochteca, sometimes attributed to Coyoacan (Sahagún 1959, Book 9:49; Durán 1967:185).

The extent of Coyoacan's territory varied over time and in relation to its political fortunes. In early Colonial times its territory was similar to that of the late pre-Hispanic period, but this area may have been only a vestige of its former size under the Tepaneca empire (which collapsed in 1428). After Coyoacan was defeated and became a dependency of the Triple Alliance, its rulers' control over land within its territory diminished greatly.

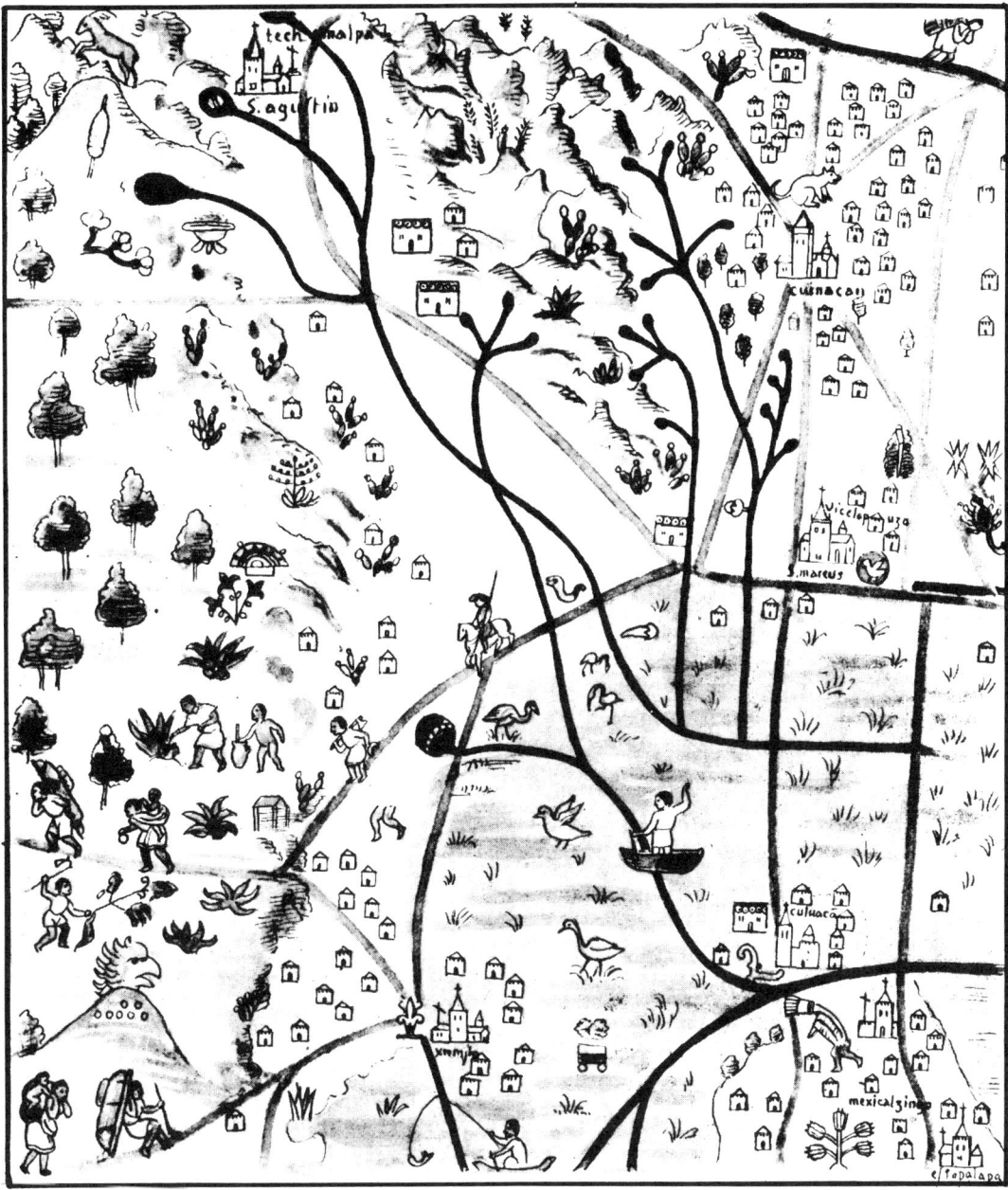

Fig. 6-3. Coyoacan, as pictured on the mid-sixteenth century Santa Cruz map (from Linné 1948). The place-glyph for Coyoacan (upper right) is a coyote on the Santa Cruz map. Elsewhere Coyoacan's glyph is a figure of a coyote with a hole in it, or a coyote's head over a hill symbol. The Nahuatl name of the town means "place where there are coyotes" or "place of the coyote" (Peñafiel 1885:83). Alternately, coyohuac means "thin coyote" (ibid.).

Political Organization of Coyoacan

Officials and Titles

Documents describing pre-Hispanic Coyoacan present few details and have only a limited time-depth. No traditional history of Coyoacan itself has been preserved, and its development can be traced only in the general Valley of Mexico histories and from Colonial legal documents and genealogies. As a result, only a limited part of its prehistoric political structure can be reconstructed. The available documents emphasize the organization of officials involved in the organization of labor and the collection of taxes, so by necessity the discussion that follows emphasizes these types of officials.

Coyoacan was ruled by one tlatoani. Subject to him were other tlatoque, and towns and villages without tlatoque were governed by administrators. Other indigenous officials explicitly mentioned in Colonial documents are tlaillotlac, meaning high official or judge, and boundary-setting officials: mixcouatlailotlac, acoçacatl, tocuiltecatl (Anderson, Berdan, and Lockhart 1976:224).

Colonial documents describe in detail the administration of labor and tribute collection in Coyoacan, and from these examples, an idea of the structure of pre-Hispanic labor and tribute-collection organization may be gained. In the 1550s, for example, tribute collection and labor organization was carried out by a tequitlato (Spanish mandón), who was supervised by a regidor. Individuals held these offices for many years. They collected taxes every three months in the form of money and cacao beans. They also collected taxes to purchase the materials used in corvée labor. One such mandón administered 30 houses, consisting of 51 tribute payers in the barrio of Culnaculzingo, in Tacubaya. The regidor is identified as a "principal," indicating elite status; the tequitlato is not (Carrasco and Monjarás-Ruiz 1976:18-22). This tequitlato described his job as follows:

> In these thirty houses he says that he has the charge of gathering together the people of these thirty houses to go to build public works, and to pay tributes and for whatever other things for which they have to be assembled. [Carrasco and Monjarás-Ruiz 1976:21]

The duties of the tequitlato described here resemble those of the pre-Hispanic tequitlato described by Zorita (1963:228).

Market officials collected taxes from merchants who traded in Coyoacan's market. They are mentioned in Colonial documents as having done this from "tiempo inmemorial," and Cortés reported seeing officials collecting taxes from merchants at canoe entrances to Tenochtitlan, suggesting that this indeed was a pre-Hispanic practice (Cortés 1971:108). The market tax collector (65 years old in 1578) said that merchants paid in goods or cacao beans every market day (Mondays in the 1550s). One Indian said that these taxes went partially to the alguacil who distributed 200 cacao beans to the *cacique*, one-half tomin of chiles to the alguacil of the barrio of Omac, and 400 cacao beans to the mayordomo for the expenses of rural judges and other rural administrators coming to town to see the gobernador and alcaldes. Others said the tax went to the gobernador for municipal expenses, and yet others said it went exclusively to the *cacique* and always had (AGN, Vínculos, Vol. 242, Exp. 1, Fols. 41-47; Carrasco and Monjarás-Ruiz 1978:42-43).

Other offices that possibly were carry-overs from pre-Hispanic times were listed in a document from the mid-1500s. A list of "tepantlaca" from various locations in Coyoacan's territory suggests that 380 individuals were either palace dependents (a similar word, tecpantlaca, means "palace people"), relatives of the *cacique*, or administrators (from tepan, which means "over someone or something"). In keeping with what is known about pre-Hispanic administrative practices, they could have been both administrators and relatives (see Anderson, Berdan, and Lockhart 1976:152-54; Carrasco 1976; Hicks 1984:163). It is possible that these 380 people administered Coyoacan's outlying dependencies in some way, but no documents were available for this study with which to clarify the matter further (see Table 6-2).

Administration of Dependencies

Officials in Coyoacan's sujetos were organized in a manner similar to those of the urban center, but there were fewer, and the administrative structure was simpler. In Tacubaya, a tlatoani related to the rulers of Azcapotzalco ruled before the Spanish Conquest (Carrasco and Monajarás-Ruiz 1976:66). Under his authority in the 1550s were officials, referred to both as "regidores" and "principales" who administered the 11 barrios or wards of the town (ibid.:7-19). Sons followed fathers in holding these offices. For instance, Pedro Mexical, referred to as "principal y jefe de los mandones" and also as "regidor y principal," in the barrio of Culnacalzingo in Tacubaya had been in office for 20 years in 1553. It was said that he was

> ... chief because the father of Don Toribio who is now governor made him principal of the said barrio, and ... that he has the charge of assembling the people of the ward for public works and tribute, and that for this he has those persons named Juan Tustle and Pedro Suchil, and because of the aforesaid, he receives neither a salary nor any tribute, nor do they work fields [for him], nor is there any other thing that he is paid. [Carrasco and Monjarás-Ruiz 1976:22]

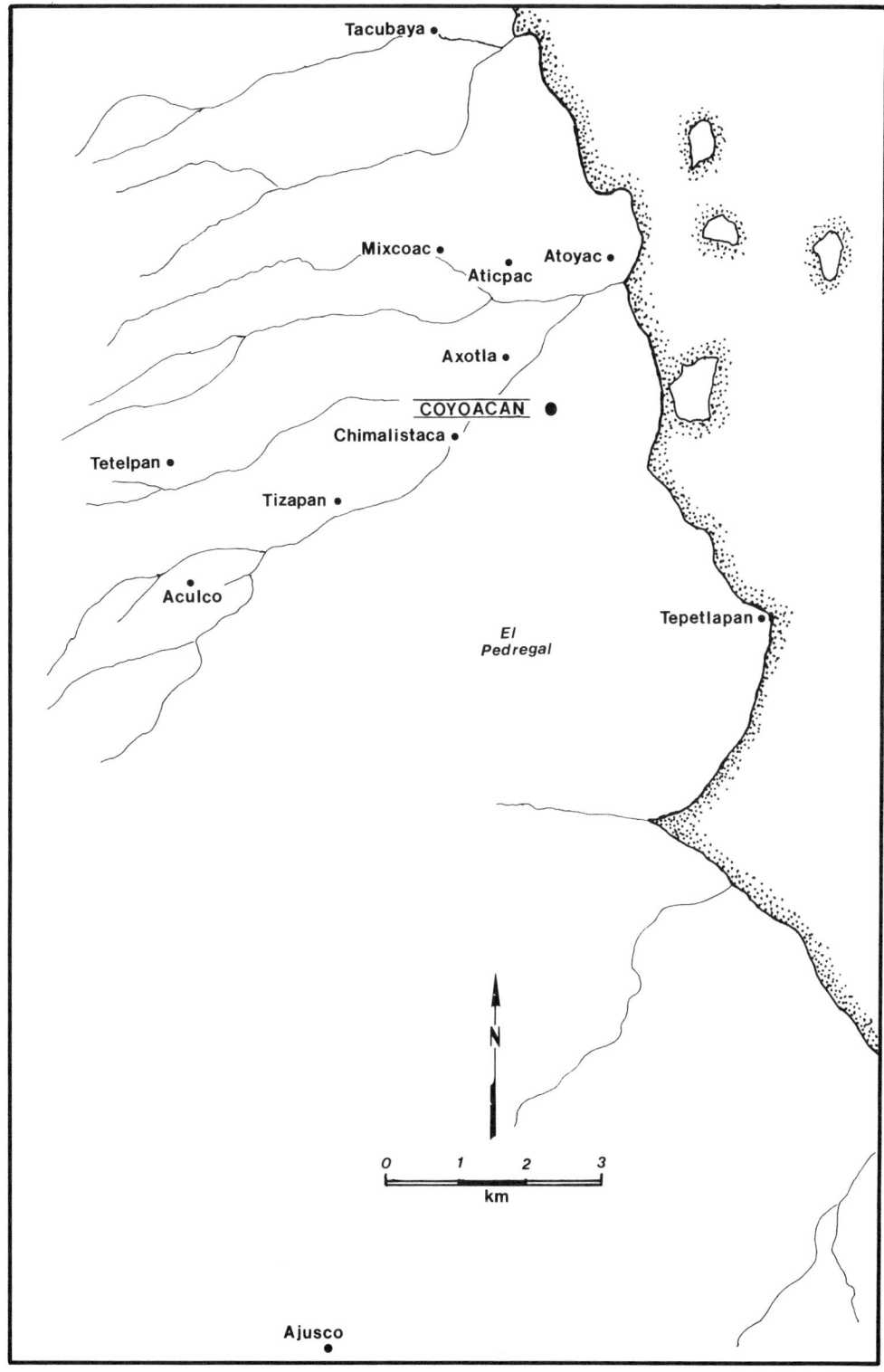

Fig. 6-4. Coyoacan's territory, with some of its dependencies.

TABLE 6-2
DEPENDENTS AND/OR ADMINISTRATORS
RESPONSIBLE TO DON JUAN, 1550

To Don Juan belong 29 men and widows who are tepantlaca of his:

At Chimaliztaca are 7 men
At Atlauhcamilpan, 7 men
At Mixcouac, 4 men
At Xochitenco, 4 men
At Chinancaltonco, 4 men
At San Jerónimo, 12 men
At Tlacoyiacan, 18 men
At Hueycalco, 8 men and 2 youths
At Auacatitlan, 21
At Acopilco, 25 and 6 youths
At Pachiocan, 2 men
At Chimalpan, 4 men
At Amantlan, 6 men
At Couatzonco, 13 men
At Tecouac, 6 men
At Acolco, 80 men
At Tlamimilolpan, 51 men
At Çacamolpan, 29 men
At Ocotitlan, 30 men and 6 youths
At Tepechpan, 6 men
And it all totals 380, and widow[s]

(Source: AGN, Tierras, Vol. 1735, Fols. 114, 149; Carrasco and Monjarás-Ruiz 1978:184; Anderson, Berdan, and Lockhart 1976:152–53)

That is, the governor had appointed him, and he received no income from the position. Under the regidor's authority were tequitlatoque. In addition, in Tacubaya, there were officials representing craftsmen and tradesmen—carpenters, masons, merchant officials, and leaders of the merchants (ibid.:19).

To summarize, the early Colonial-period documents from Coyoacan suggest that in the pre-Hispanic period, the tlatoani was assisted by a number of officials, most of whom were from the elite class. These officials administered courts, markets, and production in rural dependencies. Within the urban center and smaller towns, residential wards (barrios) consisting of 15 to 120 houses (and thus approximately 75 to 600 people) were the administrative units (see Table 6-3; Fig. 6-5).

Economic Organization of the Tlatoani's Household

Don Juan, Coyoacan's *cacique* in the mid-1500s, and his brother and father before him, collected tribute from Coyoacan's commoners. In 1560, Don Juan received food, wood, cacao, and fodder for his animals from community lands (AGN, Indios, Vol. 1, Exp. 298, Fols. 134v-135v). The community worked his fields in four places and provided men to guard his house and women to grind maize. Carpenters and stonemasons built and cared for his house. Other men worked in his gardens. Two different lists of the income he received are reproduced in Table 6-4, and Table 6-5 is a list of laborers assigned to work in his fields.

In addition, the *cacique* had an annual income of 140,780 cacaos (5 loads equalling 24,000 cacao beans plus 2½ xiquipillis [8000 units = 1 xiquipilli] or 20,000 cacao beans, plus 780) (Carrasco and Monjarás-Ruiz 1976:164) and miscellaneous produce and manufactured goods, which were the traditional income of the tlatoani.

> . . .it is true that they collected and are collecting the aforementioned cacao contained in the five loads and that this tribute of cacao is tribute that the maceguales have given him for a long time, because they gave it to him in the time of Moctezuma, and the mantas and hens also were given to him back then, and . . . this cacao that is paid to Don Juan, governor, and that which is surplus is spent in the community house, for feasts that occur on Sundays or during fiestas. [Carrasco and Monjarás-Ruiz 1976:174]

Don Juan received wood from the commoners, also a traditional income, for he said that "*este tributo de leña es tributo muy antiguo dende [sic] el tiempo de Montezuma, e antes, e solían dar las maceguales mucho más cantidad de leña de la que agora dan*"—"this tribute of wood was ancient, from the time of Moctezuma and before, and the commoners had to give much more wood before than they do at the present" (Carrasco and Monjarás-Ruiz 1976:175).

In addition to receiving produce and labor from the community, Coyoacan's tlatoani received income from teuctlalli, or "lord's lands." These were four sections of land which were worked for him by the community. These plots (see Table 6-4) provisioned the palace and official functions. In addition, Don Juan had income from patrimonial fields (itecpilal or ueuetlalli) (AGN, Tierras, Vol. 1735, Exp. 2, Fols. 125, 152; Carrasco and Monjarás-Ruiz 1978:19, 197-99; Anderson, Berdan, and Lockhart 1976:154-55; AGN, Vínculos, Vol. 242, Exp. 2, Fol. 11). According to one list, Don Juan had 11 plots in the lower region of Coyoacan and 21 in the upper region. Renteros, or tenants, worked most of these lands (AGN, Tierras, Vol. 1735, Exp. 2, Fol. 67; Carrasco and Monjarás-Ruiz 1978:137). Another

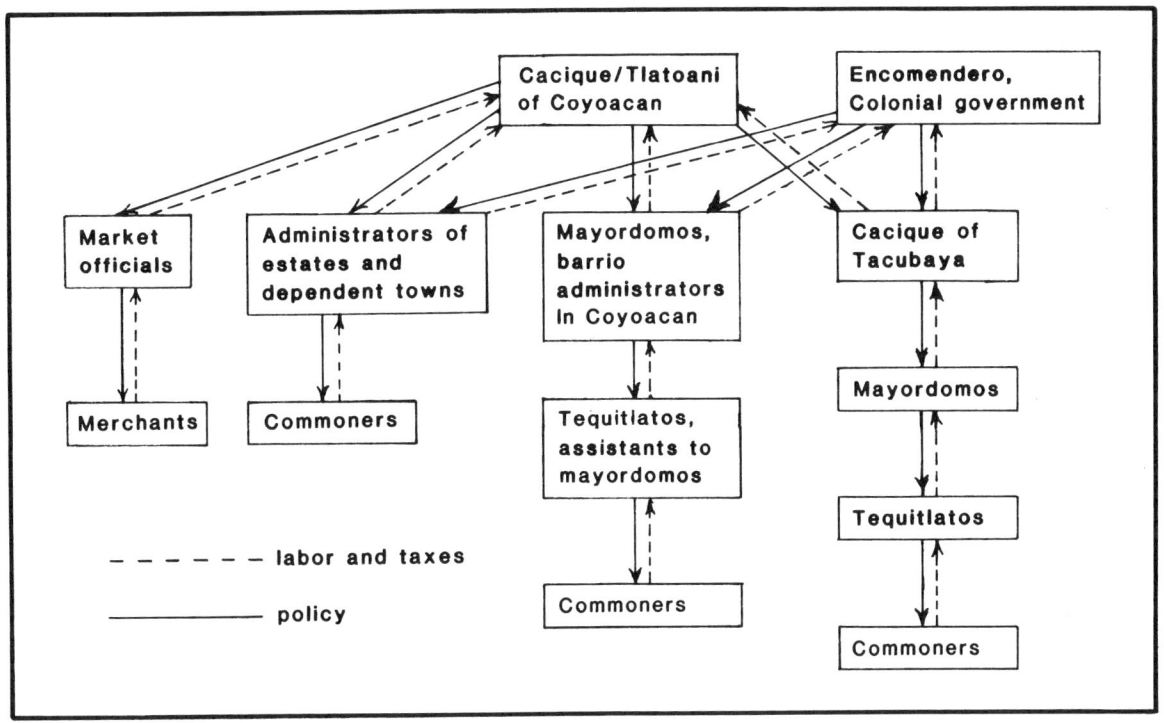

Fig. 6-5. Coyoacan's administrative organization, mid-1500s.

TABLE 6-3
NUMBER OF TRIBUTE PAYERS AND
ADMINISTRATORS IN COYOACAN, 1553
(Derived from data on 7 [of 32] wards)

Name of Ward	Number of Tribute Payers	Number of Administrators
San Agustín Atlitiauipaque	136	10
San Pedro Cuaximalpa	154	2
Zacamacuesco	100	2
Hueytetitlan	220	13 or 14
Atongo	137	6
Omaque	297	9
Amealco	125	5

Number of tribute payers per administrator in Coyoacan is 14 to 77. This is much greater than in Tacubaya, where the number ranges from 7 to 17 (see Pérez Rocha 1978:12).

list of the *cacique's* lands (which lists the rulers of Coyoacan as well) follows.

Lands that belong to the house of Coyoacan and the history of its genealogy: Tezozomoc, Maxtla, Thutzin, Totolachnetzin, Quauhpopoca, Cetotzin who later was called Don Hernando, and Don Juan de Guzmán Yztolinque. The lands are Cohuatzonco, Tecohuac, Cacamolpan, Ocotitlan, Axoccotlazchtitlan, Chimalyztacan, Atlahucamilpan, and Tlacotlyiacan. [AGN, Tierras, Vol. 1735, Exp. 2, Fols. 155-155v; Carrasco and Monjarás-Ruiz 1978:206]

In all of the documents, inherited land is distinguished from purchased land. Patrimonial lands were bequeathed to descendants in many of the wills of the nobles, and stipulations were made that certain lands were not to be sold but were to be passed on by inheritance (AGN, Tierras, Vol. 1735; Exp. 2, Fol. 32; Carrasco and Monjarás-Ruiz 1978:104).

Like the tlatoani, other elites received labor from the commoners and had land on which tenants worked. These varied greatly from person to person (Table 6-5; Carrasco and Monjarás-Ruiz 1976).

Finally, the *cacique* of Coyoacan received the market taxes. Sellers paid either cacao beans or part of their produce as tax. The tax was collected by Indian officials assigned to this specific task (Carrasco and Monjarás-Ruiz 1978:39, 41-42; AGN, Vínculos, Vol. 242, Exp. 1, Fols. 39-41). The destination of this tax was disputed; some informants said the tax went exclusively to the tlatoani and

TABLE 6-4
INCOME OF DON JUAN, TLATOANI OF COYOACAN

List 1, ca. 1556

Daily Provisions:	100 tomatoes
	100 chili peppers
	½ block of salt
	2 hens
	3 loads of wood
	3 loads of fodder
	1 load of ocote, or torch pine
Weekly:	4 tlapixque, or guards, from the community
Yearly:	400 fanegas of maize
	4 fields cultivated by the community (2 cultivated each year; 2 left fallow; at Ocoçacapan, Milpolco, Coyotleuhco, Tochco)

(AGN, Tierras, Vol. 1735, Exp. 2, Fol. 27; Carrasco and Monjarás-Ruiz 1978:100)

List 2, ca. 1560–70

Daily Provisions:	3 hens
	2 baskets of shelled maize
	400 cacao beans
	200 chili peppers
	1 block of salt
	tomatoes
	gourd seeds
	6 loads of wood
	5 loads of fodder
Daily Labor:	10 men (tlapixque) to act as guards
	8 women to grind maize
Twice Yearly:	150 cacao beans or 2 tomines from each macegual
Yearly:	Fields at 4 locations were worked (Ocoçacapan, Milpolco, Coyotleuhco, Tochco)
	10 carpenters and 10 stonemasons built and maintained Don Juan's house
	Artisans and craftsmen worked at the tlatoani's house (tecpan)

(AGN, Tierras, Vol. 1735, Exp. 2, Fols. 150–51; Anderson, Berdan, and Lockhart 1976:151; Carrasco and Monjarás-Ruiz 1978:192–93)

others said that part went to pay for community expenses and to other officials as well as to the tlatoani (Carrasco and Monjarás-Ruiz 1978:188-90, 195-96; Anderson, Berdan, and Lockhart 1976:138-49).

Rulers of Coyoacan

A list of rulers of Coyoacan is found in a Colonial document which lists the genealogy of Don Juan de Guzmán Itztollinque, who was *cacique* of Coyoacan in the 1550s. His forebears were Tezozomoc (ruler of Azcapotzalco), Maxtla (son of Tezozomoc), Thutzin (brother of Maxtla), Totlachnitzin (Maxtla's son), and Cetototzin (Don Hernando, who was ruler in 1519) (AGN, Tierras, Vol. 1735, Exp. 2, Fols. 155r-155v; Carrasco and Monjarás-Ruiz 1978:206). This list may not be complete (Don Juan may be emphasizing his descent from his most famous ancestors), for other histories mention some additional rulers. A tentative list of Coyoacan's rulers is presented in Table 6-6. The only ruler mentioned before Tezozomoc is Chalchiuhtlanitzin, lord of Culhuacan, who is reported to have ruled Coyoacan as a dependency of Culhuacan (Alva Ixtlilxochitl 1975-77, I:304). This indicates that there either was no tlatoani in Coyoacan before Tezozomoc and that the rulership of Coyoacan was a creation of the Tepaneca empire, or that the names of any previous rulers were deleted from history after the Tepaneca conquest of the town.

Ruler Succession in Pre-Hispanic Coyoacan

In Coyoacan, son usually followed father as tlatoani. Preferably this was the eldest son, but a younger son might inherit the title if the eldest could not rule. Although father-to-son inheritance of office was the Tepaneca ideal, it could not always be carried out in practice.

Coyoacan was ruled by a Tepaneca tlatoani starting in A.D. 1410, when Tezozomoc, ruler of Azcapotzalco, appointed his son Maxtla to the office. Before this, a military governor ruled, under the direction of Tezozomoc (Chimalpahin 1965:186). Maxtla ruled for 17 years, until he went to Azcapotzalco to rule the Tepaneca city-states after his father's death (some histories say he had to assassinate his older brother to do this) (Chimalpahin 1965:191; *Historia de los Mexicanos* 1941:252; Torquemada 1975, I:104, 121). Maxtla appointed his son Tecolotzin as tlatoani of Coyoacan in 1427 (Chimalpahin 1965:191).

Tecolotzin was deposed in 1427 or 1428 by the Triple Alliance. Although a Colonial document lists the rulers as Tezozomoc, Maxtla, Thutzin, Totlachnetzin, Quauhpopoca, Cetotzin (Don Hernando), and Don Juan de Guzmán Itztollinqui (AGN, Tierras, Vol. 1735, Exp. 2, Fols. 155-155v; Carrasco and Monjarás-Ruiz 1978:206), other sources name additional rulers. A ruler of

TABLE 6-5
LIST OF INDIANS ASSIGNED TO WORK THE FIELDS
OF DON JUAN, *CACIQUE* OF COYOACAN,
MIDDLE 1500s

The macehualtin of lord don Juan who are to work the land in San Agustín, and clear the ground: they begin to clear the ground at Xiuhtlan and Çacamolpan and Ocotitlan and Couatzonco. And the people of the household and the Quapoltitlan people will clear the ground for one week; Diego will direct them.

And the Acopilco people are to give Pedro de Vergara his wood, his beams, his logs for one week. Huitznacatl is to be over them.

And the people of Atlauhcamilpan are to feed people for one week. Domingo will take care of it.

And those who cultivate the fields at Cimatlan and Mixcoac are to reap wheat at Atepocaapan for one week. Juan Tlanauaua will be over them.

They are to work all the purchased lands which are scattered, beginning at Neçaualcaltitlan the seventh day; Antón Huixtopolcatl will direct them.

The people of Chimalistaca are to lead the oxen working the land for the week.

(Archivo General de la Nación, Ramo de Tierras, Vol. 1735, Exp. 2, Fols. 114, 149; Carrasco and Monjarás-Ruiz 1978:184-85; Anderson, Berdan, and Lockhart 1976:153-55)

Coyoacan named Tzotzomatzin was assassinated by Ahuitzotl, ruler of Tenochtitlan, in 1501; his son later replaced him (Durán 1964:210-16; *Anales Mexicanos* 1903:69). See Table 6-6 for a chronological list of rulers of Coyoacan, as reported by various annals from the Valley of Mexico.

Marriage Alliances of Coyoacan's Rulers

Coyoacan's rulers were Tepaneca, and their descent from Tezozomoc is emphasized in their genealogies. However, by 1519, they were also related to the rulers of Tenochtitlan and Texcoco. The ruler of Coyoacan in 1519, Cuaupopocatzin, was a cousin of the ruler of Texcoco, Cacamatzin (Díaz 1956:240), and he was married to a granddaughter of Moctezuma I's brother; she was also the daughter of the ruler of Huitzilopochco (*Crónica Mexicáyotl* 1949:131-34). Thus, by 1519, the rulers of Coyoacan were tied into the kin networks of both Tenochtitlan and Texcoco (see Fig. 6-6, a reconstruction of the genealogy of the rulers of Coyoacan).

Political Alliances of Coyoacan

An important Tepaneca city, Coyoacan was attacked and conquered early in the Tepaneca-Tenochca war. It became one of the first dependencies of Tenochtitlan, and it was assimilated into the economic and political life of the capital.

Coyoacan had ruled a number of nearby, smaller towns (*Códice Osuna* 1947:250-51; Carrasco and Monjarás-Ruiz 1976). In 1553, Don Toribio, *cacique* of Tacubaya, said that

his father and grandfather . . . were *caciques* in the pueblo [of Tacubaya]. He says that his father was called Nyculas and his grandfather Yzquas and that all descended from Pequatle who was the first grandfather that they had had, and that all had been *caciques* in that time and no one remembered anything to the contrary, because they were the first founders of this pueblo and that the founder of all was the lord of Azcapotzalco named Tezozomoctli, who was the first founder of all this land and that this is proven and affirmed by the old and ancient ones and by ancient codices. . . . [Carrasco and Monjarás-Ruiz 1976:66]

After its conquest by Tenochtitlan in 1429-30, Coyoacan remained part of the Tepaneca political confederation, which was the section of the Triple Alliance administered by Tlacopan. In this way, the Tepaneca cities retained their political and cultural identity to some degree after their conquest.

Before the Triple Alliance, there were economic and cultural links between Coyoacan and Otomí peoples, and with the towns south and west of Coyoacan (Gerhard 1972; Davies 1981). However, after conquest by Tenochtitlan, they may have had less interaction with towns to the south and west, towns to which the Tepaneca nobles had fled after the war with Tenochtitlan and Texcoco (Torquemada 1975, I:145; Durán 1967:96).

Coyoacan as a Dependency of the Aztec Empire

The Tepaneca and Mexica always had an uneasy relationship, even when the Mexica were subjects of and paid tribute to Azcapotzalco. The *Anales de Tlatelolco* report that as late as 1406, Mexica warriors were captured and sacrificed at Coyoacan (1948:53).

The Mexica conquest lists report that Coyoacan was conquered by Itzcoatl in 1429-30 (*Anales de Cuauhtitlan* 1945:47, 66; *Anales de Tlatelolco* 1948:55; *Codex Mendoza* 1925:5v; *Crónica Mexicáyotl* 1949:108-09). A Texcocan source reports that Nezahualcoyotl conquered Coyoacan in 1428 (Alva Ixtlilxochitl 1975-77, I:376, 384).

TABLE 6-6
RULERS OF COYOACAN

Name	Dates of Reign	Source
Chalchiuhtlanetzin (Ruler of Culhuacan; at this time, Coyoacan was ruled by Culhuacan)	1200s	Alva Ixtlilxochitl 1975–77, I:304
Tezozomoc (Ruler of Azcapotzalco)	?–1410	Carrasco and Monjarás-Ruiz 1978:206
Maxtla (Son of Tezozomoc; exiled in 1431)	1410–26	Chimalpahin 1965:186
Tayauh (Brother of Maxtla)	1426?	Alva Ixtlilxochitl 1975–77, I:539
Tecolotzin or Totlachnetzin (Son of Maxtla)	1427–31	Chimalpahin 1965:190; Carrasco and Monjarás-Ruiz 1978:206
Itztollinqui	1453	*Anales Mexicanos* 1903:64
Zucamacan or Tzotzomatzin (Killed by Ahuitzotl, ruler of Tenochtitlan)	?–1501	*Anales Mexicanos* 1903:69; Carrasco and Monjarás-Ruiz 1976:76
Cuauhpopocatzin (Ruler killed during the Spanish Conquest)	1509–19	*Anales de Cuauhtitlan* 1945:63; *Cronica Mexicayotl* 1949:131–34
Ce Tochtzin (Cetotzin)	1519–25	*Crónica Mexicáyotl* 1949:131–34; Carrasco and Monjarás-Ruiz 1976:76
Don Juan de Guzmán Itztollinqui (Brother of Ce Tochtzin; both were sons of Cuauhpopocatzin)	1525–69	*Crónica Mexicáyotl* 1949:131–34; Chimalpahin 1965:244

Coyoacan was one of three main Tepaneca towns, with Azcapotzalco and Tlacopan (*Crónica Mexicáyotl* 1949:101-03). After Azcapotzalco was defeated, Maxtla, Cuecuech, and Zaconcatl of Coyoacan ordered the roads leaving Tenochtitlan blocked off, so that no Mexica could trade in Coyoacan, and they harassed Mexica travelers on the roads (Durán 1967:85-86). However, Maxtla, ruler of Coyoacan, was unable to get assistance from other city-states against Tenochtitlan (ibid.:87-90). Itzcoatl and Nezahualcoyotl attacked and defeated Coyoacan, Atlacuihuayan (Tacubaya), and Huitzilopochco in 1430, and Maxtla fled south to Taxco (Torquemada 1975, I:145; Durán 1967:97-101).

Driven out of their homes by the battle, the people of Coyoacan had to pay the Mexica in order to return. According to Mexica histories, they begged Itzcoatl for peace; they gave the conquerors land and built houses for them, and they gave cloth and blankets woven of maguey fiber, precious green stones, and gold to Itzcoatl. They gave the Mexica produce from their fields (*Anales Mexicanos* 1903:62-63; Durán 1967:95-104).

In addition, people were taken from Coyoacan to Tenochtitlan as slaves, and their land was divided among the Tenochca rulers and his warriors and nobles. Many of the people of Coyoacan who had fled stayed in exile (Durán 1967:97-102). As a major Tepaneca city and a close neighbor of Tenochtitlan, Coyoacan had been dangerous; as a conquered town, its lands enriched the rulers and nobles of Tenochtitlan.

Coyoacan's dependent position in the Triple Alliance was a result of its position as part of the Azcapotzalcan polity, and undoubtedly its territory was affected in much the same way as the rest of the Tepaneca territory. According to Charles Gibson,

> . . .the wars of the late 1420's and early 1430's brought about a rapid diminution of Tepanec strength. The Tepanecs were defeated by their two foremost subjects, Acolhuacan and Tenochtitlan; Azcapotzalco was reduced to a town of lower rank; and by agreement with the Acolhua and the Tenochca, Tlacopan became the Tepanec capital, in alliance with Tenochtitlan and Texcoco. Tepanec territory thus underwent successive expansions and contractions, to the extent that a legitimate historical-geographical definition of "Tepanec territory" becomes problematic and conditional. [Gibson 1964a:137]

Coyoacan's Obligations to the Triple Alliance

According to Durán, after Coyoacan's defeat, Itzcoatl announced to his cihuacoatl, Tlacaelel, that "those who work must be rewarded and paid for their labor. My men have worked and sweated and it is proper that we now divide the lands of Coyoacan among them" (Durán 1964:71). The division was made as follows:

> The first to be awarded its share was the Royal Crown. The king, his family, the courtesans, foreign visitors, messengers from other lands—all of these would be maintained by the fruits of these new possessions. Tlacaelel was given eleven

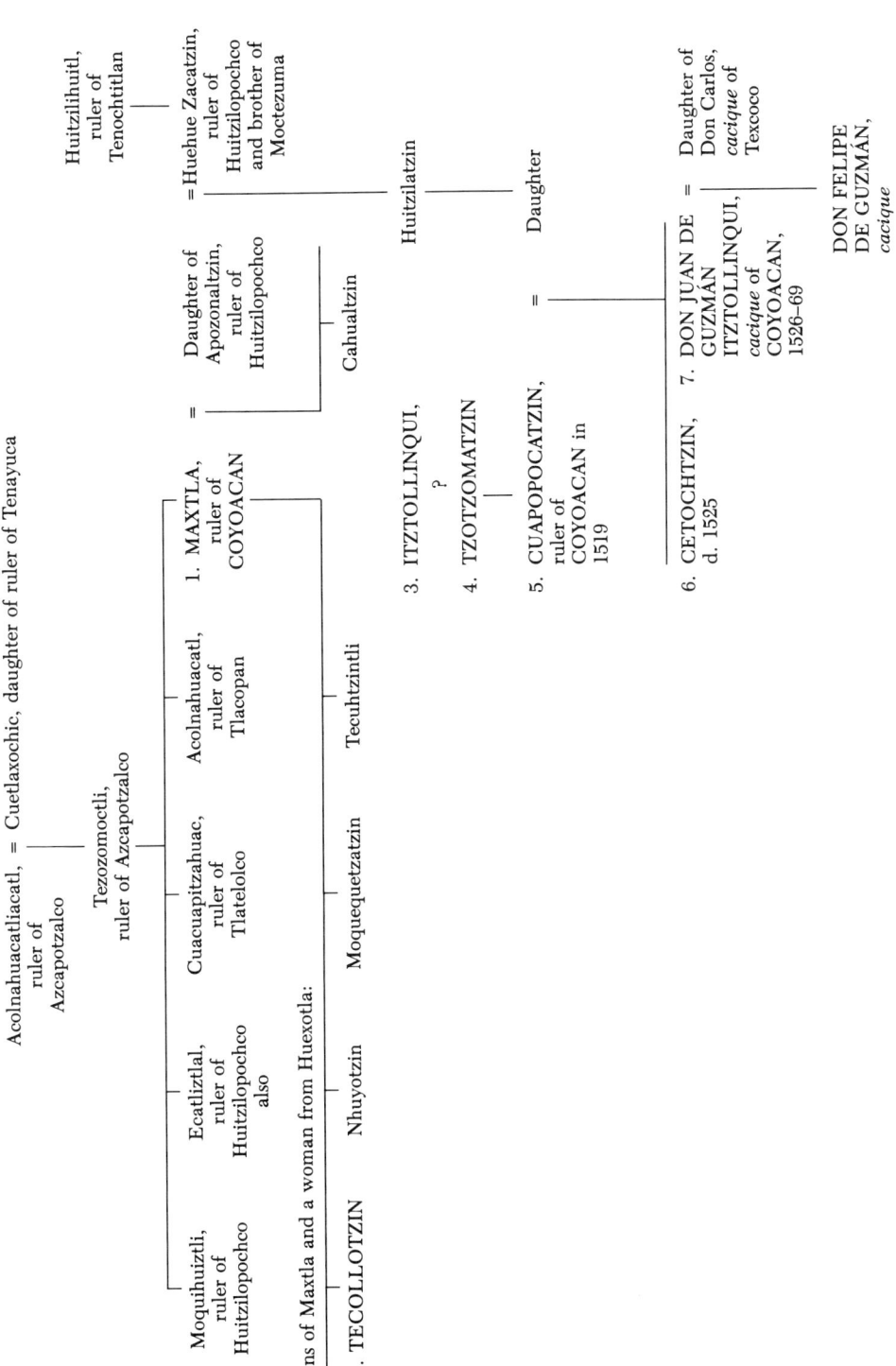

Fig. 6-6. Genealogy of tlatoque of Coyoacan (in capitals), Azcapotzalco, and Tenochtitlan (from *Anales Mexicanos* 1903:64; *Crónica Mexicáyotl* 1949:131-34; Carrasco and Monjarás-Ruiz 1976, 1978; Fernández de Recas 1961:62).

pieces of land and after him the noblemen received two or three according to their merit. [Durán 1964:71-72]

As a result, Coyoacan's tlatoani's control over land, and hence labor and produce that he actually controlled, diminished under the Triple Alliance. Sections of Coyoacan also delivered tribute to the ruler of Texcoco (Alva Ixtlilxochitl 1975-77, I:384).

As subjects of the Triple Alliance, and particularly of Tenochtitlan, Coyoacan's people were required to participate in a number of imperial activities. For these purposes they were grouped with the Tepaneca towns and directed by Tlacopan. They provided men and supplies for war (Durán 1967:156-57, 164). They formed a division of the Tepaneca troops and marched into battles with the Tepaneca division (Sahagún 1954, Book 8:52, 72; Durán 1967:164). They participated in Triple Alliance wars against Chalco, Tepeaca, the Huaxteca, Cempoala, Coixtlahuaca, Oaxaca, and Michoacan, to name a few (Durán 1967:156-57, 164, 186, 197, 285).

Coyoacan provided labor for projects in the capital such as building the temple for Huitzilopochtli in Tenochtitlan, as commanded by Moctezuma I. Tlacopan and the Tepaneca realm built the back of the temple, directed by Totoquihuaztli, lord of Tlacopan (Durán 1967:133-34). Likewise, they probably sent settlers to the colonies in Oaxaca with the Tepaneca contingent (ibid.:238). The Tepaneca provided feasts at state rituals in Tenochtitlan (Durán 1971:215, 439), though Coyoacan is not specifically mentioned. Coyoacan probably was included with Tlacopan in these ceremonies, for Durán mentions that the rulers of Coyoacan accompanied the ruler of Tlacopan in greeting Axayacatl, ruler of Tenochtitlan, with gifts when he arrived at Tlacopan after his first victory (Durán 1967:273).

Coyoacan had a contingent of long-distance traders (pochteca); they resided either in Mixcoac (Sahagún 1959, Book 9:24, 49), a town subject to Coyoacan, or in Coyoacan itself (Durán 1967:185). At the time of the arrival of the Spaniards, all long-distance pochteca trade was directed by the tlatoani of Tenochtitlan and the head pochtecatl of Tlatelolco (Sahagún 1959, Book 9).

Despite its participation in Triple Alliance activities, Coyoacan's problems with its neighbor, Tenochtitlan, continued. In 1501, Coyoacan's ruler was told by the hueytlatoani Ahuizotl to provide water for Tenochtitlan by building an aqueduct from one of Coyoacan's springs. In this very embroidered story, Coyoacan's ruler refused to build the aqueduct, saying that it would flood Tenochtitlan because the springs were so powerful. Ahuitzotl ordered the ruler killed for disobedience, and though Coyoacan's ruler was a great sorcerer, he was strangled. Ahuitzotl built the aqueduct anyway, after which the springs flooded Tenochtitlan in 1502. The aqueduct had to be torn down and the water gods appeased with many sacrifices. Ahuitzotl appointed the dead ruler's son as tlatoani of Coyoacan (Durán 1967:369-74; *Anales Mexicanos* 1903:69; *Codex Ramírez* 1920:118).

A primary reason—after security—for conquering Coyoacan was, of course, income. As mentioned, the Mexica ruler took land within Coyoacan's territory which provided tribute in goods directly to his household and to various officials. The town of Coyoacan provided labor for public works and warfare, but whether it paid regularly scheduled tribute in goods is unclear.

Officially, Coyoacan was part of the Tepaneca confederation, led by Tlacopan. It is thus listed as one of the pueblos that, with 36 others, "obeyed Tacuba [Tlacopan] in warfare, paid tributes to Tacuba, and served Tacuba with supplies of stone, lime, and other materials" (*Memorial de los Pueblos Sujetos al Señorío de Tlacupan....* in Paso y Troncoso 1940, XIV:118-22). Quantities paid to Tlacopan are not specified. It is consistent with these data that Coyoacan does not appear in the *Codex Mendoza* (it is likely that the Coyoacan in the Valley of Mexico is not the one that appears on page 47 of the codex, with the province of Xoconochco, on the coast of what is now Guatemala [see Barlow 1949:97-99]). However, Coyoacan may have been included in the highland tribute-collection province of Quahuacan (Gerhard 1972).

Coyoacan also paid tribute to Texcoco. This tribute is not quantified as far as Coyoacan itself is concerned, but Coyoacan is included with towns paying tribute of foodstuffs, textiles, skins, feathers, and other sumptuary goods to Texcoco (Paso y Troncoso and Chimalpopoca Galicia 1897; Alva Ixtlilxochitl 1975-77, I:376, 384).

In the mid-1500s, Coyoacan paid tribute in labor and food to Mexico City (Paso y Troncoso 1905-06, I:105-06), and it also delivered labor, money, and produce to Cortés (Carrasco and Monjarás-Ruiz 1976:16), to an encomendero, and to the monasteries. Its former ties with Tlacopan and Tenochtitlan-Mexico were broken by the Spanish Conquest and subsequent Colonial administration, though Coyoacan still provided labor for public works under the direction of Tlacopan (Gibson 1964a). Without more complete data, we have to conclude that Coyoacan paid labor tribute to both Tenochtitlan and Tlacopan and also paid tribute in goods directly to Tenochtitlan, first as a price for peace and later regularly through estates of Tenochca nobles.

Cohuatequitl, or public service, in the early Colonial period was extremely demanding of the Indian commoners, and protests against it resulted in an inquiry by Judge Santillán into its use in Coyoacan (published by Carrasco and Monjarás-Ruiz 1976). Despite the obvious changes that occurred in the system as a result of depopulation and increased demands following the Spanish Conquest, pre-Hispanic systems were used to organize labor for public works (Gibson 1964a), and the operation of the cohuatequitl in Coyoacan may be similar to that of the Late pre-Hispanic period. For that reason, Table 6-7 is included, which gives for one day, the assignment of tasks to various barrios of Coyoacan. It is an example of how labor was administered at one point in the Colonial period, perhaps patterned on earlier practices.

In summary, Coyoacan is reported as having paid tribute in goods to all three Triple Alliance capitals. Its labor tribute was organized by Tlacopan, and Coyoacan's rulers, warriors, and laborers served imperial demands as part of the Tepaneca division (see Fig. 6-7).

Summary and Conclusions

The Political Organization of Coyoacan

Coyoacan, a large city of ca. 24-30,000 in 1519, was administered by one tlatoani, who ruled a territory in the southwestern corner of the Valley of Mexico which included at least one town with its own tlatoani who obeyed the ruler of Coyoacan, and many small towns and villages. Coyoacan's administrative system included officials who governed and dealt out legal decisions in the dependent towns and varied officials in the urban center itself—market tax collectors, boundary-setting officials, warriors, priests, ward chiefs, and their assistants. The urban center had 2 great divi-

TABLE 6-7
LIST OF WORK ASSIGNED TO COYOACAN'S SUJETOS ON A SINGLE DAY IN 1613

Public service (cohuatequitl) for today, 10 March 1613:

Homac—They are occupied in the cathedral
Yezotitlan—in the house of the Marqués (Cortés)
Tenantitlan
Tizapan—Transport wood to the cathedral
Homaxac—They are occupied in the cathedral
Acxotlan—Marqués
Tlacopac—They go to the house of the Marqués
Santo Domingo
Aticpan Cimatlan—They work in Mexico City
Atepotzco—They are occupied with "zacate real"
Tlilhuacan—Marqués
Hueytetitlan—They work in the cathedral
Tehuitzço
San Gerónimo—They will transport wood to the cathedral
Atliytic—The church's cattle
Amealco—Both get [illegible]
Tlaltenanco
San Pedro—Gather the "zacate real"
Tlalxopan—They are occupied in Mexicaltzingo
Xochac
Tlilac—They care for the community
Tetzcolco
Tochco—They care for the community
Atoyac—Go to the house of the Marqués
Trinidad—They are occupied in the cathedral
Avzolco
Atliztacan

(AGN, Tierras, Vol. 1735, Exp. 2, Fol. 83; Carrasco and Monjarás-Ruiz 1978:152).

sions comprised of ca. 32 lesser ones (called tlaxillacaltin, barrios, or wards). The tlaxillacaltin contained 9 to 120 houses in 1551; they were administered by ward headmen assisted by tequitlatoque, or foremen, who collected taxes and organized the people for corvée labor.

The tlatoani received income in cacao beans, wood, and produce from the community. In addition, he received labor for maintaining his house and garden. The commoners worked lands for him in four places, lands which were attached to the office of tlatoani (although the tlatoani also possessed patrimonial lands). He also received market taxes, from which he paid municipal expenses, supported officials coming to town on business, or contributed to fiestas.

Coyoacan's Alliances with Other City-States

Coyoacan's own histories start with the foundation of its Tepaneca rulership, although histories of other towns say that there was a settlement at

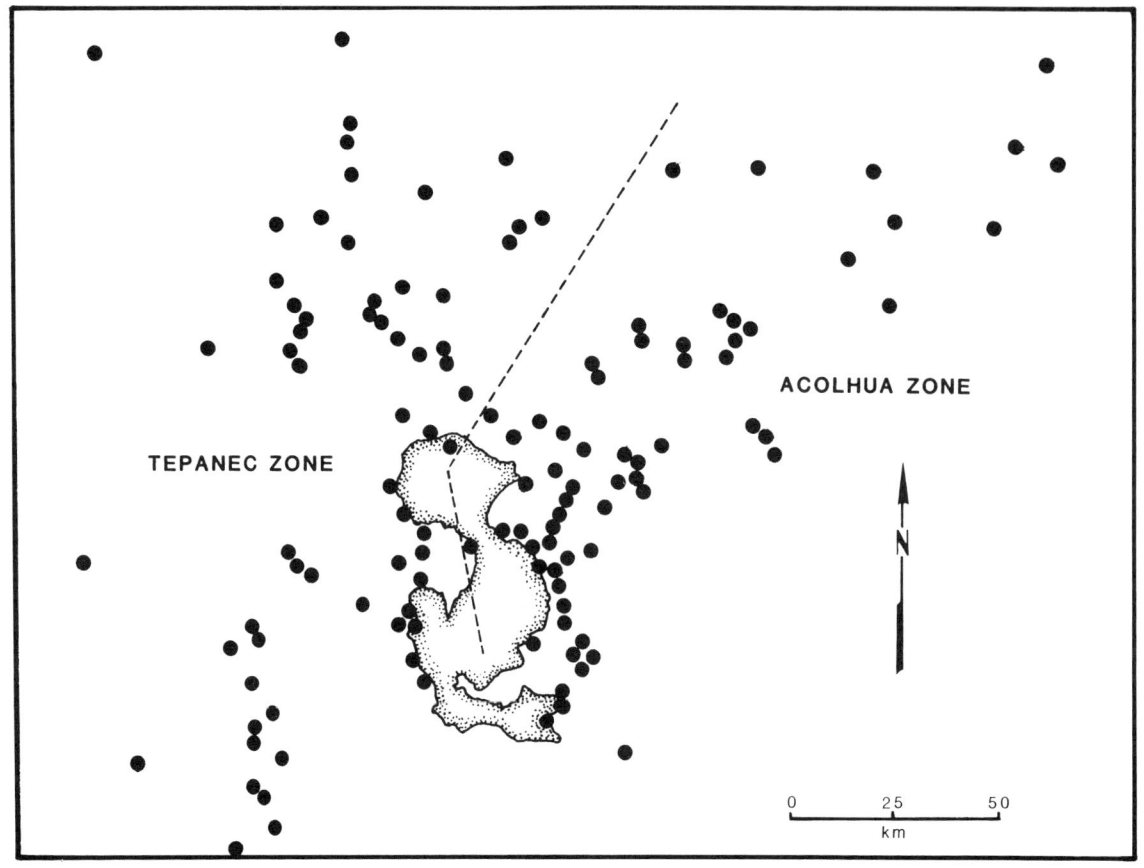

Fig. 6-7. Acolhua and Tepaneca labor zones, with Coyoacan in the Tepaneca zone (after Gibson 1971:387).

Coyoacan which was a dependency of Culhuacan before that time. As a major center in the Tepaneca political system, Coyoacan shared in ruling much of the Valley of Mexico from the middle 1300s until 1428. During the Tepaneca apogee, Coyoacan was ruled by a son of the Azcapotzalcan ruler, Tezozomoc; with the death of Tezozomoc in 1426, the Tepaneca state began to disintegrate.

As part of the Azcapotzalcan system, Coyoacan's ruler was appointed by the lord of Azcapotzalco, and the city-state of Coyoacan participated in military campaigns with Azcapotzalco. Coyoacan's people participated in ceremonies and rituals typical of Tepaneca culture. Coyoacan collected tribute from its dependencies, and one of its dependencies had a resident barrio of long-distance traders, or pochteca, who participated in the restricted commerce in sumptuary goods. This may have contributed to the large market held at Coyoacan, for the traders may have returned with some goods that could be exchanged in the market. The market was administered by the tlatoani of Coyoacan.

Coyoacan's political ties were with the Tepaneca towns and with Otomí communities to the south and west of it, towns such as Atlapulco and Xalathauhco, which aided Coyoacan in its war with Tenochtitlan, or Taxco and Ocuilco, to which its ruler fled after losing the war. Thus, before the Triple Alliance, Coyoacan was a dependency of Azcapotzalco; it was the second most important Tepaneca city. After its conquest, it was reduced to a lesser rank as a dependency of Tlacopan, the city-state which replaced Azcapotzalco as head of the Tepaneca confederation and which was a member of the Triple Alliance.

Coyoacan and Tenochtitlan

After its conquest by Tenochtitlan and Texcoco in 1428–30 Coyoacan had to pay special taxes which were imposed when the people, driven out of their

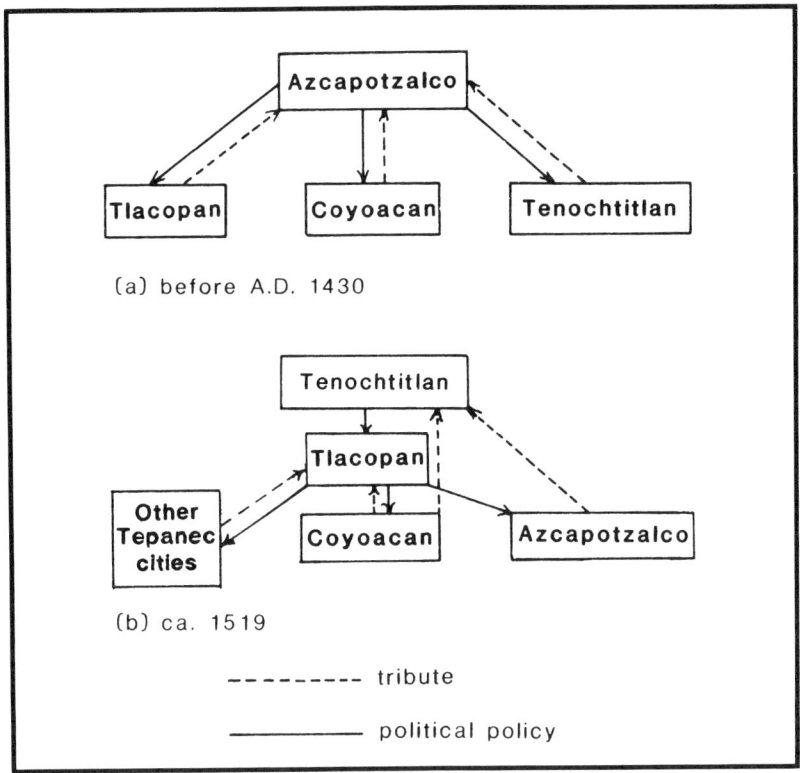

Fig. 6-8. Coyoacan's position in the Valley of Mexico's political hierarchy (a) before 1430, (b) ca. 1519.

city, begged to return. Large portions of Coyoacan's land were taken by the Mexica ruler and nobles to provide income for them. Thereafter, Coyoacan contributed to Triple Alliance activities, though there are no quantitative data on its tribute payments. It is uncertain whether or how much its territory decreased through loss of control of towns dependent upon it.

As part of the Triple Alliance, Coyoacan was, for many purposes, administered directly by Tlacopan. This is suggested by three things: (1) It does not appear in the *Codex Mendoza* or *Matrícula de Tributos* in the lists of towns paying taxes to Tenochtitlan. (2) It is listed in the tribute and labor lists of Tlacopan (see Gibson 1964a, 1964b). (3) It is listed as participating in Triple Alliance activities under the direction of Tlacopan. Thus, Coyoacan was demoted from an important dependency of Azcapotzalco to a dependency of Tlacopan along with the other Tepaneca cities.

Coyoacan's rulers were responsible to the tlatoani of Tenochtitlan. One ruler was executed for disobeying an order of Ahuitzotl, though Ahuitzotl later appointed that ruler's son as tlatoani. In the final years before the Spanish Conquest, one of Coyoacan's rulers married a woman related to the Tenochca rulers, thus bringing Coyoacan's rulers into the Tenochca dynasty.

As a dependency of Tlacopan and of Tenochtitlan, and as one of the first polities conquered by Tenochtitlan and Texcoco, Coyoacan paid tribute to all three capitals in goods and labor. It participated in Triple Alliance military campaigns and participated in imperial ceremonies and rituals, usually as part of the Tepaneca contingent. It received long-distance trade goods via its pochteca. Motolinía (1950:210) ranked Coyoacan fifth in the Valley of Mexico politically, following Tenochtitlan, Texcoco, Tlacopan, and Cuauhtitlan. Proximity to Tenochtitlan made Coyoacan important strategically, and its authority over many people and towns as well as its market made it a rich town, one which was quickly made a dependency of all three Triple Alliance members.

Chapter 7

Teotihuacan: An Acolhua City-State

The People and the Place of Teotihuacan

Aztec Teotihuacan is located in the northeast of the Valley of Mexico, in the center of the Teotihuacan Valley near the famous Classic-period ruins of the same name (Fig. 7-1). The *Relación geográfica* of 1580 described the Colonial settlement of San Juan Teotihuacan as follows:

> The capital, San Juan, and all its subordinate towns lie on a plain and the farthest of the latter is situated at a distance of two leagues from the capital. Towards the North, a league distant, is a great mountain which the natives name Tenan, which in Spanish means "mother," because many small hills issue from it. Another hill, medium sized, shelters the southeastern portion of the plain. In the territory of the subordinate towns there is a lack of water and the natives drink stored rain water. In the capital there is an abundance of water and many springs close together that feed a large river on which the natives have a mill. The water of said river irrigates two leagues of land, which is the whole length of its course. It passes by the towns of Acolman, Tepechpan, Tequizistlan, and the boundary of Texcoco, and empties itself into the lagoon. This region yields an abundance of fodder and food supplies. [Nuttall 1926:53-54]

A sub-valley within the Valley of Mexico, the Teotihuacan Valley runs from northeast to southwest; it is about 35 km long and covers about 600 km². The valley floor ranges between 2440 m in elevation in the southwest to 2300 m in the northeast. The southern border of the valley is the Patlachique mountain range, while the northern border is a series of volcanic hills, the highest of which—Cerro Gordo—rises to 3050 m above sea level. Between these volcanic hills are low valleys. The spring-fed Río Teotihuacan runs from the center of the valley into Lake Texcoco (Sanders 1970:74-75).

The *Relación geográfica* of 1580 describes the Teotihuacan Valley as high and cool. Crops grown there included "native cherries of the edible cacti" (tuna), agaves, maize, beans, amaranth, and chia (*Salvia*), as well as Spanish vegetables and wheat.

Although another town in the valley, Tequizistlan, specialized in salt extraction and weaving cotton and agave fibers into cloth, agriculture was Teotihuacan's foremost industry (Nuttall 1926:78-79, 81).

The Urban Center of Teotihuacan

Settlement History and Population Estimates

An archaeological survey of the Teotihuacan Valley has produced maps of prehistoric settlements and estimates of the valley's population during all the ceramic prehistoric periods. The valley contained the huge Classic-period site of Teotihuacan (see Millon 1973, 1976), which contained up to 125,000 people and covered up to 20 km². Teotihuacan was the largest Classic site in the entire Valley of Mexico, but by A.D. 750-950, its population had begun to disperse. By the Late Aztec period (A.D. 1350-1520), the area contained six small city-states: Teotihuacan, Acolman, Otumba, Tepexpan, Chiconauhtla, and Tezoyuca (Sanders 1968:99). Each of the six Late Aztec-period towns in the Teotihuacan Valley contained the residence of a tlatoani, or hereditary ruler, whose domain included the surrounding territory and widely dispersed lands with tribute-paying commoners living on them. In this period, 31% of the population lived in the towns, 30% lived in large villages, and the remaining 30% lived in small villages and hamlets (Sanders, Parsons, and Santley 1979:208; Fig. 7-2).

Scatters of Aztec pottery suggest that the Aztec site of Teotihuacan contained as many as 10,000 people, and the *relación's* estimate of 1600 tribute payers suggests a population of 8000 (which included the center and 17 outlying hamlets) in 1580 (Paso y Troncoso 1905, VI:220; Nuttall 1926:56). Other documentary estimates are ambiguous, for

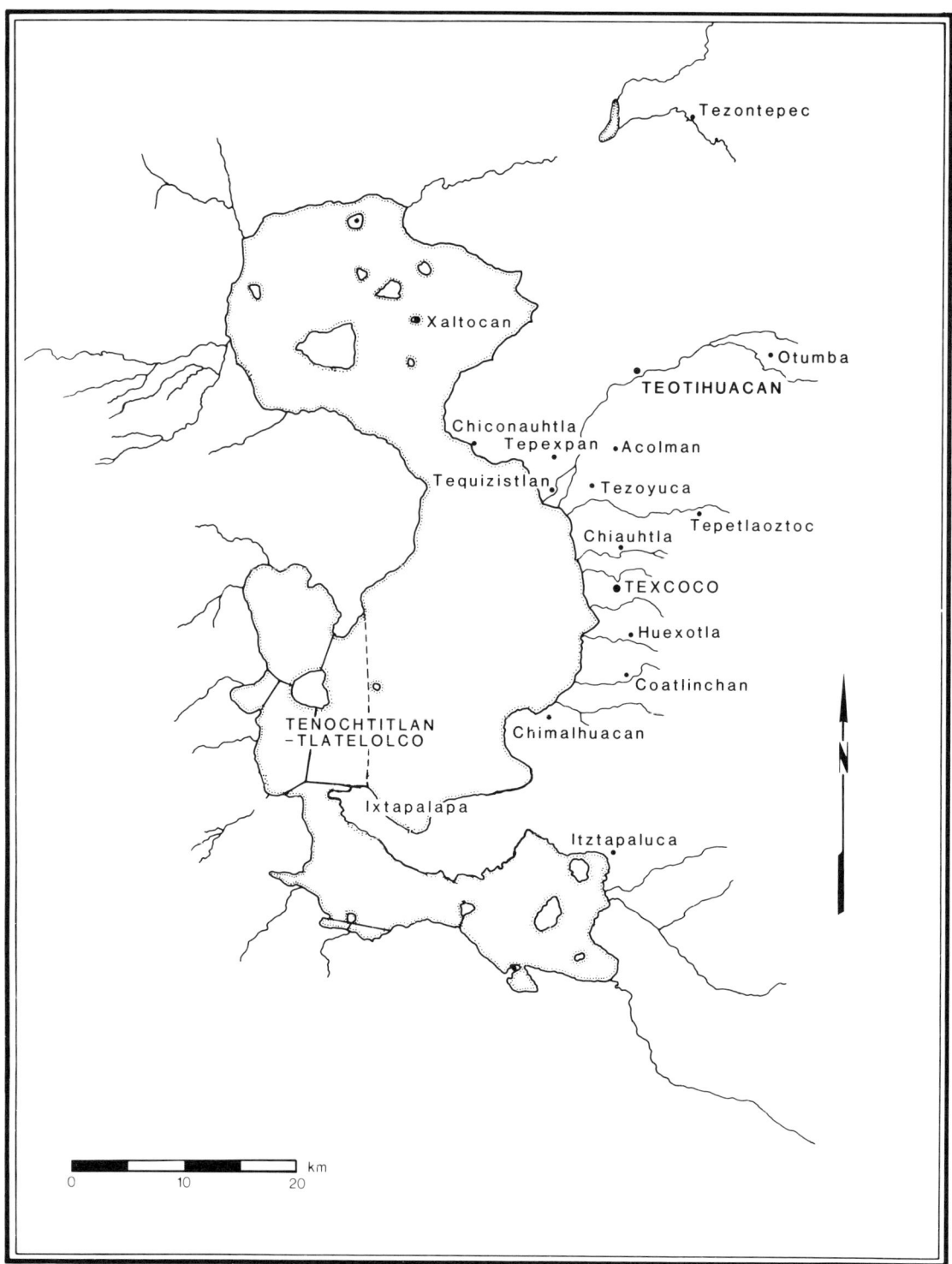

Fig. 7-1. Location of Teotihuacan in the Valley of Mexico.

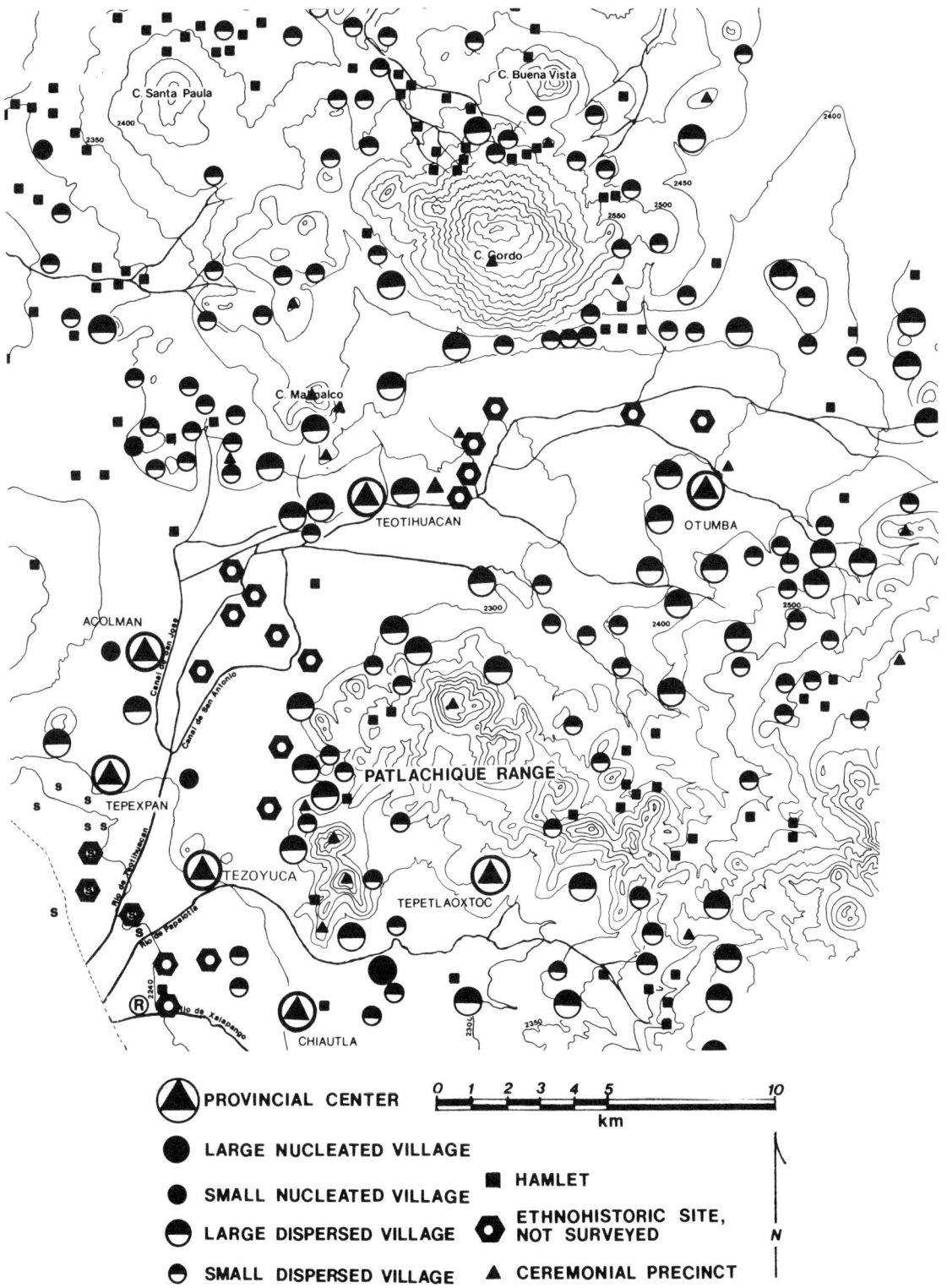

Fig. 7-2. Late Aztec period settlements in the Teotihuacan area. [Portion of Map 18, Late Horizon, reprinted from *The Basin of Mexico: Ecological Processes in the Evolution of a Civilization*, by William T. Sanders, Jeffrey R. Parsons, and Robert S. Santley, Copyright 1979, by Academic Press, Inc.]

they do not record the exact area involved (as discussed by Sanders 1970), and the area was depopulated early in the Colonial period by epidemics, an additional problem in judging the size of the pre-Hispanic population (Paso y Troncoso 1905, VI:220; Sanders 1965, 1970; Gerhard 1972:274).

Much of Late Aztec Teotihuacan (TA22) is covered by modern San Juan Teotihuacan, and the archaeological survey reported that, "the survey has not revealed ceremonial and urban core zones similar to those found in other Aztec towns. No evidence of an urban core was found in the area of the present villa" (Sanders 1965:83). Unlike other towns in the valley, such as Otumba or Tepexpan, there was no evidence of a pyramid temple within the town. Not surprisingly, "the attached barrios have a more rural way of life and settlement pattern (excepting possibly Purificación) although the population density of San Juan Evangelista is relatively high (2200/km^2)" (ibid.).

The Teotihuacan Valley settlement pattern was "a continuous band of . . . settlement of variable density and ranging in width from 500-1500 m." It "extended for 5000 m along the piedmont from Maquixco to San Martin. This would have been the largest Aztec population cluster in the Valley" (Sanders 1965:84). Apparently, in Aztec times, the town and its hamlets were scattered throughout the area that had been covered by the much larger Classic period site. Use of the Classic-period pyramids and ceremonial center by the Aztec-period population perhaps reduced the need for an urban ceremonial center in the town.

Despite its unassuming archaeological remains, the Postclassic Aztec settlement of Teotihuacan was an important site in Aztec political geography. It was the residence of a hereditary ruler, or tlatoani, who governed a number of subordinate villages and scattered "estates." Although no pre-Hispanic codices depict the town, its name glyph, seen in the *Códice Xolotl* (1951), is a pyramid with rays over it. The Nahuatl name Teotihuacan means "place of the gods" (teutl means "god or spirit") (Paso y Troncoso 1905, VI:219, 270; Alva Ixtlilxochitl 1975-77, I:272). A nearby village, called San Martín in the Colonial period, was called Teotiloyan or Neteotiloyan, meaning "place where everyone goes to worship" (Gamio 1922, I:68), referring to its location within the perimeter of the Classic site.

The Urban Structure of Aztec Teotihuacan

In reference to the town's appearance, the writer of the 1580 *relación* reported:

> The natives say that in ancient times this town was thickly populated by a great number of inhabitants. . . . The town was not founded on a regular plan, but consists of a number of scattered houses. The inhabitants of said town are a polished people of a good understanding who always live on the produce of their land. [Nuttall 1926:56]

The town's climate was described as cold and damp because it was "situated among canals and fountains all proceeding from flowing springs" (Nuttall 1926:52). The houses were made of stone and adobe, with flat roofs. "The houses of the principal personages are curiously and elaborately constructed" (ibid.:80).

The *Relación geográfica* map of 1580 depicts the center of San Juan Teotihuacan as built at the intersection of roads, with the Río San Juan running out of it. The center includes a large church, a tianguiz (market), and a square with "comunidad," or government building, written by it. On the periphery are other Colonial additions—a hospital, a mill, and a shop. Further out are the pyramids, glossed "oracle of Montezuma" (Fig. 7-3). On the 1580 map, the seven barrios (Atezcapan, Huitznahuac, Calputitlan, Atempa, Cozotlan, Zacatla, and Tlacaxoloc) are not labeled (Gamio 1922, II:518; AGN, Vínculos, Vol. 232, Fols. 15-20), but Atezcapan and the other barrios appear on a map from 1764 (Fig. 7-4).

Compared to other towns in the Teotihuacan Valley, San Juan Teotihuacan appeared to the observer in 1580 to be the most urbanized. The other towns—Tequizistlan, Tepexpan, and Acolman—were "built without order," with scattered houses, and no streets (Nuttall 1926:56). In contrast to the "polished people of good understanding" in Teotihuacan, the people of the other towns had "medium intelligence" (Tequizistlan) or were "well disposed but dull of understanding" (Acolman). In Tepexpan, "The foremost or chief natives are of medium understanding and the rest are rude and dull" (ibid.:55). Thus, although Teotihuacan lacked pyramids or other large public buildings in its center, it retained in the Colonial period evidence of its former status as the center of a province and the residence of rulers, in the form of its well built houses and sophisticated residents.

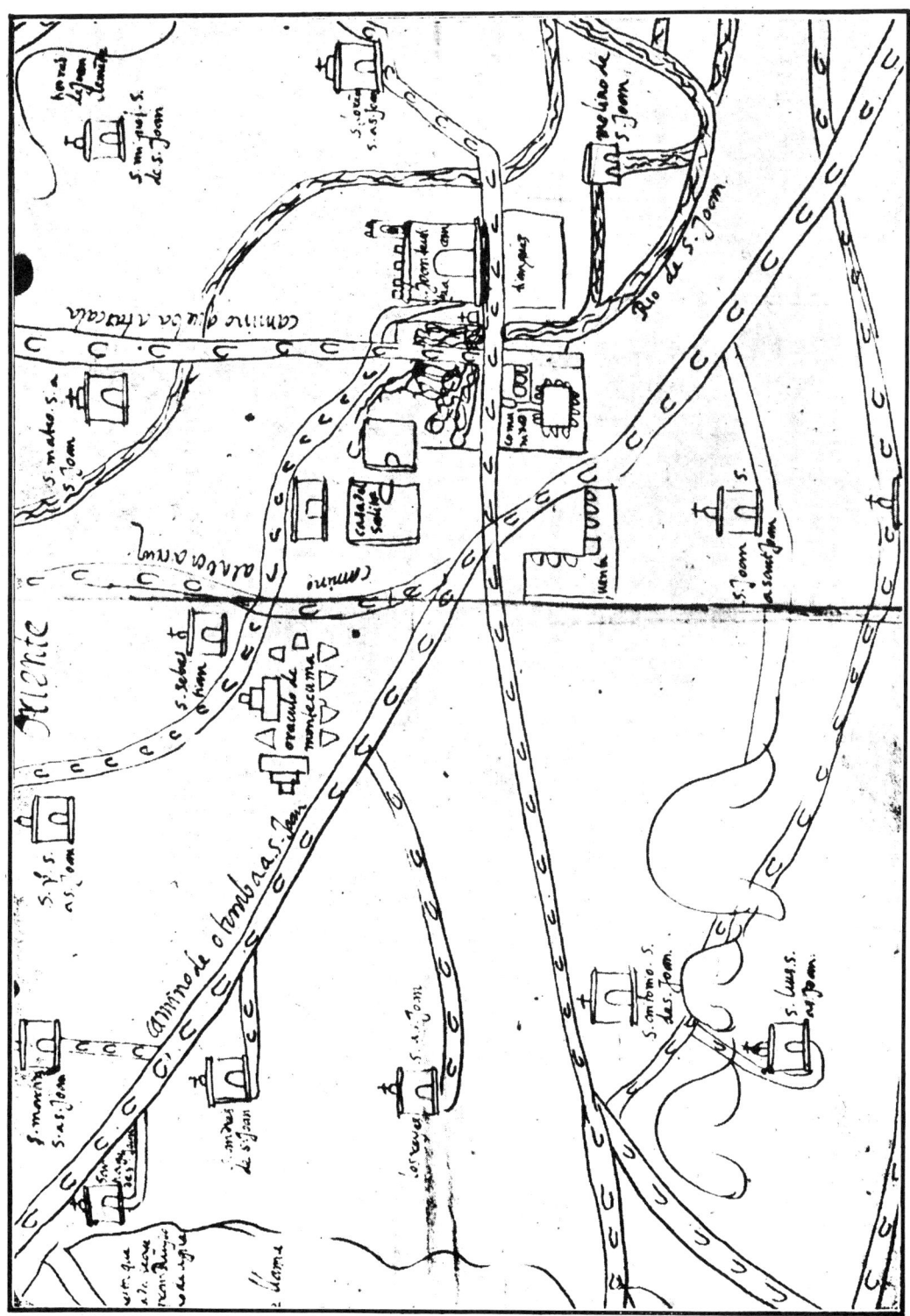

Fig. 7-3. Enlargement of a portion of the *Relación geográfica* map of 1580, showing the town of San Juan Teotihuacan (from Paso y Troncoso 1905, VI).

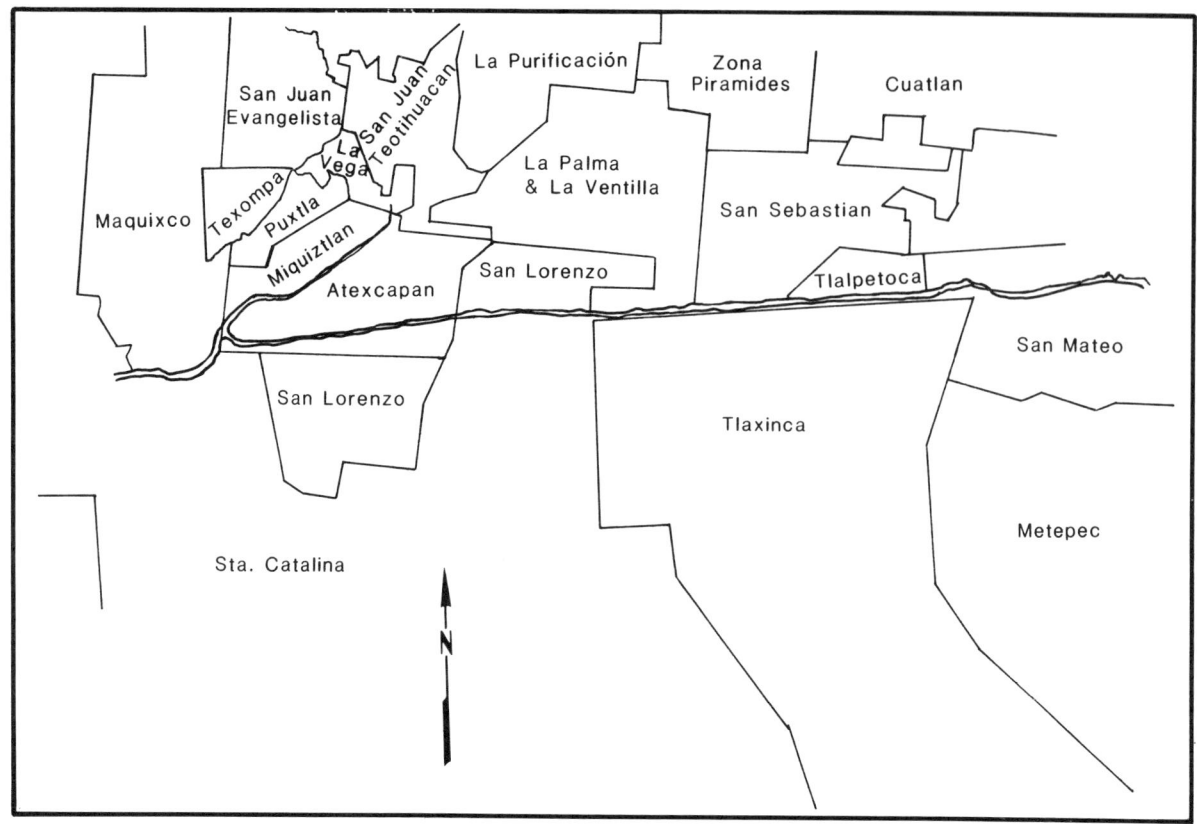

Fig. 7-4. Map of San Juan Teotihuacan's barrios, 1764 (after Munch 1976:36).

The People of Teotihuacan

The majority of people in Teotihuacan spoke Nahuatl. Otomí and Popoloca minorities lived in the area as well (Durán 1967:557; Nuttall 1926:56; Gerhard 1972:273).

The Postclassic people of the area were known as Acolhua. They claimed descent from Chichimec immigrants who founded Huexotla, Coatlinchan, and Texcoco, and later formed the Acolhua state based in Coatlinchan and later in Texcoco (Alva Ixtlilxochitl 1975-77, I:299-308; *Códice Xolotl* 1951). The political history of Teotihuacan is intimately interwoven with that of Texcoco.

Aztec Teotihuacan obtained prestige from its proximity to the ruins of Classic-period Teotihuacan. These ruins contained the "oracle where the Indians of Mexico and those of all other surrounding towns idolatrized" (Nuttall 1926:62).

In the Postclassic period, the natives described the Classic-period ruins as remains of a "Toltec" city, and the Colonial Texcocan historian Alva Ixtlilxochitl reported the nearby ruins and pyramids to be those of the greatest and most powerful Toltec city: "Among the most prominent [of Toltec cities] was Teotihuacan, city and place of the gods. It was a major city and more powerful than Tula, being the sanctuary of the Toltecs. It had the largest and very high temples and the most awesome buildings in the world, that today are visible as ruins and other great curiosities" (Alva Ixtlilxochitl 1975-77, I:272). The Toltecs worshipped the sun ("Tonacateuhtli") and his woman, the moon (ibid.). The city had a great market which met every 20 days (ibid.:283). When the Postclassic residents of Teotihuacan attributed the pyramids to the Toltecs, they were referring not to the archaeological site of Tula but to the legendary Toltec culture, a golden age of learnedness and skill with which they wished to be associated.

Religion and Ritual at Aztec Teotihuacan

The 1580 *relación* says that the natives of Teotihuacan worshipped the brothers of the moon: Huitzilopochtli and Mictlantecuhtli (Paso y Troncoso 1905, VI:222). They used the ancient ceremonial center, which was described in the *relación* of 1580.

> On [the] summit [of the highest pyramid] was a stone idol they named Tonacatecuhlli, made of very hard, rough stone all of one piece. It was eighteen feet long, six feet wide, and six feet thick, and faced West.
>
> In the level space in front of the temple, there was another small one eighteen feet high, on which was an idol smaller than the first, named Micttlantecuhtli, Lord of the Underworld. . . . to the north was another [pyramid] temple slightly smaller than the first, which was called the "Hill of the Moon," on top of which was another great idol nearly eighteen feet high which they named the Moon. Surrounding this [pyramid] temple were many others in the largest of which were six other idols called "the Brethren of the Moon," to all of which the priests of Montezuma, the lord of Mexico, with the said Montezuma came to offer sacrifices, every twenty days. [Nuttall 1926:68]

In addition, the archaeological survey reported numerous isolated ceremonial centers (a type of site common to the Aztec period) in the Teotihuacan Valley. These are single pyramids or plaza complexes located on natural hilltops. At these sites, ceremonial pottery but no residential structures are found (Sanders 1965:88).

Like other central Mexican people, the Postclassic inhabitants of Teotihuacan celebrated 18 monthly festivals, one every 20 days. The *relación* adds that every four-year period ended with a feast, but that "in the bissextile [leap] year there were five days in excess and they then held a feast in a large square that was situated between the two pyramids" (Nuttall 1926:69). (If this is correct, they deviated from the Mexica practice of having five extra days every year [nemontemi] during which special ceremonies were performed.)

Since Teotihuacan was part of the Acolhua (Texcocan) state, its rulers may have participated in Acolhua state rituals. Important among these were offerings to the rain deity, Tlaloc, made on mountaintops (Wicke and Horcasitas 1957). Texcocan deities included Tezcatlipoca, Huitzilopochtli, Quetzalcoatl, Tlaloc, Huehueteotl, Chalchiuhtlicue, and Mixcoatl. Nezahualcoyotl, who ruled Texcoco from 1430-72 and was one of the founders of the Triple Alliance, worshipped an "unseen god" (Alva Ixtlilxochitl 1975-77, I:447, II:126-26, 137). The sources do not say to what extent the Teotihuacanos participated in rituals at Texcoco. Moreover, the town's only explicitly recorded role in state rituals is that the ruler of Tenochtitlan made pilgrimages to the ancient pyramids (Nuttall 1926:68).

Territorial Organization of Teotihuacan

The polities in the Teotihuacan Valley appear on the 1580 *Relación geográfica* map, and Gibson (1964b:45-46) noted the interdigitation of Colonial cabeceras and sujetos in this area, due to the arrangement of lands created by the Acolhua state administrative system (Fig. 7-5). A strategy for promoting stability in both the Acolhua and Mexica political systems was to give local rulers income-producing estates detached from the town in which they had their palaces (Bray 1972; Evans 1980b). The area controlled by Teotihuacan's ruler consisted of a number of nearby villages as well as several more far-flung towns. In the Acolhua state, rulers were assigned lands whose residents paid tribute to them; these lands of lordship, or "señorío," were assigned to each tlatoani by Nezahualcoyotl when he reorganized the Acolhua state in the 1430s. Despite the general pattern of interdigitation of territories, Teotihuacan's sujetos were nonetheless more nucleated than those of Acolman or Tepexpan.

A diachronic analysis of the expansion or contraction of Teotihuacan's territory would be speculative, due to the scarcity of data. Teotihuacan was part of Huexotla's total territory before its conquest by Azcapotzalco. Later, after 1430, it was reorganized as part of the Acolhua state, by Nezahualcoyotl. The Colonial-period territory retained this composition for a time, until the towns were changed by congregaciones of Indians which were instituted starting in 1600 (Gamio 1922, I:378-81; Munch 1976).

Teotihuacan's territory was bounded by Texcoco, Tepetlaoztoc, Oztoticpac, and Quauhtlacinco on the south and east, and on the north by Maquixco, Tezontepeque and Azatecameca, and on the west by the territory of Temascalapa, Tepexpan, and Acolman (AGN, Vínculos, Vol. 232, Fols. 84-94; Alva Ixtlilxochitl 1975-77, II:308-30). Its 17 sujetos (ca. 1580) were San Lorenzo Aztecapa, San Miguel Tlotezcac, San Mateo Tenalco, San Sebastián Chimalpan, Santa María Aguatlan, San Francisco

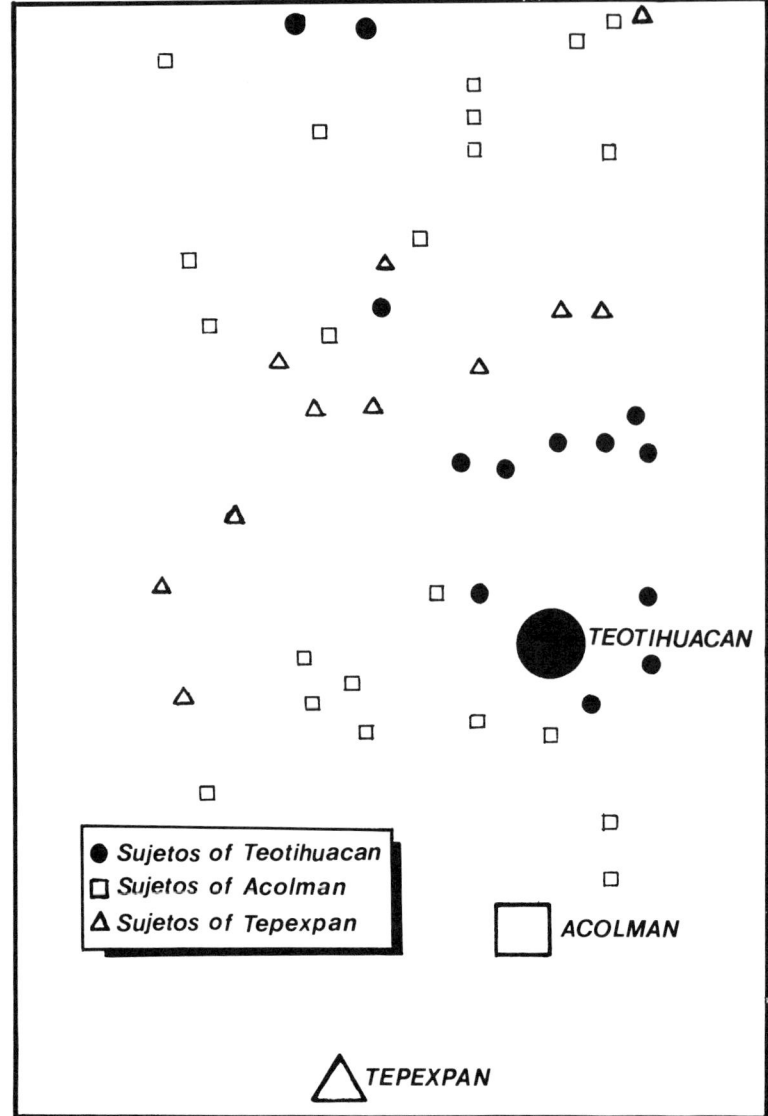

Fig. 7-5. Diagram of the interspersed dependencies (sujetos) of Teotihuacan, Acolman, and Tepexpan in 1580 (map in Paso y Troncoso 1905, VI; diagram after Gibson [1964b:46]).

Macatlan, San Pedro Tlaguican, San Martín Teacal, Santiago Tolman, San Andrés Oztolpachuacan, Los Reyes Aticpac, San Antonio Tlajomulco, San Agustín Ohuayucan, San Pedro Ocotitlan, San Miguel Tlalguac, San Luis Xiuhquemeccan, and San Juan Evangelista Tlaylotlacan (Nuttall 1926:60-61).

Teotihuacan's Political System

Officials and Titles

In 1519, Teotihuacan was governed by a single tlatoani. Apparently the ruler had no title other than tlatoani, although the tlatoani appointed by Nezahualcoyotl in 1434-35 at the time of the reorganization of the Acolhua state and the foundation of the Triple Alliance, abandoned the title atecpanecatl, a title associated with the former Tepaneca lords of the area (Chimalpahin 1965:194; Davies 1981:135). The tlatoani ruled from his tecpan, or "ruler's house" (AGN, Vínculos, Vol. 232, Fol. 66; Alva Ixtlilxochitl 1975-77, II:297).

The ruler of Teotihuacan was one of 14 major officials of the Acolhua state. He also held the position of judge within the state. Quetzalmamalitzin I possessed the title of Capitán General (no Nahuatl title is given) for the nobles; that is, he judged legal cases involving nobles of the provinces in his section of the Acolhua state (see Table 2-3). The lord of Otumba judged cases concerning commoners of the same provinces (Alva Ixtlilxochitl 1975-77, II:89). The tlatoani of Teotihuacan also served as a leader in the Acolhua armies and as an advisor to the ruler of Texcoco (see *Mapa Quinatzin*, in Robertson 1959:Pl. 46), along with the lords of the other 14 provinces ruled by tlatoque (Table 2-2).

Beyond the tlatoani, no other officials in the political system of Teotihuacan are described explicitly in documentary sources pertaining to Teotihuacan alone. Among commoners, legal disputes were resolved by the "chieftain or elder of the quarter," according to the *Relación geográfica* of 1580 (Nuttall 1926:72-73). The laws regarding theft, adultery, and escapes of slaves, resemble the codified laws of Texcoco (Nuttall 1926:72-73; Alva Ixtlilxochitl 1975-77, I:101-05).

From the description of the religious rites, we can infer that religious specialists may have performed rites at the pyramids, and since the rulers received tribute from various estates, there may have been tribute collectors (Guzmán 1938:93-94; *Tratado* 1904:445). From the sources available, however, one must conclude that the administrative system of Teotihuacan was quite simple and involved few officials.

Rulers and Succession to Rulership

The first recorded ruler of Teotihuacan was Xolotl, who founded a Chichimec state in Tenayuca, ca. A.D. 1120. Xolotl gave the province of Huexotla, which included Teotihuacan, to a noble named Tochintecuhtli (Guzmán however, points out that probably there were other intervening rulers [see Guzmán 1938:102]).

Teotihuacan was ruled as part of the polity of Huexotla until Quiyauhtzin, Huexotla's ruler, divided his territory between two of his sons. From then on, Teotihuacan was ruled by its own tlatoani. The list of rulers is presented in Table 7-1.

Figure 7-6 presents the genealogy of the rulers of Teotihuacan. Succession to rulership correlated with the individual's relationship to the previous ruler, and with marriage to the daughter of the previous ruler. The rulers were always related to, or dependents of, a higher political authority, either the rulers of Xolotl's kingdom, or those of Tex-

TABLE 7-1
RULERS OF TEOTIHUACAN

Approximate Dates of Reign	Tlatoque or *Caciques* of Teotihuacon
? –1283	Xolotl, ruler of Tenayuca
?1298–1357	Tochintecuhtli, ruler of Huexotla
1357–1382	Quiyauhtzin, ruler of Huexotla
?1382–1409	Cohuazanac, ruler of Huexotla
1409–1419	Huetzin II, first ruler of Teotihuacan
1419–1431	Totomochtzin, ruler under Azcapotzalco
1434–1486	Quetzalmamalitzin, appointed by Nezahualcoyotl
1486–1490	Cotzatzin
1491–1520	Xiuhtototzin
1521–1525	Manahualtzin
1525–1533	Juan Tlazolyaotzin
1533–1563	Francisco Verdugo Quetzalmamalitzin
1563–1580	Ana Cortés
1580–1597	Francisca Cristina Verdugo
1597–1639	Ana Cortés Ixtlilxochitl
	Other Colonial-period *caciques*....

(Source: Munch 1976; see also Guzmán 1938)

coco (*Tratado* 1904:433-34; Guzmán 1938; Alva Ixtlilxochitl 1975-77, II; Carrasco 1974, 1984).

Marriage Alliances of Teotihuacan's Rulers

The historical sources give little information about Teotihuacan before the formation of the Acolhua state. The first ruler of Teotihuacan, Huetzin, was the son of Quiyauhtzin, ruler of Huexotla, and a princess from Chalco (*Tratado* 1904:442-43; Munch 1976:60; Alva Ixtlilxochitl 1975-77, II:22). After the reorganization of the Acolhua state, ca. 1430-33, intermarriage between Teotihuacan's rulers and daughters of the Texcocan rulers became the practice. The favored marriage pattern was between the provincial ruler and a daughter of the Texcocan ruler's first wife—who was almost always a daughter of the tlatoani family of Tenochtitlan (Gamio 1922, I:534-37; Carrasco 1974:239). When the fifth ruler of Teotihuacan left only two daughters at his death, and no sons, both daughters married the same man, a son of the ruler of Texcoco (*Tratado* 1904:448; Guzmán 1938:96; see Fig. 7-6).

In summary, marriages linked the rulers of Acolhua city-states with noble lineages from the Acolhua capital (Carrasco 1974, 1984). As a result, the rulers of Teotihuacan were close relatives of the rulers of Texcoco, and once-removed from those of Tenochtitlan. Marriage alliances between Teotihuacan's rulers and ruling lineages of city-states at the same level in the Acolhua political hierarchy or with towns outside the Acolhua state are not recorded (a similar pattern is found in the marriages of the rulers of neighboring Tepexpan, who married elites from Tenochtitlan before A.D. 1430, but who later married those of Texcoco, as a result of the Texcocan ruler's intervention in elite marriages in Tepexpan [Alva Ixtlilxochitl 1975-77, II:118-20; *Tira de Tepechpan* 1978]).

Income of Teotihuacan's Rulers

Documents supplying data about the economic support of Teotihuacan's administrators concentrate on the income of the tlatoque and their families. In 1611, during legal proceedings regarding inheritance of the lands of the *cacicazgo* of Teotihuacan, one witness speaking on behalf of the descendants of the pre-Hispanic tlatoque of Teotihuacan summarized the rights and position of the ruling lineage:

> I have heard said that Don Francisco Quetzalmamalitzin and Xiuhtototzin, his father, and the rest of his ancestors were native lords of this pueblo and its subject towns, and as such native lords who were of this pueblo, they served them and gave them tribute and recognition and obedience, for they were great and lords, and I, this witness, saw that in the time when Don Francisco Quetzalmamalitzin lived, the natives of this pueblo came to him with tribute and acknowledgment of labor and produce, and they occupied themselves with working his fields for him and repairing his houses and with other services that they did for him. [AGN, Vínculos, Vol. 232, Fol. 77]

Don Francisco Quetzalmamalitzin left the lordship to his daughter in 1563, and he described it as the "kingdom and patrimony that includes all the lands of the town and its wards, that is divided into seven parts, from which the commoners and community pay tribute." In the same document, he leaves the land, houses, ("tecpas casas"—lord's houses) and everything called pillalli (nobles' lands) to his wife and daughter (AGN, Vínculos, Vol. 232; Alva Ixtlilxochitl 1975-77, II:283).

The lands controlled by the pre-Hispanic rulers (ca. 1430) and those owned by the early Colonial descendants of these rulers are listed in Tables 7-2 and 7-3. As the tlatoani families of Texcoco and Teotihuacan continued to intermarry, additional lands were added to the rulers' income, accounting for the differences in names of territory owned at different times (these differences can also be explained because there may have been several names for a particular plot or section). Table 7-4 itemizes the income of the tlatoani of Teotihuacan.

In addition to tribute from particular plots of land, Teotihuacan's lords may have received tribute from other nearby towns in exchange for letting them use water from the Río Teotihuacan. This practice is suggested by a lawsuit in 1589 in which the people of San Juan Teotihuacan petitioned for payment for water that had gone to Acolman: "We say that for many years in this area it has been the custom that because we allow the water that originates in our town to be carried to the town of Acolman and its villages, particularly for use by the mill of that town, it has given us and contributed each year blankets, feathers, and other things valuing more than 100 pesos" (AGN, Tierras, Vol. 1520, Exp. 5). They claimed that they hadn't been paid in five years, and that they had received payment for water for irrigation (not just for the Colonial-period mill) from "time immemorial." The disputants from Acolman admitted that they had paid Teotihuacan fowl, tortillas, tamales, cacao beans, Spanish wine, and pulque equal to 20 gold pesos each year, and that they had paid this tax for the preceding 5 years (ibid.). Elsewhere, it has been noted that the town of Teotihuacan "owned" the springs and collected an annual water tax from the towns below it and suggested that with the largest market and control of the water, Teotihuacan would have been able to dominate other towns in its valley (Sanders 1965:100).

Thus, the documents available for this study indicate that the tlatoani of Teotihuacan and his household received a sizable income from commoners in Teotihuacan and from villages outside the town. However, this economic system did not operate in isolation, and pertinent to understanding the operation of Teotihuacan is its relationship to Tenochtitlan and Texcoco.

Teotihuacan's Political Alliances

The *Relación geográfica* informants of 1580 said of Teotihuacan's history that:

> In heathen times its people constituted a republic which recognized no authority but that of its natural lords who were [of the race] named Chichimecas until Netzahualcoyotzin, lord of Texcoco, made war and tyrannized over the whole territory, killing sons of Tetzotzomoctzin, lord of Azcapotzalco, to whom all rendered allegiance. After the death of Tetzotzomoctzin the said Netzahualcoyotzin made

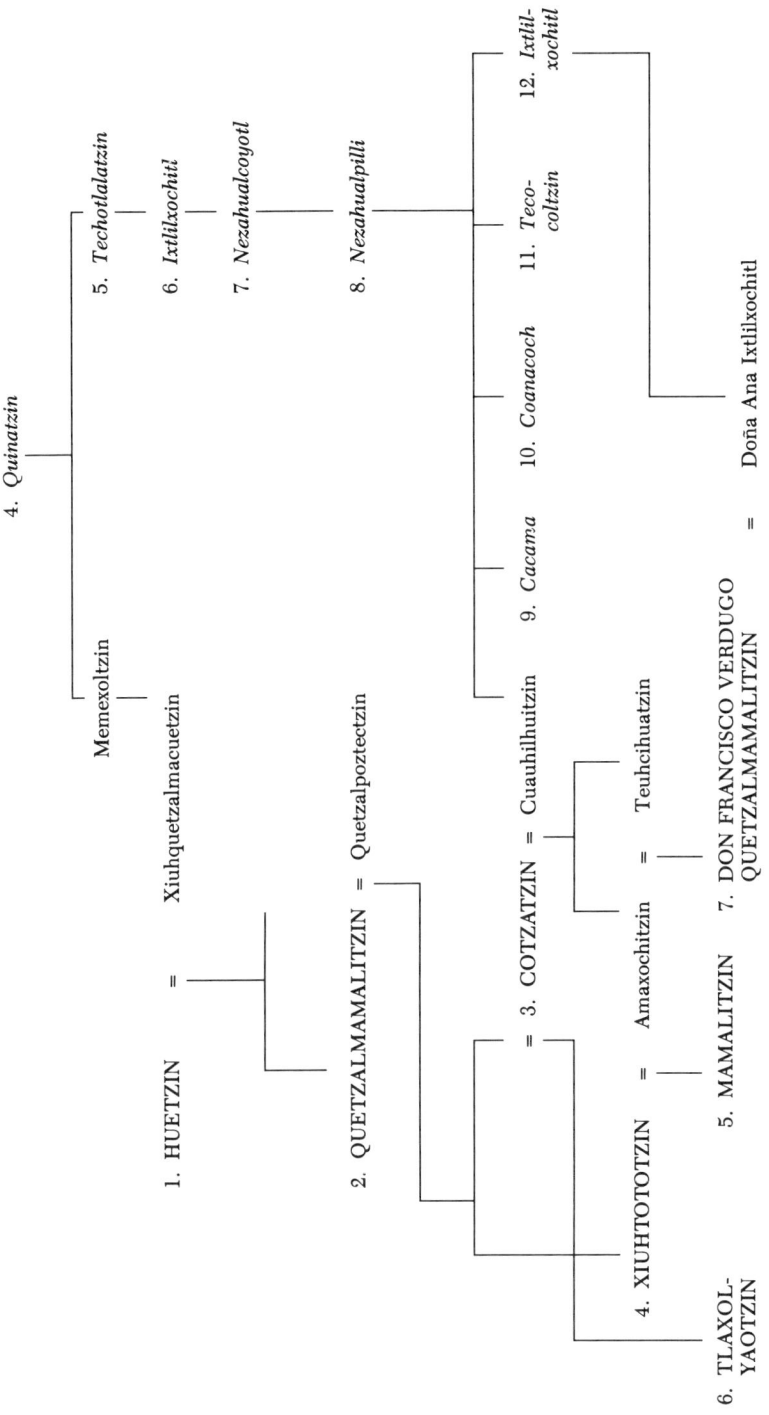

Fig. 7-6. Rulers of Teotihuacan (in capitals) and their marriages to women of the ruling family of Texcoco (in italics) (after Carrasco 1984).

TABLE 7-2
LANDS PAYING TRIBUTE TO THE TLATOANI OF TEOTIHUACAN

Tribute Lands Given in 1435	Dowry Lands from Nezahualcoyotl	Conquered Pueblos that Paid Tribute	Lands Belonging to Nezahualcoyotl's Daughter
Portions of land in:	Huexocalco	Mazahuacan	Acahuac
Texcoco	Quaxatlaco	Caltecoyan	Tequicistlan
Huexotla	Zacatlaco	Ecatzinco	Atliziutlan
Coatlinchan	Tepoxaco	Tlacapehuacan	Apan
Tepetlaoztoc	Texochihuacan	Ayahualolco	Xoxoquitepetl
Atezoyocan	Chimalpan	Chalco Quauhtlalpam	Zempoalan
Chiuhnauhtlan	Chalchihuacan		
Tenochtitlan	Tenango in Chalman:	Added and given to	
Tlatelolco	Tlaxolotl	Quetzalmamalitzin's sons:	
Ecatepec	Cazotlan	Palaces in	
	Tzapotlan	Xohuacan	
	Tolman near Temascalopan	Tecipilpan Mixquitlatlan	
	(All of the above are in the pueblo of Teotihuacan)		

(from Guzmán 1938:94–95; *Tratado* 1904:444–45)

TABLE 7-3
PROPERTY OF DON FRANCISCO QUETZALMAMALITZIN FROM HIS WILL, 1563

Tribute Paying Land in the Following Pueblos:
   Atezcapan[1]
   Huitznahua
   Calpoltitlan
   Cozotlan
   Atempan
   Zacatla
   Tlacaxoloc
Houses:
   "Casas tecpas" in Mizquititlan, Xihuacan, Aticpac
   Other houses in: Axopilco, Tlacoxalco, Tecuicmillpan
Other Lands in:
   Nextlateltitlan
   Cacalomillpan
   Tecuicmillpan
   Chicuacenazco (irrigated)
   Millchayahuac
   Tonatiuhyahuipan
   Cacatlatloxomolco

[1]Size of fields in Atezcapan, left to son:
   "20 palos de largo y de ancho 19" (20 × 19 units)
(AGN, Vínculos, Vol. 232, Fols. 10–15)

himself powerful by making an alliance with Montezuma, lord of Mexico. They divided between themselves the lands of the towns of Teotihuacan and Acolman. The inhabitants of Teotihuacan, in recognition of their overlordship, paid them as tribute, every eight days, some blankets made of coarse agave fiber, named *ichtilmates*, and some loads of agave leaves named *metlontli*. [Nuttall 1926:67-68]

The *relación* informants are decidedly anti-Texcocan, perhaps viewing the remote past as more pleasant than the recent past when the town was ruled by Texcoco and Tenochtitlan; this attitude contrasts sharply with that of Alva Ixtlilxochitl (1975-77), who wrote later and from the point of view of the Texcocan nobility, in ca. 1610.

Major events in Teotihuacan's development according to Alva Ixtlilxochitl, whose writings are the most detailed, can be briefly summarized as follows. About A.D. 1200, when Teotihuacan was founded, it was part of Xolotl's Chichimec confederation. It then became part of the subsequent Acolhua political system ruled by Techolatzin (1357-1409) and Ixtlilxochitl (1409-18) (Offner 1979:128-44, 152). From approximately 1298-1409, Teotihuacan was governed by the ruler of Huexotla and did not have its own tlatoani. In the late 1300s Teotihuacan was established as the seat of a tlatoani when Huexotla's domain was divided between the ruler's two sons.

Teotihuacan, along with Texcoco, was conquered by the Tepaneca (Azcapotzalcan) state, ca. 1418, and governed along with the other Acolhua polities until ca. 1428. The Tepaneca, according to Ixtlilxochitl, used Texcoco, Coatlinchan, and Huexotla as administrative centers, replacing their indigenous rulers with sons of the Azcapotzalcan ruler, Tezozomoc. When the area was initially conquered, a captain of Tezozomoc's army called together the leaders of the three aforementioned towns, along with those of Teotihuacan and Tepexpan, and gave them orders as to who would receive

TABLE 7-4
TRIBUTE RECEIVED BY TEOTIHUACAN'S RULERS

From Towns Outside Teotihuacan's Territory	From Towns Within Teotihuacan's Territory
large blankets	6 bundles of mustard seed
large sashes	5 bundles of large blankets
feathered robes	10 bundles of white blankets
bows	1 handful + 10 of fine feathers
arrows	1 bundle + 5 of woven blankets
skirts	6 bundles of large blankets
silver	1 measure + 630 cacao beans
jade	72 fowl
feathers	? people to work for the tlatoani
clubs and shields	5 bundles of white mantas of cotton and maguey
sandals	7 bundles of maguey cloth
fowl	10 men to carry things
cocoa	5 bundles of 4-cornered blankets
chili peppers	140 loads of torch pine
salt	120 mats
wood for fire	60 woven seats
pine kindling	10 sets of baskets
pine nuts	? molcajetes
laying hens	10 pots
blouses	1 set of plates
skirts	2 sets of jars
aprons	
tending of forests and fields called "ruler's lands" or tlatocatlalli and war (captured) lands, or "yaotlalli"	Provided Daily for the Palace: 7 fanegas of corn 40 fowl 280 cacao beans 7 crates of tomatoes 7 crates of chili peppers 700 long chili peppers 7 crates of pumpkin seeds 7 measures of salt 30 loads of firewood 70 women to grind corn 7 water-carriers 32 men to work milpas ("ruler's lands")
"This was the tribute of the pueblos that have been mentioned" (Guzmán 1938:93–94).	"This was the charge and service that they did for the lords in Teotihuacan" (Guzmán 1938:94).

land and who would govern towns (Alva Ixtlilxochitl 1975-77, I:344-45).

Teotihuacan as a Dependency of Texcoco

In 1428, Texcoco, Tenochtitlan, and other city-states overthrew the Azcapotzalcan polity, and Nezahualcoyotl, the son of the previous Acolhua ruler, returned to rule in Texcoco. Nezahualcoyotl is credited with building the Texcocan state system and even with inventing most of the imperial system of the Triple Alliance (particularly by Alva Ixtlilxochitl, his descendant, but also by Pomar [1941] and by Piña Chan in recent literature [1976]). Nezahualcoyotl reorganized the Acolhua state into 14 polities with tlatoque and 8 calpixqui-administered provinces. Teotihuacan was ruled by a tlatoani, the son of the former ruler. Within the organization of the Texcocan state, Teotihuacan's roles were as follows.

With 15 other towns, Teotihuacan provided supplies and labor to maintain the Texcocan palace for six months of each year. They provided wood, charcoal, mats, and other items needed in the palace. People from these 15 provinces swept, carried water, and cared for fields in which corn and other produce was grown for the ruler (Torquemada 1975, I:167; Alva Ixtlilxochitl 1975-77, II:114).

Teotihuacan's ruler was one of 14 advisors (the

tlatoque of 14 city-states) to the Acolhua ruler. He is pictured on the *Mapa Quinatzin* (Robertson 1959:Pl. 46) at the right of the Acolhua ruler in the palace. In this capacity, Teotihuacan's tlatoani led armies, and one tlatoani of Teotihuacan, Quetzalmamalitzin, was called "Capitán General" of the kingdom of Texcoco (Alva Ixtlilxochitl 1975-77, II:145, 213).

The tlatoani of Teotihuacan was a judge for legal cases involving nobles in the "Milpa" divison of the Acolhua state (ibid.:89; see Chapter 2).

Like other provinces in the Acolhua state, Teotihuacan's territory contained fields which paid tribute in produce to Texcoco's nobles. Likewise, the tlatoani of Teotihuacan received income from fields in other city-states' territories.

> And when Lord Nezahualcoyotl reapportioned the lands, he gave some in this pueblo to lords of Mexico and to the lords of Culhuacan, and in the same manner also, he gave lands to the lord of Teotihuacan who also had lands and vassals in several places who brought tribute to him. [Guzmán 1938:94-95]

Teotihuacan's tlatoani received parcels of land in Texcoco, Huexotla, Coatlinchan, Tepetlaoztoc, Atezoyocan, Acolman, Chiconauhtla, Tenochtitlan, Tlatelolco, and Ecatepec (ibid.:95). According to the same document, the ruler of Teotihuacan also received land as part of a dowry when he married Nezahualcoyotl's daughter. She also had lands of her own paying tribute to her, which she was given by her father (see Table 7-2 for a list of these lands; unfortunately, no measurements are provided by which to calculate the amount of land involved—a description and some quantities of tribute paid to Teotihuacan's tlatoani appear in Table 7-4, however). All these parcels of land stayed in the family of the rulers of Teotihuacan, and with others belonging to the Texcocan ruler's family, they are mentioned in Colonial litigation regarding possesions of the *cacicazgo* of Teotihuacan (AGN, Vínculos, Vol. 232; Munch 1976).

The terms used for land indicate how land was allocated for state purposes. Documents dealing with Teotihuacan mention the following types: tequitlalli, or tribute lands; tlatocatlalli, or lands supporting the tlatoani; tecpantlalli, or lands supporting the tlatoani's court; tetzcoco tlatocatlalli, or lands paying tribute to Texcoco's ruler; and pillalli, or nobles' lands, which paid tribute to nobles. Pillalli included lands that could be inherited by the tlatoani's children, including the lands belonging to Nezahualcoyotl's daughter, which were to be inherited by the eldest son exclusively, by order of Nezahualcoyotl (Guzmán 1938:95).

Thus, Teotihuacan provided labor and goods to the Texcocan state, as well as soldiers for war, led by its tlatoani. Its territory contained parcels of land which commoners worked to provide income for nobles in Teotihuacan, Texcoco, and other city-states such as Culhuacan. As mentioned previously, Teotihuacan also had obligations to Tenochtitlan, and these will be discussed below.

Teotihuacan as a Tributary Province of Tenochtitlan

The amount of tribute paid by Teotihuacan to Texcoco or Tenochtitlan is not quantified, but simply itemized. The town paid wood and other items needed for daily maintenance of the Texcocan palace for 6 months each year. Nezahualcoyotl of Texcoco and Moctezuma of Tenochtitlan divided lands of Teotihuacan and Acolman between them (Nuttall 1926:67-68). The *relación* says that the inhabitants of Teotihuacan paid them tribute every eighty days, in the form of blankets made of agave fiber and loads of agave leaves (ibid.:68). This is very little, and perhaps the informants in 1580 wanted to minimize the quantity paid in order to reduce their own tribute to the Spaniards.

In his study of the *Codex Mendoza*, Barlow included Teotihuacan in the "Acolhuacan" tributary province, even though it is not pictured in the document (Barlow 1949:69). The tribute paid from this area was 2000 bundles of white mantas, 1200 bundles of rich thin mantas in three styles, 400 loincloths, 400 women's skirts and blouses, 121 warrior costumes with shields, 4 wooden bins of agricultural produce—1 each of maize, beans, chia, and amaranth (Barlow 1949:71-72). These items are the same as those paid to the tlatoani to Teotihuacan, but there is no record of how or if they were passed on to Tenochtitlan.

However, of the 14 lordships in the Acolhua state, only two (Tepexpan and Tezoyuca) appear in the *Codex Mendoza* (1925:21v-22r). Other tribute-collection points were in towns outside the seats of tlatoque, though in city-state territories (such as Aztaquemeca, outside of Otumba, or Quauhyocan, a sujeto of Acolman, or Tlachyahualco, subject to Tepexpan [see Barlow 1949:69-70]). The place-names appearing as part of Acolhuacan province in the *Codex Mendoza* also do not overlap with the tribute-collection centers of the Acolhua state (Table 2-2). Apparently tribute-collection centers were not placed in city-state centers as often as they were placed in towns governed by administrators. These data, however, do not exclude the possibility that the city-state centers' rural areas paid tribute to Tenochtitlan. As we have seen in the cases of Amecameca and Cuauhtitlan, imperial tribute centers were often placed outside of the town centers that were the residences of tlatoque and that were political centers (perhaps to avoid obvious conflict with local rulers' jursidictions); throughout the Valley of Mexico, the tribute-collection hierarchy and the political decision-making hierarchy had become largely differentiated by the early 1500s.

Summary and Conclusions

Historical Summary

The Postclassic polity of Teotihuacan, according to native historians, was affiliated with the Chichimec political realm of Xolotl (ca. A.D. 1224-83), and with the succeeding Acolhua (Texcocan) state (A.D. 1430-1520). Initially part of the polity of Huexotla, Teotihuacan was ruled by its own tlatoani starting in 1409, when Huexotla's ruler divided his territory between his two sons. This line of rulers survived the disruption of the Azcapotzalcan conquest and the subsequent Azcapotzalcan-Tenochca war (1428-30), for a member of the ruling lineage was reinstated when Nezahualcoyotl, ruler of Texcoco, reorganized the Acolhua state (ca. 1430-33). Following the formation of the Triple Alliance, Teotihuacan was closely controlled administratively by Texcoco. Its people also paid tribute to Texcoco and directly to Tenochtitlan, until the Spanish Conquest in 1519.

Internal Organization

Teotihuacan was a town of up to 10,000 people, located in the center of the Teotihuacan Valley. Lacking an elaborate urban center, the huge Classic-period pyramids near the town served as its ritual center. Teotihuacan's internal administrative organization consisted of one tlatoani and his dependents, and lower-level officials such as ward chiefs and tribute collectors. The tlatoani drew income from the town's sujetos and from estates outside the town. Though territorial dispersion was common in the area, Teotihuacan controlled a more concentrated territory than its neighbors in the Teotihuacan Valley and may have controlled their access to water.

Teotihuacan as a Dependency of the Triple Alliance Capitals

Under the Triple Alliance, and as a province within the Acolhua state, Teotihuacan performed few independent functions, economic or political. However, it was an important ritual site for the ruler of Tenochtitlan.

As a dependency of the Acolhua state, Teotihuacan was one of 14 provinces whose tlatoque also served as advisors to the ruler of Texcoco. The tlatoani of Teotihuacan was a regional judge who decided cases dealing with the elite class of one-third of the state. He also served as a military chief and, with warriors from Teotihuacan, participated in Triple Alliance wars. The tlatoani of Teotihuacan was appointed by Texcoco's ruler, and after 1430, incumbents of the office married women from the ruling lineage of Texcoco, and thus were brothers-in-law of the Texcocan rulers.

Although a political dependency of Texcoco, Teotihuacan paid tribute to both Texcoco and Tenochtitlan. Teotihuacan provided palace maintenance (furnishing labor and subsistence goods) along with other provinces for 6 months of each year. Fields in its territory were divided among the rulers of Texcoco, Tenochtitlan, Culhuacan, and Teotihuacan, so that Teotihuacan's commoners paid tribute in local agricultural products and crafted goods to at least four lords. Some of the Teotihuacan rulers' income came from estates farther away, a conscious strategy of the Acolhua state to separate rulers from their local bases of support (and hence to decrease their independence and ability to secede). Texcocan control over the lordship of Teotihuacan was further increased by dowry lands given to the daughters of Texcocan rulers who married rulers of Teotihuacan; these dowry lands were located within Teotihuacan's territory (in contrast to lands given to the Teotihuacan rulers [sons-in-law], which were further removed from the

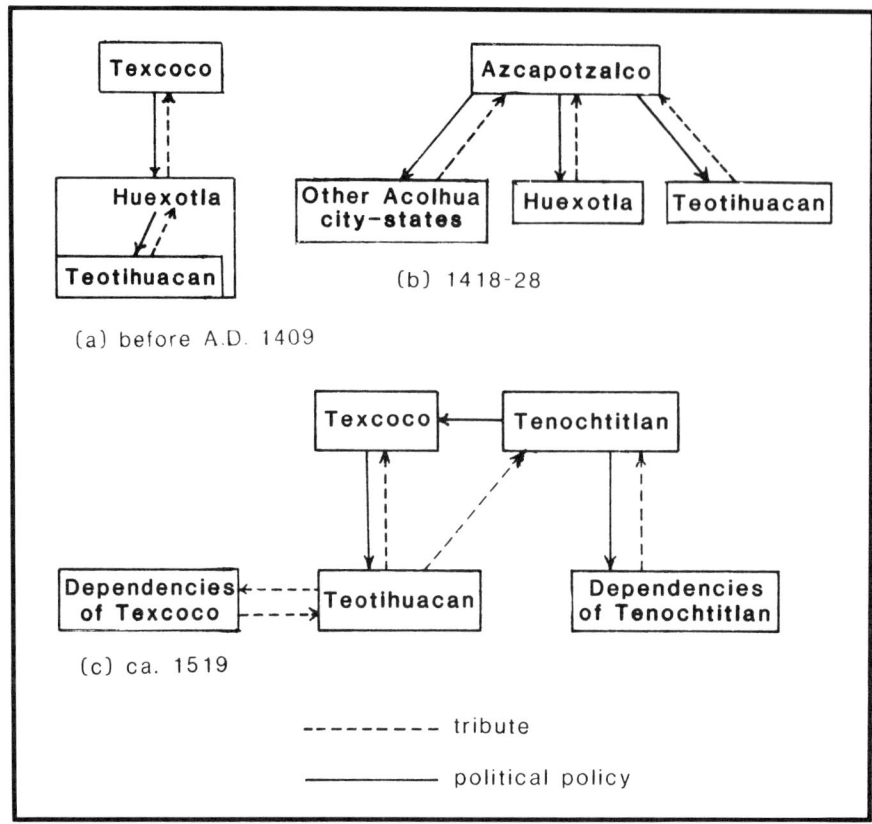

Fig. 7-7. Diagram of Teotihuacan's place in the Valley of Mexico political hierarchy, (a) before A.D. 1409, (b) A.D. 1418-30, (c) ca. A.D. 1519.

town) (Guzmán 1938:95). Few data on long-distance trade or market exchange are available, so it is unclear to what extent they were important redistributive mechanisms in this area.

To conclude, Teotihuacan was politically a secondary center within the Acolhua state. Its position in the Valley of Mexico political hierarchy at various times is diagrammed in Figure 7-7.

Chapter 8

Conclusions: The Aztec Empire as Seen from Its Dependencies

City-States

In the Valley of Mexico in the Postclassic period (A.D. 1150-1520), the basic political unit was the city-state, or altepetl. Each city-state consisted of an urban center and its surrounding territory. The word altepetl also meant "king" or "sovereign," and each polity was ruled by a hereditary ruler, called tlatoani, or "speaker."

According to their own histories, most city-states in the Valley of Mexico were founded after the fall of Tula (ca. A.D. 1168), and archaeological evidence suggests that the urban centers associated with these polities expanded in population between 1350 and 1520 (Sanders, Parsons, and Santley 1979; Parsons et al. 1982). Archaeological evidence reveals that although sites of some of the city-states were founded before the historic period, others (such as Tenango and Malacachtepec) developed later than their histories claim (Parsons et al. 1982:351).

City-states sometimes allied with others to form confederations or leagues, and the Aztec empire, originally an alliance of three city-states, grew by accretion, absorbing other city-states by alliance and by conquest. The Aztec empire in 1519 consisted of 489 towns within 38 provinces and covered much of Mesoamerica (Barlow 1949). This study has concentrated on the operation of the empire's central area rather than on its entirety, and it has focused on city-states in the Valley of Mexico. The imperial capital, Tenochtitlan, promoted greater involvement of these nearby city-states in imperial activities, in an attempt to create a stable, pacified area around itself.

This study of political processes has analyzed in detail the operation of five city-states within the center of the empire. It has examined the nature of political organization at the city-state level, and it has examined variation among five polities before and after their conquest by the empire. This comparative, regional approach was chosen in order to avoid the limitations of single community studies, which can result in one polity being regarded as typical of all polities. Political interactions between five city-states and the capital have been compared, in order to achieve a regional perspective on the operation of the empire. The case studies in Chapters 3-7 provide data for comparing city-states' location, size, political affiliation, and political organization before conquest. Finally, the study examined the city-states after their incorporation into the empire, to assess how much autonomy they retained, what functions were taken over by the empire and which were not, and to what extent the first-conquered polities were more "Mexicanized" than those that had been part of the empire for a shorter time. The next few pages present a summary of these findings.

Organization of Five Aztec City-States: A Comparison

Territories

City-state territories varied greatly in size, as shown in Figure 8-1, which compares the extent of five city-states. Since indigenous and Colonial-period documents do not delineate the exact boundaries of these city-state territories, the size of the territory of each city-state studied here has been approximated by drawing a line around its dependent towns. The estimated territory sizes are: Cuauhtitlan, 900 km^2; Coyoacan, 420 km^2; Xochimilco, 250 km^2; Amecameca, 125 km^2;

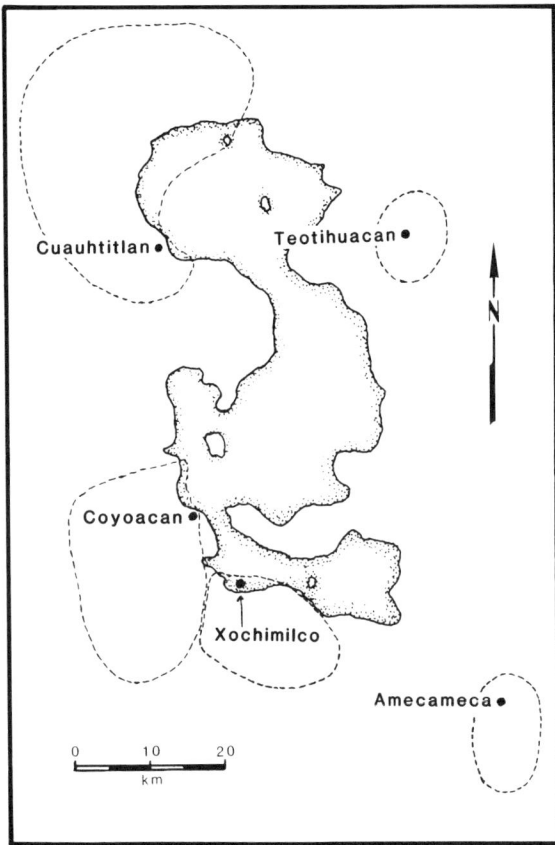

Fig. 8-1. Comparison of estimated sizes of the territories of five city-states in approximately A.D. 1500. Since exact boundaries are unknown, limits for each city-state are indicated by a line that encloses all its dependent towns. Cuauhtitlan = 900 km²; Coyoacan = 420 km²; Xochimilco = 250 km²; Amecameca = 125 km²; Teotihuacan = 100 km².

Teotihuacan 100 km². The largest territories shown in Figure 8-1 are those of Cuauhtitlan and Coyoacan. These large city-states governed not only their own urban centers and their immediate hinterlands; they also administered other urban centers and their territories (cf. Ramírez de Fuenleal 1870).

The size of the population available for labor affected the income of the rulers. Greater territorial size meant that the ruler of Cuauhtitlan, for instance, could call on a greater number of corvée laborers to build his palace and temple, have canals made, etc., as recorded in the *Anales de Cuauhtitlan* (see Chapter 4). Of the five city-states examined here, those with larger territories—Coyoacan, Cuauhtitlan, and Xochimilco—had large ceremonial-civic centers as well as extensive canals and causeways, whereas the smaller (and in this case, less centralized) polities—Teotihuacan and Amecameca—did not have as much monumental public-building construction in their urban centers. In addition, it follows that larger territories provided more manpower for military ventures and, with more available warriors, the larger polities would be politically more influential.

The territorial sub-units within city-states included (1) wards of the urban center, or tlaxillacaltin, (2) rural villages and hamlets, (3) rural lands with resident laborers who paid tribute in produce from the land directly to the tlatoani, and (4) towns with their own tlatoque who took orders from a higher-ranking tlatoani. In addition, the tlatoque of some city-states (among them Cuauhtitlan and Teotihuacan) controlled portions of land outside their own territories, from which laborers paid tribute to them.

The span of city-state rulers' control varied in relation to territorial size. Amecameca's teteuctin controlled only their own urban barrios and probably outlying villages, although there is no information delineating exactly how the 13 surrounding villages were administered. In contrast, in "a remarkable instance of tlatoani encroachment..." (Gibson 1964b:39), Cuauhtitlan expanded to govern city-states which had been ruled previously by independent lords. Xochimilca territory extended originally far to the south and east of the urban center of Xochimilco and included a number of dependent tlatoque. Coyoacan's ruler governed many towns and villages, at least one with a tlatoani. Teotihuacan, which was created as a city-state by the division of Huexotla's territory between two sons of its ruler, and which was always a dependency of a larger polity, did not expand in size by absorbing other polities. Its territory encompassed only villages and hamlets in the Teotihuacan Valley and a few villages outside the valley.

Urban Centers

Among the city-states studied here, larger territories did not necessarily correlate with larger urban centers ca. 1519. The larger centers were in Coyoacan (25,000-30,000), Xochimilco (20,000-25,000), and Cuauhtitlan (ca. 10,000-15,000), while the smaller were in Teotihuacan and Amecameca (ca. 5,000-10,000). The data acquired in the course of this study have demonstrated that political events affected the size of Aztec city-state territories and that these territories changed over time. Thus, by 1519 Xochimilco, one of the largest urban centers, administered a reduced territory, and Cuauhtitlan, an urban center smaller than either Xochimilco or Coyoacan, administered a much larger territory. Sizes and populations of Aztec urban centers in the period between A.D. 1100 and 1520 are of course only estimates, since most Aztec urban sites are now covered by modern occupation (Sanders, Parsons, and Santley 1979).

All city-states contained a ruler's palace, and most contained civic-ceremonial buildings and a marketplace. Beyond these functional uniformities, the city-states' urban centers varied greatly in form. Cuauhtitlan apparently was constructed around a temple plaza complex, built ca. 1350, following years of dispersed settlement (see Chapter 4). It had four urban administrative divisions whose residents, along with those of dependent towns, contributed labor for projects such as canal building, temple construction, and warfare (*Anales de Cuauhtitlan* 1945:34). The town of Amecameca, founded later, had little civic-ceremonial construction (its people visited a shrine on a nearby mountain) although it had palaces and temples (Cortés 1971:80). The town had seven divisions, each founded by a separate lineage, and each was the residence of its "chief," or teuctli. The town of Teotihuacan, founded among the pyramids of the Classic-period site, was dispersed in form (Sanders, Parsons, and Santley 1979), although it was reported to have had more elaborate architecture than other nearby towns and villages (Nuttall 1928). Xochimilco consisted of three divisions, each one the residence of a tlatoani (Carrasco 1977). It contained a market and port, as well as canals and bridges, and outside the town were extensive chinampa plots (Cortés 1971:198-99; Torquemada 1975, II:159). The urban design of the large city of Coyoacan is not well-described, but it is reported to have contained fine houses, temples, and a market; the urban center comprised two major administrative divisions with up to thirty-two subdivisions (Carrasco and Monjarás-Ruiz 1976; Pérez Rocha 1978).

City-State Officials

The city-states' administrative hierarchies were headed by one or more tlatoque. In those ruled by multiple tlatoque (such as Xochimilco and Amecameca), each tlatoani governed a designated territory which included a palace, lands, and dependents. One of the multiple tlatoque was usually selected to carry out special tasks such as diplomatic missions or negotiations with confederations or other governments, and one of multiple tlatoque could be selected for temporary offices, such as war leader.

Tlatoque were supreme rulers of their city-states. They meted out justice within their territories. They ensured the material and spiritual well-being of their people. From documents about Cuauhtitlan there are explicit references to the local lord acting as a religious functionary and, in Amecameca, a "ruler priest" is mentioned. Probably most tlatoque provided feasts and made public sacrifices. The tlatoani was the highest-ranking official in the city-state, and as such he collected tribute in goods and labor from his people. Rulers of Xochimilco and Cuauhtitlan are recorded as having distributed items collected as tribute to their followers two or four times per year.

City-state rulers were assisted by various officials. The highest offices were held by nobles. In Xochimilco, three to four officials served as general-purpose advisors to each of the three tlatoque (Carrasco 1977). In Cuauhtitlan, before its conquest by the Aztec empire, leaders of four divisions assisted the ruler in administering that city-state's dependencies for public works, foreign affairs, and warfare (*Anales de Cuauhtitlan* 1938:224). In Amecameca, rulers were assisted by their closest relatives (Chimalpahin 1965:73).

The titles of the highest-level administrators are recorded more commonly than are descriptions of their duties. Titles were in many cases granted to elites and sometimes to commoners as rewards for participation in warfare; such titles conferred status or rank, and they did not always entail specific obligations. When a noble who had received a title became an advisor to a ruler, his administrative duties fell within a wide range of general policy-making and advising the ruler. The highest-ranking offices in the city-states examined here thus seem to be somewhat undifferentiated, like those of the council of four advisors to the ruler of Tenochtitlan.

Ranked below the highest-level advisors, whose activities have been described above, were nobles who ruled dependent towns; for instance, the ruler of Tacubaya took orders from the ruler of Coyoacan (Carrasco and Monjarás-Ruiz 1976). In Cuauhtitlan, individuals called tlacateuctli, tlacochteuctli, or tlacochcalcatl administered dependent towns (*Anales de Cuauhtitlan* 1938:180, 281-82; 286-87). Some were nobles appointed by the tlatoani; others were hereditary lords of these towns (ibid.:180, 286-87).

Titles of officials who performed more specialized tasks also appear in the chronicles. Documents describing both Cuauhtitlan and Coyoacan mention officials in charge of boundary measurements, and a Colonial document from Amecameca mentions an individual who maintained land maps and deeds (AGN, Tierras Vol. 2674, Exp. 1). Priestly titles are mentioned in sources describing Amecameca, and here the priests in some cases participated in rulership with the teteuctin, or lords (Chimalpahin 1965:201).

Officials at the lowest levels had explicit duties. In Coyoacan, certain officials collected market taxes, and officials who led artists' and craftmen's guilds are recorded in documents from Coyoacan and Xochimilco. Under the supervision of nobles, or principales, were barrio officials called tcquitlato, calpixqui, and tepixqui. These officials organized corvée labor and payment of taxes at the ward or barrio level. In most cases persons holding the office of tequitlato were commoners (Carrasco and Monjarás-Ruiz 1976:18-22). However, evidence suggests that offices held by both commoners and nobles were either inherited or were at least most likely to pass from father to son (Carrasco and Monjarás Ruiz 1976; Carrasco 1977).

Central-Place Functions of City-States

Political Decision-making. In each city-state, the urban center was functionally the central place in the territory. A town was the city-state's center because it was the residence of the ruler and contained his palace. The city-state center was the location where all the highest policy decisions were made and where rituals involving all the communities in a city-state were performed. The tlatoani and his assistants directed many of these organizing functions. These activities varied in content and structure from one city-state to another, as seen in Chapters 3-7, but the general categories of activities are listed below.

Rituals. The city-state's principal center was the location of calendrical rites for the territory. Towns had distinctive deities, and annual rites were performed in Xochimilco, Cuauhtitlan, and Coyoacan. In Amecameca and Teotihuacan some important rituals were performed at shrines near the urban center—a sacred hill and the Classic-period pyramids—rather than in urban temples.

Protection and Warfare. The urban center sometimes provided protection during wars (for instance, the Xochimilca burned their bridges and used their canals as moats against the Spaniards). The tlatoani usually led the warriors into battle.

Law and Courts. The tlatoani dispensed justice, according to local traditions of the city-state or, as in the case of the Acolhua city-states, according to standardized codes of his political confederation. He appointed judges to posts in dependencies, and in Teotihuacan, barrio leaders are specifically mentioned serving as judges.

Public Works. The tlatoani initiated the planning, building, and maintenance of canals, aqueducts, and causeways, as well as construction of temples and palaces. Assistants to the tlatoani organized and directed these projects. The ruler of Teotihuacan oversaw use of water from springs located in the town.

Economic Administration. The tlatoani received tribute from commoners in his territory. This tribute consisted mainly of subsistence goods provided at daily, weekly, and monthly intervals, and, at longer intervals, cloth or other craft goods manufactured in the city-state, and sometimes cacao beans. City-state tlatoque and their households regularly received labor from the community for the maintenance of their houses and the cultivation of their fields. Tlatoque are reported to have given some of the materials collected to city-state officials at specified intervals (two to four times annually), usually in a ceremonial context. For higher authorities, the tlatoani served as the organizer of labor tribute from his territory.

Markets. The city-state's urban center was the focus of exchange, and markets were held at definite intervals. The five city-states studied here all were said to have had large markets. Market officials collected taxes from traders in Coyoacan and in Xochimilco. One divison of Amecameca (Panohuaya) held a regional market.

Rulership

As discussed in the preceding chapters, Aztec city-states were ruled by one or more hereditary rulers, or tlatoque. Noble lineages preceded the founding of city-states, according to traditional histories. As in Tenochca and Acolhua historical mythology, the origin myths of three of the five city-states examined here state that each community was settled by immigrating leaders and their people. Some of these groups claimed to have descended from "primitive" hunters carrying bows and arrows (Chichimeca); other groups claimed to be descendants of more cultured ancestors (Toltecs), who were related to the rulers of the great Classic-period city of Tula.

Cuauhtitlan was said to have been founded ca. A.D. 804, by an individual named Mixcoatl and his followers (*Anales de Cuauhtitlan* 1945), and the Xochimilca were said to have settled in the Valley of Mexico ca. A.D. 1100 (Durán 1964:10). Amecameca's seven ruling lineages arrived separately, between the late 1200s and early 1300s (Chimalpahin 1965:53, 72-73, 174-76, 203-05; see Chapter 3), and they claimed different origins. The Nonoalca, who arrived with nobles, painted books, practiced xochiyaotl, and worshipped Tezcatlipoca, called themselves "palace people" and had "Toltec" culture traits; the other groups claimed Chichimec deities and origins (ibid.; see Chapter 3).

Teotihuacan's ruling lineage was said to have been established around A.D. 1409, when the kingdom of Huexotla was divided between two sons of the ruler, and Coyoacan's ruling lineage was established by the Azcapotzalcan ruler, Tezozomoc, in the late 1300s. In the case of Teotihuacan, a permanent Acolhua rulership was firmly established ca. 1434, when the Acolhua state was formed. Thus, both Teotihuacan's and Coyoacan's ruling lineages were established by the rulers of city-states on which they were dependent, and the rulers of these city-states were related by blood or marriage to the rulers of their capital.

Long historical traditions served to legitimize a noble lineage's right to hold the teuctli or tlatoani office and adjunct positions and to receive tribute in goods and services from the commoners. In exchange, commoners would be protected from war, invasion, chaos, and famine. They would also receive spiritual leadership—protection from natural disasters, etc., through intervention with deified ancestors and with natural forces.

In Nahua culture, deities and early chiefs, leaders, or heroes frequently have similar names, suggesting that such leaders may have been deified after death, and that these deified ancestors became protector gods of city-states. Over time, their status as heroes or protectors became embellished by association with natural forces with which they were thought to be able to intercede (López Austin 1973). In this study, examination of specific lineages has disclosed that in Cuauhtitlan, early rulers resided near the temple of Mixcoatl (*Anales de Cuauhtitlan* 1945:31-34). Mixcoatl was the name of an ancient war chief and also the city's protector deity. In Amecameca, at least one ruler was called "ruler-priest," or Teohua Teuctli (*Crónica Mexicáyotl* 1949:47). Both examples demonstrate a strong link between rulership and the supernatural. Lineages of rulers existed prior to the settlement of some city-states, and the ancestors and protector gods that aided the chiefs and their people in migrating and finding land on which to settle were believed to aid them in later times when they were settled in towns and territories.

A special relationship to deities may explain partially the status of ruling lineages and of the nobility in Nahua culture. Ancestry often provides a rationale for social stratification, and in Central Mexico in the Late Postclassic period, there was competition to claim ancestry from Toltec rulers, Chichimec lords, or other powerful rulers. The prestige of noble ancestry promoted the practice of arranging marriages with offspring of high-status noble lineages (for instance, Acamapichtli of Tenochtitlan married a "Toltec" princess from Culhuacan, and his offspring then could claim Toltec ancestry).

The recorded histories of city-states are most often the history of their nobles (sometimes one of the few surviving bits of information about a city-state is its list of rulers). In the period when city-states were being settled in the valley, the noble lineages could be regarded as isomorphic with city-states. In this period, peaceful division of territory sometimes occurred as a result of inheritance; for example, a lordship was created in Teotihuacan through division of Huexotla's territory between two sons of the ruler. At this time, lineages seem to have been regarded as more significant in defining a city-state than were territorial boundaries.

Conflicts between city-states in Early Aztec times can be characterized as struggles between lineages for land, space, and commoners to provide them with income. Early expansionist polities were controlled by a single lineage. For instance, the

Azcapotzalcan system was formed of Azcapotzalco, ruled by Tezozomoc, and several second-level city-states in which Tezozomoc's sons were placed as rulers. This method of organization was a way of expanding the span of direct control over conquered towns while at the same time getting competitive heirs out of the capital.

Later, when the Triple Alliance lords controlled the Valley of Mexico, rulership of city-states by indigenous noble lineages was still the explicit rule. However, rulership of city-states became connected to a valley-wide elite network centered at Tenochtitlan and Texcoco; for instance, sons of Tenochca rulers governed Ixtapalapa and Ecatepec in 1519. That inheritance was still a strong force is demonstrated by the fact that the Texcocan ruling dynasty was involved in a succession struggle at the time of the Spanish Conquest, with the result that its territory was eventually divided between two brothers. However, in the Late Aztec period, as Chapters 3-7 have demonstrated, rulership became a concern of the empire.

Succession to Rulership

City-states were the seats of tlatoque, offices traditionally filled by inheritance (with certain qualifications, skills, and experience required). However, a change brought about by the Aztec imperial system was that the personnel occupying tlatoani offices were sometimes changed as a function of political policy. Few conquered city-states were actually able to maintain orderly father-to-son succession, and maintaining a lineage's position was a struggle. As Chapters 3-7 have demonstrated, disruption in succession to the office of tlatoani occurred in Cuauhtitlan, Amecameca, Xochimilco, and Coyoacan. The rulers of small city-states struggled to keep members of their lineages as rulers; the imperial rulers attempted to appoint administrators responsive to imperial demands rather than to local loyalties. The empire often chose to seat pro-Mexica relatives of rulers (sons, brothers, cousins) in tlatoani offices of conquered city-states. Sons of Mexica nobles and local noblewomen (as in Amecameca), or sons of local lords and Mexica noblewomen (as in Chalco) were favored by the empire for appointment to tlatoani offices. As Chapters 3-7 have shown, the most drastic measures taken by the empire to control city-state administration were to impose an entirely new ruling lineage on a polity (as in Cuauhtitlan) or to set up a parallel Mexica lordship (as in Xochimilco and Azcapotzalco) in the city-state. Frequently the empire appointed a military ruler (quauhtlatoani) for a time and later appointed a tractable descendant of the former ruler, usually an individual educated in Tenochtitlan.

In summary, although city-states were originally by definition the seats of hereditary rulers, in the Valley of Mexico, under Aztec administration, succession to the office of tlatoani of dependent city-states was disrupted more and more often by imperial intervention, a result of the capital's goal of weaving a pan-valley elite network which emanated from the capital.

Marriage Alliances of Ruling Lineages

One way for tlatoque to maintain political power was through interdynastic marriage alliances. Marriage alliances were particularly beneficial with neighboring rulers because they promoted the formation of territorial mutual-interest blocs and, with more powerful lineages, they helped to secure protection. The rulers of Aztec city-states examined in this study formed marriage alliances in an attempt to maintain control of their territories.

The rulers of Amecameca tended to form alliances with towns to the east and south—for instance, with Huexotzinco. These alliances were convenient when the Amecamecan nobles fled from inter-valley conflicts which began in the 1370s. Following its conquest by Tenochtitlan, Amecameca's elites formed marriage alliances with the cihuacoatl branch of the Tenochca dynasty. Local elite women married Tenochca men; their sons (educated in Tenochtitlan) returned to become Amecameca's rulers under the empire.

Cuauhtitlan's rulers married elite women from the southern valley towns of Chapultepec and Culhuacan before the Triple Alliance. Under the Triple Alliance, the last Cuauhtitlan ruler before the Spanish Conquest married a daughter of Moctezuma II, making the lordship of Cuauhtitlan part of the Tenochca dynasty (although this ruler's secondary wives were from Tepaneca towns in his territory).

Teotihuacan's rulers all married daughters of the Texcocan rulers, making them sons-in-law of the Acolhua rulers; when a ruler of Teotihuacan was survived only by daughters, his two daughters both married a relative of the Acolhua ruler. Wife-giving to provincial rulers was the pattern throughout the Acolhua state (see Carrasco 1984).

Thus, the Tenochca and Acolhua rulers attempted to make the rulers of their dependencies part of their paramount dynasties. The Acolhua state's 14 provincial rulers were relatives of the Texcocan ruler. The Mexica also incorporated the tlatoani lineages of dependent city-states into the Mexica ruling lineage. This occurred in Chalco, Amecameca, Xochimilco, Cuauhtitlan, Coyoacan—city-states chosen for case-study here—and in other Mexica dependencies such as Chalco (Rounds 1979; Brumfiel 1983; Carrasco 1984). The valley was divided into two sections, Acolhua and Mexica, with the rulers of each section at the head of a lineage network. Tenochtitlan's and Texcoco's ruling families intermarried, and marriages between nobles of dependencies and their immediate capital were, of course, politically more advantageous to the dependency than were marriage alliances between dependencies at equal levels. Moreover, second-level ruling families of the Acolhua and Mexica territories did not intermarry, as evidenced dramatically by a story recounted by Ixtlilxochitl which describes the Acolhua ruler Nezahualcoyotl's assassination of a provincial ruler in Tepexpan and his subsequent marriage to the widow. Following this, Tepexpan's rulers were allied by marriage to the Acolhua rulers and no longer had marriage alliances with the nobility of Tenochtitlan (Alva Ixtlilxochitl 1975-77, I:450; *Tira de Tepechpan* 1978). In sum, marriage alliances, formerly a method of strengthening the political bargaining power of individual lineages and creating regional blocs of lineages, were manipulated to benefit imperial ends.

City-States before the Empire

The above discussion has focused largely on the internal organizations of city-states, and we now turn to a discussion of the city-states' political context. The many city-states that were founded in the Valley of Mexico at the period which is the chronological beginning of this study—A.D. 1150-1350—evolved following the demise of earlier capitals—Teotihuacan and Tula. Their increasing population size is apparent in the archaeological record (Parsons 1976; Sanders, Parsons, and Santley 1979); they began to establish permanent boundaries and urban centers. Their histories written down in the 1500s report this early period as a time of relative independence; but by the late 1300s, an atmosphere of conflict between polities had developed, as the city-state of Azcapotzalco began to expand and to conquer other polities (Davies 1973a, 1973b; Carrasco 1971).

The expansionist Azcapotzalcan polity, ruled by Tezozomoc, and aided by its allies, the Tenochca of Tenochtitlan, began conquering other city-states. Between 1371 and 1428 the Azcapotzalcans conquered the major Acolhua cities (Huexotla, Coatlinchan, Teotihuacan, etc.), plus Xochimilco, Cuauhtitlan, and others. From these conquests grew the political environment in which the Triple Alliance appeared, when Texcoco, Tenochtitlan, and other polities subject to Azcapotzalco rebelled in 1428.

The Aztec Empire's Center

Confederations of City-States in the Valley of Mexico

The rebellion against Azcapotzalco was achieved by confederations of city-states. The confederations, or leagues, had long-standing diplomatic interaction and were formed for mutual defense. Two large confederations were the Acolhua and the Xochimilca. The Chalca cities formed a confederation of several separate but equal polities. The Mixquica, Cuitlahuaca, and Culhua confederations were small but separate entities. Of the pre-Triple Alliance confederations, the Acolhua and Tepaneca were the most durable. These two large confederations were hierarchically organized, with one city-state as capital, and with the ruler of the capital directing rulers of dependent city-states (see Fig. 2-4).

Confederations were political organizations formed for mutual defense and conquests, but they often were chartered on shared origin legends and geographical proximity. They were not ethnic groups or tribal groups. Although confederations such as the Chalca, Mixquica, Xochimilca, and Cuitlahuaca had independent decision-making powers in the period prior to the Aztec empire's domination of the valley, after conquest by Tenochtitlan, they became administrative units which supplied labor, taxes, and warriors. The central dependencies of Tenochtitlan and Texcoco were called on more often than the peripheral ones for participation in festivals, public works, and war, and these tasks were administered at the confederation level.

Obligations of dependencies of the empire were both *scheduled*—tribute was delivered every 80 days—and *ad hoc*, such as providing labor for public works, providing soldiers, sending gifts and representatives to coronations and funerals in the capitals, and providing people for colonies. Some of the confederations' obligations are described below.

Confederations provided food at rituals, particularly at the festival of Huey Tecuilhuitl, or "Great Feast of the Lords" (Durán 1971:215). Rulers of nearby, allied city-states viewed the human sacrifices at this festival as did "unfriendly rulers," who were sneaked into the city after dark (Durán 1967:172-75). This ritual was performed with the unfriendly lords present in order to impress them into submission (Sahagún 1951, Book 2:53).

For the festival of Huey Tecuilhuitl, after the sacrifices,

> for ten days there was eating and banqueting in [the City of] Mexico. Each one of the nearby provinces was obliged to contribute and feed the lords. The Chalcas provided on the first day, the Tepaneca on the second, others on the third. Thus each had its turn, providing splendid, rich foods and drinks: chocolate, pinole, great quantities of pulque, all striving to give the best. On one day this was done for the princes, on another for the knights, on another for the Tequihuas, on another for the Cuachique Otomis. [Durán 1971:215]

In addition, the wards of Tenochtitlan furnished feasts for the warriors, and these festivals were sponsored sometimes by the Chalca, Tepaneca, or Xochimilca (ibid.:439).

Leaders of confederations participated in pilgrimages to shrines such as Cerro Tlaloc. All the nobles of Mexico

> ...King Moteczoma together with all the great men of Mexico—knights, lords, and nobles—came to the celebration on the great mountain. Nezahualpiltzintli, King of Acolhuacan, [arrived] with all the nobility of his land and kingdom. At the same time came the rulers of Xochmilco and of Tlacopan with their leading chieftains. So everyone came to the Mountain of Tlalocan: the entire nobility of the land, princes and kings, and great lords, both from this side of the snowy mountain [Iztaccihuatl] and from the other, Tlaxcala and Huexotzinco. [Durán 1971:156-57]

At this ceremony (Huey Tzontli, or "great vigil") sumptuous offerings were given to the idols: first by the ruler of Tenochtitlan, second by the ruler of Texcoco, third by the ruler of Tlacopan, and finally by the rulers of Xochimilco and all the rest. If a ruler couldn't attend, he sent an envoy with offerings. The neighboring towns, below the mountain, prepared feasts for the celebrants, after which they returned to their cities, usually by canoe (Durán 1971:159).

Confederations provided the organization for contributions to imperial public works. For instance, in building Huitzilopochtli's temple in Tenochtitlan, each confederation was assigned the construction of a different side. Texcoco and its provinces completed the front; Tlacopan and the Tepaneca realms completed the rear; the Chalca completed the left side; the Xochimilca completed the right side; the Otomí carried sand; and the people from the *tierra caliente* or hot lands supplied lime (Durán 1967:227). Other such projects were aqueduct-building and rebuilding Tenochtitlan following a flood (ibid.:373, 381). Rulers received gifts from the Tenochtitlan's tlatoani, after which the commoners were told what supplies to provide and when to send workers (Durán 1967:227-28; see Rojas 1977; Gibson 1956, 1964a, 1964b).

Confederations were required to provide warriors and supplies for war. When war was declared, the ruler of Tenochtitlan sent messengers to the rulers of cities telling them what to prepare.

> Moteczoma and Tlacaelel then began to prepare their men for war, and sent messengers to the neighboring cities to obtain great quantities of toasted maize cakes, toasted grains of corn, and maize flour. They also obtained great quantities of bean flour, salt and chili, pumpkin seeds, together with pots, plates, grinding stones and mats in order to make tents and huts in the field. [Durán 1964:99]
>
> Then messengers were dispatched to Texcoco, Xochimilco, Culhuacan, Chalco, Cuitlahuac, Coyoacan, and Azcapotzalco so that they all would supply provisions, shields, swords, and arrows for war. All the lords of the pueblos mentioned said that it pleased them to do what he wished, and that they were at his service, treating the messengers hospitably. Then they ordered the supplies to be provided, and they carried them to the place where the battle was to be. [Durán 1967:156-57]

Thus, in addition to regularly scheduled tribute, the dependencies had to provide warriors, food, supplies, and bearers to carry the supplies when war was declared.

The army was composed of squadrons of soldiers organized by confederation: Mexica, Acolhua, Chalca, Xochimilca, Tepaneca, etc. (Durán 1967:157;

Sahagún 1954, Book 8:52). After wars, leaders and warriors received from the ruler of Tenochtitlan gifts such as jewels and feathered capes. Sometimes spoils were divided among participants, but details of this distribution are not known (Durán 1967:388-89).

Confederations sent colonists to Triple Alliance colonies in Oaxaca, Alauiztla, Oztompan, and Teloloapan. Groups were sent from Tenochtitlan, Texcoco, Tlacopan, Xochimilco, Chalco, and the *tierra caliente* (Morelos) (Durán 1967:238, 353, 355). When settlers were sent to Oaxaca, the rulers of Texcoco and Tlacopan each sent 60 families, and 600 men and their families were sent from Mexico to Oaxaca and given land there. The administrator of this colony was Moctezuma's cousin Atlazol (ibid.:238).

Administration of Dependencies of the Empire

The Aztec empire included a central area, in which administrative control was tighter, as opposed to the newly-conquered periphery where administrative controls were fewer (Katz 1958:20-21; Davies 1973a: 110-114). These nearer areas were subject to more administrative controls, but they received protection, food reserves against famine, and public works such as irrigation canals, chinampas, and aqueducts (Adams 1979:68). These city-states formed the central support area of the empire. Their tlatoque or cuauhtlatoque (rulers or military governors) and other officials were directly responsible to the rulers of Tenochtitlan, Texcoco, or Tlacopan. Thus, the center of the empire was comprised of polities having special relationships of an administrative nature with the capital. Polities in this category were not necessarily located in the Valley of Mexico, but most were, and for that reason dependencies in the valley were chosen for this study. In the following paragraphs, I will summarize the effects of conquest by the capital on city-states; then I will summarize the Triple Alliance activities in which city-state rulers usually participated.

City-states became part of the Aztec empire through alliance or conquest. As is well known, the empire itself was formed by the alliance of Tenochtitlan, Tlacopan, and Texcoco. Other Valley of Mexico city-states were assimilated by conquest (see Kelly and Palerm 1952, for chronological lists of conquests by each Mexica ruler). In the Valley of Mexico, the towns and territories of the Tepaneca (Azcapotzalco and Coyoacan), were divided up among Mexica nobles. Then the Mexica conquered the "chinampa" polities—Xochimilco, Cuitlahuac, Mixquic, Huitzilopochco, and Culhuacan. Much later, the Chalca towns were conquered and assimilated. With Chalco and Xochimilco conquered, the Triple Alliance had easier access to areas which produced cotton, fruit, and other prized tropical products (Parsons et al. 1982). As city-states were conquered, they incurred (1) imposition of tribute payments of both goods and labor; (2) imposition of special tasks (for instance, the Xochimilca had to build a causeway from Coyoacan to Tenochtitlan); and occasionally (3), temporary or permanent loss of a tlatoani, i.e., the local ruler was replaced by a Mexica military governor, although frequently the ruling lineage was reinstated later.

Following a peace settlement, the nobles of the conquered city-states were obligated to the capital in three important ways:

First, rulers of dependencies were considered part of the Mexica tlatoani's court, and their presence at the capital was required for part of each year. Cortés noted:

> There are in the city many large and beautiful houses, the reason for this being that all the chiefs of the land, who are Mutezuma's vassals, have houses in the city and live there for part of the year; and in addition there are many rich citizens that also have very good houses. [Cortés 1971:107]

Second, provincial tlatoque were confirmed or installed at the capital. Broda (1978:231) notes that the lords of city-states directly subject to Tenochtitlan were confirmed at the capital; for instance, Chalca rulers went to Tenochtitlan for a four-day fast and were installed by Tizoc, the Mexica ruler (Chimalpahin 1965:219). Rulers of Cuauhtitlan and Xochimilco were appointed by the Mexica ruler as well, and at one point, the Mexica ruler appointed the ruler of Coyoacan (see Chapters 4, 5, 6). Although Motolinía says that the lords of city-states subject to Texcoco and Tlacopan/Tacuba were confirmed at these capitals and that only the rulers of Texcoco and Tlacopan were confirmed at Tenochtitlan (Motolinía 1967:284), the data collected in this study suggest that Tenochtitlan had taken over the right to appoint rulers in Tlacopan's territory. The data from Teotihuacan, however, confirm that the Texcocan ruler appointed the rulers of Teotihuacan and other Acolhua city-states (see Chapter 7).

Third, nobles from dependencies regularly participated in rituals and sometimes sponsored feasts at the capital. At these ceremonies, the ruler of Tenochtitlan presented them with gifts or exchanged gifts with them. For instance, nobles from all the cities came to a feast at the coronation of a ruler of Tenochtitlan. These included all rulers of dependencies, as well as the rulers of independent states. The rulers of Michoacan, Cuextlan, Meztitlan, the Totonac polities, Tlaxcala, Cholula, Huexotzinco, the Mixteca, Anauac, and Tehuantepec; that is, all the "lords of foreign lands," and "all the lords posted on the shores of the ocean, and all the lords of the cities encircling Mexico— the ruler of Texcoco and the ruler of Tlacopan" (Sahagún 1954, Book 8:64-65) attended imperial coronations. At these ceremonies they received gifts from the new ruler, as did noblemen, brave warriors, lords, judges, rulers of youths, singers, keepers of gods, fire priests, and all other priests of Tenochtitlan (ibid.). It is likely that these ceremonial exchanges symbolized the relationships between the sovereign and his dependents or between the sovereign and his equals.

City-States and The Aztec Empire

Goals of the Empire

As stated in Chapter 1, empires attempt to obtain a monopoly over exchange and over goods produced in an extensive area; they seek to achieve this by force and by administrative policy. Ancient empires were limited by their ability to communicate over long distances and by their means to record and process information coming from their many subjects. An expanding empire such as that of the Aztec would seek to create from nearby polities a stable "heartland," or center. The Aztec empire did so by absorbing indigenous leaders of dependencies into its bureaucracy or by appointing bureaucrats from the capital. Dependencies were not demoted to uniformly low-level, undifferentiated rural centers. Instead, they attained varied positions in the larger, hierarchical organization.

Relationships between the conquered and the conquerors are asymmetrical, and conquered polities produce goods and supply labor for their capital. In a hierarchical, complex system, not every function becomes centralized, and formerly independent centers retain control over some activities. However, a dependency's span of control will vary according to its position in the larger hierarchy.

When polities are absorbed into a larger system, changes are made in their decision-making structures, and an increased number of dependencies affects the capital as well. Increased size requires more administrators and more kinds of them (or conversely, a growing elite-administrative class may create a demand for more tribute or more dependencies). Let us now turn to a discussion of the effects of conquest by the Aztec empire on city-states in the Valley of Mexico.

Effects of Conquest

In 1428, polities subject to Azcapotzalco rebelled, aided by a polity from outside the valley (Huexotzinco). The polities of Tenochtitlan and Texcoco then together formed the new Triple Alliance, putting Tlacopan, a Tepaneca city, in nominal charge of the Tepaneca (Azcapotzalcan) area. Soon after, Tenochtitlan embarked on a series of conquests, and by 1440 it had conquered most of the valley. It conquered Coyoacan in 1428-30, Xochimilco in 1430, Cuauhtitlan in 1435, and Chalco gradually between 1440 and 1465.

Conquest resulted in changes in the political organizations of city-states. Figure 8-2 presents schematically the relation of each polity studied to the capital and to others in its region before and after the Triple Alliance. This diagram illustrates promotion, demotion, or regional reorganization of the polities. Figure 8-2 reveals how inclusion into the Aztec empire affected five city-states differentially.

Amecameca and the Chalca city-states were not centralized before being conquered by the Mexica; instead, they joined together in an *ad hoc* manner, and they delegated and divided the tasks of diplomacy and directing battles to rulers of different towns. After conquest, the ruler of Tenochtitlan appointed military governors, replacing the Amecamecan rulers for 20 years. After 20 years, five rulerships were reinstated, but two were never replaced, streamlining the Amecamecan system of many rulers. Amecameca was administered through the city of Tlalmanalco (Chalco), which was promoted from one of several equal city-states to provincial capital.

The defeat of Azcapotzalco was at first exploited advantageously by the rulers of Cuauhtitlan, who

CONCLUSIONS

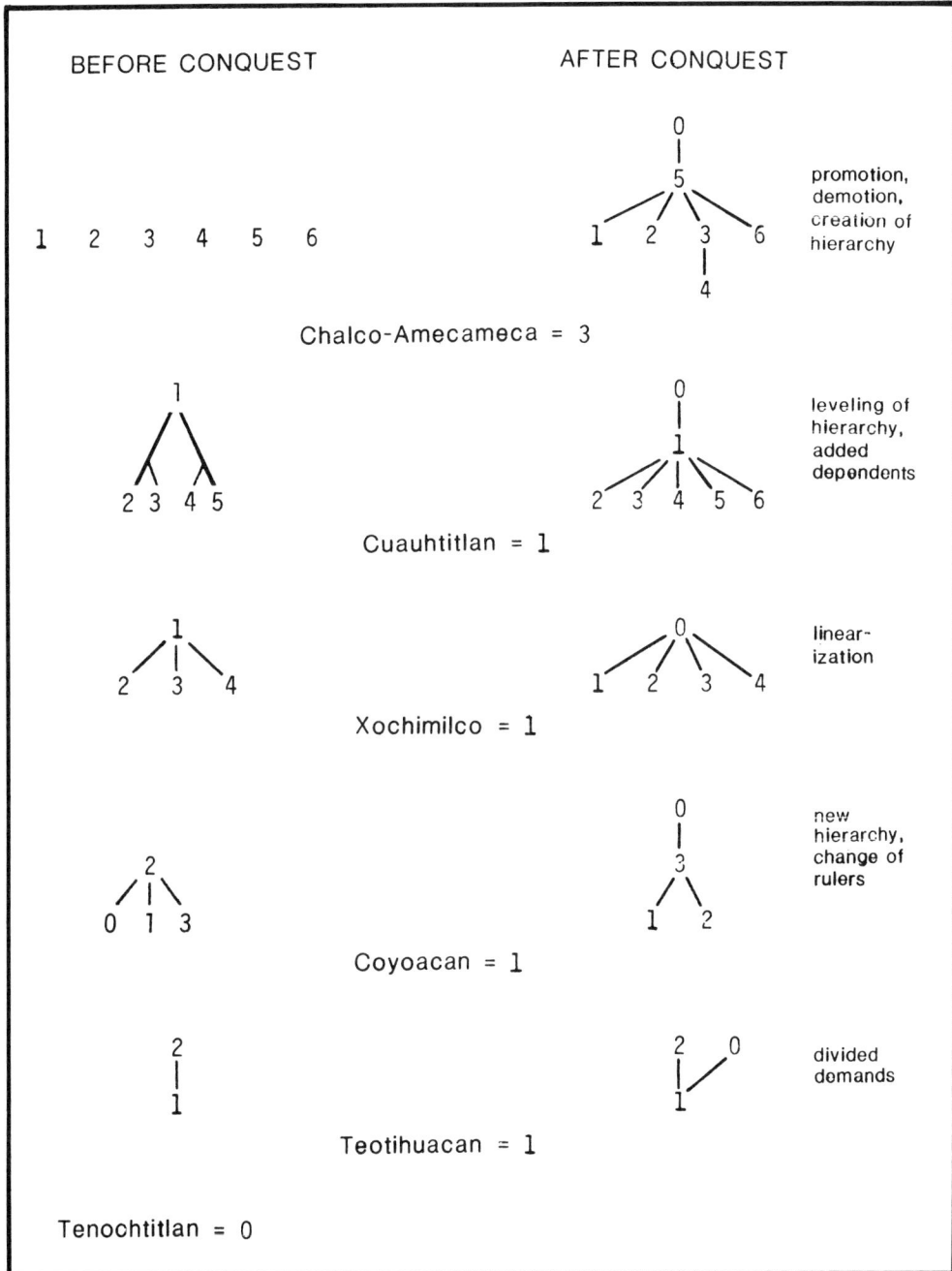

Fig. 8-2. Change in five local political hierarchies following conquest by the Aztec empire. Above, the acephalous Chalca polities were hierarchically organized by the Mexica; Cuauhtitlan gained dependencies; Xochimilco lost some control over its dependencies; Coyoacan was administered by a new capital, and Teotihuacan served two (instead of one) capitals.

were Tepaneca, but who had been Mexica allies in the rebellion. This alliance was short-lived, for Cuauhtitlan was conquered by Tenochtitlan in 1435. Cuauhtitlan's earlier rulers had divided the large province of Cuauhtitlan into four administrative sections headed by nobles from Cuauhtitlan with whom they shared rulership. This organization was altered after conquest by the Aztec empire, and Cuauhtitlan's tlatoani was left as administrator of the urban center and the dependent towns, while the middle level of management—the administrators of the four divisions—was eliminated. As an imperial provincial administrator, Cuauhtitlan's ruler received as rewards "war lands"—income-paying areas outside his own territory—while Tenochca nobles were granted estates within Cuauhtitlan's territory.

The Xochimilca territory was initially ruled by at least two tlatoque with separate domains. Later, at least two rulers governed from the urban center of Xochimilco. After Xochimilco's inclusion into the Aztec state system, an additional tlatoani office was added, and this ruler's tecpan became the tribute-collection headquarters for the province. The ruler of one Xochimilca tecpan seems consistently to have been the most prominent in political relations with other polities: its tlatoani is mentioned most frequently in the sources from other polities. After conquest by the empire, the wide-ranging Xochimilca territory was reduced to a small area between the lake and the sierra, and lords of its formerly subject towns may have been partially responsible to and appointed by Tenochtitlan's rulers (Paso y Troncoso 1905, VI:286; Gibson 1964b:13). As in other conquered areas, lands in Xochimilco were divided among Triple Alliance nobles.

For Coyoacan, inclusion in the Triple Alliance meant a change of capital and subjugation to Mexica and Acolhua tribute demands. As a defeated Tepaneca city, Coyoacan became a dependency of Tlacopan rather than of Azcapotzalco, and it was responsible to Tlacopan for supplying labor and produce, as well. Mexica nobles appropriated many fields which were to provide them with income.

Postclassic Teotihuacan exemplifies one of the two types of territories created by and administered by the Acolhua state. The Acolhua (Texcocan) region was reorganized after 1430 when Nezahualcoyotl regained the office of ruler of the region. He appointed 14 tlatoque to govern single provinces, and 8 provinces were governed by calpixque. The tlatoani of Teotihuacan served as an advisor to the Acolhua ruler and was an important state judicial official. Both the lands of Acolhua rulers and their jurisdiction in judicial matters were interdigitated by Texcoco's ruler. After the formation of the Triple Alliance, sections of Teotihuacan's territory paid tribute to Tenochtitlan and to various Acolhua lords, while Teotihuacan's ruler received income from lands in the territories of polities both in the Acolhua zone and outside it.

There is a progression apparent if the five city-states studied here are examined in the order of their conquest by the empire, even in so short a period (approximately 37 years; ca. 1428-65). Those within large political systems already, such as Teotihuacan, became more closely integrated into these systems by elite intermarriage and through the intermingling of lands from which the rulers gained support. Coyoacan and Xochimilco were conquered and were closely integrated into imperial activities at an early date, and lands within these city-states were divided among the rulers and nobles of Texcoco and Tenochtitlan. Cuauhtitlan's tlatoani was replaced by a cuauhtlatoani, and its four second-level administrative offices were eradicated. Later, a tlatoani appointed by Moctezuma ruled Cuauhtitlan. Amecameca, conquered later, was subjected to reorganization and bureaucratic control. When tlatoque were reappointed, these rulers were appointed by Tenochtitlan's ruler and were sons of women who married Tenochca lords. From the later-conquered polities we have more evidence of varied political organizations before their conquest and of efforts by Tenochtitlan to institute centralized and hierarchically organized bureaucracies following their conquest.

The Political Hierarchy

Following conquest of the Valley of Mexico city-states by Tenochtitlan and Texcoco, there were three to four levels of political decision-making. These levels were: (1) The imperial level—at Tenochtitlan—at which all decisions were made regarding conquests and foreign policy; at this level, Tenochtitlan's ruler was assisted by the rulers of Texcoco and Tlacopan; (2) internal administration and policy of three states, controlled by the tlatoani of Texcoco, the tlatoani of Tlacopan, and the tlatoani and cihuacoatl of Tenochtitlan; (3) the tlatoque or cuauhtlatoque of individual city-states in each area; (4) tlatoque subject to those at Level 3; and (5) administrators of towns and villages.

At the founding of the empire, the pattern was probably close to that pictured in Figure 8-3. However, due to nesting of polities geographically and

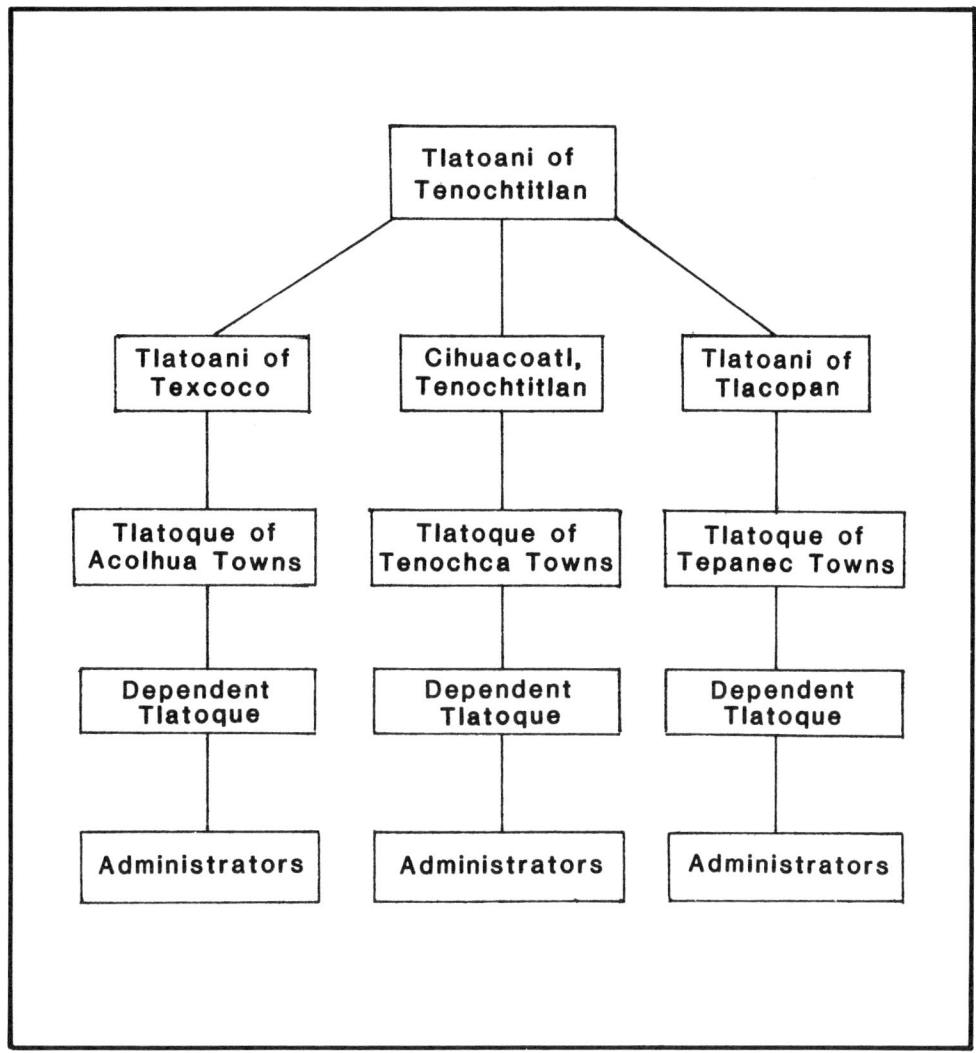

Fig. 8-3. Levels of decision-makers in the Triple Alliance political hierarchy.

instances of linearization, whereby an intermediate decision-maker was bypassed, by 1519 some towns at Level 4 or 5 were directly controlled by rulers at Levels 1 or 2 (Chimalpahin 1965; Paso y Troncoso 1940, X:120; Alva Ixtlilxochitl 1975-77; Guzmán 1938; Durán 1967:83). Some communities, such as Cuauhtitlan in the Tepaneca zone, appear from their chronicles to have been directly responsible to Tenochtitlan politically (though perhaps responsible to Tlacopan as well, for labor tribute). Teotihuacan was politically responsible to Texcoco but paid tribute to Tenochtitlan (as documented more specifically in Chapter 7). This hierarchy is diagrammed in Figure 8-4.

The Tribute Hierarchy

The imperial tribute hierarchy (as based upon the *Codex Mendoza* [1925; Barlow 1949]) differed from the political hierarchy, and it was more centralized. In the central part of the valley, the tributary provinces and the political provinces were different (Fig. 8-5; Table 8-1). This divergence in hierarchies occurred because: (1) some city-states were grouped after conquest into new tributary provinces, with one city-state promoted to tribute-collection center; (2) certain towns paid tribute directly to Tenochtitlan or Texcoco, bypassing the regional centers; (3) tlatoque did not collect tribute in

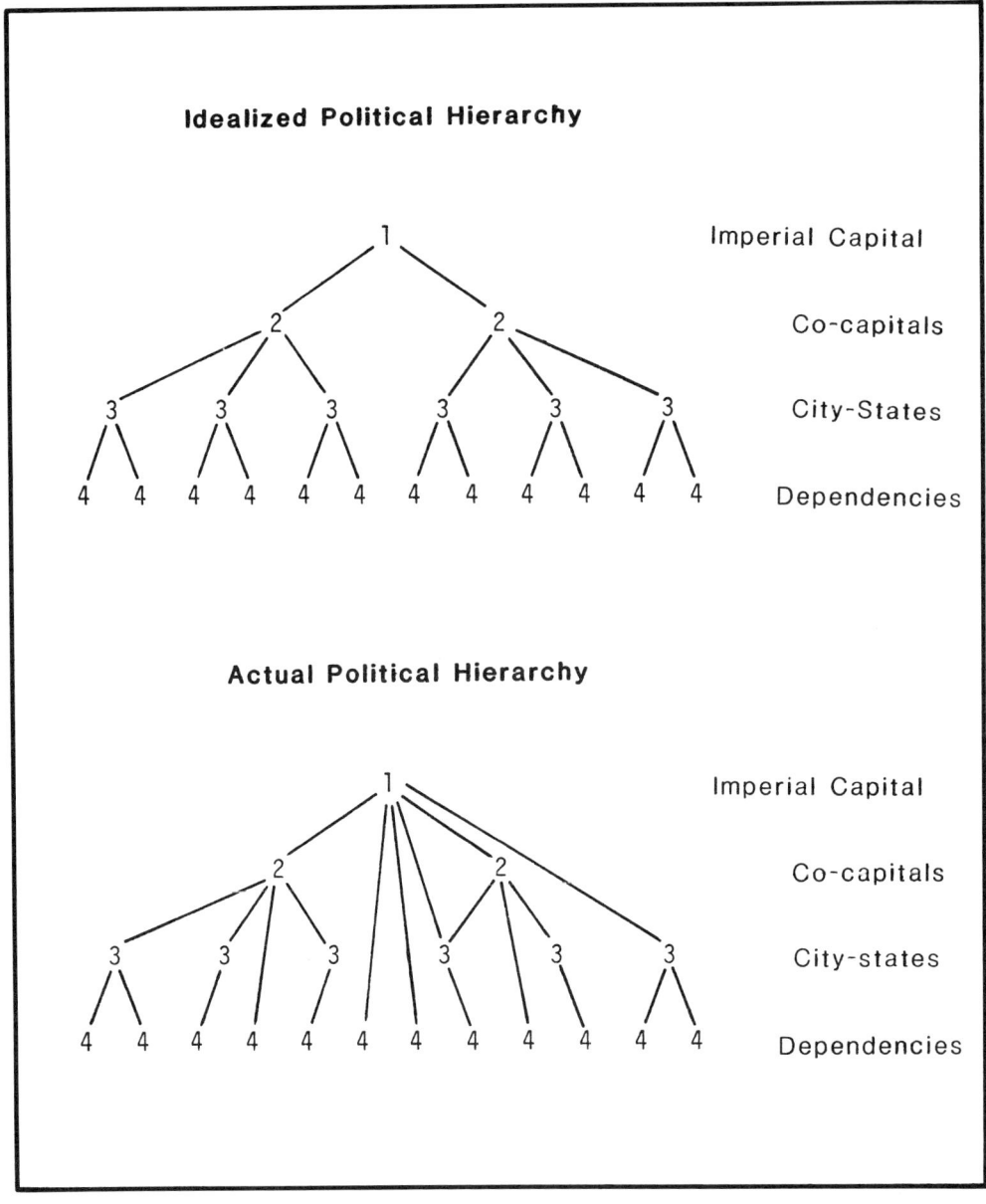

Fig. 8-4. The actual versus idealized political hierarchy in the Valley of Mexico. "Actual" hierarchy diagrams relationships in 1519.

city-state urban centers and pass it on to Tenochtitlan and Texcoco—tribute was instead collected by calpixque at separate centers and then taken on to the capital (Barlow 1949; Gibson 1971).

The channeling to the capitals of tribute paid by the five city-states examined here shows considerable variety: Cuauhtitlan paid tribute directly to Tenochtitlan. Xochimilco paid to Tenochtitlan via Petlacalco, a separate tribute-collection zone in the center of the valley. Amecameca paid tribute to Tenochtitlan via Tlalmanalco. Teotihuacan paid to both Texcoco and Tenochtitlan, while Coyoacan paid tribute to Tlacopan, Texcoco, and Tenochtitlan.

The tribute hierarchy in the valley, according to the *Codex Mendoza* included five major divisions of tribute payers (Table 8-1; Fig. 8-5). Actually, tribute payment was more complicated. Sometimes towns paid tribute to two capitals, and lands within the dependent city-states paid income to individual nobles at the capitals. Mexica nobles

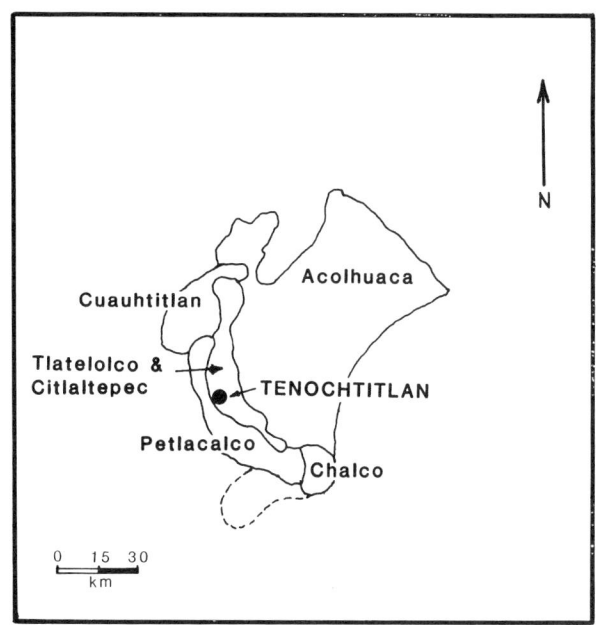

Fig. 8-5. Location of tributary provinces in the Valley of Mexico (from Barlow, 1949). The province of Acolhuaca extends outside the valley. The dotted line indicates the extent of Chalco province according to Barlow; however it probably only included that part enclosed in a solid line (see Parsons et al. 1982).

had estates in the territories of the five city-states examined in this study, as they did in many dependencies. Texcocan rulers received tribute from estates in Xochimilco's and Coyoacan's territories and, of course, from Teotihuacan, which was within the Texcocan state. The presence of such estates is similar to the situation in the Mixteca Alta in the Late Postclassic and early Colonial periods, where *caciques*' lands, included in their *cacicazgo*, were sometimes not within the political territory of their town (Spores 1967:155). However, while this occurred as a result of inheritance and dowry-giving in both the Valley of Mexico and the Mixteca Alta, in the Valley of Mexico, lands were also reassigned by the rulers of Tenochtitlan and Texcoco as rewards to their allies and for other political reasons.

Tribute in Labor

Labor tribute followed a different system from tribute in goods. It was not controlled as directly from the capital as was the collection of goods; instead it was administered through the second level of decision-making. For labor tribute there was a division of the valley into two (Fig. 6-7; Gibson 1956, 1964a, 1971:387), and perhaps three, sections—east and west, or Acolhua and Tepaneca—or Acolhua, Tepaneca, and a Mexica area consisting of Tenochtitlan's southern dependencies such as Xochimilco and Chalco. The chinampa cities and the Chalco area were directly responsible to the Mexica (Durán 1967:227, 373, 381), and the Chalca worked on buildings at Texcoco as well (Chimalpahin 1965:216). At times, laborers from everywhere worked at each capital (Alva Ixtlilxochitl 1975-77, II:92).

Marriage Alliances

In order to form an effectively administered central area, Tenochtitlan sought to integrate city-states' rulers more closely into its activities. To do so, it arranged marriages between its elites and those of the dependencies, who were in many cases the administrators of those dependencies.

City-state ruling lineages varied greatly in genealogical proximity of their elites to those of the capital. While the Aztec were not explicitly as concerned with the status and ranking of lineages as were the Mixtec (Spores 1974) or the Quiché (Carmack 1981), it appears that the rulers preferred to deal with relatives as administrators who might be more loyal or trustworthy than non-relatives. Sisters and daughters of the imperial rulers were sent to marry rulers of dependencies. As a result, by 1519, city-state elites formed a network of related rulers.

This pattern is demonstrated in the histories of the city-states studied here. Generally, marriage alliances were arranged by rulers of the capitals with rulers of city-states directly dependent upon them. Thus, geographically, marriage alliances formed two areas, corresponding to the territories of the two major powers, Tenochtitlan and Texcoco. For instance, the last ruler of Cuauhtitlan before the Spanish Conquest was married to a daughter of Moctezuma. The ruler of Coyoacan also was related by marriage to the ruling lineage of Tenochtitlan. One of the rulers of Xochimilco was related to rulers of Tenochtitlan, while one of the Amecameca tlatoque at the time of the Spanish Conquest was descended from the second most important lineage in Tenochtitlan. (This suggests a pattern of less important branches of the Tenochca ruling lineage having marriage alliances with less important dependencies.) The ruler of Teotihuacan was a brother-in-law of the tlatoani of Texcoco. This intra-valley network of elites evolved over time from

TABLE 8-1
**HIERARCHY OF IMPERIAL TRIBUTE PAYMENT IN THE VALLEY OF MEXICO,
ACCORDING TO CODEX MENDOZA**

LEVEL 1: IMPERIAL CAPITAL	Tenochtitlan				
LEVEL 2: PROVINCES	Citlaltepec & Tlatelolco	Petlacalco	Cuauhtitlan	Acolhuacan	Chalco
LEVEL 3: TRIBUTE COLLECTION POINTS	Tzonpanco Xaltocan Puputlan Iztacalco Chalco Atenco	Tecoloapan Petlacalcatl Huizilopochco Tzapotitlan Cuitlahuac Olac Xico Mixquic Cocotlan Tepopulan	Tepoxaco Tepotzotlan Tehuiloyoca Huehuetoca Cuexcomahuaca Xilotzinco	Pachuca Epacoyuca Tlaquilpa Tezontepec Cenpoalan Tetlyztaca Pepepulco Tizayuca Huiçilan Temazcalapa Teacalco Tonanytla Teotihuacan Matixco Ecatepec Tepechpan Teçoyuca Tepetlaoztoc Chimalhuacanatoyac Chicaloapan Coatepec Chalco Acolman Acolhuaca Otompan	Quauhxumulco Tepuztlan Amecameca

(from Barlow 1949)

many different lineages; marriage alliance was an important diplomatic strategy before the Aztec empire and it was used by Tenochtitlan's rulers, as well (see Fig. 8-6, which shows some of these relationships).

Centralization vs. Autonomy

Through a comparison of five areas, this study has revealed that in the Valley of Mexico, the imperial tribute hierarchy was the most centralized and was not congruent with the less centralized administrative hierarchy, which was based on complex and preexisting political and lineage relationships that had developed before the foundation of the empire. Labor tribute tended to follow the administrative hierarchy; but more importantly, laborers, warriors, and supplies were called up through well-established, pre-imperial confederation lines. After the foundation of the empire, the conquered city-states' independent political activities were curtailed. They no longer initiated their own diplomatic missions. Their rulers were required to be present in Tenochtitlan and Texcoco much of the year, as well as at state rites such as coronations, funerals, and state religious rites.

Another pre-imperial intra-valley network was that of the pochteca, who were centered at Tenochtitlan and Tlatelolco but who had divisions in 10 other cities. This organization, controlled by the tlatoani of Tenochtitlan and the head pochtecatl, was exclusive and centralized (see Fig. 2-13).

Imperial activities—other than warfare—that took place outside the capital were infrequent, but included rituals which took place at open air shrines. The Tenochca ruler made regular visits to at least two sacred places in the Acolhua area: the pyramids at Teotihuacan and Monte Tlaloc (south of Texcoco). Other pilgrimages were made to hills in Chalco and outside Chapultepec and Ixtapalapa. A pilgrimage map of rituals would show some rites occurring outside the capital at particular mountains, springs, and lakes, and city-states like Teotihuacan gained prestige from having these shrines within their territory.

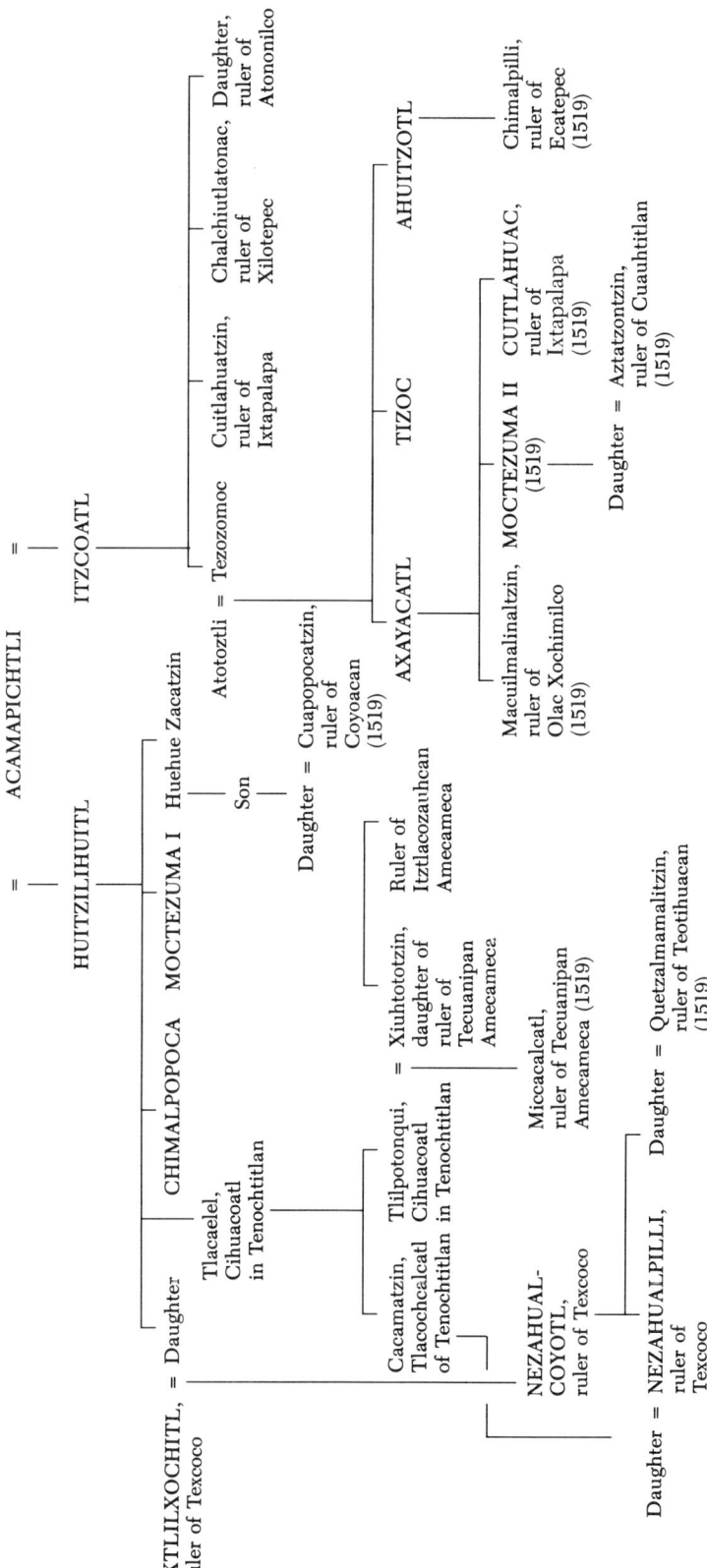

Fig. 8-6. Marriage alliances between the ruling lineages of Tenochtitlan and Texcoco and the rulers of other Valley of Mexico city-states. Names in capitals are rulers of Tenochtitlan or Texcoco.

In summary, in the central area of the Aztec empire, political control became hierarchical and somewhat centralized. Administrators were appointed to carry out policy from the capital. Similar to the political hierarchy was the organization of labor tribute. A separate but even more centralized hierarchy for collection of tribute in goods was instituted. Long-distance trade in sumptuary goods was centralized and controlled by Tenochtitlan.

Conclusions

City-states were differentially affected by inclusion in the Aztec empire. Some dependencies remained organized in their pre-imperial confederations and participated in imperial activities as part of these units; others became directly subject to Tenochtitlan. In less centrally organized areas, such as Chalco, more bureaucratic machinery was imposed for administration, and in more hierarchically organized areas like Cuauhtitlan, the indigenous organization was simplified to adapt it to imperial administration.

Although city-state rulers became part of the Aztec empire's political organization, they continued to be the political leaders within their territories. They continued to receive tribute from their commoners (as well as from estates outside their own territories, in some cases). In large provinces, there is evidence that rulers and their assistants directed local craft specialists and oversaw the markets. Local city-states retained their traditional deities and rituals, but their rulers participated in imperial ceremonies. Within the Aztec imperial system, administration by the capital was adapted to dependencies' indigenous political organizations, and each city-state retained its political identity, despite its participation in the empire's activities.

Glossary of Some Nahuatl and Spanish Words

ALCALDE: Colonial-period judge and cabildo member
ALGUACIL: Constable
ALMUD: One-twelfth of a fanega
ALTEPETL: City, state, ruler
ALTEPETLALLI: Town land
BARRIO: Town subdivision
BRAZA: Unit of measure; commonly two varas (1.67 m)
CABALLERIA: Unit of agricultural land; about 105 acres
CABECERA: Head town
CACICAZGO: Territory belonging to a *cacique*
CACIQUE: Colonial term for local ruler
CALMECAC: Pre-conquest school
CALPIXQUI (pl. CALPIXQUE): Tax collector and administrator
CALPULLALLI: Land belonging to a calpulli
CALPULLI (pl. CALPULTIN): Territorial unit or the occupants of the unit
CAMELLON: Chinampa
CASAS DE COMUNIDAD: Buildings for community government
CEMMITL: Braza (1.67 m)
CHIA: New World sage (*Salvia*)
CHINAMPA: Raised field
CIHUACOATL: "Snake Woman"; title of Aztec official
CIHUAPILLI: Female pilli
CIUDAD: City
COATEQUITL: Institution of labor assignment
CONGREGACIÓN: Concentration of scattered populations
CUAUHNOCHTLI: Administrator
CUEZCONPIXQUI: Official in charge of granaries; tribute collectors
ENCOMENDERO: Possessor of an encomienda
ENCOMIENDA: Grant of Indians, mainly as tribute payers, or the area of the Indians granted to a Spaniard
ESTANCIA: Subordinate Indian community; farm
FANEGA: Unit of dry measure; about 1.5 bushels
HUAUHTLI: Amaranth
HUEYTLATOANI: Great tlatoani
HUIPIL: Woman's blouse
HUITZILOPOCHTLI: Mexica deity
JUEZ (pl. JUECES): Judge
LLAMAMIENTO: Summons, usually for labor
MACEGUAL (Sp.; Nahuatl, MACEHUALLI): An Indian commoner
MAGUEY: Agave, a plant processed for pulque and fiber
MANDÓN: Subordinate town officer
MANTA: Blanket
MATRÍCULA: List, generally of tribute
MAYEQUE: Indians of a subordinate or sub-macegual class
MAYORDOMO: Majordomo; custodian
MEDIDA: Measure
MERCED: Grant, generally of land
METATE (Sp.; Nahuatl, METATL): Grinding stone
MILPA: Cultivated field
NAUHTEUCTLI: Four related teuctli offices
OCOTL: Torch pine
PARCIALIDAD: Large section of a town
PETATE: Mat
PILLALLI: Land of a pilli
PILLI (pl. PIPILTIN): Literally, son; designates offspring of a teuctli or noble
POCHTECATL (pl. POCHTECA): Merchant

PRINCIPAL: Member of the Indian upper class; nobleman
PUEBLO: Town
PUEBLO POR SÍ: Independent town; cabecera
PULQUE: Fermented beverage made from maguey
QUAUHTLATOANI: Military governor; "eagle ruler"
QUAXOCHPIXQUI: Officials in charge of arsenals or garrisons
REGIDOR: Colonial town official; councilman
REPARTIDOR: Official in charge of a labor repartimiento
REPARTIMIENTO: Labor draft
SEÑORÍO: Lordship, kingdom, *cacicazgo*, "city-state"
SEÑOR NATURAL: Tlatoani
SERVICIO: Service, labor, or provision of goods
SUJETO: Subject town
TASACIÓN: Tribute or tribute assessment record
TECCALLI: Ruler's house
TECPAN: Territory and dependents of an Indian lord
TECPANPOUQUE (TECPANTLACA): People of the tecpan
TECPANTLALLI: Land of the tecpan
TEOTLALLI: Land cultivated to support the temples and patron gods
TEOPIXQUI: Priest
TEPIXQUI (pl. TEPIXQUE): Guardian
TEQUITL: Tax or labor service
TEQUITLATO (pl. TEQUITLATOQUE): Calpulli or town officer; tax collector or mayordomo
TÉRMINOS: Limits, boundaries
TERRAZGUERO: Tenant farmer; received part of harvest in return for labor
TEUCTLI (pl. TETEUCTIN): Noble, lord, ruler
TIANQUIZ: Market
TIERRA CALIENTE: Hot country
TIZOCYAHUACATL: Military title, official
TLACATECCATL: Title granted to warrior
TLACOCHCALCATL: Military title, official
TLACOTLI: Slave or slave-like person in Indian society
TLACUILO: Indian draftsman or scribe
TLALMILLI: Land plot of a barrio
TLAMACAZQUI: Priest
TLATOANI (pl. TLATOQUE): Indian ruler of a community
TLATOCATLALLI (TLATOCAMILLI): Land of a tlatoani
TLAXILLACALLI: Residential ward, "barrio"
TOCHOMITL: Rabbit fur textile
TOMIN: Unit of money, equal to twelve grains of gold (ca. .575 g)
TORTILLA: Thin pancake of maize meal
TRIBUTARIO: Tribute payer
TRIBUTO: Tribute
VARA: Staff of office; unit of measure, about .84 m
VIEJO: Elder
VISITA: Tour of inspection
VISITADOR: Inspector
XIQUIPILLI: Unit of 8000
XOCHIYAOTL: War of flowers, or ritual war
ZONTLE: Four hundred

Bibliography

Archives and Collections of Documents Used in this Study

Archivo General de la Nación, México (abbreviated AGN in text)
Biblioteca Nacional de México
Archivo Histórico, Museo Nacional de Antropología e Historia, México
Biblioteca, Museo Nacional de Antropología e Historia, México
Latin American Collection, University of Texas, Austin
Ayer Collection, Newberry Library, Chicago
William L. Clements Library, University of Michigan, Ann Arbor

Published Sources

Acosta Saignes, Miguel
    1945   Los Pochteca. *Acta Antropológica* 1, Pt. 1.
    1946   Los Teopixque. *Revista Mexicana de Estudios Antropológicos* 8:147-205

Adams, Robert McCormick
    1966   *The Evolution of Urban Society.* Chicago: Aldine Publishing Company.
    1979   Late Prehispanic Empires of the New World. In: *Power and Propaganda, A Symposium on Ancient Empires,* Mogens Trolle Larson, ed., pp. 59-73 (Mesopotamia: Copenhagen Studies in Assyriology 7.) Copenhagen: Akademisk Forlag.

Alva Ixtlilxochitl, Fernando de
    1975- *Obras Históricas.* 2 Vols. Edmundo O'Gorman, ed.
    1977   México: Universidad Nacional Autónoma de México, Instituto de Investigaciones Históricas.

Alvarado Tezózomoc, Hernando
    1975   *Crónica Mexicana.* México: Editorial Porrúa, S.A.

Anales de Cuauhtitlan
    1938   *Die Geschichte der Konigreiche von Colhuacan und Mexico.* Text mit uberzetzung von Walter Lehmann. Quellenwerke zur alten Geschichte Amerikas aufgezeichnet in den Sprachen der Eingeborenen, 1. Stuttgart: Kohlhammer (reprinted 1974).
    1945   *Códice Chimalpopoca. Anales de Cuauhtitlan y Leyenda de los Soles.* Traducción por Primo Feliciano Velázquez. México: Universidad Nacional Autónoma de México, Instituto de Investigaciones Históricas. Primera Serie Prehispánica 1 (reprinted 1975).

Anales de Tlatelolco
    1948   *Anales de Tlatelolco: Unos Anales Históricos de la Nación Mexicana y Códice de Tlatelolco.* Heinrich Berlin and Robert H. Barlow, eds. México: Antigua Librería Robredo de José Porrúa e Hijos. Fuentes para la Historia de Mexico, 2.

Anales Mexicanos
    1903   Anales Mexicanos—México Azcapotzalco, 1426-1589. Traducción por José Fernando Ramírez. *Anales del Museo Nacional de México,* Época 1, 7:49-74.

Anderson, Arthur J.O., Frances Berdan, and James Lockhart
    1976   *Beyond the Codices: The Nahua View of Colonial Mexico.* Berkeley: University of California Press.

Andrews, J. Richard
    1975   *Introduction to Classic Nahuatl.* Austin: University of Texas Press.

Anonymous Conqueror
    1866   El Conquistador Anónimo: Relación de Algunas Cosas de la Nueva España, y de la Gran Ciudad de Temestitlan México; Escrita por un Compañero de Hernan Cortés. In *Colección de Documentos para la Historia de México.* Joaquín García Icazbalceta, ed., Vol. 1:568-99. México: Antigua Librería Robredo.

Anunciación, Fray Domingo de
    1940   Parecer de Fray Domingo de la Anunciación, Sobre el Modo que Tenían de Tributar los Indios en Tiempo de la Gentilidad. . . . *Epistolario de Nueva España,* Francisco del Paso y Troncoso, ed., Vol. 7:259-66. México: Biblioteca Histórica Mexicana de Obras Inéditas, Segunda Serie.

Archivo General de la Nación, México
    1933   *Códices Indígenas de Algunos Pueblos del Marquesado del Valle de Oaxaca.* México: Talleres Gráficos de la Nación.
    1935   *Documentos Inéditos Relativos a Hernán Cortés y Su Familia.* México: Publicaciones del Archivo General de la Nación, 27.
    1964   *Nuevos Documentos Relativos a los Bienes de Hernán Cortés.* México: Archivo General de la Nación y Universidad Nacional Autónoma de México.

Aubin, Joseph Marius Alexis
    1886   Mapa de Tepechpan. *Anales del Museo Nacional de Antropología e Historia,* Época 1, 3:368.

Balandier, Georges
    1970   *Political Anthropology.* New York: Pantheon.

Bandelier, Adolph F.
    1877   On the Art of War and Mode of Warfare of the Ancient Mexicans. *Tenth Annual Report of the Peabody Museum of Archaeology and Ethnology*:95-191.
    1880   On the Social Organization and Mode of Government of the Ancient Mexicans. *Twelfth Annual Report of the Peabody Museum of Archaeology and Ethnology*:557-699.

Barlow, Robert H.
    1945   Some Remarks on the Term "Aztec Empire." *The Americas* 1:344-49.

1947 Review of Primo Feliciano Velázquez, *Códice Chimalpopoca*. *Hispanic American Historical Review* 27:520-26.
1947- La Fundación de la Triple Alianza (1427-33). *Ana-*
1948 *les del Instituto Nacional de Antropología e Historia* 3:147-55.
1949 The Extent of the Empire of the Culhua Mexica. *Ibero-Americana* 28. Berkeley: University of California Press.
1951 El Códice de los Alfareros de Cuauhtitlan. *Revista Mexicana de Estudios Antropológicos* 12:5-8.
1963 Documentos de la Zona de Chalco y Amecameca (1560- 1702). *Tlalocan* 4:239-54.

Berdan, Frances M.F.
1975 Trade, Tribute, and Market in the Aztec Empire. Ph.D. dissertation, The University of Texas, Austin.

Berry, Brian J.L., Edgar C. Conkling, and D. Michael Ray
1976 *The Geography of Economic Systems*. Englewood Cliffs, N.J.: Prentice Hall.

Beyer, Hermann
1924 Los Bajo Relieves de Santa Cruz Acalpixcan. *El México Antiguo* 2:1-13.

Blanton, Richard E.
1972 Prehispanic Settlement Patterns of the Ixtapalapa Peninsula Region, Mexico. Department of Anthropology, The Pennsylvania State University, *Occasional Papers in Anthropology* 6.
1975 Texcoco Region Archaeology. *American Antiquity* 40:227-30.
1976a Anthropological Studies of Cities. *Annual Review of Anthropology* 5:249-64.
1976b The Role of Symbiosis in Adaptation and Sociocultural Change in the Valley of Mexico. In *The Valley of Mexico*, edited by Eric R. Wolf, pp. 181-201. Albuquerque: University of New Mexico Press.
1980 Cultural Ecology Reconsidered. *American Antiquity* 45:145-51.

Blanton, Richard E., Stephen A. Kowalewski, Gary Feinman, and Jill Appel
1982 Monte Albán's Hinterland, Part 1: The Prehispanic Settlement Patterns of the Central and Southern Parts of the Valley of Oaxaca, Mexico. *Memoirs of the Museum of Anthropology, University of Michigan* 15. Ann Arbor.

Blau, Peter M., and Richard M. Schoenherr
1971 *The Structure of Organizations*. New York: Basic Books.

Borah, Woodrow, and Sherburne F. Cook
1963 The Aboriginal Population of Central Mexico on the Eve of the Spanish Conquest. *Ibero-Americana* 54. Berkeley: University of California Press.

Bosch Gimpera, Pedro
1966 Pueblos e Imperios. *Revista Mexicana de Estudios Antropológicos* 20:9-39.

Bray, Warwick
1968 *The Everyday Life of the Aztecs*. New York: G.P. Putnam's Sons.
1972 The City-State in Central Mexico at the Time of the Spanish Conquest. *Journal of Latin American Studies* 4(2):161-85.
1978 Civilising the Aztecs. In *The Evolution of Social Systems*, J. Friedman and M.J. Rowlands, eds., pp. 373-98. Pittsburgh: University of Pittsburgh Press.

Broda, Johanna
1978 Relaciones Políticas Ritualizadas: El Ritual como Expresión de una Ideología. In *Economía, Política e Ideología en el México Prehispánico*, Pedro Carrasco y Johanna Broda, eds., pp. 221-25. México: Centro de Investigaciones Superiores, Instituto Nacional de Antropología e Historia y Editorial Nueva Imagen.

Brumfiel, Elizabeth
1980 Specialization, Market Exchange, and the Aztec State: A View from Huexotla. *Current Anthropology* 21:259-78.
1983 Aztec State Making: Ecology, Structure, and the Origin of the State. *American Anthropologist* 85:261-84.

Calnek, Edward E.
1972 Settlement Pattern and Chinampa Agriculture at Tenochtitlan. *American Antiquity* 37:104-15.
1975 Organización de los Sistemas de Abastecimiento Urbano de Alimentos: El Caso de Tenochtitlán. In *Las Ciudades de América Latina y Sus Áreas de Influencia a Través de la Historia*, Jorge E. Hardoy y Richard P. Schaedel, comps., pp. 41-60. Buenos Aires: Ediciones SIAP.
1976 The Internal Structure of Tenochtitlan. In *The Valley of Mexico*, Eric R. Wolf, ed., pp. 287-302. Albuquerque: University of New Mexico Press.
1978 The City-State in the Basin of Mexico: Late Prehispanic Period. In *Urbanization in the Americas from Its Beginnings to the Present*, R. Schaedel et al., eds., pp. 463-70. The Hague: Mouton.

Carmack, Robert
1981 *The Quiché Mayas of Utatlán: The Evolution of a Highland Guatemala Kingdom*. Norman: University of Oklahoma Press.

Carrasco, Pedro
1950 *Los Otomíes. Cultura e Historia Prehispánica de los Pueblos Mesoamericanos de Habla Otomiana*. México: Biblioteca Enciclopédica del Estado de México.
1966 Documentos Sobre el Rango de Tecuhtli en los Nahuas Tramontanos. *Tlalocan* 5:133-60.
1971 Social Organization of Ancient Mexico. In *Handbook of Middle American Indians*, Vol. 10, *Archaeology of Northern Mesoamerica*, Pt. 1, Gordon F. Ekholm and Ignacio Bernal, eds., pp. 349-75. Austin: University of Texas Press.
1974 Sucesión y Alianzas Matrimoniales en la Dinastía Teotihuacana. *Estudios de Cultura Náhuatl* 11:234- 40.
1976 Los Linajes Nobles del México Antiguo. In *Estratificación Social en la Mesoamérica Prehispánica*, by Pedro Carrasco, et al., pp. 19-36. México: Instituto Nacional de Antropología e Historia.
1977 Los Señores de Xochimilco en 1548. *Tlalocan* 7:229-65.
1980 Comment on Brumfiel. *Current Anthropology* 21:468.
1984 Royal Marriages in Ancient Mexico. In *Explorations in Ethnohistory: Indians of Central Mexico in the Sixteenth Century*, Herbert R. Harvey and Hanns Prem, eds., pp. 41-81. Albuquerque: University of New Mexico Press.

Carrasco, Pedro, et al.
1976 *Estratificación Social en la Mesoamérica Prehispánica*. México: Instituto Nacional de Antropología e Historia.

Carrasco, Pedro, and Johanna Broda, eds.
1978 *Economía, Política e Ideología en el México Pre-*

hispánico. México: Centro de Investigaciones Superiores del Instituto Nacional de Antropología e Historia.

Carrasco, Pedro, and Jesús Monjarás-Ruiz, eds.
1976 *Colección de Documentos Sobre Coyoacán, Vol. 1 (Visita del Oidor Gómez de Santillán al Pueblo de Coyoacán y Su Sujeto Tacubaya en el Año de 1553).* México: Instituto Nacional de Antropología e Historia, Colección Científica 39.
1978 *Colección de Documentos Sobre Coyoacán, Vol. 2 (Autos Referentes al Cacicazgo de Coyoacán que Proceden del AGN).* México: Instituto Nacional de Antropología e Historia, Colección Científica 65.

Carta de los Caciques e Indios de Suchimilco
1563 Carta de los Caciques e Indios de Suchimilco a Su Magestad . . . 2 de mayo de 1563. In *Colección de Documentos Inéditos Relativos al Descubrimiento, Conquista y Organización de las Antiguas Posesiones Españolas de América y Oceania, Sacados de los Archivos del Reino, y Muy Especialmente del de Indias,* Vol. 13:292-301. Madrid: José María Pérez (1970 reprint of 1864-84 edition).

Caso, Alfonso
1936 *La Religión de los Aztecas.* México: Enciclopedia Ilustrada Mex. 1.
1942 Aztecas de México. *Cuadernos Americanos* 8:145-81.
1956 Los Barrios Antiguos de Tenochtitlan y Tlatelolco. *Memorias de la Academia Mexicana de la Historia* 15:7-63.
1963 Land Tenure Among the Ancient Mexicans. *American Anthropologist* 65:863-78.
1966 La Época de los Señoríos Independientes, 1232-1427. *Revista Mexicana de Estudios Antropológicos* 20:147- 54.
1971 Calendrical Systems of Central Mexico. In *Handbook of Middle American Indians,* Vol. 10, *Archaeology of Northern Mesoamerica,* Pt. 1, Gordon F. Ekholm and Ignacio Bernal, eds., pp. 333-49. Austin: University of Texas Press.
1973 *La Política Indigenista en México, Métodos y Resultos.* 2nd ed. México: Instituto Nacional Indigenista y Secretaría de Educación Pública (1st ed., 1954).

Castillo F., Victor M.
1972 Unidades Nahuas de Medida. *Estudios de Cultura Náhuatl* 10:195-223.

Chang, Kwang Chih
1983 Settlement Patterns in Chinese Archaeology: A Case Study from the Bronze Age. In *Prehistoric Settlement Patterns: Essays in Honor of Gordon R. Willey,* Evon Z. Vogt and Richard M. Leventhal, eds., pp. 361-74. Albuquerque: University of New Mexico Press and Peabody Museum of Archaeology and Ethnology.

Charlton, Thomas H.
1972 Population Trends in the Teotihuacan Valley, A.D. 1400-1969. *World Archaeology* 4(1):106-23.

Chimalpahin Quauhtlehuanitzin, Domingo Francisco de San Antón Muñón
1889 *Anales. Sixième et Septième Relations (1258-1612).* Rémi Siméon, ed. and trans. Paris: Maisonnueve.
1950 Diferentes Historias Originales de los Reynos de Culhuacan y México, y de Otras Provincias. *Mitteilungen aus dem Museum für Volkerkunde in Hamburg* 22.
1958 Das Memorial Breve Acerca de la Fundación de la Ciudad de Culhuacan und weitere ausgewählte Teile aus den "Diferentes Historias Originales. . . ." Walter Lehmann and Gerdt Kutscher, trans. *Quellenwerke zur alten Geschichte Amerikas aufgezeichnet in den Sprachen der Eingeborenen* 7. Stuttgart.
1963 Die Relationen Chimalpahin's zur Geschichte Mexico's. Teil I: Die Zeit bis zur Conquista 1521. Aztekischer text herausgegeban von Günter Zimmermann. *Universität Hamburg Abhandlung aus dem Gebeit der Auslandskunde* 68.
1965 *Relaciones Originales de Chalco Amequemecan Escritas por Don Francisco de San Antón Muñon Chimalpahin Cuauhtlehuanitzin.* Sylvia Rendón, trans. México: Fondo de Cultura Económica.
1975 *Compendio de la Historia Mexicana . . . Extracts from a Lost Manuscript.* John B. Glass, ed. Gordon Whittaker, trans. Lincoln Center, Mass.: Conemex.
1978 *Historia Mexicana. A Short History of Ancient Mexico.* John B. Glass, ed. Lincoln Center, Mass.: Conemex.

Christaller, Walter
1933 *Die Zentralen Orte in Süddeutschland.* Jena: Zeiss. [Translated as Central Places in Southern Germany, 1966, Englewood-Cliffs, N.J.: Prentice Hall]

Civiera Taboda, Miguel, and María Elena Bribiesca
1977 *Guía Descriptiva de los Ramos que Constituyen el Archivo General de la Nación.* México: Archivo General de la Nación.

Cline, Howard F., ed.
1973- *Guide to Ethnohistorical Sources. Handbook of*
1975 *Middle American Indians,* Vols. 12-15. Robert Wauchope, gen. ed. Austin: University of Texas Press.

Cline, Susan L.
1980 Land Tenure and Land Inheritance in Late 16th Century Culhuacan. Paper presented at the annual meetings of the American Anthropological Association, Washington, D.C., December, 1980.

CODICES:
Boturini
1964 Códice Boturini. In *Antigüedades de México Basadas en la Recopilación de Lord Kingsborough,* José Corona Núñez, ed., Vol. 2:7-29. México: Secretaría de Hacienda y Crédito Público.

Mendoza
1925 *Colección de Mendoza o Códice Mendocino.* Jesús Galindo y Villa, ed. México: Museo Nacional (reprinted by Editorial Cosmos).

Osuna
1947 *Códice Osuna.* Luis Chávez Orozco, ed. México: Instituto Indigenísta Interamericano.

Ramírez
1920 Codex Ramírez. In: The Sources and Authenticity of the History of the Ancient Mexicans. *University of California Publications in American Archaeology and Ethnology* 17(1):1-150.

Telleriano-Remensis
1963 *Pictografía Mexicana del Siglo XVI.* Carmen Cook de Leonard, ed. México: Echaniz.

Xolotl
1951 *Códice Xólotl.* Charles E. Dibble, ed. Mexico: Universidad Nacional de México and the University of Utah.

Coe, Michael
   1964   The Chinampas of Mexico. *Scientific American* 211:90-98.
   1966   *Mexico*. New York: Praeger.

Colin, Mario
   1966- *Índice del Documentos Relativos a los Pueblos del*
   1968   *Estado de México*. Ramo de Tierras del Archivo General de la Nación (1966); Ramo de Mercedes (1967); Ramo de Indios (1968). México: Biblioteca Enciclopédica del Estado de México.

Cook, Sherburne F., and Woodrow Borah
   1960   The Indian Population of Central Mexico, 1531-1610. *Ibero-Americana* 44. Berkeley: University of California Press.

Cook de Leonard, Carmen, and Ernesto Lemoine Villicāna
   1954- Materiales para la Georgrafía Histórica de la Re-
   1955   gión Chalco-Amecameca. *Revista Mexicana de Estudios Antropológicos* 14(Pt. 1):289-95.

Corona Sánchez, Eduardo J.
   1973   Desarrollo de un Señorío en el Acolhuacan Prehispánico. Tesis, Maestro de Etnología, Escuela Nacional de Antropología e Historia, México.
   1976   Estratificación Social en el Acolhuacan. In *Estratificación Social en la Mesoamérica Prehispánica*, by Pedro Carrasco et al., pp. 102-17. México: Instituto Nacional de Antropología e Historia.

Cortés, Hernán
   1971   *Letters from Mexico*. A.R. Pagden, trans. New York: Grossman Publishers.

Coyoacan
   1927   Información de los Méritos y Servicios de D. Juan Señor, Natural de Cuyuacan, y Petición del Mismo a Su Magestad. México 8 de junio de 1536. Francisco del Paso y Troncoso, ed. *Anales del Museo Nacional de México*, Época 4, 5:354-59.

Crónica Mexicana. See Alvarado Tezózomoc 1975.

Crónica Mexicáyotl
   1949   *Crónica Mexicáyotl*, por Hernando Alvarado Tezczómoc. Adrián León, trans. México: Universidad Nacional Autónoma de México.

Davies, Claude Nigel
   1973a *The Aztecs, A History*. London: Macmillan.
   1973b *Los Mexicas: Primeros Pasos Hacia el Imperio*. México: Universidad Nacional Autónoma de México, Instituto de Investigaciones Históricas, Serie de Cultura Náhuatl, Monografía 14.
   1981   *The Toltec Heritage: From the Fall of Tula to the Rise of Tenochtitlan*. Norman: University of Oklahoma Press.

Díaz del Castillo, Bernal
   1956   *The Discovery and Conquest of New Spain, 1517-1521*. Genaro García, ed. A.P. Maudslay, trans. New York: Farrar, Strauss, and Giroux.

Díaz Lozano, Enrique
   1925   Excavaciones Practicadas en el Pueblo de Coyoacan, D.F. *Ethnos* 1:60-66.

Dibble, Charles E.
   1940   The Ancient Aztec Writing System. *University of Utah Anthropological Papers* 2:7-28.
   1971   Writing in Central Mexico. In *Handbook of Middle American Indians*, Vol. 10, *Archaeology of Northern Mesoamerica*, Pt. 1, Gordon F. Ekholm and Ignacio Bernal, eds., pp. 322-32. Austin: University of Texas Press.

Durán, Fray Diego
   1964   *The Aztecs. The History of the Indies of New Spain*. Doris Heyden and Fernando Horcasitas, trans. New York: Orion Press.
   1967   *Historia de las Indias de Nueva España e Islas de la Tierra Firme*. Vol. 2. Ángel María Garibay K., ed. México: Editorial Porrúa.
   1971   *Book of the Gods and Rites of the Ancient Calendar*. Fernando Horcasitas and Doris Heyden, trans. Norman: University of Oklahoma Press.

Durand Forest, Jacqueline de
   1974   Los Grupos Nahuas y sus Divinidades según Chimalpahin. *Estudios de Cultura Náhuatl* 11:37-44.

Eisenstadt, Shmuel N.
   1963   *The Political Systems of Empires*. New York: Free Press.

Evans, Susan T.
   1980a Spatial Analysis of Basin of Mexico Settlement: Problems with the Use of the Central Place Model. *American Antiquity* 45:866-75.
   1980b A Settlement Systems Analysis of the Teotihuacan Region, Mexico, A.D. 1350-1520. Ph.D. dissertation, Department of Anthropology, Pennsylvania State University.

Farías Galindo, J.
   1964   Xochimilco Histórico y Arqueológico. *Boletín de la Sociedad Mexicana de Geografía y Estadística* 98:155-200.

Feldman, Lawrence H., and Teresita Majewski, eds.
   1977   *Indexing Early Central Mexican Documents: A Report of the Results of the "Systematic Subject Indexing of Early Central Mexican Documents" Research Tools Pilot Project Made to the National Endowment for the Humanities*. Columbia, Missouri: Museum of Anthropology, University of Missouri.

Fernández de Recas, Guillermo S.
   1961   *Cacicazgo y Nobilario Indígena de la Nueva España*. México: Universidad Nacional Autónoma de México, Instituto Bibliográfico Mexicano, Biblioteca Nacional de México 5.

Flannery, Kent V.
   1972   The Cultural Evolution of Civilizations. *Annual Review of Ecology and Systematics* 3:399-426.

Foster, Elizabeth Andros
   1950   See Motolinía, 1950

Fried, Morton H.
   1960   On the Evolution of Social Stratification and the State. In *Culture in History*, Stanley Diamond, ed., pp. 713-31. New York: Columbia University Press.
   1967   *The Evolution of Political Society*. New York: Random House.

Galarza, Joaquín
   1963   Codex San Andrés (Juridiction de Cuautitlan). Manuscrit Pictographique du Musée de l'Homme de Paris. *Journal de la Société des Américanistes* n.s. 52:61-90.
   1964   Codex Procès de Cuauhtitlan—8 Avril 1568. Manuscrit Pictographique de la Bibliothèque Nationale de Paris. *Baessler-Archiv* n.s. 12(1):193-225.

Gallegos, Gonzalo
   1927   Relación Geográfica de Culhuacan, 1540. *Revista Mexicana de Estudios Históricos* 1(6):171-73.

Gamio, Manuel, ed.
   1922   *La Población del Valle de Teotihuacán*. 3 Vols.

México: Secretaría de Agricultura y Fomento/Dirección de Antropología, Mexico.

García Mora, Carlos
- 1981 *Naturaleza y Sociedad en Chalco-Amecamecan.* México: Biblioteca Enciclopédica del Estado de México 107.

Gerhard, Peter
- 1970a A Method for Reconstructing Precolumbian Political Boundaries in Central Mexico. *Journal de la Société de Américanistes* n.s. 59:27-41.
- 1970b El Señorío de Ocuituco. *Tlalocan* 6:97-114.
- 1972 *A Guide to the Historical Geography of New Spain.* Cambridge: Cambridge University Press.

Gibson, Charles
- 1956 Llamamiento General, Repartimiento, and the Empire of Acolhuacan. *Hispanic American Historical Review* 36:1-27.
- 1960 The Aztec Aristocracy in Colonial Mexico. *Comparative Studies in Society and History* 2:169-96.
- 1964a The Pre-Conquest Tepanec Zone and the Labor Drafts of the Sixteenth Century. *Revista de Historia de América* 57-58:136-45.
- 1964b *The Aztecs Under Spanish Rule. A History of the Indians of the Valley of Mexico, 1519-1810.* Stanford: Stanford University Press.
- 1971 Structure of the Aztec Empire. *Handbook of Middle American Indians*, Vol. 10, *Archaeology of Northern Mesoamerica*, Pt. 1, Gordon F. Ekholm and Ignacio Bernal, eds., pp. 376-94. Austin: University of Texas Press.

González Aparicio, Luis
- 1973 *Plano Reconstructivo de la Región de Tenochtitlan.* México: Instituto Nacional de Antropología e Historia.

Griffin, James B., and A. Espejo
- 1947 La Alfarería Correspondiente al Último Período de Ocupación Nahua del Valle de México. *Tlatelolco a Través de los Tiempos* 6:3-20.

Guzmán, Eulalia
- 1938 Un Manuscrito de la Colección Boturini que Trata de los Antiguos Señores de Teotihuacan. *Ethnos* 3(4- 5):89-103.

Haggett, Peter
- 1966 *Locational Analysis in Human Geography.* New York: St. Martin's Press.

Hassig, Ronald Ross
- 1979 Trade, Tribute, and Transportation: Sixteenth-Century Political Economy of the Valley of Mexico. Ph.D. dissertation, Department of Anthropology, Stanford University.

Hicks, Frederick
- 1978 Los Calpixque de Nezahualcoyotl. *Estudios de Cultura Náhuatl* 13:129-52.
- 1979 Un Parecer Sobre Tributos del Siglo XVI y el Caso de los Renteros de un Señor Chalca. *Boletín, Escuela de las Ciencias Antropológicas de la Universidad de Yucatán* 7(38):18-28.
- 1982 Tetzcoco in the Early 16th Century: The State, the City, and the Calpolli. *American Ethnologist* 9(2):230-49.
- 1984 Rotational Labor and Urban Development in Prehispanic Texcoco. In *Explorations in Ethnohistory: Indians of Central Mexico in the Sixteenth Century*, H. R. Harvey and Hanns J. Prem, eds., pp. 147-74. Albuquerque: University of New Mexico Press.

Historia Tolteca-Chichimeca
- 1976 *Historia Tolteca-Chichimeca.* Paul Kirchhoff, Liña Odena Güemes, and Luis Reyes García, eds. México: Instituto Nacional de Antropología e Historia.

Historia de los Mexicanos por Sus Pinturas
- 1941 Historia de los Mexicanos por Sus Pinturas. In *Nueva Colección de Documentos para la Historia de México*, Joaquín García Icazbalceta, ed., pp. 209-40. México: Editorial Chávez Hayhoe.

Jiménez Moreno, Wigberto
- 1954- Síntesis de la Historia Precolonial del Valle de
- 1955 México. *Revista Mexicana de Estudios Antropológicos* 14(1):219-36.

Johnson, Gregory A.
- 1973 Local Exchange and Early State Development in Southwestern Iran. *University of Michigan, Museum of Anthropology, Anthropological Papers* 51.
- 1978 Information Sources and the Development of Decision-Making Organizations. In *Social Archeology: Beyond Subsistence and Dating*, Charles L. Redman et al., eds., pp. 87-112. New York: Academic Press.

Karttunen, Frances
- 1983 *An Analytical Dictionary of Nahuatl.* Austin: University of Texas Press.

Katz, Friedrich
- 1956 Die Sozialökonomischen Verhältnisse bei den Azteken im 15. und 16. Jahrhundert. *Etnographish-Archaeologische Forschungen* 3, Pt. 2. Berlin: Veb. Deutscher Verlag der Wissenschaften.
- 1958 The Evolution of Aztec Society. *Past and Present* 13:14-25.

Kelly, Isabel, and Ángel Palerm
- 1952 The Mexican Conquests. Appendix B, in The Tajín Totonac, Part I: History, Subsistence, Shelter, and Technology. *Smithsonian Institution, Institute of Social Anthropology, Publication* 13.

Kirchhoff, Paul
- 1954- Land Tenure in Ancient Mexico. *Revista Mexicana*
- 1955 *de Estudios Antropológicos* 14:351-61.
- 1956 Composición Étnica y Organización Política de Chalco Según las Relaciones de Chimalpahin. *Revista Mexicana de Estudios Antropológicos* 14:297-302.

Kubler, George, and Charles Gibson
- 1951 The Tovar Calendar. *Memoirs of the Connecticut Academy of Arts and Sciences* 11.

Lattimore, Owen
- 1962 *Studies in Frontier History. Collected Papers, 1928-1958.* London: Oxford University Press.

Lehmann, Walter
- 1938 See Chimalpahin, 1958.

Lemoine Villicaña, Ernesto, ed.
- 1961 Visita, Congregación y Mapa de Amecameca de 1599. *Boletín del Archivo General de la Nación*, Segunda Serie, 2:5-46.

León-Portilla, Miguel
- 1960 The Concept of the State Among the Ancient Aztecs. *The Alpha Kappa Deltan* 30(1):7-13.
- 1963 *Aztec Thought and Culture: A Study of the Ancient Nahuatl Mind.* Norman: University of Oklahoma Press.
- 1969 *Pre-Columbian Literatures of Mexico.* Grace Lobanov and Miguel León-Portilla, trans. Norman: University of Oklahoma Press.

1971   Códice de Coyoacan—Nómina de Tributos, Siglo XVI. *Estudios de Cultura Náhuatl* 9:57-74.

León y Gama, Antonio de
    1927   Descripción de la Ciudad de México, Antes y Después de la Conquista. *Revista Mexicana de Estudios Antropológicos* 1 (Suppl.):8-58.

Lewis, Oscar
    1951   *Life in a Mexican Village: Tepoztlan Restudied*. Urbana: University of Illinois Press.

Libro de las Tasaciones
    1952   *El Libro de las Tasaciones de Pueblos de la Nueva España, Siglo XVI*. Francisco González de Cossío, ed. México: Archivo General de la Nación.

Linné, Sigvald
    1948   *El Valle y la Ciudad de México en 1550.* . . . *The Ethnographical Museum of Sweden*, n.s., Publication No. 9. Stockholm.

Litvak King, Jaime
    1971   *Cihuatlan y Tepecoacuilco: Provincias Tributarias de México en el Siglo XVI*. México: Universidad Nacional Autónoma de México, Instituto de Investigaciones Históricas, Serie Antropológica, 2.

Lloyd, Peter C.
    1965   The Political Structure of African Kingdoms: An Exploratory Model. In *Political Systems and the Distribution of Power*, Michael Banton, ed., pp. 63-112. London: Tavistock Publications.

Lockhart, James
    1982   Views of Corporate Self and History in Some Valley of Mexico Towns: Late Seventeenth and Eighteenth Centuries. In: *The Inca and Aztec States, 1400-1800; Anthropology and History*, George A. Collier and John D. Wirth, eds., pp. 367-93. New York: Academic Press.

López Austin, Alfredo
    1961   *La Constitución Real de México-Tenochtitlan*. México: Universidad Nacional Autónoma de México, Instituto de Historia, Seminario de Cultura Náhuatl.
    1973   *Hombre-Dios: Religión y Política en el Mundo Náhuatl*. México: Universidad Nacional Autónoma de México, Instituto de Investigaciones Históricas.
    1974   Organización Política en el Altiplano Central. *Historia Mexicana* 23:515-50.

López de Velasco, Juan
    1971   *Geografía y Descripción Universal de las Indias Recopilada por el Cosmógrafo-Cronista Juan López de Velasco desde el Año de 1571 al de 1575.* . . . Madrid: Ediciones Atlas.

Lösch, August
    1954   *Die räumliche Ordnung der Wirtschaft/The Economics of Location*. H. Woglom and W.F. Stolper, trans. New Haven: Yale University Press.

Luttwak, Edward N.
    1976   *The Grand Strategy of the Roman Empire*. Baltimore: Johns Hopkins University Press.

Madsen, William
    1960   *The Virgin's Children: Life in an Aztec Village Today*. Austin: University of Texas Press.

Malacachtepec Momoxco
    1953   *Fundaciones de los Pueblos de Malacachtepec Momoxco*. México: Vargas Rea.

Marcus, Joyce
    1973   Territorial Organization of the Lowland Classic Maya. *Science* 180:911-16.
    1976   *Emblem and State in the Classic Maya Lowlands: An Epigraphic Approach to Territorial Organization*. Washington, D.C.: Dumbarton Oaks; Trustees for Harvard University.
    1982   The Aztec Monuments of Acalpixcan. Appendix 4, in Prehispanic Settlement Patterns in the Southern Valley of Mexico: The Chalco-Xochimilco Region, by Jeffrey R. Parsons, Elizabeth Brumfiel, Mary H. Parsons, and David Wilson, pp. 475-85. *Memoirs of the Museum of Anthropology, University of Michigan* 14.
    1983a   On the Nature of the Mesoamerican City. In *Prehistoric Settlement Patterns: Essays in Honor of Gordon R. Willey*, Evon Z. Vogt and Richard M. Leventhal, eds., pp. 195-242. Albuquerque: University of New Mexico Press and Peabody Museum of Archaeology and Ethnology, Harvard University.
    1983b   Lowland Maya Archaeology at the Crossroads. *American Antiquity* 48(3):454-488.

Matos Moctezuma, Eduardo
    1978   El Proyecto Templo Mayor. *Boletín del Instituto Nacional de Antropología e Historia*, Época 3, 24 (Octubre-Diciembre).

Matrícula de Tributos
    1974   Matrícula de Tributos. Comentarios, paleografía y versión por Victor M. Castillo Farreras. *Historia de México* 2:321-96. Barcelona: Salvat.

Memorial de los Pueblos Sujetos al Señorío de Tlacupan
    1939-   Memorial de los Pueblos Sujetos al Señorío de
    1942   Tlacupan, y de los que Tributaban a México, Tezcuco y Tlacupan. In *Epistolario de Nueva España*, Francisco del Paso y Troncoso, ed., Vol. 14:118-22. México: Biblioteca Histórica Mexicana de Obras Inéditas, Ser. 2.

Mendieta, Fray Gerónimo
    1971   *Historia Eclesiastica Indiana: Obra Escrita a Fines del Siglo* XVI. México: Porrúa.

Millon, René
    1973   *Urbanization at Teotihuacan, Mexico. Vol. 1, The Teotihuacan Map, Part One: Text*. Austin: University of Texas Press.
    1976   Social Relations in Ancient Teotihuacan. In *The Valley of Mexico*, Eric R. Wolf, ed., pp. 205-48. Albuquerque: University of New Mexico Press.

Molina, Fray Alonso de
    1970   *Vocabulario en Lengua Castellana y Mexicana y Mexicana y Castellana* [1571]. México: Editorial Porrúa, S.A.

Monjarás-Ruiz, Jesús
    1977   Nacimiento y Consolidación de la Nobleza Mexica. Tesis Profesional, Escuela Nacional de Antropología e Historia, México.

Monzón, A.
    1949   *El Calpulli en la Organización Social de los Tenochca*. Mexico: Universidad Nacional Autónoma de México, Publicaciones del Instituto de Historia, 1st. ser., 14.

Moreno, Manuel M.
    1962   *La Organización Política y Social de los Aztecas*. México: Universidad Nacional Autónoma de México (reprint of 1931 ed.)

Morgan, Lewis Henry
    1878   *Ancient Society*. New York.

Motolinía, Toribio de Benavente
    1950   *Motolinia's History of the Indians of New Spain*. Elizabeth Andros Foster, trans. Documents and Narratives Concerning the Discovery and Con-

quest of Latin America, n.s., 4. Berkeley: The Cortés Society.
1967 *Memoriales*. Luis García Pimentel, ed. México: Editorial Aviña Levy.

Munch G., Guido
1976 *El Cacicazgo de San Juan Teotihuacan Durante la Colonia, 1521-1821*. México: Instituto Nacional de Antropologiá e Historia, Colección Científica, Historia, 32.

Muñoz Camargo, Diego
1892 *Historia de Tlaxcala*. Publicada y anotada por Alfredo Chavero. Edición facsimile 1966. México: Oficina Tip. de la Secretaría de Fomento.

Nicholson, Henry B.
1960 The Mixteca-Puebla Concept in Mesoamerican Archaeology: A Reexamination. In *Men and Cultures*, A. Wallace, ed., pp. 612-17. Philadelphia: University of Pennsylvania Press.
1971 Religion in Pre-Hispanic Central Mexico. In *Handbook of Middle American Indians*, Vol. 10, *Archaeology of Northern Mesoamerica*, Pt. 1, Gordon F. Ekholm and Ignacio Bernal, eds., pp. 395-446. Austin: University of Texas Press.

Noguera, Eduardo
1969 Excavaciones en Sitios Postclásicos del Valle de México. *Anales de Antropología* 6:197-231.
1970 Exploraciones Estratigráficas en Xochimilco, Tulancingo y Cerro de la Estrella. *Anales de Antropología* 7:91-130.

Nuttall, Zelia
1926 Official Reports on the Towns of Tequizistlan, Tepechpan, Acolman, and San Juan Teotihuacan Sent by Francisco de Castañeda to His Majesty, Phillip II, and the Council of the Indies, in 1580. *Papers of the Peabody Museum, Harvard University* 11:45-86.

Offner, Jerome
1979 Law and Politics in Aztec Texcoco. Ph.D. dissertation, Department of Anthropology, Yale University.

Olivera, Mercedes
1976 El Despotismo Tributario en la Región de Cuauhtinchan-Tepeaca. In *Estratificación Social en la Mesoamérica Prehispánica*, by Pedro Carrasco, Johanna Broda et al., pp. 181-206. Mexico: Instituto Nacional de Antropología e Historia.

Parsons, Jeffrey R.
1970 An Archaeological Evaluation of the Códice Xolotl. *American Antiquity* 35:431-40.
1971 Prehistoric Settlement Patterns in the Texcoco Region, Mexico. *Memoirs of the Museum of Anthropology, University of Michigan* 3.
1974 The Development of a Prehistoric Complex Society: A Regional Perspective from the Valley of Mexico. *Journal of Field Archaeology* 1:81-108.
1976 The Role of Chinampa Agriculture in the Food Supply of Aztec Tenochtitlan. In *Cultural Change and Continuity*, Charles Cleland, ed., pp. 233-57. New York: Academic Press.

Parsons, Jeffrey R., Elizabeth Brumfiel, Mary H. Parsons, and David J. Wilson
1982 Prehispanic Settlement Patterns in the Southern Valley of Mexico: The Chalco-Xochimilco Region. *Memoirs of the Museum of Anthropology, University of Michigan* 14.

Paso y Troncoso, Francisco del, ed.
1905- *Papeles de Nueva España*. Segunda Serie, Geografía y Estadística. 7 Vols. Madrid: Tipográfico
1906 Sucesores de Rivadeneyra.
1912 *Códice Kingsborough. Memorial de los Indios de Tepetlaoztoc*. . . . Madrid: Hauser y Menet.
1939- *Epistolario de Nueva España (1505-1818)*. 16
1942 Vols. México: Biblioteca Histórica Mexicana de Obras Inéditas, Segunda Serie.

Paso y Troncoso, Francisco del, and Faustino Chimalpopoca Galicia, eds.
1897 Lista de los Pueblos Principales que Pertenecían Antiguamente a Tetzcoco. *Anales de Museo Nacional de México*, Época 1, 4:48-56.

Peñafiel, Antonio
1885 *Nombres Geográficos de México*. México: Oficina Tipografía de la Secretaría de Fomento.
1900 *Teotihuacan, Estudio Histórico y Arqueológico*. México: Oficina Tipografía de la Secretaría de Fomento.

Pérez Rocha, Emma
1975 La Tierra y el Hombre en la Villa de Tacuba en la Época Colonial. Tesis Profesional, Escuela Nacional de Antropología e Historia, S.E.P.-I.N.A.H., México.
1978 *Servicio Personal y Tributo en Coyoacan: 1551-1553*. México: Centro de Investigaciones Superiores del I.N.A.H., Cuadernos de la Casa Chata 8.

Pérez-Zavallos, Juan Manuel
1981 Organización del Señorío Xochimilca. In *Xochimilco en el Siglo XVI*, by Ludka de Rebeca Ramos, Juan Gortari Krauss, and Manuel Pérez-Zevallos, pp. 105-54. México: Centro de Investigaciones Superiores del I.N.A.H., Cuadernos de la Casa Chata 40.

Piña Chan, Román
1976 Los Chichimecas y los Mexicas. In *Los Señores y Estados Militaristas*, Román Piña Chan, ed., pp. 159-82. México: Instituto Nacional de Antropología e Historia, Panorama Histórico y Cultural 9.

Pollard, Helen P.
1980 Central Places and Cities: A Consideration of the Protohistoric Tarascan State. *American Antiquity* 45:677-96.

Pomar, Juan Bautista
1941 Relación de Tezcoco. In *Nueva Colección de Documentos para la Historia de México*, Joaquín García Icazbalceta, ed., Vol. 3:1-64. México: Editorial Chávez Hayhoe.

Prem, Hanns J., ed.
1974 *Matrícula de Huexotzinco (Ms. Mex. 387 der Bibliothèque Nationale, Paris)*. Graz: Akademische Druck- und Verlagsanstalt.

Radin, Paul
1920 Sources and Authenticity of the History of the Ancient Mexicans. *University of California Publications in American Archaeology and Ethnology* 17(1):1-150.

Ramírez de Fuenleal, Sebastián
1870 Carta a Su Magestad . . . 1532. In *Colección de Documentos Inéditos del Archivo de Indias*, Joaquín Fernández Pacheco, ed., Vol. 13:250-61. Madrid.

Redfield, Robert
1930 *Tepoztlan: A Mexican Village*. Chicago: University of Chicago Press.

Relación de la Genealogía
    1941 Relación de la Genealogía de los Señores que han Señoreado esta Tierra de la Nueva España. In *Relaciones de Texcoco y de la Nueva España. Nueva Colección de Documentos para la Historia de México*, Joaquín García Icazbalceta, ed., Vol. 3:240-56. México: Editorial Chávez Hayhoe.
Relación de Zempoala y su Partido
    1949 Relación de Zempoala y su Partido, 1580. *Tlalocan* 3:29-41.
Relación de Tequisquiac, Citlaltepec y Xilocingo
    1957 Relación de Tequisquiac, Citlaltepec, y Xilocingo, Ignacio Bernal, ed. *Tlalocan* 3:289-308.
Reyes García, Luis
    1977 Genealogía de Doña Francisco de Guzmán, Xochimilco, 1610. *Tlalocan* 7:31-35.
    1979 Comentario. In *El Trabajo y los Trabajadores en la Historia de México. Labor and Laborers through Mexican History*, pp. 66-69. México: El Colegio de México and University of Arizona Press.
Robertson, Donald
    1959 *Mexican Manuscript Painting of the Early Colonial Period.* New Haven: Yale University Press.
Rojas, Teresa
    1977 *La Organización del Trabajo para las Obras Públicas: El Coatequitl y las Cuadrillas de Trabajadores.* México: Centro de Investigaciones Superiores del I.N.A.H., Cuadernos de la Casa Chata 2.
    1979 El Tributo en Trabajo en la Construcción de las Obras Públicas de México Tenochtitlan. Paper presented at the Seminario sobre el Modo de Producción Tributario en Mesoamérica, Mérida, Yucatán; 12-15 noviembre de 1979.
Rounds, J.
    1979 Lineage, Class, and Power in Aztec History. *American Ethnologist* 6:73-86.
Roys, Ralph L.
    1943 The Indian Background of Colonial Yucatan. *Carnegie Institution of Washington,* Publication 548.
Sahagún, Fray Bernardino de
    1950- *Florentine Codex: General History of the Things*
    1969   *of New Spain*, Arthur J.O. Anderson and Charles E. Dibble, trans. 12 Vols. Sante Fe: School of American Research and The University of Utah.
Sahlins, Marshall D., and Elman R. Service, eds.
    1960 *Evolution and Culture.* Ann Arbor: University of Michigan Press.
Sanders, William T.
    1965 *The Cultural Ecology of the Teotihuacan Valley.* University Park, Pa.: Pennsylvania State University, Department of Anthropology.
    1970 The Population of the Teotihuacan Valley, the Basin of Mexico, and the Central Mexican Symbiotic Region in the 16th Century. In The Teotihuacan Valley Project Final Report, Vol. 1, William T. Sanders et al., eds., pp. 385-457. Department of Anthropology, The Pennsylvania State University, *Occasional Papers in Anthropology* 3.
    1976 The Natural Environment of the Basin of Mexico. In *The Valley of Mexico*, Eric R. Wolf, ed., pp. 59-68. Albuquerque: University of New Mexico Press.
    1981 Ecological Adaptation in the Basin of Mexico: 23,000 B.C. to the Present. In Supplement to *Handbook of Middle American Indians*, Vol. 1, Archaeology, Jeremy A. Sabloff, ed., pp. 147-97. Austin: University of Texas Press.
Sanders, William T., Jeffrey R. Parsons, and Robert S. Santley
    1979 *The Basin of Mexico: Ecological Processes in the Evolution of a Civilization.* New York: Academic Press.
Sanders, William T., and Barbara J. Price
    1968 *Mesoamerica: The Evolution of a Civilization.* New York: Random House.
Santley, Robert S.
    1980 Disembedded Capitals Reconsidered. *American Antiquity* 45:132-45.
Scholes, France V., and Eleanor B. Adams, eds.
    1957 *Información Sobre los Tributos que los Indios Pagaban a Moctezuma—Año de 1554.* México: Documentos para la Historia de México Colonial 4.
    1958 *Sobre el Modo de Tributar los Indios de Nueva España a Su Magestad—1561-1564.* México: Documentos para la Historia del México Colonial 5.
Service, Elman R.
    1955 Indian-European Relations in Colonial Latin America. *American Anthropologist* 57:411-25.
    1971 *Primitive Social Organization: An Evolutionary Perspective.* 2nd ed. New York: Random House.
    1975 *Origins of the State and Civilization.* New York: W.W. Norton and Co.
Siméon, Rémi
    1885 *Dictionnaire de la Langue Nahuatl ou Mexicaine.* Paris: Imprimerie Nationale. Graz, Austria: Akademische Druck- und Verlagsanstalt (reprinted in 1971).
Simon, Herbert
    1969 *The Science of the Artificial.* Cambridge, Mass.: M.I.T. Press.
Skinner, George William
    1977 Cities and the Hierarchy of Local Systems. In *The City in Late Imperial China*, G. William Skinner, ed., pp. 275-352. Stanford: Stanford University Press.
Smith, Carol, ed.
    1976 *Regional Analysis.* Vol. 2: *Social Systems.* New York: Academic Press.
Smith, Michael E.
    1979 The Aztec Marketing System and Settlement Pattern in the Valley of Mexico: A Central Place Analysis. *American Antiquity* 44:110-25.
Soustelle, Jacques
    1962 *Daily Life of the Aztecs on the Eve of the Spanish Conquest.* New York: Macmillan.
Southall, Aidan
    1965 A Critique of the Typology of States and Political Systems. In *Political Systems and the Distribution of Power*, Michael Banton, ed., pp. 113-40. London: Tavistock Publications.
Spores, Ronald
    1967 *The Mixtec Kings and Their People.* Norman: University of Oklahoma Press.
    1973 Special Problems in Methodology. In *Research in Mexican History*, Richard E. Greenleaf and Michael C. Meyer, eds., pp. 25-48. Lincoln: University of Nebraska Press.
    1974 Marital Alliances in the Political Integration of Mixtec Kingdoms. *American Anthropologist* 76:297-311.

Steponaitis, Vincas P.
  1978 Location Theory and Complex Chiefdoms: A Mississippian Example. In *Mississippian Settlement Patterns*, Bruce D. Smith, ed., pp. 417-53. New York: Academic Press.
  1981 Settlement Hierarchies and Political Complexity in Nonmarket Societies: The Formative Period in the Valley of Mexico. *American Anthropologist* 82:320-63.
Swartz, Marc J., V.W. Turner, and A. Tuden, eds.
  1966 *Political Anthropology*. Chicago: University of Chicago Press.
Thompson, J. Eric S.
  1933 *Mexico Before Cortez*. New York: Charles Scribner's Sons.
Tira de Tepechpan
  1978 *Tira de Tepechpan; Códice Colonial Procedente del Valle de México*. Edición y comentarios por Xavier Noguez. 2 Vols. México: Biblioteca Enciclopédica del Estado de México.
Torquemada, Fray Juan de
  1975 *Monarquía Indiana*. 3 Vols. México: Porrúa [reprint of 1615 ed.].
Tratado de Principado y Nobleza de Pueblo de San Juan Teotihuacan...
  n.d. Tratado de Principado y Nobleza de Pueblo de Sn. Juan Teotihuacan Como se Contiene en las Antiguos Papeles de Nobleza que por Mandado de Su Magestad Confirmo la Real Audencia.... Manuscript in Nahuatl and Spanish, Museo Nacional de Antropología e Historia, México, Colección Paso y Troncoso, Leg. 52.
  1904 Los Primeros Señores de Teotihuacan. In *Obras del Alfredo Chavero, Tomo I, Escritos Diversos* (Biblioteca de Autores Mexicanos, 52). México: Tipografía de Victoriano Agüeros.
Trautmann, Wolfgang von
  1968 Untersuchungen zur indianischen Siedlungs- und Territorialgeschichte im Becken von Mexico bis zur frühen Kolonialzeit. *Hamburgischen Museums für Völkerkunde und Vorgeschichte, Beitrage zur Mittleamerikanischen Völkerkunde* 7.

Vaillant, George C.
  1938 Correlation of Archaeological and Historical Sequences in the Valley of Mexico. *American Anthropologist* 40:535-73.
  1941 *The Aztecs of Mexico: Origin, Rise, and Fall of the Aztec Nation*. Garden City, New York: Doubleday.
West, Robert C., and Pedro Armillas
  1950 Las Chinampas de México. *Cuadernos Americanos* 50:165-92.
White, Leslie A.
  1949 *The Science of Culture*. New York: Grove Press.
Wicke, Charles R., and Fernando Horcasitas
  1957 Archaeological Investigations on Mt. Tlaloc, Mexico. *Mesoamerican Notes* 5:83-95.
Willey, Gordon R.
  1979 The Concept of the Disembedded Capital in Comparative Perspective. *Journal of Anthropological Research* 35(2):123-37.
Wright, Henry T.
  1977 Recent Research on the Origin of the State. *Annual Review of Anthropology* 6:379-97.
  1978 Towards an Explanation of the Origin of the State. In *Origins of the State: The Anthropology of Political Evolution*, R. Cohen and E.R. Service, eds., pp. 49-68. Philadelphia: Institute for the Study of Human Issues.
Wright, Henry T., and Gregory Johnson
  1975 Population, Exchange, and Early State Formation in Southwestern Iran. *American Anthropologist* 77:267-89.
Zantwijk, Rudolf van
  1967 La Organización de Once Guarniciones Aztecas: Una Nueva Interpretación de los Folios 17v y 18r del Códice Mendocino. *Journal de la Société des Américanistes* 56(1):149-60.
  1969 La Estructura Gubernamental del Estado de Tlacupan (1430-1520). *Estudios de Cultura Náhuatl* 8:123-55.
Zorita, Alonso de
  1963 *Life and Labor in Ancient Mexico: The Brief and Summary Relation of the Lords of New Spain*. Benjamin Keen, trans. New Brunswick, N.J.: Rutgers University Press.

Resumen en Español

Capítulo I. Introducción

Presentamos en este libro un análisis comparativo sobre la evolución de los sistemas administrativos del Postclásico en el Valle del México, tomando como base las estructuras políticas de cinco señoríos: Amecameca, Cuauhtitlán, Xochimilco, Coyoacán y Teotihuacán. Examinamos asimismo los cambios administrativos resultantes del surgimiento de una nueva organización política regional: el imperio Azteca. Por eso, se revisaron, en primer lugar, las estructuras administrativas de dichos señoríos considerándoseles como unidades independientes durante la fase Azteca Temprano. Al respecto, las crónicas indican que en esta fase existieron diferentes grupos étnicos que fundaron en el Valle de México de 40 a 60 entidades políticas independientes, las mismas que tuvieron tradiciones étnicas, históricas, rituales y políticas distintas. En segundo lugar, se examinaron los cambios políticos y administrativos acaecidos en la fase Azteca Tardío, a causa de la conquista de las cinco ciudades por Tenochtitlán y Texcoco.

El estudio de los datos nos permite proponer que el imperio Azteca no solamente transformó los sistemas de tributación, sino también la organización administrativa de las ciudades subordinades en el Valle de México. Sin embargo, debemos indicar que los cambios en las estructuras administrativas de cada provincia no fueron iguales. Por otro lado, los pueblos conquistados continuaron manteniendo sus propias organizaciones políticas, además de la jerarquía regional dentro del señorío.

Las fuentes utilizadas en la realización de este trabajo incluyen documentos de los primeros años de la conquista e informes arqueológicos concernientes con las cinco regiones. En esta investigación empleé únicamente la información relacionada con estas cinco regiones, evitando la proposición de generalizaciones aventuradas a causa del uso indiscriminado de datos de origen geográfico heterogéneo.

En mi opinión las fuentes más importantes son las crónicas que describen la historia prehispánica (los *Anales de Cuauhtitlán*, por ejemplo). Las que se ocupan de los señoríos en forma individual dan cuenta de las migraciones, los cambios de poder de un grupo a otro, las estructuras políticas y las guerras. También existen otras fuentes como los documentos judiciales del siglo xvi. A su vez los testamentos y genealogías tienen información sobre las posesiones y relaciones de los miembros de la élite en tiempos prehispánicos. Por otro lado, la documentación judicial y administrativa del siglo xvi, proveniente de los archivos, trata sobre la situación colonial pero refleja también ciertas características de origen prehispánico, complementando de este modo la información proveniente de otras fuentes. También, las *Relaciones Geográficas* del siglo xvi, las descripciones que proporcionan los conquistadores, los mapas y los códices, ofrecen datos valiosos sobre los señoríos.

Capítulo II. Señoríos del Valle de México

Las crónicas y los documentos del siglo xvi se ocupan ampliamente del sistema político de Tenochtitlán, capital del imperio Azteca. Los relatos de Alva Ixtlilxóchitl describen el estado de Acolhuacán y la ciudad de Texcoco. Sin embargo, en el Valle de México hubo otros 40 a 60 señoríos. En náhuatl "señorío" se conoce con el nombre de *altepetl*, es decir "pueblo o rey" (Molina 1970:4). Un *altepetl* consistía de una ciudad, un territorio bajo su dominio y un gobernante o *tlatoani*. El señorío era la sede de un *tlatoani* y su linaje. Los documentos del siglo xvi llamaban señorío o *cacicazgo* a una ciudad-estado.

Las organizaciones políticas regionales comprendían varios señoríos que en conjunto constituían una confederación, formada como resultado de una alianza para protegerse mutuamente. En la fase

Azteca Temprano hubo siete confederaciones en el Valle de México: los mexica o tenochca, los acolhua, los tepaneca, los chalca, los cuitlahuaca, los xochimilca, y los mixquica. En este trabajo los señoríos representan diversas confederaciones y, en consecuencia, facciones políticas diversas.

El imperio Azteca se inició a base de tres confederaciones cuyos centros fueron: Tenochtitlán, Texcoco y Tlacopán. En el Valle de México, Tenochtitlán y Texcoco se convirtieron en dos estados poderosos y tenían subyugados a los pueblos vecinos sea por conquista o por alianza. Como se recordará, al momento del contacto con los españoles Tenochtitlán se había encumbrado como el lugar más poderoso de Mesoamérica.

Uno de los objetivos primordiales del imperio Azteca era extender sus dominios para así incorporar nuevos contribuyentes. La expansión Azteca se realizaba mediante violentas incursiones o por medios pacíficos; en estos últimos las alianzas y la diplomacia jugaban un papel transcendental. Los gobernantes o *tlatoque* de Tenochtitlán y Texcoco incorporaron a sus cortes y a las jerarquías metropolitanas a los *tlatoque* de los pueblos sometidos del Valle de México. Este hecho permitió el surgimiento de una jerarquía administrativa con *tlatoque* y nobles de señoríos con tradiciones y estructuras internas diversas, ocasionando cambios estructurales en los sistemas políticos de los señoríos subordinados al imperio. Los señoríos dependientes que se hallaban en el Valle de México ocupaban una área segura, debido a su cercanía a Tenochtitlán y Texcoco.

Capítulo III. Amecameca

Las relaciones de Chimalpahin y otros documentos proporcionan numerosos datos sobre los sucesos prehispánicos de Amecameca. De acuerdo a las relaciones, Amecameca fue fundada por seis grupos chichimecas y un grupo nonoalca. Estos siete grupos conquistaron y ocuparon la región entre 1268 y 1304.

En Amecameca estos pueblos fundaron siete parcialidades, cada una gobernada por un señor o *teuctli*. Los *teuctin* gobernaban siete territorios independientes, nombrando un *teuctli* en tiempo de guerra o en otras situaciones políticas, quien se desempeñaba temporalmente como jefe militar o embajador.

Antes de ser sometidos, los amecameca tenían un sistema político sin jerarquía permanente. Situación similar existía también en la vecina región chalca. Amecameca se alió con los pueblos ubicados en el sureste del Valle de México, dando lugar a la confederación chalca. La alianza incluyó a los señoríos de Chalco Atenco, Tenango, Atlauhtla, Chimalhuacán Chalco, Tepetlixpan, Amecameca, y otros. El objetivo fue la mutua protección y no hubo una capital permanente.

Hacia el año de 1385 las ciudades chalcas fueron atacadas por los tenochca y tepaneca, siendo conquistadas todas las ciudades chalcas y finalmente Amecameca en 1465. Luego de la conquista los *teteuctin* de Amecameca fueron reemplazados por *cuauhtlatoque* o gobernantes militares de Tenochtitlán. Sin embargo, dos décadas después, en los años 1484-88, fueron restituidos en sus antiguos cargos cinco *teteuctin* de Amecameca. Aquellas divisiones que no tenían *teteuctin* permanecieron como parcialidades dependientes de otros *teteuctin*. Los nuevos nobles *teteuctin* fueron consecuencia del matrimonio entre dignatarios de Tenochtitlán y doncellas nobles de Amecameca.

Los tenochca impusieron en la región chalca una jerarquía política, liderada por la ciudad de Tlalmanalco. Ésta fue una cabeza de provincia que incluía a todos los señoríos chalcas. Así, Amecameca pasó a depender de Tlalmanalco y Tenochtitlán. El imperio Azteca implantó pues un ordenamiento administrativo y un régimen tributario en la región chalca.

Capítulo IV. Cuauhtitlán

Según la crónica anónima, los *Anales de Cuauhtitlán* (1938, 1945), Cuauhtitlán fue fundada por los chichimeca en el año 804. En sus inicios fue una ciudad pequeña pero en el siglo XIV se convirtió en un centro con cuatro parcialidades grandes, contando con un templo, una plaza y un palacio.

Cuauhtitlán estaba bajo el mando de un *tlatoani*. Los *tlatoque* de esta ciudad gobernaban con la ayuda de cuatro oficiales de la nobleza. Estos se desempeñaban también como embajadores y cada uno tenía a su cargo cuatro divisiones administrativas de Cuauhtitlán. Las divisiones comprendían un distrito como cabecera y dos pueblos dependientes. A su vez, estas cuatro divisiones tributaban y daban servicios al *tlatoani* y al palacio de

Cuauhtitlán. Por otro lado, el *tlatoani* redistribuía—según los *Anales*—cuatro veces al año el tributo recibido.

Cuauhtitlán fue conquistada por Tenochtitlán en el año 1435 y posteriormente los *tlatoque* de Tenochtitlán modificaron la administración de Cuauhtitlán. Los cuatro oficiales dejaron de funcionar como administradores regionales. Esta medida fue adoptada por Tenochtitlán en un esfuerzo por hacer más eficiente la tributación y el manejo de la provincia. Los pueblos dependientes de Cuauhtitlán pasaron a ser directamente gobernados por ocho administradores. Además, Citlaltepec, un pueblo subordinado a Cuauhtitlán, fue gobernado por un administrador nombrado por el *tlatoani* de Tenochtitlán. En realidad, estos cambios permitieron una administración más eficaz pues se eliminó un nivel (los cuatro oficiales) en la jerarquía administrativa de Cuauhtitlán. Asimismo, poco antes del contacto con los españoles, el *tlatoani* de Cuauhtitlán era designado por el *tlatoani* de Tenochtitlán, además de nombrar un *calpixque* en Cuauhtitlán para recoger el tributo.

Cuauhtitlán, una vez sujeta al imperio Azteca, redujo su jerarquía política al eliminarse un nivel de administradores. Esta situación al parecer es distinta a la producida en la región chalca y en Amecameca, en donde Tenochtitlán impuso una jerarquía administrativa regional.

Capítulo V. Xochimilco

Xochimilco fue fundada en el siglo xii por los xochimilca, quienes vinieron del norte del Valle de México. La ciudad de Xochimilco fue cabeza de un gran territorio que cruzaba la Sierra de Ajusco, extendiéndose hasta la Sierra Madre Oriental. Fue también el asentamiento principal de la confederación xochimilca.

Según los relatos históricos, Xochimilco tenía al principio dos *tlatoque* quienes gobernaban dos divisiones de la ciudad: Tecpan y Tepetenchi. Sin embargo, Xochimilco fue conquistada por los tenochca en el año 1430, surgiendo un tercer *tlatoani* que gobernaba Olac, una parcialidad de la ciudad de Xochimilco. Según el *Códice Mendocino* Olac fue el centro para la recolección. Se dice también que el gobernante de Olac descendía del linaje de los *tlatoque* de Tenochtitlán.

Luego que Xochimilco fue conquistada, éste sufrió algunos cambios en su estructura administrativa. En primer lugar, es destacable el hecho que Tenochtitlán impuso un nuevo señorío con un *tlatoani* de procedencia tenochca. Al igual que en otros señoríos, los *tlatoque* locales gobernaban con el permiso del *tlatoani* de Tenochtitlán y la ciudad de Xochimilco y sus pueblos daban tributo y servicio a Tenochtitlán.

Capítulo VI. Coyoacán

Las fuentes indican que en los siglos xii y xiii hubo una ciudad llamada Coyoacán subordinada a Culhuacán. Sin embargo, la historia del señorío de Coyoacán se inicia con el *tlatoani* Maxtla, hijo de Tezozómoc, quien gobernó Coyoacán desde 1410 hasta 1428.

Coyoacán fue conquistada por los tenochca en los años 1429 y 1430, dividiendo su territorio de tal manera que permitiera una tributación más eficaz. Antes de su sometimiento por Tenochtitlán, Coyoacán era la segunda ciudad más importante del estado Tepaneca, pero al incorporarse al imperio Azteca pasó a depender de Tlacopán. Coyoacán tributaba directamente a Tenochtitlán y conjuntamente con Tlacopán daba servicios a la capital imperial.

Los *tlatoque* de Coyoacán pertenecían al linaje de los reyes de Azcapotzalco y al ser conquistados por Tenochtitlán se produjeron alteraciones en la sucesión de los *tlatoque* de Coyoacán por sus similares de Tenochtitlán. Así por ejemplo, Ahuitzotl asesinó a un *tlatoani* de Coyoacán que desoyó sus órdenes. Si bien es cierto que Ahuitzotl reinstauró el linaje de los reyes de Coyoacán, las genealogías revelan que en 1519 el *tlatoani* de Coyoacán estaba aliado por motivos matrimoniales con el linaje de los *tlatoque* de Tenochtitlán.

Dado que Coyoacán era un centro tepaneca importante, fue uno de los primeros en ser conquistado por los tenochca y acolhua. Luego de este suceso Coyoacán perdió su posición secundaria en la jerarquía política de Azcapotzalco, pasando a depender de Tenochtitlán y Tlacopán.

Capítulo VII. Teotihuacán: Un Señorío Acolhua

Teotihuacán tiene una historia común conjuntamente con los señoríos acolhuas, figurando Huexotla, Coatlinchan y Texcoco. Las crónicas indican que el asentamiento correspondiente al Postclásico fue eregido por Xólotl, el gran Chichimecatl Teuctli del siglo xiii. Tlotzin, nieto de Xólotl, concedió a su hijo Tochinteuctli el gobierno de los pueblos de Huexotla, Oztotícpac, Chiauhtla y Teotihuacán. Este último se convirtió en señorío en el año 1409, fecha en que Tochinteuctli repartió sus tierras entre sus dos hijos, correspondiendo a Huetzin el señorío de Teotihuacán.

En 1418 las ciudades de la región acolhua fueron conquistadas por Azcapotzalco, y después de la fundación de la Triple Alianza Nezahualcóyotl, señor de Texcoco, devolvió a los señores acolhuas sus ciudades, quedando Quetzalmamalitzin, hijo de Huetzin, al mando del señorío de Teotihuacán. Como se recordará, Quetzalmamalitzin contrajo matrimonio con una hija de Nezahualcóyotl y a partir de esta fecha los *tlatoque* de Teotihuacán siempre se casaron con las hijas de los reyes de Texcoco.

Los *tlatoque* de Teotihuacán eran oficiales de alto rango en el estado de Acolhua, desempeñándose como jueces regionales y consejeros en el palacio de Texcoco.

En realidad, Teotihuacán siempre estuvo subordinado a Texcoco y esto se comprueba por los servicios de mantenimiento que los *macehualtin* de dicha ciudad, así como los provenientes de otros poblados, prestaban durante seis meses al palacio de Texcoco. A esto se agrega la tributación que obligatoriamente debían cumplir con el estado. Por otro lado, debemos anotar que las tierras pertenecientes a los *tlatoque* de Teotihuacán, Acolmán y Tepetlaóztoc, fueron divididas por el *tlatoani* de Texcoco, reduciendo así la posibilidad de un intento separatista.

Después de la fundación del imperio Azteca es posible que Teotihuacán y la provincia de Acolhuacán tributaron también a Tenochtitlán. Ciertamente Teotihuacán es el típico ejemplo de un señorío profundamente sometido a un centro regional, en este caso Texcoco. Teotihuacán tenía realmente una estructura administrativa sencilla y se hallaba en gran manera bajo el control político del *tlatoani* de Texcoco.

Capítulo VIII. El Imperio Azteca y Sus Provincias

El análisis de los cinco señoríos del Valle de México permite proponer algunas conclusiones concernientes con la formación del sistema político en el centro del imperio Azteca. Así, durante la hegemonía de la Triple Alianza en el valle, tanto los *tlatoque* de Tenochtitlán y Texcoco recogían el tributo de los pueblos subordinados. Para cumplir este cometido se gestó una nueva jerarquía que incluyó *calpixque* de muchos rangos encargados de cobrar el tributo. Sin embargo, para los efectos de gobierno los *tlatoque* de Tenochtitlán y Texcoco debieron hacer uso de las propias jerarquías administrativas que tradicionalmente tenían estas ciudades. En consecuencia no existió una jerarquía política-administrativa centralizada como caracterizó a la jerarquía tributaria. En tal sentido, las jerarquías políticas a veces quedaban en manos de los *tlatoque* de las ciudades subordinadas, ya que con esta medida los dignatarios de Tenochtitlán y Texcoco trataban de utilizarlos como oficiales imperiales.

En Teotihuacán y en otras ciudades el señorío se instituyó incorporando a miembros de los linajes reales de Tenochtitlán y Texcoco. En otros casos el imperio depuso a los *tlatoque* locales y en algunas provincias cambió la jerarquía administrativa regional. Así por ejemplo, disminuyó el prestigio de Coyoacán y existen evidencias que en Xochimilco se añadió un señorío, cuyo linaje era tenochca. Asimismo, en ciudades como Amecameca, que carecían de una jerarquía política permanente, el imperio imponía una jerarquía. Finalmente, en las ciudades en que existía una jerarquía más elaborada, Cuauhtitlán por ejemplo, el imperio redujo el número de oficiales como parte de su política para menguar la jerarquía local.